P9-EEA-840

AUGUSTANA UNIVERSITY COLLEGE
LIBRARY

The BALLOT

AND ITS

MESSAGE

Voting in Canada

NEW CANADIAN READINGS

General Editor: J.L. Granatstein

Titles currently available

Michael D. Behiels, ed., *Quebec Since 1945: Selected Readings*

David J. Bercuson, ed., *Canadian Labour History: Selected Readings*

Carl Berger, ed., *Contemporary Approaches to Canadian History*

Hartwell Bowsfield, ed., *Louis Riel: Selected Readings*

Kenneth S. Coates and William R. Morrison, eds., *Interpreting Canada's North: Selected Readings*

Terry Crowley, ed., *Clio's Craft: A Primer of Historical Methods*

Robin Fisher and Kenneth Coates, eds., *Out of the Background: Readings on Canadian Native History*

J.L. Granatstein, ed., *Canadian Foreign Policy: Historical Readings*

Norman Hillmer, ed., *Partners Nevertheless: Canadian–American Relations in the Twentieth Century*

Michiel Horn, ed., *The Depression in Canada: Responses to Economic Crisis*

Douglas McCalla, ed., *The Development of Canadian Capitalism: Essays in Business History*

Douglas McCalla, ed., *Perspectives on Canadian Economic History*

R.C. Macleod, ed., *Lawful Authority: Readings on the History of Criminal Justice in Canada*

Morris Mott, ed., *Sports in Canada: Historical Readings*

Fernand Ouellet, *Economy, Class, and Nation in Quebec: Interpretive Essays*, ed. and trans. Jacques A. Barbier

Michael J. Piva, ed., *A History of Ontario: Selected Readings*

Patricia E. Roy, ed., *A History of British Columbia: Selected Readings*

John Saywell and George Vegh, ed., *Making the Law: The Courts and the Constitution*

Gilbert A. Stelter, ed., *Cities and Urbanization: Canadian Historical Perspectives*

Veronica Strong-Boag and Anita Clair Fellman, eds., *Rethinking Canada: The Promise of Women's History*, 2nd edition

Joseph Wearing, ed., *The Ballot and Its Message: Voting in Canada*

Graeme Wynn, ed., *People, Places, Patterns, Processes: Geographical Perspectives on the Canadian Past*

NEW CANADIAN READINGS

THE BALLOT

AND ITS

MESSAGE

VOTING IN CANADA

EDITED BY

JOSEPH WEARING

TRENT UNIVERSITY

Copp Clark Pitman Ltd.
A Longman Company
Toronto

© *Copp Clark Pitman Ltd., 1991*

All rights reserved. No part of this work covered by the copyrights hereon may be reproduced or used in any form or by any means—graphic, electronic, or mechanical—without the prior written permission of the publisher.

Any request for photocopying, recording, taping, or for storing on information storage and retrieval systems of any part of this book shall be directed in writing to the Canadian Reprography Collective, 379 Adelaide Street West, Suite M1, Toronto, Ontario M5V 1S5.

ISBN 0-7730-5131-7

executive editor: Brian Henderson
editing: Melanie Sherwood
series design: Susan Hedley
cover design: Liz Nyman
typesetting: Andrea Weiler and Marnie Morrissey
printing and binding: Webcom Limited

Canadian Cataloguing in Publication Data

Main entry under title:

Wearing, Joseph
The ballot and its message

Includes bibliographical references.
ISBN 0-7730-5131-7

1. Voting - Canada, I. Title.
JL193.W42   1991   324.971   C90-095886-3
                 ᒪ9819

Copp Clark Pitman Ltd.
2775 Matheson Blvd. East
Mississauga, Ontario
L4W 4P7

associated companies: *Longman Group Ltd., London ·
Longman Inc., New York · Longman Cheshire Pty., Melbourne ·
Longman Paul Pty., Auckland*

Printed and bound in Canada

1 2 3 4 5   5131-7   95 94 93 92 91

OTABIND

Bound to stay open

Publisher's Note

Otabind (Ota-bind). This book has been bound using the patented Otabind process. You can open this book at any page, gently run your finger down the spine, and the pages will lie flat.

FOREWORD

○

We all (or most of us) vote. But how many of us truly know why we vote the way we do? The impact of party, class, religion, region, gender, and age, not to say a dozen additional important factors, on our ballot tend to be overlooked by most of us, but not by political scientists. The study of voting behaviour is a highly developed art in Canada, as the articles in this collection so clearly demonstrate. And Joseph Wearing, Professor of Political Science at Trent University and editor of this volume, is one of the leaders in the field.

The articles collected here analyse the effects of political, social, and economic factors, and discover much about the patterns of voting behaviour. Reading this text closely might even help Canadians cast their votes more rationally, and more effectively.

J.L. Granatstein
General Editor

AUGUSTANA UNIVERSITY COLLEGE
LIBRARY

CONTENTS

○

FOREWORD _____ *vii*

INTRODUCTION _____ *1*

section *1* PARTY IDENTIFICATION _____ *8*
Partisan Instability in Canada: Evidence from a New
Panel Study • LAWRENCE LEDUC, HAROLD D. CLARKE,
JANE JENSON AND JON H. PAMMETT _____ *9*

Short-term Forces and Partisan Change in Canada:
1974–1980 • HAROLD D. CLARKE AND
MARIANNE C. STEWART _____ *19*

section *2* IDEOLOGICAL AND SOCIAL
FACTORS _____ *53*
Ideology and Unstable Party Identification in Canada: Limited
Rationality in a Brokerage Party System • H. MICHAEL
STEVENSON _____ *54*

Explaining the Religious Basis of the Canadian Partisan
Identity: Success on the Third Try • WILLIAM P. IRVINE ___ *86*

The Reproduction of the Religious Cleavage in Canadian
Elections • RICHARD JOHNSTON_____ *92*

Comment on "The Reproduction of the Religious Cleavage
in Canadian Elections" • WILLIAM P. IRVINE _____ *105*

The Geography of Class and Religion in Canadian Elections •
RICHARD JOHNSTON _____ *108*

section *3* CLASS AND VOTING _____ *136*
Class Voting and Class Consciousness in Canada • JON H.
PAMMETT_____ *137*

Social Class, Left/Right Political Orientations, and Subjective
Class Voting in Provincial and Federal Elections • RONALD
D. LAMBERT, JAMES E. CURTIS, STEVEN D. BROWN AND
BARRY J. KAY _____ *157*

The Failure of the New Democratic Party: Unions, Unionists,
and Politics in Canada • KEITH ARCHER_____ *182*

section *4* THE ECONOMY AND VOTING_____ *194*
The Economy and Political Support: The Canadian Case •
KRISTEN MONROE AND LYNDA ERICKSON _____ *195*

Inflation, Unemployment and Canadian Federal Voting
Behaviour • KEITH ARCHER AND MARQUIS JOHNSON_____ *223*

section 5   *RECENT FEDERAL ELECTIONS* ____ *236*

Voting Behaviour and the Outcome of the 1979 Federal
Election: The Impact of Leaders and Issues • HAROLD D.
CLARKE, JANE JENSON, LAWRENCE LEDUC AND
JON PAMMETT _____ *237*

Great Debates: The Televised Leadership Debates of 1979 •
LAWRENCE LEDUC AND RICHARD PRICE _____ *266*

The Character of Electoral Change: A Preliminary Report from
the 1984 National Election Study • BARRY J. KAY, STEVEN D.
BROWN, JAMES E. CURTIS, RONALD D. LAMBERT AND JOHN
M. WILSON _____ *283*

Free Trade and the Dynamics of the 1988 Canadian
Election • RICHARD JOHNSTON, ANDRÉ BLAIS, HENRY E.
BRADY AND JEAN CRÊTE _____ *315*

section 6   *VOTING AND GENDER* _____ *340*

Does Gender Make A Difference in Voting Behaviour? •
PETER WEARING AND JOSEPH WEARING _____ *341*

FURTHER READING _____ *351*

INTRODUCTION

T he simple act of voting, of marking an "X" on a ballot, repeated twelve million times in one day, can overthrow a government without a single shot being fired. Each individual's act, fused with others' into a truly awesome power, is the culmination of a complex decision-making process. A lifetime's experience, observation, and discussion under the leviathan of the modern state comes together in that simple decision whether or not to renew the present government's lease on power or to replace it with another. Can one help being fascinated with how we and our fellow citizens arrive at our decision?

The question is more than just a kind of academic voyeurism, because it helps us to answer some very basic questions in politics. What do elections mean? Does an election mandate a government to carry out a particular policy or does it simply empower it to act according to its own best judgement? Has the electorate chosen a prime minister or simply dismissed an old one?

The raw material for answering these questions is provided in the survey research data of the National Election Studies, funded by the Social Sciences and Humanities Research Council, from every federal election since 1965 (with the exception of the 1972 poll). As political scientists have analysed the data, utilising increasingly sophisticated statistical methods, they have made considerable progress in unravelling the many considerations and influences that go into the simple act of voting.[1]

The articles and papers collected here are among the most important to appear in the 1980s, and are testimony to the high level of scholarship in this field. Taken together, they provide many insights into our voting behaviour, although many mysteries remain. Nor do the voters themselves remain static as they are being studied—a further testimony (if indeed one were needed) to the incredible complexity of human behaviour.

The study of voting behaviour draws on insights from disciplines such as psychology, economics, sociology, and statistics. The articles in Section 1 look at voting from a psychological perspective with a focus on enduring party loyalty or "party identification" (the usual term). According to this approach, voters develop an affection for one particular party and this colours their views of parties, leaders, and issues.

The concept of party identification was first developed in the US, where it is perhaps more applicable than elsewhere. In many states, a voter registers as a Democrat or Republican in order to be able to vote in the party primary. Although the turnout in primaries is low, the number of Americans who vote in primaries is proportionately much higher than the number who choose party candidates in other countries. American voters, unlike those in parliamentary democracies, also have the opportunity to develop the notion of maintaining an overall loyalty for one party, while occasionally voting for another. This they do when they "ticket split" on the so-called "long ballot" for offices at the national, state and local levels. Because parliamentary voters typically vote for only one candidate on election day, many do not differentiate between identifying with a party and voting for it. When asked for their party identification, they tend to name the party of the candidate they voted for most recently.

While party identification has to be applied more cautiously with respect to Canadian voters, it is still a useful tool in examining party alignment within the electorate. How have these alignments fared over time? Are Canadian voters in the process of changing their allegiances? In other words, are we now in a period of realignment? Or are more voters declaring that they have *no* allegiances, ushering in a period of dealignment? Are most participants voting contrary to their stated allegiances, marking a deviating or volatile period? Currently, both British and white American voters appear to be in a period of dealignment. (Black Americans are more staunchly Democratic than ever.) Canadian voters, on the other hand, are not dealigning, according to LeDuc, Clarke, Jenson and Pammett, but they do change their party identification more often. These observations, however, may not be valid beyond the time-frame of their research (1974–80), since an article in Section 5 by Kay, Brown, Curtis, and Lambert finds evidence of a shift in party identification in 1984, of, in other words, a *realignment*.

LeDuc, Clarke, Jenson and Pammett attempt to explain why Canadians have a lower level of continuous identification with one party than occurs in the US or the UK. Not only do Canadian voters often develop separate party loyalties at federal and provincial levels ("split-identifiers"), but they are also particularly sensitive to short-term forces associated with new issues, government performance, and changes in party programs or leaders. By contrast, socio-demographic variables (such as region, religion, and social class) are only weakly related to party identification and vote, according to the authors.

Clarke and Stewart explore further the unstable nature of party allegiance in Canada. Although this instability is partly explained by younger voters having weaker party ties than their elders, the difference between the two groups is not a marked one. As in the previous article, reasons for switching party identification are due mostly to short-term factors, such as negative feelings about a party's leader and the party's overall performance. Concern about particular issues, on the other hand, are of less importance in explaining changing party allegiances.

The articles in Sections 2 and 3 essentially challenge the thesis that Canadian voters are governed by short-term factors and that long-term influences, such as class and religion, are very weak. In Richard Johnston's words, "the Canadian party system, far from lacking a social base, is profoundly rooted in tribal loyalties."

The article by Stevenson deals with both party identification and class. He challenges a commonly held view that Canadian party politics must, of necessity, be grounded on "an un-ideological centre" and questions whether random changes of mood by an irrational, disillusioned electorate are the primary cause of unstable partisan allegiances. On the contrary, he finds slight though significant evidence that ideological considerations were an important component in the switching of party allegiances from 1977 to 1981 and that class support for the two older parties became more differentiated rather than more similar. Younger voters were more sensitive to class and ideological concerns than older voters. Surprisingly, such post-materialist issues as the environment were less instrumental in changing the party allegiances of young voters than traditional class questions such as income redistribution.

Both Irvine and Johnston are intrigued by the very different support that political parties receive from Catholics and Protestants, even though religious issues no longer have much importance in federal politics. Irvine cites political socialization within the family to explain the phenomenon. Because just under half the electorate identifies with the same party as one or both of their parents, they are said to have "inherited" their party allegiance, and they are also likely to share their parents' religious preferences. So, a link between religion and party—arising from an earlier period when religious issues *did* dominate politics—may have been passed unwittingly from one generation to another. Conversely, when children do not inherit their families' political loyalties, then the political–religious link disappears.

Johnston, on the other hand, argues that inheritance alone cannot explain the persistence of a religious cleavage in the way Canadians vote. Voters can be said to acquire their political allegiances in either of two ways: through inheritance (those who vote the same as their parents) or through recruitment (those who vote differently from their parents). If the religious link were a factor only in the inheritance process, then the contrasting party allegiances of the two religious groups would diminish over time, but that has not happened. The explanation lies in the fact that, mathematically, a party system can approach an equilibrium in which each party's relative size is maintained from one generation to another, but only when the transition rates (i.e., both inheritance and recruitment) vary according to the size of each party. Thus a larger party needs both higher inheritance and higher recruitment rates simply to maintain its position. It will not grow indefinitely since it follows logically that the larger the party, the smaller its potential recruitment base. In this context Johnston uses two terms that may be unfamiliar to the reader. "Asymptotic" means that the parties will steadily approach but never actually achieve this equilibrium. A "stochastic process" is one governed by the laws of probability.

In the Canadian case, the Liberal party's consistently higher level of support by Catholic voters cannot be due only to the inheritance factor. The recruitment rate also has to be high for the cleavage to persist to the same degree over time. In fact, a comparison of the two Liberal columns in table 3 of Johnston's article shows that, among Catholics, the recruitment rate for Liberal children of non-Liberal voters is consistently higher than for Protestants. Johnston concludes by examining various social forces outside the family that influence Catholic voters.

In a later article Johnston examines the interplay of several long-term social factors—religion, union membership and geography. Canadian voters, he suggests, do not see the three major parties only along one simple left–right spectrum with the NDP on the left, the Conservatives on the right and the Liberals in the centre. If they did, the Liberals would always be the first or second choice of every voter. It would be illogical, for example, for a right-wing voter to give his or her first preference to the Conservative party and second preference to the NDP. Table 3 shows, however, that 16.6 per cent of voters outside Quebec gave the Liberal party as their last choice. To solve this conundrum, Johnston hypothesizes that a large number of voters are chiefly concerned to rank the parties on an ethno-religious basis and he believes this to be associated with the division of the population between Catholics and non-Catholics (which is a shorthand indicator of the ethno-religious cleavage). The opposing ends of this second spectrum are occupied by the Conservative and Liberal parties. Depending on the circumstances, a voter may shift from one spectrum to the other, and Johnston finds that one relevant "circumstance" is the size of the Catholic population within a province. When small, the left–right spectrum is uppermost in voters' minds; whereas a large Catholic population induces voters to think along a Catholic versus non-Catholic axis. He concludes: "Where Catholics are numerous, class, or union/nonunion, differences are suppressed. But where Catholics are few, class differences, at least in NDP voting, can flourish. This pattern is especially marked in provincial elections."

Not all of Johnston's expectations are borne out and one could question his assumption that union membership is an indicator of working-class allegiance, especially now when union membership is growing faster in the relatively well-paid public sector and the low-paid service sector is notably less unionized.

The sociological approach is further developed in Section 3, specifically with respect to the role of social class in Canadian voting behaviour. Pammett examines various hypotheses that seek to explain the low level of class consciousness in Canada. The majority of Canadians see themselves as middle class, and survey research does not uncover an appreciable number of discontented, class-conscious workers. Even those voters with a union member in the family are more likely to see themselves as middle class rather than working class—a reflection no doubt of the relative prosperity of those workers who are organised. A small number of voters *do* make a class analysis of society in which class conflict is inevitable; but slightly more of them are middle class than working class! Ironically, the NDP gets its best support from voters in non-manual occupations who see themselves as members of the working class, but they comprise only 3 per cent of the electorate. Class politics might conceivably emerge if the PC party adopted a right-wing, middle-class ideology, attacking universal social programs, for example, and thus raising "an opposing class consciousness." In 1987, Pammett doubted the PC party would pursue such a program. A year later, the Liberal and New Democratic parties attempted to convince voters that such an agenda lay hidden within the Conservative government's Free Trade Agreement with the US, and there is some evidence of more class voting than usual in the 1988 federal election.

Do voters see the parties as favouring one class or another, and are these *subjective* perceptions related to *objective* measures of social class: income, occupation and education? The question is explored by Lambert, Curtis, Brown and Kay. Each respondent in their survey was asked to rank his or her preferred party (both federal and provincial) on a seven-point scale, one being "for the lower social classes," and seven "for the higher social classes." Using these indicators, class voting was more evident in provincial than in federal elections. The highest level of class voting occurred in BC, Alberta and Saskatchewan provincial elections. The lowest was in Quebec. Total explained variance was substantially improved when two other *subjective* variables were added: respondents were asked to place themselves on a left–right spectrum and within a class hierarchy. Not surprisingly, those who described themselves as right-wing and upper class tended to vote for a party they saw favouring the higher social classes. More remarkably, adding the two subjective variables pushed Ontario and Manitoba into the group of provinces with a high level of class voting in provincial elections.

Additional support for the thesis that subjective class awareness has a greater impact on voting than objective factors such as income, education and occupation is provided in the article by Archer on the NDP and unions. Members of trade unions that are affiliated with the NDP are more inclined than those in non-affiliated unions to see themselves as members of the working class and to have a favourable view of the NDP. They also vote NDP in greater numbers. For the NDP, a disturbing feature of this research lies in the steadily declining percentage of union members who are in NDP-affiliated locals.

In contrast to the foregoing approaches, which see voters as being motivated by their emotions or their group loyalties, a quite different approach to voting behaviour is inspired by the economists' view of people as essentially rational beings. These theories see the voter as a rational actor who judges the governing party on its past and on its proven record in delivering those benefits which the voter values highly. A much more difficult assessment comes when estimating how effective the opposition party (or parties) would be in delivering those same benefits. The voter then makes a choice. To economize the effort involved in having to make a rational decision every voting day, the voter tends to give the benefit of the doubt to one party—a short-hand calculation that is likely to become entrenched over the years, unless some dramatic event (a depression, a war, a scandal) upsets the calculation. (The end result is not so very different from the process of party identification discussed earlier, except that the latter is a more emotional process, the former more rational.) Although Canadian political scientists have shown less interest in the rational approach, Section 4 does provide two articles that test various hypotheses on how economic conditions might affect support for the three federal political parties.

According to the findings of Monroe and Erickson, Canadians believe that the federal government is responsible for controlling inflation and unemployment. In light of this, one might expect to see voters either passing judgement on the governing party's economic performance or casting their votes according to perceptions as to which party is better equipped to deal with inflation or unemployment. Neither hypothesis is born out with respect to support for either of the two older parties, apparently because voters see no significant differences between them on economic policies. Economic fluctuations do affect NDP support, but not in the expected way. The rational theory suggests that voters should be attracted to the NDP's more radical prescriptions when the party in power (either the Liberals or the Conservatives) has allowed increasing unemployment to soil its record. But the voters do the opposite. Support for the NDP rises in times of prosperity. The study suggests that perhaps voters exercise a different kind of rationality. They regard the party's social welfare programs as luxury goods, which the country can afford only in good times, rather than as antidotes to economic decline.

The article by Archer and Johnson indicates that, under certain conditions, the voters may indeed distinguish between the Liberals and Conservatives on economic questions. They use the terms "sociotropic" and "egocentric economic voting" in testing whether the individual is sensitive to general economic conditions or whether, as in the second case, the voter is concerned only with his or her own economic situation. Only the first seems to be an important factor in voting behaviour. In two recent elections economic issues were especially salient: inflation in the 1974 election, and unemployment in the 1984 election. In the first election, inflation did not affect the outcome, partly because Trudeau's popularity helped the Liberal government overcome the issue's negative impact. In the second election, Turner's unpopularity did nothing to mitigate the public's concern over unemployment—something that worked to the PC party's advantage.

In Section 5, three recent federal elections are analysed. Clarke, Jenson, LeDuc and Pammett show that the 1979 election can be seen as a case study of how parties attempt to devise a winning strategy in a situation where none really has an advantage. None of the three leaders was especially popular and no issue was dominant. Because Joe Clark, in certain respects, was his party's biggest handicap, the party developed a strategy of "aggregating several 'issue publics'"—of finding several issues, each of which was important for a segment of the electorate. The strategy worked, but not enough to give the party a decisive victory. Those who switched their votes between 1974 and 1979 moved disproportionately to the PCs. New voters, however, favoured the Liberals, as did those for whom the leader was an important factor in their voting decision. As for the NDP, it gained votes from Liberals between 1974 and 1979, but lost a good number to the Conservatives. Not surprisingly, the election produced a minority government.

Televised debates between the three party leaders have become an important part of campaign mythology, but whether they actually make a difference to the outcome is another question. In attempting to answer it, LeDuc and Price are very sensitive to the problem of establishing causality and the direction it takes. Paradoxically, those who watched the debates assessed Clark's performance more negatively than Trudeau's or Broadbent's, but they were also more likely to have voted Conservative. The authors suggest that the direction of causality may indeed have been reversed. That is, those who had already decided to vote Conservative were more likely to have watched the debates, which simply reinforced their voting decision. Similarly, the debates did not produce a higher turnout at the polls from those who had watched them. Instead, what seems to have happened is that those who intended to vote made a point of watching the debates. Undoubtedly, the 1979 debates had a minimal impact because they occurred just nine days before the election. The 1984 and 1988 debates were held earlier and were also more dramatic in content. A comparison of the three debates would be particularly instructive for showing the relative impact of televised debates on voting behaviour.

The Conservative landslide victory of 1984 raises a fundamental question that interests Kay, Brown, Curtis, Lambert and Wilson. Was it a flash-in-the-pan (a deviating election), or had a major realignment of the parties occurred? This is not easily answered, partly because it is only after the passage of time that we can be sure that a long-term shift in voter loyalties has really set in. Moreover, Canadian voters have been notorious vote switchers in the past. The number of switchers did increase in 1984, although the increase was not as great as the election results would suggest. What made 1984 switchers distinctive is that they showed a greater consensus about the direction of their switching than had been the case in several preceding elections. The PC party made its biggest gains among groups that had previously been most alienated from the party, most notably Quebeckers and

French Canadians. Consequently, the patterns of support for each party emerging from the 1984 election were remarkably uniform throughout the country, compared with the regional and socio-demographic cleavages of preceding elections. Evidence for arguing that the election was a short-term, deviating election can perhaps be deduced from the authors' findings that more voters than usual decided how to vote during the campaign period and especially after having watched the televised leaders' debates. On the other hand, the shift in party identification suggests that 1984 may have been a realigning election—at least for the two older parties. They recognise, nevertheless, that in Canada, unlike the US, party identification tends to be a shorter-term phenomenon accompanying a change in party vote.

The 1988 federal election is an especially fascinating subject for study. First, unlike most elections, one issue was dominant—the Free Trade Agreement (FTA) with the US. Second, support for the three major parties shifted dramatically in the course of the campaign. Third, the election provides a good case study of the perennial controversy about whether published polls have an impact on voter intentions. In examining these questions, Johnston, Blais, Brady and Crête explain one paradox of the campaign. Because opposition to the FTA grew steadily throughout the campaign, one might have expected its only supporter, the PC party, to have done worse than it did—possibly to have lost the election. The party's majority victory is largely explained by the manner in which it continuously squeezed support from its natural base, FTA supporters. At the start of the campaign just two thirds of FTA supporters intended to vote Conservative, but by the end, the party's share of the pro-FTA camp climbed to a remarkable 88 per cent.

Finally, we provide an initial investigation of a surprisingly overlooked aspect of Canadian voting behaviour—that of Canadian women. Although considerable research has been done on women's participation in the political process and obstacles to that participation, there has been relatively little analysis of what women do when they get to the polls. A gender gap does exist, but not always in the expected direction. Unlike the historical pattern in other western democracies, Canadian women are not more conservative than men; indeed they are less conservative, especially those with a university education. Some of this difference is related to differing policy concerns, although not always on issues where one might expect it. For example, men and women divide about the same over abortion; but concern over controlling the deficit sets highly educated men apart from their peers of the opposite sex and from the rest of the population. It remains to be seen whether the parties will begin appealing to the gender gap in the areas where it exists.

NOTES

1. Because some of the statistics are quite complex, it might be appropriate to remind the reader that the material can be read at several different levels, depending on one's familiarity with statistics. Some readers will want to examine the methodology closely. Others that have only a rudimentary understanding of statistics can still follow the conclusions, although they would obviously not be able to question the methodology itself.

section

1

PARTY IDENTIFICATION

PARTISAN INSTABILITY IN CANADA: EVIDENCE FROM A NEW PANEL STUD$Y^\diamond$

LAWRENCE LeDUC
HAROLD D. CLARKE
JANE JENSON
JON H. PAMMETT

o

The concept of party identification derives from more general precepts of social psychological theory which stress the importance of reference groups in processes of attitude formation and the development of a sense of personal identity. Political scientists who have traced the origins of the concept often cite Wallas's[1] description of political parties as objects that could be "loved and trusted" by individuals because they could be recognized from one election to another as being the same thing. Since the publication of the seminal work by Campbell and his colleagues,[2] the notion that voters develop partisan identities and that these self-perceptions serve as a powerful influence on voting choice has provided the basis for much of our theoretical understanding of the forces that act on individual voting behaviour. As Miller notes in a review of the evolution and application of the concept:

> Party identification has become one of the ubiquitous concepts in national and cross-national electoral analysis. In one version or another, the concept has been used in innumerable studies of mass politics and has now been described or otherwise analyzed in at least fifteen different countries.[3]

Although the concept of an enduring psychological predisposition in favour of a political party appears to have a high degree of theoretical generality, it would seem particularly applicable to polities characterised by a relatively stable two-party system combined with electoral arrangements in which a large number of voting

---

$^\diamond$ *American Political Science Review* 78 (June 1984): 470–84.

choices are required. In systems that do not possess one or both of these attributes, the meaning of the concept is less certain. Thus, although the concept of party identification has been applied to the study of electoral behaviour in several countries, its utility in models of voting choice in non-American settings has been questioned, particularly in political milieux with multiparty systems, electoral systems less complex than that of the United States, or both.[4]

The importance of comprehending the characteristics of partisanship in different political systems goes beyond questions related to the determinants of individual voting behaviour. In particular, patterns and levels of instability in individual partisan ties are relevant for understanding aggregate change in party systems over time. A key indicator, for example, of hypothesised patterns of dealignment in several contemporary Western political systems has been an observed increase in the number of individuals without strong psychological attachments to political parties.[5] Similarly, hypotheses regarding partisan realignment involve the initial abandonment of an established party tie, followed by its replacement with an equally strong attachment to another party, either simultaneously or within some definable period of time. Theories of dealignment, therefore, postulate increased or increasing levels of partisan instability at the individual and aggregate levels, whereas theories of realignment require a specific sequence of events at both levels culminating in a changed but once again stable party system and pattern of identification.

In the past decade, two research developments have helped to advance our theoretical understanding of the concept of party identification along the lines suggested by Miller in his discussion of its cross-national applications quoted above. One of these has been the study of party identification in countries with party and electoral systems considerably different from those of the United States. A second, related, development has been a growing recognition of the need for accurate data on changes in party identification over time. To date, theoretically fruitful cross-national comparisons have been hampered by the absence in many countries of panel survey data which would permit reliable measurement of cross-time change in party identification at the individual level. Recall data utilised for this purpose, although suggestive of general patterns, are subject to challenge on methodological grounds and are limited in the amount of information they can yield regarding the actual dynamics of partisanship.[6]

Juxtaposing the results of the handful of existing panel studies suggests the existence of interesting and potentially important cross-national differences in key characteristics of party identification. Analyses of the three US panel studies to date (1956–1960, 1972–1976, and 1980) have found relatively high levels of directional stability in individual partisanship,[7] findings consistent with earlier conceptions of party identification as an enduring psychological tie between the voter and the party system. Studies in other countries, in contrast, have disclosed a greater tendency for party identification to travel with the vote, thereby suggesting that partisanship in non-American political settings is more responsive to the various short-term forces associated with particular elections. In one of the earlier and best known comparisons, Butler and Stokes noted the strong tendency in Britain for partisan change to accompany vote switching although they did not question the overall utility of a concept of partisan self-image in the British case.[8] In the Netherlands, however, Thomassen's finding that party identification was *less* stable than vote across a three-year period prompted him to conclude that the role of party identification in explaining voting behaviour in that country was doubtful.[9]

The findings of such panel surveys should be considered in conjunction with the results of recent analyses of nonrecursive models of electoral choice that demonstrate that party identification should be conceptualized as endogenous to the matrix of forces operative in the electoral arena during particular time periods.[10] Rather than being unmoved movers, the strength and, in some instances, even the direction of party identification are subject to the short-term effects of voters' prospective and retrospective evaluations of candidates and parties.

Although American panel survey data indicate high levels of continuity in the direction of party identification, there is evidence that, in certain circumstances, the directional stability of party identification in the United States is not impervious to short-term forces. In particular, the panel study by Jennings and Niemi suggests that levels of directional change in partisanship can be substantial. Their research shows that, in the late 1960s and early 1970s at least, levels of partisan change varied across generations, with the identifications of younger persons being considerably less stable than those of their parents.[11] Secondary analysis of their data by Markus shows that tendencies toward partisan change were at least partly a function of reactions to salient political issues.[12] Such findings notwithstanding, the weight of the evidence suggests that, in the American case, short-term forces primarily influence the strength rather than the direction of party identification. In this respect, the United States stands in contrast to other countries such as Britain and the Netherlands, where it appears that such forces can have sizable effects on both the directional stability and the strength of partisan attachments.

In sum, recent studies in the United States and elsewhere indicate that the nature of party identification remains imperfectly understood. Clearly, the hither-to-prevailing conception of party identification as a stable, exogenous force in models of voting behaviour and election outcomes seems inadequate, both in the American case and a fortiori, in other Western polities where requisite research has been conducted. Taken together, existing evidence suggests that the theoretical status of party identification in such models, and the more general utility of the concept for cross-national inquiry, cannot be definitively established until more is learned about the characteristics of partisan attachments in different political milieux.

In this article, we attempt to deepen and extend our understanding of the party identification concept by examining some of its crucial properties in one contemporary liberal democracy—Canada.[13] Generally, it can be anticipated that a number of the important aspects of party identification in Canada will resemble those of the British case more closely than those of the United States or the Netherlands. The Canadian party system, with two major parties and a strong third party, is similar to that of Britain in the 1970s, and the electoral systems of the two countries are identical. However, Canada, unlike Britain or the Netherlands, is also a federal system. Surprisingly little is known about patterns of partisanship at multiple levels of government in federal polities. Unlike other federal systems such as the United States, West Germany, or Australia, provincial politics in Canada often are quite distinctive, with party systems such as those of Quebec or British Columbia differing greatly from that of the national arena. The opportunity to investigate more fully the question of dual loyalties, and the particular meaning that these may have for broadening our understanding of the party identification concept, makes the Canadian case an important one for cross-national research.

An examination of party identification in Canada is facilitated by the availability of a major new three-wave panel study which greatly enhances our ability to measure the stability of the components of partisanship in this country and to make direct comparisons with the known properties of party identification elsewhere.[14] Specifically, we are able to investigate the nature and extent of instability of party identification in Canada, as well as some of the characteristics of Canadian party identification deriving from the existence of autonomous federal and provincial party systems. If provincial and federal partisanship are mutually reinforcing, then those whose identification is consistent across the two levels of the political system should be more likely to be stable than those whose identification is inconsistent. Furthermore, if it were argued, as the classic literature might suggest, that cross-level inconsistency in partisanship represents a state of cognitive dissonance, then it can be expected that changes in provincial partisanship will be in the direction of federal partisanship (or vice versa), i.e., in the direction of consistency. If, however, in a decentralized federal system such as Canada's, inconsistent identification reflects a more general independence of political orientation toward the two levels of government, one would not anticipate a trend toward resolution in favour of consistency, but rather an approximately equal flow in both directions.

The value of the Canadian panels for investigating these and related questions is enhanced by the timing of recent federal elections, which provide a rare opportunity to contrast movement over a relatively limited period of time (1979–1980) with that over considerably longer intervals (1974–1979, 1974–1980). A three-wave panel also possesses a great advantage over one containing only two waves in that it is possible to distinguish patterns of sustained change from simple volatility. For example, one can distinguish persons who change partisanship for a short period only and then return to a former identification from those who change or abandon partisanship on a more permanent basis. The existence of recent panel studies for comparable time periods in both Britain and the United States provides an additional bonus, in that it permits more accurate comparisons of patterns of partisanship in Canada with those in other countries, thereby advancing our understanding of the theoretical generality of the party identification concept.

To orient readers unfamiliar with the Canadian case, we may observe that data on party identification in Canada (figure 1) depict an electorate in which the vast majority of voters identify at least "fairly strongly" with a party. Similar to the British case, but in contrast to that for the United States, the number of respondents who classify themselves as independents or who decline a party identification is small. Also, unlike the results of recent surveys in Britain and the United States, the percentage of Canadians reporting only a weak partisan attachment is relatively

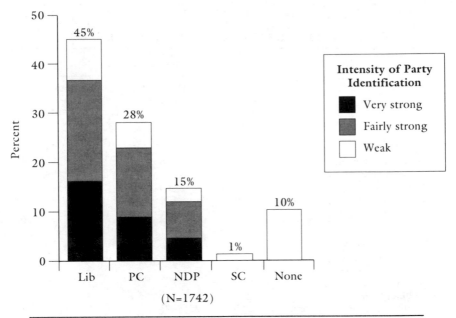

FIGURE 1   *DIRECTION AND INTENSITY OF FEDERAL*
PARTY IDENTIFICATION IN CANADA:
1980 NATIONAL SAMPLE

small.[15] Again dissimilar to the British and American cases, no sustained pattern of aggregate change is suggested by the Canadian data, the direction and strength of identifications in 1980 being generally very similar to the results of every national survey conducted since 1965.[16] Identification with the Liberal party, long the dominant party in Canadian federal politics, continues to exceed that for all other parties by a substantial margin. Percentages of respondents identifying with the Progressive Conservative or the New Democratic parties, the second and third largest federal parties, are substantially smaller than that for the Liberals, and are likewise at levels very similar to those for previous national surveys. Social Credit, an erratic factor in Canadian politics since the 1930s, has witnessed its level of partisan support erode very slowly over the past decade and a half (from 6% in 1965 to 1% in 1980), and it is no longer a significant political force in national politics.

In both direction and intensity of partisanship, then, the survey data portray a seemingly stable party system and a partisan electorate. Of course aggregate stability should not be taken to imply individual stability. Nevertheless, it is clear that party identification in Canada has not been subject to extensive weakening or dealignment, and it is unlikely, although not impossible, that these data mask an ongoing process of sustained realignment or other secular change. Whether this portrait of aggregate stability reflects patterns of stability at the individual level is an empirical question that can best be addressed via the panel surveys.

TABLE 1   *TURNOVER IN PARTY IDENTIFICATION AND VOTING BEHAVIOUR: 1974–1979 AND 1979–1980 CANADIAN PANELS (%)*

	Party Identification			
	Same party in both waves	Different parties	Moving to or from non-identification*	Total
1974–1979 Panel**				
Voting for the same party in 1974 and 1979 elections	48	4	8	60
Voting for different parties in 1974 and 1979	7	10	5	22
Moving to or from nonvoting	10	4	4	18
Total	65	18	17	100
1979–1980 Panel*				
Voting for the same party in 1979 and 1980 elections	58	3	7	68
Voting for different parties in 1979 and 1980	7	7	3	17
Moving to or from nonvoting	10	3	2	15
Total	75	13	12	100

* Includes respondents reporting nonidentification in both waves (3% in 1974–1979 and 3% in 1979–1980).
** Diagonal percentages. $N = 1213$. Excludes nonvoters in both elections.
* Diagonal percentages. $N = 1558$. Excludes nonvoters in both elections.

THE DIRECTIONAL STABILITY OF PARTISANSHIP

Although the Canadian party system appears stable in the aggregate, it is nevertheless a system that contains large numbers of "flexible" partisans, including many who report instability of partisanship at some time in the past.[17] The Canadian electorate likewise contains durable party identifiers, for whom long-term forces are powerful predictors of voting choice.[18] To investigate individual-level stability in partisanship, we examine first the turnover of party identification and vote between two proximate pairings of elections (1974–1979 and 1979–1980) as shown in table 1. We use 3 x 3 tables for this purpose because it is desirable to include nonidentifiers in the analysis and to distinguish clearly between the adoption of a new party identification and the abandonment of a former one. The inclusion of nonidentifiers is especially important for comparative purposes. Butler and Stokes' finding, for example, that party identification in Great Britain has a greater tendency to travel with vote than in the United States has been shown to derive largely from their decision to include British Liberal party identifiers in the analysis while excluding American Independents.[19] When both groups are included, the conclusion drawn is somewhat different. The same point may be inferred from Converse's study of the dynamics of partisanship in the United States.[20] Although his analysis of the 1956–1960 panel shows little actual turnover of party identification, a much higher level of instability is evident if movement from identification to independence and vice versa is considered. Similar arguments may be applied with respect to non-voters. The exclusion of nonvoters eliminates a type of electoral change that is known to be an important element of the dynamics of both individual voting behaviour and electoral outcomes.[21] Linkages between nonvoting and partisan instability therefore require careful examination.

During the five years between the 1974 and 1979 elections, less than half of the panel (48%) was stable with regard to both party identification and vote (table 1). Between the 1979 and 1980 elections, the comparable figure is only 58%, although these two contests occurred within a nine-month span. This finding suggests that time alone is of limited importance in accounting for partisan instability. Time is seemingly less important than the existence of opportunities for change, such as those provided by exposure to short-term forces generated by events such as elections. Relatedly, a noticeable proportion of the movement in both the 1974–1979 and 1979–1980 cases is accounted for by the entry and exit of transient voters including, in each instance, 10% of the panel who fail to vote in one of the paired elections but who show no change in their partisanship. This effect represents the mobilization or demobilization of persons whose identifications are directionally stable over the period surveyed. To this group may be added an additional complement of transient voters who do show changes in partisanship— 8% in the 1974–1979 panel and 5% in the 1979–1980 panel—but whose partisan leanings, or lack thereof, are reflected in their voting choice in only one of the elections in question. This category divides about equally in both instances between those shifting between parties and those moving between partisanship and nonidentification.

Particularly interesting is the cell (7% in each panel) that combines stability of partisanship with variability in voting choice, because it is this group that most closely fits the concept of partisanship described in the early American voting studies. Although this cell demonstrates that the Canadian electorate contains individuals whose partisanship survives periodic changes in voting behaviour, it is perhaps of greater importance to note that this group is considerably smaller than is commonly reported in American studies and that it is smaller than (in the case of 1974–1979 panel) or equal to (in the 1979–1980 panel) the proportion of the electorate for whom partisanship travels with vote (centre cell of table 1).[22] These two groups, found in the centre and centre-left cells of each panel in table 1, represent two basic types of partisan-vote change. Clearly, there are Canadian voters whose partisanship is durable, supported by various long-term forces that may change only slowly, if at all. For these individuals, party identification is more stable than voting choice in any given election. But there are also those for whom partisanship is as unstable as voting choice itself, changing with the vote in response to various short-term forces associated with elections.

There is, it may be noted, a third group of individuals who do not fit either of the two basic types described above, but who collectively account for a significant portion of the total movement found in both panels, namely persons who decline to identify with a party in one or both of the two waves of the respective panels. In the American studies, these are commonly referred to as "independents," but the term "independent" is rarely used in Canadian politics, either by survey respondents or by analysts. Although Canada, unlike the United States, does not have a large or increasing contingent of political independents, the role of nonidentification in the dynamics of partisanship in Canada is an important one. At a given point in time only about one voter in ten does not report a party identification at the federal level (see figure 1) and, if federal and provincial identifications are considered together, the percentage of voters lacking a party tie in some form is even smaller. However, this nonpartisan tenth of the electorate is not a fixed entity. In each of the two-wave panels (1974–1979, 1979–1980), the percentage of respondents who maintain continuous nonidentification is only 3%, and the percentage doing so across all three waves (1974–1979–1980) is about the same. In Canada, therefore, most nonidentifiers are not a permanently unaligned contingent of voters, but rather individuals caught at any given time in the process of movement from one party identification to another or away from a party and back again. Like a single frame clipped from a strip of movie film, nonidentification in Canada is a static fragment of a dynamic process.

Although this pattern suggests that the number of true independents is actually very small in Canada, it also may be interpreted to mean that the phenomenon of nonidentification is somewhat more widespread than it appears in a single cross-section survey. Although only one voter in ten reports nonidentification in any given wave, and only 3% do so continuously, 22% of the total panel report nonidentification in one of the three waves. Nonidentification reflects electoral behaviour less than does partisan change in that it occurs as often in conjunction with stable voting preferences as with a change of vote or a move to nonvoting. In the aggregate, it is as important a source of instability across time as directional partisan change.

The various types of movement across all three waves of the panel are summarised in table 2. Over the three waves, 41% of the respondents display stability of partisanship and vote. As noted, nonidentification occurs in conjunction with both

TABLE 2   SUMMARY OF TURNOVER IN PARTY IDENTIFICATION AND VOTING BEHAVIOUR IN THREE PANEL WAVES: 1974–1979–1980 *(Percentages of Total Sample)**

| | Party Identification | | |
Vote	Same in three waves	Changing at least once	Moving to or from non-identification**
Voting three times for the same party	41	3	7
Switching at least once	11	16	9
Not voting at least once	13	6	6

* *N* = 791. The table excludes nonvoters in all three elections. Rows and columns do not total, and do not total to 100%, because not all categories are mutually exclusive. A respondent, for example, who switched in one pair of elections and did not vote in the other is counted in two cells. The same is true of those who moved to or from nonidentification and also changed party identification.

** Includes 2% of sample that reported continuous nonidentification.

stability and instability of voting choice. The three other main types of movement in the panel are delineated by the cells italicised for emphasis in table 2, each of which represents a distinctive type of movement of party identification or vote or both. Sixteen per cent of the sample report a change in partisanship together with a change in vote in at least one wave of the panel, whereas 11% report partisan stability combined with at least one voting switch. The third of these cells, at 13%, consists of those who report the same party identification across the three waves, but were not mobilized to vote in all three elections. Together with the fully stable group and those moving to or away from nonidentification, these represent the main categories of stability and change in partisanship and voting in the Canadian electorate.

In assessing the picture of party identification in Canada presented by these data, a comparison with other countries is useful: table 3 replicates and summarises the analysis up to this point with the use of panel studies in the United States and Britain conducted over approximately the same period and with similar research designs and virtually identical measures.[23] Of the three countries, Canada has the smallest percentage of respondents maintaining the same party identification across all three panel waves. The meaning of this statistic is illustrated by the particular characteristics of party identification in each country. The percentage reporting a change in the direction of party identification in the United States is significantly lower than in Britain or Canada, reflecting the unusually stable character of US party identification even during a politically volatile period.[24] Similar to Canada, Britain displays a relatively high degree of directional change in party identification, but is distinguished by the much smaller role played by moves to or from nonidentification. Partisan instability in Canada, then, is greater than in Britain or the United States because it incorporates both of these features, whereas the other two countries display only one of them in significant numbers.

When voting choice is taken into account (table 3), the picture changes considerably. The three countries differ only slightly with regard to vote switching between elections, although Canada is still the most volatile of the three. But it is the very high incidence of nonvoting which distinguishes the United States from the other two cases and results in the relatively small percentage of Americans (39%) who report voting for the same party across the three elections. Also distinctive in the American case is the combination of high levels of stability in party identification with considerable volatility in voting behaviour (table 3). Although Canada stands between Britain and the United States in terms of the percentage maintaining a stable identification and vote, it is in fact quite similar to Britain in displaying a greater tendency for party identification to travel with the vote. Overall, then, although there are some distinctive features in the patterns of partisanship and voting in Britain and Canada, it is the United States that appears to constitute the special case.

To this point, the primary concern has been to measure levels of partisan and electoral change and to distinguish broadly between certain types of change, e.g., variations in the direction of party identification, moves to and from nonidentification, and the re-entry and exit of nonvoters. We should recognise, however, that variations in partisanship, particularly when measured across a pair of elections, may conform to a number of different patterns, some of which constitute an enduring

TABLE 3   *TURNOVER OF PARTY IDENTIFICATION AND VOTE IN THREE-WAVE PANELS IN CANADA, THE UNITED STATES, AND GREAT BRITAIN(%)*

	Canada 1974–1979– 1980	United States 1972–1974– 1976	Britain 1974 (Feb.)– 1974 (Oct.)– 1979
Party Identification			
Same in three waves	59+	68	73
Changing at least once	23	11	23
Moving to or from non- identification++	22	24	6
Voting Behaviour			
Voting for the same party in three elections	49	39◆	57
Switching at least once	33	28	28
Abstaining at least once◆◆	24	39	19
Specific Partisanship/Vote Patterns			
Same party identification and vote in three-panel waves	41	33	52
Changing both party and vote at least once	16	4	13
Same party identification, but switching vote at least once	11	19	11
Same party identification but abstaining at least once◆◆	13	25	11
N	791	772	706

+ The percentages total more than 100% because categories are not mutually exclusive.
++ Includes continuous nonidentifiers in all three waves: Canada, 2%; United States, 4%; Britain, less than 1%.
◆ For House of Representatives.
◆◆ But excluding nonvoters in all three elections, which makes a significant difference only for the United States in which 17% of the total sample report not voting for Congressional candidates in all three elections.

change and others of which might be more properly classified as ongoing volatility or fluctuation. For example, individuals who abandoned a party tie in 1979 but returned to it in 1980 might be said to have followed a classic pattern of short-term deviation, rather than one of longer-term partisan change. In contrast, voters who adopted a new party tie in 1979 and kept it through the 1980 election are displaying a potentially more permanent alteration of partisan attachment. The three-wave panel can be of considerable value in isolating and identifying these types of move-ment which, if systematic, may suggest patterns of realignment or dealignment. When a change of partisanship occurs in the second wave of the panel, it is possible to use the third wave to confirm the nature of that change. Where the variation occurs in the third (1980) wave, however, no additional information is available that would permit a more detailed classification. Within these limitations, it is possible to classify patterns of partisan stability and change in the three-wave panel.

TABLE 4   SUMMARY OF STABILITY AND CHANGE
PATTERNS IN PARTY IDENTIFICATION:
THREE-WAVE PANEL, 1974-1979-1980 (%)

Stable Partisanship (same party identification in all three waves)	59
Homing Pattern (returning to initial party identification)	6
Alignment and Realignment (moving to a new party identification)	14
Dealignment Pattern (abandoning party identification)	6
Volatility Pattern (all multiple changes)	7
Indeterminate Change (third wave change only)	8
	100

N = 854

Such a classification is presented in table 4. The first category comprises the 59% of the panel who have directionally stable partisan ties across the three waves of the panel. More than half of these persons are Liberals, indicating the extent of the advantage this party traditionally has enjoyed in Canadian federal politics. The remaining 41% report directional differences in party identification at some point in the six-year period and display a myriad of specific patterns of partisan change. However, most of these can be grouped into broad types that are readily associated with familiar processes of electoral and partisan change. Thus, slightly more than 6% of the total sample display what might be called a homing pattern of partisanship, that is, abandoning a party identification in 1979 but returning to it in 1980. Most of these are also Liberals, a finding consistent with the temporary decline in Liberal voting associated with that party's defeat in the 1979 election and its subsequent return to power in 1980. A somewhat larger proportion of the panel (14%) displays a pattern consistent with an ongoing process of alignment or realignment, involving a change in 1979 which was subsequently confirmed in the 1980 interview. Given the differing circumstances of the 1979 and 1980 elections, there is every reason to suspect that these represent "real" alterations in partisanship which may have consequences beyond voting choice in specific elections. Although no single party benefits substantially from these sustained changes, fewer than a third moved toward the Liberals, whereas more than two-thirds favoured either the Conservatives or the NDP. The term "alignment/realignment" is appropriate in describing the patterns of movement of these respondents as individuals, but it should not be understood as necessarily having such consequences for the party system as a whole. Rather, it appears to be a fragment of the ongoing process of interchange among the parties, in which each gains and loses a certain number of new adherents.

This general pattern is echoed by the small complement of respondents who appear to have undergone a process of dealignment, in which the abandonment of a partisan tie has not been accompanied by the assumption of a new one. This group is exceedingly small in Canada, particularly in comparison with the United States, which has shown marked tendencies toward dealignment in recent years.[25] In the former country, the number of nonidentifiers assuming a party tie is nearly as great as the number of identifiers abandoning one, leaving the size of the nonidentifier group virtually constant across the period covered by the national surveys. Clearly, dealignment has not been an important part of the process of partisan change in Canada. Some of the change patterns, of course, do not fit any of the categories detailed above, either because variation occurs only in the third wave of the panel and therefore cannot be classified, or because it is part of a pattern of multiple movement. Of the latter group (7% of the sample), it might be said that the pattern is one of simple volatility—ongoing instability devoid of any clear directional component. Although some of the respondents in this category may eventually settle into a pattern of stable partisanship, it is likely that this group is more representative of that segment of the electorate for whom partisanship is continuously unstable, buffeted by a variety of short-term forces associated with varying perceptions of parties, party leaders, and issues.

CROSS-LEVEL CONSISTENCY

In federal systems, the relationship between partisanship at the federal (national) and provincial (state) levels is relevant to any examination of the properties of party identification generally. Although investigations of cross-level variation in party identification in other federal systems such as the United States and Australia have disclosed that few voters maintain multiple partisan allegiances,[26] there is good reason to believe that the marked differences between the federal and provincial party systems in Canada might be associated with greater cross-level variability. Canadian political parties at different levels of the federal system are quite distinct, even in those provinces where they carry the same name, which may affect partisan attachments in a direct and meaningful way. In several provinces, there are strong provincial parties which either are absent entirely from the federal scene or which fail to compete successfully for support at the federal level. The Parti Québécois in Quebec and Social Credit in British Columbia are good present-day examples of this phenomenon, and historically there have been several important provincial political movements which have had no exact federal counterpart. In addition, a number of provinces such as Manitoba, Saskatchewan, and Ontario have political parties that, although they bear the same names, cannot, to paraphrase Wallas, be recognised as being the same thing at different levels of government. Even in the Atlantic provinces, where federal and provincial party alignments are relatively similar, the nature of individual-level partisan linkages at the two levels must be treated as an empirical question. Separate measures of federal and provincial party identifications used in the Canadian surveys provide an opportunity to study multiple-level identifications as a component of partisanship in a decentralized federal system.[27]

The survey data show that only a minority of Canadians maintain a fully consistent party identification across levels of the federal system with respect to both direction and intensity, although about two-thirds do so with regard to direction alone. The proportion of fully consistent identifiers in the nation as a whole has remained virtually constant across the three waves of the panel (44% in 1974 and 45% in 1980), indicating that inconsistency of partisanship across level is an established feature of Canadian politics and not merely part of a transitional phase of a general partisan realignment or the rejection in some provinces of federal parties in favour of provincial ones. Although cross-level inconsistency is greater where the provincial party systems are most distinctive (e.g., in Quebec, British Columbia, and Alberta), it is of more than minor importance in the partisan fabric of virtually every province. In Ontario, for example, barely half of the provincial respondents (e.g., 51% in 1980) are fully consistent across level, whereas 17% of Ontarians in the most recent survey report split (i.e., directionally different) identifications at the two levels of government. Even in the Atlantic provinces, where partisan consistency tends to be greater than elsewhere, there is substantial variation in both direction and intensity between federal and provincial identification. For example, 58% of Nova Scotians and 60% of Newfoundlanders reported fully consistent identification in 1980, whereas 9% and 13%, respectively, were split party identifiers.

The panel data also provide an opportunity to investigate relationships between patterns of change in federal and provincial party identification. In the aggregate, approximately the same proportions of respondents report changes in provincial as in federal partisanship across the three-wave panel, and the nature of these changes is very similar. Fifty-six per cent maintain the same provincial party identification throughout, whereas 29% show at least one change in provincial party attachment (compare table 3). Twenty per cent of the panel report a move to provincial nonidentification at some point, about the same as the percentage doing so federally. Such moves, however, may be either related to, or completely independent of, changes in federal partisanship. Respondents whose party identification was inconsistent across level in 1974 are somewhat more likely to have reported a change in either federal or provincial identification over the course of the three-wave panel (r = .23). But this does not necessarily imply a move in the direction of consistency. As noted above, one might hypothesise that inconsistency of identification is an inherently unstable condition, creating a dissonance which must eventually be resolved in favour of one level or the other. Alternatively, the salience of both levels of government and the federalist nature of the Canadian party system suggest that this may not be the case. If the adoption of two separate identifications is consonant with the broader realities of Canadian politics, and if these identifications are to some degree compartmentalised within their respective spheres of relevance (i.e., federal and provincial politics), then no dissonance will be created and inconsistency will prove to be relatively enduring, both at the individual level and in the aggregate.

For the three-wave panel taken as a whole, slightly fewer than half (47%) remain consistent with regard to direction of partisanship across the three interviews, whereas 14% maintain a position of inconsistency, a total of 61% showing no change in directional consistency. A change in partisan consistency indicates, by definition, that identification with either a federal or provincial party has changed across the period examined. When both direction and intensity of partisanship are taken into account, treating changes in intensity alone as "partial inconsistency," only 19% are found to maintain a position of continuous and full consistency, and only 29% of the panel show no change at all in cross-level consistency over the six-year period (data not shown).

These are impressive levels of change over a relatively short period of time, but they do not reflect any kind of drive toward consistency on the part of individual partisans. Approximately equal numbers move away from a position of federal–

TABLE 5 CHANGES IN CONSISTENCY OF FEDERAL AND
PROVINCIAL PARTY IDENTIFICATION: 1974–
1979, 1979–1980, AND THREE-WAVE PANELS, BY
STABILITY OF IDENTIFICATION (%)

	1974–1979	1979–1980	Three-Wave Panel
Stable identifiers (federal and provincial)			
Remaining fully consistent	41	38	34
Remaining partially consistent	12	11	4
Remaining inconsistent	15	23	14
Becoming fully consistent	17	15	19
Becoming partially consistent	15	13	18
Other+	—	—	11
	100%	100%	100%
N	647	1028	360
Unstable identifiers (federal or provincial)			
Remaining consistent	21	17	13
Remaining inconsistent	19	26	15
Becoming consistent	30	27	24
Becoming inconsistent	30	30	31
Other+	—	—	17
	100%	100%	100%
N	577	557	411

+ Denotes all non-monotonic patterns in three-wave panel.

provincial consistency as move toward such a position. This is best seen within categories of partisan change (table 5). Of those who report a change in either federal or provincial partisanship between any two waves, there is in fact a slightly greater tendency in the direction of inconsistent rather than consistent federal–provincial party identification. Similarly, among those who report changes in intensity only, the move is as likely to be to a new position of partial consistency as to one of full consistency. In short, it is not possible to infer from the patterns of change shown in either of the panels in table 5 that changes in the direction or intensity of party identification represent tendencies toward the resolution of dissonant federal–provincial identifications. The alternative conclusion, that inconsistent partisanship is commonplace in the Canadian political environment and not in itself a source of great dissonance, appears much more convincing.

THE DYNAMICS OF PARTISANSHIP: SUMMARY AND CONCLUSION

The separate treatment of intensity, stability, and consistency presented above should not obscure the fact that a number of different types of change can occur either simultaneously or in sequence. Persons who moved to nonidentification, for example, are likely to report a subsequent partisan change. Similarly, persons who

Degree of Change

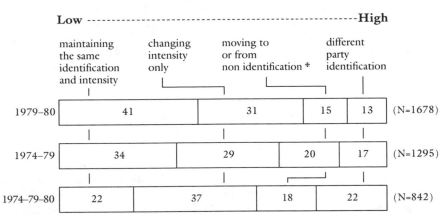

FIGURE 2 *SUMMARY OF CHANGES IN FEDERAL PARTY
IDENTIFICATION: 1979-1980, 1974-1979, AND
THREE-WAVE PANELS (Percent of total samples)*

* Includes continuous nonidentifiers—3% of 1979–1980 and 1974–1979 panels, and 2%
of three-wave (1974–1979–1980) panel.

change the direction of their party identification are prone to alter partisan intensity
as well, either at the same time or subsequently. Such changes, however, are not all
of the same magnitude. Variation in the direction of party identification is of a
higher order than a change in intensity, even when the two occur together. Thus,
to summarise the various types of movement analysed above, one may think in
terms of a hierarchy of partisan change, arraying the three panels along single
dimensions as shown in figure 2. In these distributions, individuals reporting
changes of several different types across a period are classified in terms of the higher
type only, thereby producing an ordering of the degrees of partisan movement
found in a panel. It is particularly instructive to note that nearly four-fifths of the
three-wave panel report some type of variation in federal partisanship over the
six-year period, although a large number of these are changes in intensity only.[28]
The effects of time may be seen in the higher level of change shown by the
1974–1979 panel generally in comparison with that for 1979–1980, with the
exception that intensity is as likely to vary over the shorter period as the longer one.
This is not to say that change across the 1979–1980 panel is trivial. Indeed, only
two respondents in five had not altered the direction or strength (or both) of their
party identifications over the nine months separating the two interviews.

    How can we account for the substantial instability in identification with
political parties in Canada? Part of the explanation lies in the weakness of
sociodemographic correlates of both party identification and vote and the corresponding sensitivity of attitudes and behaviour to short-term forces.[29] At both the

federal and provincial levels, Canadian party images are dominated by issue- and policy-related items, and by references to governmental performance and leadership, and such factors are frequently cited by respondents as reasons underlying a change in party identification.[30] These images tend to change easily in response to new issue concerns or changes in party programs or leaders. Ideological or group-based images, historically an important psychological source of the stability of party ties in many countries,[31] are distinctly weaker elements of the structure of political party images in Canada.[32]

Also conducive to partisan change are highly salient federal and provincial party systems which compete for the attention and allegiance of the electorate. The substantial separation of these party systems diminishes opportunities for cross-level reinforcement of partisan attitudes at either level. Such opportunities are further inhibited by structural factors such as the independent timing of federal and provincial elections and the more generally decentralized nature of the federal system. Many Canadians respond to the cues from two quite distinct party systems by maintaining two separate partisan identities and seem to find no inherent psychological conflict in so doing. At any point in time, then, a sizable minority of voters hold multiple partisan identities, a phenomenon not commonplace even in other federal polities, and all voters are continually exposed to two distinct sets of party images associated with parties operating in recognisably different party systems. These conditions enhance the likelihood of partisan change at both levels of the federal system.

In conclusion, it should be emphasised that we do not interpret our findings as suggesting that the properties of party identification in Canada are *sui generis*. Rather, as noted in the introduction, research over the past two decades in a number of countries has demonstrated sufficient instability in party identification over time to generate a debate on the cross-national utility of the concept. In comparative perspective, it appears that a strong tendency to combine a stable party identity with considerable variation in voting behaviour remains a peculiarly American phenomenon, perhaps attributable to the institutional features of the US electoral system. This debate and any American idiosyncracies notwithstanding, it remains possible to argue that the party identification concept has widespread applicability. Citizens in many countries readily identify with political parties, and such identifications can and do provide cues that affect both perception and behaviour.[33] However, as the Canadian data illustrate, the bases of such identifications are not necessarily long-term, and identifications are not necessarily stable. Although the party identifications of a substantial minority of Canadian voters are durable, that is, strong, stable allegiances resistant to the corrosive effects of short-term forces, there is a majority whose partisan identities are flexible, being amenable to change in response to such forces.

When reflecting upon the broader significance of this mix of partisan types in the Canadian electorate, it is significant to note that this phenomenon is not simply a function of processes of generational replacement or cataclysmic political upheavals.[34] Rather, the process of partisan change is an ongoing one, with individual-level variations in party identification frequently being associated with reactions to such mundane occurrences as the varying salience of issues, changing party leader images, and the conduct of election campaigns. Such events and conditions, of course, are hardly unique to Canada, but rather constitute much of the substance of normal politics in all contemporary liberal democracies. This fact, taken together with evidence that in a number of these polities the relationship between social cleavages and party systems has weakened discernibly over the past two decades,[35] suggests that patterns of partisanship not unlike those documented in this article may characterise an increasing number of Western European and Anglo-American political systems. The ratio of what we have termed durable and flexible partisans will likely vary from one such system to another, but in all cases, the latter may be a significant and growing proportion of the electorate. To determine if this is so, and thereby to enhance our understanding of the theoretical utility of the party identification concept for comprehending both individual political behaviour and broader system-level processes of political stability and change in the 1980s, additional cross-national comparative inquiries will be essential.

NOTES

1. G. Wallas, *Human Nature and Politics* (London: Constable, 1920), 83.

2. A. Campbell, P. Converse, W. Miller, and D. Stokes, *The American Voter* (New York: Wiley, 1960); Campbell et al., *Elections and the Political Order* (New York: Wiley, 1966).

3. W. Miller, "The Cross National Use of Party Identification as a Stimulus to Political Inquiry," in *Party Identification and Beyond*, ed. I. Budge, I. Crewe, and D. Farlie (New York: Wiley, 1976), 21.

4. Budge, et al., ed., *Party Identification and Beyond*.

5. I. Crewe, J. Alt, and B. Sarlvik, "Partisan Dealignment in Britain," *British Journal of Political Science* 7 (1977): 121–90. N. Nie, S. Verba, and J. Petrocik, *The Changing American Voter* (enlarged ed.) (Cambridge, Mass.: Harvard University Press, 1979).

6. B. Gutek, "On the Accuracy of Retrospective Attitudinal Data," *Public Opinion Quarterly* 42 (1978): 390–401. R. Niemi, R. Katz, and D. Newman, "Reconstructing Past Partisanship: The Failure of the Party Identification Recall Questions," *American Journal of Political Science* (*AJPS*) 24 (1980): 633–51. B. Weir, "The Distortion of Voter Recall," *AJPS* 19 (1975): 53–61.

7. P. Converse, "On the Possibility of Major Political Realignment in the South," in *Elections and the Political Order* by Campbell et al. (New York: Wiley, 1966). P. Converse and G. Markus, "Plus ça change...the New CPS Election Study Panel," *American Political Science Review* (*APSR*) 73 (1979): 32–49.

8. D. Butler and D. Stokes, *Political Change in Britain* (London: Macmillan, 1969), 35–36.

9. J. Thomassen, "Party Identification as a Cross-National Concept: Its Meaning in the Netherlands," in *Party Identification and Beyond*, ed. Budge et al. (1976).

10. For example, B.E. Cain, "Dynamic and Static Components of Political Support in Britain," *AJPS* 22 (1978): 849–66; H.D. Clarke and M.C. Stewart, "Dealignment of Degree: Partisan Change in Britain, 1974–83" (Revised version of a paper presented at the Annual Meeting of the Southern Political Science Association, Atlanta, Georgia, November, 1982); M.P. Fiorina *Retrospective Voting in American National Elections* (New Haven, Conn.: Yale University Press, 1981); J.E. Jackson, "Issues, Party Choices and Presidential Votes," *AJPS* 19 (1975): 161–85; G.B. Markus, "The Political Environment and the Dynamics of Public Attitudes: A Panel Study," *AJPS* 23 (1979): 338–59; G.B.

Markus, "Political Attitudes During an Election Year: A Report on the NES Panel Study," *APSR* 76 (1982): 538–60; G.B. Markus and P. Converse, "A Dynamic Simultaneous Equation Model of Electoral Choice," *APSR* 73 (1979): 1055–70; B.I. Page and C.C. Jones, "Reciprocal Effects of Policy Preferences, Party Loyalties and the Vote," *APSR* 73 (1979): 1011–89; W.P. Shively, "The Development of Party Identification among Adults: Exploration of a Functional Model," *APSR* 73 (1979): 1039–54.

11. M.K. Jennings and R. Niemi, *Generations and Politics* (Princeton, N.J.: Princeton University Press, 1981), 48–52.

12. Markus, "The Political Environment and the Dynamics of Public Attitudes."

13. An examination of the characteristics of party identification in Canada based on cross-sectional studies may be found in W. Irvine, "Explaining the Brittleness of Partisanship in Canada" (Paper presented at the Annual Meeting of the Canadian Political Science Association, Edmonton, June, 1975); J. Jenson, in "Party Loyalty in Canada: The Question of Party Identification," *Canadian Journal of Political Science* (*CJPS*) 8 (1975): 543–53; J. Jenson, "Party Strategy and Party Identification," *CJPS* 9 (1976); 27–48; J. Meisel, *Working Papers in Canadian Politics* (Montreal: McGill-Queen's Press, 1975); P. Sniderman, H.D. Forbes, and I. Melzer, "Party Loyalty and Electoral Volatility," *CJPS* 7 (1974): 268–88; See also H.D.Clarke, J. Jenson, L. LeDuc, and J. Pammett, *Political Choice in Canada* (Toronto: McGraw-Hill Ryerson, 1979). For a comparison using panel data of party identification in Canada with other countries, see L. LeDuc, "The Dynamic Properties of Party Identification: A Four Nation Comparison," *European Journal of Political Research* 9 (1981): 257–68. On the dynamics of partisanship in Quebec, see H.D. Clarke, "The Parti Québécois and Sources of Partisan Realignment in Contemporary Quebec," *Journal of Politics* 45 (1983): 64–85.

14. The 1974–1979–1980 National Election and Panel Studies were conducted by Harold Clarke, Jane Jenson, Lawrence LeDuc, and Jon Pammett with funding from the Social Sciences and Humanities Research Council of Canada. Field work for the studies was conducted by Canadian Facts, Ltd. (Toronto). The 1974 survey employed a national cross-sectional sample of 2562 respondents interviewed immediately after the 1974 federal election. Details concerning the study design may be found in L. LeDuc, H. Clarke, J. Jenson, and J. Pammett, "A National Sample Design," *CJPS* 7 (1974): 701–708. After the 1979 federal election, 1295 of these respondents were re-interviewed as part of the 1979 Election Study to form a 1974–1979 panel. A total of 822 of the original respondents were interviewed after the 1980 federal election to form a three-wave panel, together with 926 new respondents, drawn in a 1979 cross-sectional sample. These two groups together form a second (1979–1980) panel of 1748 respondents. Weights are applied in all three panels to approximate national cross-section samples of the Canadian electorate. Further information on these studies may be obtained from the principal investigators or from the Inter-University Consortium for Political and Social Research.

15. L. LeDuc, "Is There Life after Dealignment? Partisan Change in Canada, Great Britain, and the United States" (Paper presented at the workshop on electoral behaviour, European Consortium for Political Research Joint Sessions, Freiburg, West Germany, March, 1983).

16. Clarke et al., *Political Choice in Canada*; Meisel, *Working Papers.*

17. The concept of flexible partisanship is developed at some length in Clarke et al., *Political Choice in Canada*, 135–64 and 301–19. In the 1974 national sample, respondents were classified as flexible if they reported no party identification or weak identification (34 per cent), if they recalled having changed

their party identification in the past, or if they held differing federal and provincial partisan identities (30 per cent). On this basis, 63 per cent of the sample were classified as flexible in partisanship by reason of holding at least one of these attributes. Similar proportions are found in the 1979 and 1980 national samples.

18. Clarke et al., *Political Choice in Canada*, 343–48.

19. B.E. Cain and J. Ferejohn, "A Comparison of Party Identification in the United States and Great Britain," *Comparative Political Studies* 14 (1981): 31–47.

20. Converse, "On the Possibility of Major Political Realignment in the South."

21. Clarke et al., *Political Choice in Canada*.

22. For example, if partisanship and vote in Canada and the United States are compared directly across the twowave panels, it is evident that the relationship between party identification and vote differs even though the proportion who report both stable partisanship and vote is nearly identical. Considering only those respondents in the 1974–1979 Canadian panel and the 1972–1976 US panel who report both a party identification and a vote, the following pattern is obtained:

	Party Identification	
Vote	Stable	Unstable
Canada		
Stable	70	5
Variable	10	15/100%
United States		
Stable	71	4
Unstable	22	3/100%

For more than 90 per cent of those reporting a change in both party identification and vote, the direction of movement is the same for both.

Congressional rather than presidential vote is used in these analyses because it provides the nearest approximation to the Canadian and British electoral system. Also, there are three congressional elections (1972, 1974, and 1976) available in the panel but only two presidential elections (1972 and 1976), thereby facilitating direct comparison with table 4. However, if presidential rather than congressional vote is used in a two-wave analysis similar to that shown above, the percentage reporting the same party identification and vote is 68 per cent rather than 71 per cent. Other cells vary from those shown above by only 1 per cent when presidential vote is used.

23. For purposes of this analysis, identical definitions of party identification are used in the US and British studies. The US data were collected by the Center for Political Studies, University of Michigan, and made available by the Inter-University Consortium for Political and Social Research. The British data were collected by Bo Sarlvik and Ivor Crewe and made available by the SSRS Survey Archive, University of Essex. In both cases, neither the principal investigators nor the archives are responsible for the analyses or interpretations of the data reported here.

24. The political instability associated with the Vietnam war–Watergate period in American politics and the landslide character of two of the last three presidential elections provide simple but powerful testimony on this point.

25. Nie et al., *The Changing American Voter*, chap. 4.

26. D. Aitkin, *Stability and Change in Australian Politics* (Canberra: Australian National University Press, 1977), 44–47; D. Aitkin and M. Kahan, "Australia: Class Politics in the New World," in *Electoral Behaviour: A Comparative Handbook* ed. R. Rose (New York: Free Press, 1974), 446; M.K. Jennings and R. Niemi, "Party Identification at Multiple Levels of Government," *American Journal of Sociology* 72 (1966): 100.

27. A separate "state party identification" question has rarely been asked in US national studies. In the Australian surveys, level of party identification has

been probed only as a follow-up to the general party identification question. In the three Canadian studies, however, full sequences covering direction and such variables as intensity were asked for each level.

28. If changes in provincial party identification also are included, the percentage showing no change across the three-wave panel is reduced to 17 per cent.

29. A multivariate analysis of the effects of seven sociodemographic variables (region, religion, language-ethnicity, social class, age, sex, and community size) shows that no more than 10% of the variance in electoral behaviour could be explained by such factors, Clarke et al., *Political Choice in Canada*, 124–27. Similarly, Rose (R. Rose, ed., *Electoral Behavior: A Comparative Handbook*, 13–20) ranked Canada twelfth on a list of 15 countries in terms of the amount of variance in individual voting behaviour that could be explained by region, religion, and occupation. See also W. Irvine and H. Gold, "Do Frozen Cleavages Ever Go Stale?" *British Journal of Political Science* 10 (1980): 213–25.

30. Respondents in the 1974 National Election Study who recalled having in the past identified with a different political party from their current one (36%) were asked to indicate their reasons for changing parties. The responses distributed as follows: policy, 31%; leaders/leadership, 25%; party performance, 16%; local candidate, 13%; personal reasons, 7%; all other, 9%. Equivalent responses from the 1979 and 1980 surveys are very similar.

31. S.M. Lipset and S. Rokkan, "Cleavage Structures, Party Systems and Voter Alignments," in *Party Systems and Voter Alignments*, ed. S.M. Lipset and S. Rokkan (New York: Free Press, 1967).

32. Clarke et al., *Political Choice in Canada*, 194–202.

33. Miller, "The Cross National Use of Party Identification."

34. Clarke et al., *Political Choice in Canada*, chap. 5; LeDuc, "The Dynamic Properties of Party Identification."

35. Crewe et al., "Partisan Dealignment in Britain"; R. Inglehart, "Changing Paradigms in Comparative Political Behavior" (Paper presented at the Annual Meeting of the American Political Science Association, New York, September, 1982); E.C. Ladd, Jr., and C.D. Hadley, *Transformations of the American Party System* (New York: Norton, 1978); S.M. Lipset, *Political Man: The Social Bases of Politics*, 2d ed. (Baltimore: Johns Hopkins University Press, 1981).

SHORT-TERM FORCES AND PARTISAN CHANGE IN CANADA: 1974-1980◇

HAROLD D. CLARKE
MARIANNE C. STEWART

○

The theoretical attractiveness of the concept of party identification derives in large measure from its presumed utility for explaining processes of political stability and change. In the wake of pathbreaking studies in the United States,[1] the widespread existence of party identification within an electorate was seen as a key factor prompting political stability at both individual and systemic levels.[2] This hypothesis was predicated on the assumption that for the vast majority of persons, partisan attachments, once developed, remained stable. In the past decade studies conducted in a variety of political settings have challenged this assumption.[3] Changes in the intensity and direction of party identification, often over relatively restricted time periods, occur more frequently than hitherto expected.

Mounting evidence of the mutability of partisan attachments has prompted a reconsideration of the status of the concept of party identification in models of voting behaviour. While some analysts[4] at least implicitly have retained the social-psychological conceptualization of party identification adopted by Campbell et al.,[5] others[6] have opted for a redefinition of the concept consistent with retrospective voting theories, i.e., as a "running tally" of evaluations of the performance of parties and their leaders. Such conceptual differences notwithstanding, however, following Jackson,[7] recent studies share the assumption that the finding of considerable, individual-level partisan instability can only be accommodated by developing models that designate party identification as endogenous to the set of forces influencing electoral choice.[8] Although differing in detail, the results of this research consistently substantiate the hypothesis that party identification responds to short-term forces operating in the political arena during particular time intervals.

◇ *Electoral Studies* 4, 1 (1985):15–35.

To date, however, the range of political systems in which hypotheses regarding short-term determinants of party identification have been tested is extremely restricted, with virtually all of the relevant research being conducted in Great Britain and the United States. A principal reason for this limited focus of inquiry has been the paucity of suitable data in other political settings. To study processes of individual-level stability and change, panel data are essential.[9] The availability of data from recently completed, national panel studies of the Canadian electorate permits us to investigate forces affecting partisan attachments in a system where individual- and aggregate-level characteristics of party identification differ from the American and British cases.[10]

The Canadian data were generated by three national post-election surveys carried out in 1974, 1979, and 1980.[11] These surveys contain interlocking panels such that it is possible to map aggregate and individual-level partisan change between adjacent elections, i.e., 1974–79, 1979–80, as well as over the entire 1974–80 period.[12] After doing so and considering possible replacement effects on the incidence of partisan change, this paper investigates the extent to which partisan attachments reflect short-term forces associated with party leader images and issue perceptions. The paper concludes by arguing that properties of Canada's national party system and the results of ongoing interparty competition within this system condition levels and patterns of partisan change over particular time intervals.

PATTERNS OF PARTISANSHIP

Previous research has established that Canadian political attitudes and behaviour are characterised by considerable aggregate stability coupled with individual-level instability. Certainly, this pattern describes the available data on party identification.[13] At the aggregate level the average shift in percentage of individuals identifying with the Liberals in the five national election studies conducted to date has been less than 5 per cent (see table 1). For the other three federal parties, mean shifts in the percentage of identifiers have been even smaller: 2.5 per cent for the Progressive Conservatives, and 1.3 per cent for the NDP and Social Credit. Similarly, the number of nonidentifiers[14] in successive surveys has changed by only 2.3 per cent on average. Moreover, as table 1 shows, with the exception of the steady decline in

TABLE 1   DIRECTION OF FEDERAL PARTY
IDENTIFICATION IN CANADA, 1965–80

Party Identification	1965	1968	1974	1979	1980
	%	%	%	%	%
Liberal	43	50	49	42	45
Progressive Conservative	28	25	24	29	28
NDP	12	11	11	13	15
Social Credit	6	5	3	3	1
No identification	11	9	13	13	10
(N =)+	(2615)	(2706)	(2411)	(2604)	(1761)

+ Missing data and "other" party identifiers removed.

TABLE 2   *STRENGTH OF FEDERAL PARTY*
IDENTIFICATION IN CANADA, 1965-80

Strength of Party Identification	1965	1968	1974	1979	1980
	%	%	%	%	%
Very strong	24	26	27	26	31
Fairly strong	43	43	40	42	42
Weak/leaning	22	23	20	19	17
No identification	11	9	13	13	10
(N =)	(2615)	(2706)	(2411)	(2624)	(1761)
Mean strength of party identification+	1.8	1.8	1.8	1.8	1.9

+ Strength of party identification scored: very strong = 3, fairly strong = 2, weak/leaning = 1, no identification = 0.

Social Credit fortunes (from 6 per cent in 1965 to 1 per cent in 1980), there are no discernible trends in the national party identification percentages. Rather, these figures vary erratically over the five surveys.

The impressive aggregate stability of party identification in Canada is mirrored in data on the strength of partisan attachments (see table 2). In contrast to Great Britain and the United States,[15] there is no trend in Canada toward a diminution in the strength of party identification, either in terms of a growing proportion of nonidentifiers (as in the United States) or a general weakening of party ties (as in Great Britain).[16] In fact, as table 2 shows, the percentage of nonidentifiers has varied irregularly from a low of 9 per cent in 1968 to a high of 13 per cent in 1974 and back to 10 per cent in 1980, with an index of the mean strength of partisanship increasing only slightly over this period—from 1.8 to 1.9. Overall, then, there is no evidence of the operation of dealignment processes comparable to those identified in the British and American cases.

At the level of the individual the picture is very different. As noted above, panel data are essential for an accurate mapping of patterns of partisanship at this level. Such data (for 1974-79 and 1979-80) reveal that during the past decade substantial numbers of Canadians have shifted the direction and/or the strength of their partisan ties between successive elections. During the earlier (1974-79) period nearly one-third (32.3 per cent) changed the direction of their identifications—16.1 per cent shifted from one party to another (e.g., from Liberal to Progressive Conservative) while 16.2 per cent moved to or from the status of nonidentifier (table 3). The magnitude of comparable figures for the shorter (nine-month) interval between the 1979 and 1980 elections is less, albeit still impressive; 23.8 per cent of the 1979-80 panelists were directionally unstable, with 12 per cent moving from one party to another and 11.8 per cent shifting to or from nonidentification. Across the three-wave, 1974-79-80 panel some 41 per cent altered their party ties. As table 3 also shows, stable nonidentifiers were not a large segment of the electorate; such persons constitute 5.4 per cent and 4.0 per cent of the 1974-79 and 1979-80 panels respectively.

The impression of considerable individual-level instability in party identification conveyed by the panel data on the direction of partisanship is reinforced by

TABLE 3   *PATTERNS OF FEDERAL PARTY*
IDENTIFICATION, 1974–79 AND 1979–80

A. 1974–79	Party Identification 1974				
Party Identification 1979	Liberal	PC	NDP	SC	None
Liberal	35.2	1.5	1.3	0.6	3.6
PC	6.5	19.2	1.3	0.5	3.3
NDP	2.5	1.0	6.7	0.1	1.0
SC	0.4	0.3	0.2	1.2	0.5
None	4.4	1.8	0.8	0.8	5.4
					/100%+

$V = 0.50, p \leq 0.001$

B. 1979–80	Party Identification 1979				
Party Identification 1980	Liberal	PC	NDP	SC	None
Liberal	37.6	3.1	1.1	0.5	2.9
PC	2.5	23.1	0.7	0.2	2.3
NDP	1.6	1.6	10.8	0.3	0.7
SC	0.1	0.1	0.1	0.7	0.3
None	1.9	1.9	1.2	0.6	4.0
					/100%+

$V = 0.58, p \leq 0.001$

+ Cell percentages computed in terms of total panel Ns: 1974–79 = 1299, 1979–80 = 1690, missing data and "other" parties excluded.

analyses of shifts in the *strength* of party ties. Overall, less than half of the panel respondents reported the same intensity of party attachment in successive interviews. Moreover, instability in partisan intensity was not confined to persons who altered the *direction* of their partisanship. Rather, many directionally stable identifiers also varied the intensity of their party ties—47 per cent switched intensity between 1974 and 1979, and 44 per cent did so between 1979 and 1980 (table 4). Comparable figures for the directionally unstable partisans are 59 per cent and 50 per cent respectively. Thus, even over a relatively brief time span such as that between the 1979 and 1980 elections, partisan instability characterised a large segment of the Canadian electorate.

SOURCES OF PARTISAN CHANGE

In general, the literature on party identification has focussed on two sources of partisan change, namely replacement and conversion.[17] Replacement refers to changes in the composition of an electorate brought about by demographic processes, cataclysmic events (e.g., wars, natural disasters) or alterations in franchise-eligibility criteria. Conversion, in contrast, refers to changing attitudes, beliefs and opinions among a group of persons eligible to vote in a series of successive elections. Depending upon their nature and the political context within which they occur, replacement and conversion processes may operate either slowly or rapidly and may serve as the principal source of either realignment or dealignment in party systems.

TABLE 4   PATTERNS OF STRENGTH OF FEDERAL PARTY
IDENTIFICATION 1974-79, 1979-80

	Directionally Stable Identifiers	Directionally Unstable Identifiers
A. 1974–79	%	%
Stable strength	53	41
Increasing strength/acquisition	25	29
Decreasing strength/abandonment	22	30
$V =$	0.28	0.06
$p \leq$	0.001	N.S.
B. 1979–80		
Stable strength	57	50
Increasing strength/acquisition	27	31
Decreasing strength/abandonment	17	19
$V =$	0.33	0.21
$p \leq$	0.001	0.001

In the Canadian context the changing age composition of the electorate would seem to be the only plausible source of replacement effects on the individual-level instability in partisanship observed above. In 1970 the age of majority was reduced from 21 to 18. This reinforced postwar demographic trends (i.e., the "baby boom") that worked to yield a very sizable component of younger voters throughout the 1970s. Indeed, by the time of the 1979 election, census data show that some 40 per cent of the voters had joined the electorate after Pierre Trudeau became Liberal leader in 1968, and only approximately 28 per cent first became eligible to cast their ballots prior to World War II. It is possible that these younger voters constituted an age cohort for whom party ties have relatively little meaning. Alternatively, following Converse's well-known argument regarding the time-related reinforcement tendencies of partisan allegiance, political life-cycle processes may not have had sufficient time to "lock in" the party identifications of many members of this large group of younger voters.[18]

As frequently has been observed, it is difficult to separate life-cycle and generational processes empirically.[19] Analyses based on cross-sectional surveys are fraught with difficulties, and the six-year span of the Canadian panels is of insufficient duration to address directly the possible significance of time-related reinforcement effects on partisan stability. For present purposes, however, these obstacles are not insuperable. Both life-cycle and generational explanations of proclivities toward partisan change refer to the composition of an electorate, and both explanations posit the existence of age-group differences in such proclivities. Thus, as an initial analysis, it is sufficient to observe the relationship between age and the incidence of partisan change in the panels. If this relationship is strong, we will have prima facie evidence of the possible significance of a compositional explanation of partisan instability in contemporary Canada. If, in contrast, the relationship is weak, it may be concluded that this phenomenon must be explained largely in terms other than replacement effects associated with the age composition of the electorate.

Empirically, relationships between age and partisan change in the 1974–79 and 1979–80 panels are statistically significant, but quite modest in magnitude. For the first of these the percentage of directionally unstable identifiers decreases monotonically from 40 per cent among persons 23 to 34 years of age to 24 per cent among those 65 and over ($V=0.08$, $p \leq 0.05$).[20] A similar pattern is evident in the 1979–80 panel with the percentage of unstable partisans decreasing from 32 per cent among persons 22 or younger to 21 per cent among those 65 and over ($V=0.10$, $p \leq 0.001$). These relationships are consonant with life-cycle or age cohort interpretations of the likelihood of partisan instability. Importantly, however, the observed relationships, while statistically significant, are not very strong,[21] with sizable percentages of voters in every age group exhibiting partisan mobility. Thus, age-related differences, however interpreted, cannot provide an adequate basis for explaining partisan instability.

As noted, it is unlikely that replacement effects other than those associated with the age composition of the electorate could account for partisan instability in the Canadian context. No large, new group of voters was enfranchised after the lowering of the age of majority in 1970, and no large group made a precipitous exit from the electorate. However, it is conceivable that the observed changes in party identification in the late 1970s represent conversion effects, with specific groups of voters realigning themselves in response to the economic and constitutional difficulties that gripped the Canadian polity in this era. This was a period in which large numbers of Quebeckers expressed deep dissatisfaction with the national political system and shifted their support in provincial politics to the Parti Québécois, a party avowedly dedicated to severing Quebec's political ties with the rest of Canada.

Indeed, the election of this party as the provincial government of Quebec in November 1976 plunged the country into a "Crisis of Confederation." Compounding this crisis was a protracted conflict between Ottawa on the one hand, and the western provinces and Newfoundland on the other, over the control of revenue generated by energy and other natural resources. This struggle was catalysed by the 1973 Arab oil embargo, and it intensified markedly as the process of constitutional renewal became a dominant item on the national political agenda in the aftermath of the PQ electoral victory.[22]

Such profound economic and political structural issues, of course, are precisely what the classic literature on party identification argues should provide an impetus for individual partisan change and an accompanying aggregate realignment or dealignment.[23] We have already seen (tables 1 and 2) that such aggregate changes in partisanship did not occur. Still, it is quite conceivable that these issues accounted for individual partisan switching by prompting certain segments of the electorate (e.g., Westerners, Québécois) to alter previously established partisan allegiances. In this scenario the net effects of such switches would be muted if the groups involved were of approximately equal size but moved in opposing directions.

There is, in fact, little evidence that partisan change was confined to any particular segment of the electorate. Table 5 reports the results of probit analyses[24] of changes in party identification using several socio-economic and demographic variables (i.e., age, gender, community size, region, ethnicity, and socio-economic status) as predictors.[25] For three of the four analyses age is negatively associated with

TABLE 5   PROBIT ANALYSES: PARTISAN CHANGE AND
SOCIO-ECONOMIC AND DEMOGRAPHIC
VARIABLES

A. 1974–79	Switching from Governing Party			Switching, All Parties		
	MLE	SE	MLE/SE	MLE	SE	MLE/SE
Constant	0.154	0.383	0.402	0.238	0.248	0.957
Age	−0.011	0.003	−3.082+	−0.010	0.002	−4.306+
Gender	0.071	0.107	0.665	−0.003	0.072	−0.037
Community size	0.033	0.028	1.162	−0.001	0.019	−0.043
Region/ethnicity: Atlantic	−0.272	0.200	−1.362	0.120	0.132	0.912
Quebec–French	−0.320	0.142	−2.251+	−0.078	−0.106	−0.743
Quebec–Non-French	−0.567	0.210	−2.705+	−0.120	0.135	−0.890
Prairies	0.419	0.171	2.447+	0.336	0.107	3.128+
British Columbia	0.369	0.183	2.013+	0.206	0.127	1.623
Socio-economic status	−0.010	0.004	−2.459+	−0.006	0.003	−2.130+
Estimated R^2 =		0.121			0.050	
B. 1979–80						
Constant	−0.608	0.427	−1.423	−0.328	0.211	−1.554
Age	−0.007	0.004	−1.828	−0.010	0.002	−4.923+
Gender	0.134	0.129	1.040	0.059	0.065	−0.905
Community size	−0.006	0.036	−0.171	0.016	0.018	0.916
Region/ethnicity: Atlantic	0.104	0.207	0.505	−0.026	0.124	−0.212
Quebec–French	0.942	0.268	3.517+	0.132	0.094	1.396
Quebec–Non-French	0.183	0.375	0.489	0.066	0.118	0.564
Prairies	0.052	0.161	0.321	0.041	0.096	0.426
British Columbia	−0.333	0.250	−1.333	0.181	0.115	1.574
Socio-economic status	−0.002	0.005	−0.517	0.001	0.002	0.554
Estimated R^2 =		0.076			0.031	

+ $p \leq 0.05$
MLE = Maximum likelihood estimates of probit parameters
SE = Standard error

partisan change, a result anticipated by the data reported previously. A number of the region ethnicity variables also are associated with partisan switches, particularly when movement away from the governing Liberal Party between 1974 and 1979 is considered. As for socio-economic status, it is negatively related to partisan switching in the 1974–79 but not the 1979–80 panel.

More importantly, none of these variables is able to explain large portions of variance in partisan change. The estimated R^2 for the four analyses ranges from a low of 3.1 per cent for general partisan switching between 1979 and 1980 to a high of 12.1 per cent for switching away from the Liberals between 1974 and 1979. Clearly, if salient economic and constitutional issues were prompting individual-level partisan change, their effects were generalized, rather than being confined to specific groups of voters defined in terms of regional, ethno-linguistic, demographic, or socio-economic cleavages in the population. Moreover, the failure of several of the variables that achieve statistical significance in 1974–79 to do so in 1979–80 suggests that any issue effects on particular groups were transitory.

SHORT-TERM FORCES AND PARTISAN CHANGE

Materials presented above indicate that individual-level partisan mutability is widespread in contemporary Canada and that the propensity to alter party ties is not confined to particular age cohorts or other easily identified segments of the population. Explanations of the observed propensity to alter partisan attachments cast in terms of electoral replacement effects or the conversion of selected groups of voters reacting to issues associated with the political circumstances of the time appear inadequate. As an alternative, it may be suggested that shifts in party identification are an ongoing and quite pervasive phenomenon in Canada, one that may be accounted for largely by short-term forces operative in the political arena during any given time interval. Such an explanation would accord well with recent work in other Anglo-American political settings. Studies such as those by Fiorina, Franklin and Jackson, Alt, and Clarke and Stewart have argued that the short-term effects of party leader images and party/issue linkages are important causes of variations in the intensity and/or direction of party identification in Great Britain and the United States, with the effects of these forces not being confined to particular groups of voters or crisis situations.[26] It is plausible that such forces operate in a similar fashion in Canada as well.

TABLE 6   REASONS FOR CHANGING FEDERAL PARTY
IDENTIFICATION, 1974, 1979, 1980

		1974	1979	1980
		%	%	%
Party leader	Positive	6.9+	9.5+	7.9+
	Negative	14.2	15.0	17.3
	Unspecified	4.8	1.9	4.1
Local candidate	Positive	3.9	4.1	3.2
	Negative	1.7	1.8	1.7
	Unspecified	4.7	1.2	1.4
Specific party policy	Positive	4.0	5.6	6.8
	Negative	8.2	7.3	6.2
	Unspecified	6.4	6.0	6.0
General party policy	Positive	4.6	7.6	7.4
	Negative	4.6	4.9	5.5
	Unspecified	6.6	0.2	1.6
Party performance	Positive	2.7	4.3	4.4
	Negative	9.9	14.9	15.4
	Unspecified	1.0	0.2	0.0
Regional, provincial,	Positive	0.6	0.7	0.8
local factors	Negative	1.9	1.1	0.6
	Unspecified	1.2	0.5	0.5
Majority/minority government		2.7	0.4	0.5
Other		17.8	16.1	12.9
Can't remember, don't know		7.8	9.1	5.0
(N =)		(800)	(831)	(656)
Total: Positive		21.2	29.3	29.3
Negative		35.6	40.5	42.1

+ Multiple response

Prima facie evidence on this point is provided by the reports of voters themselves regarding why they switched party identification.[27] These data (see table 6) are interesting in several respects. First, the reasons offered for partisan change are quite diverse and no single category is markedly more popular than the others. In all three surveys the most frequently mentioned reason concerns negative reactions to a party leader. Such reactions, however, are cited by no more than slightly over 17 per cent of those in any of the surveys. Other types of reasons are cited even less frequently.

Second, there is little evidence to indicate that changes in partisanship reflect long-term factors. General party policies, for example, are cited by fewer than 16 per cent of the respondents in any of the surveys, and regional/provincial/local factors are scarcely present—being mentioned by 3 per cent or less in each case. The "party performance" category which might include a preponderance of generalized long-term satisfactions or dissatisfactions, rather than short-term grievances, contains less than 20 per cent in each survey. Even if the reasons falling into all of these categories are assumed to capture relatively enduring factors, there are many voters who report changing their party ties for reasons that are seemingly unconnected to longer term forces.

Third, issues and policies, while clearly present in the responses, do not dominate as explanations of partisan change. Other reasons, particularly reactions to party leaders and party performance, are equally popular. Moreover, detailed inspection of the issue, leader and performance responses and evidence on the content of voters' issue concerns and party leader and party images combine to suggest that many of these reasons are related to short-term factors.[28] Proximate reactions to both issues and party policies as well as feelings about currently salient political figures, events and conditions seem to play important roles in prompting movement in party identification.

Fourth, and finally, persons switching partisan ties evidently do not wait for something to *attract* them to a new party. Rather, in each of the three surveys, pluralities of respondents supply *negative* reasons for altering their party ties (table 6). This is significant in that partisan change may be hypothesised to occur at any time there is disenchantment with a present party's leaders, policies, or performance. Voters evidently are willing to "take a chance" on a new party without having to perceive that the "grass is greener on the other side." Stated somewhat more formally, partisan change is rendered more likely in that it does not require a conjunction of dissatisfaction with a current party with perceptions of a desirable alternative. The former is sufficient.

ISSUES

Voters' descriptions of their reasons for switching party identification indicate that issues play a role in the process of partisan change. However, previous analyses of overtime variations in voting behaviour and party popularity in the interims between elections suggest that this role frequently is complex.[29] Even highly salient issues do not "speak by themselves" but rather are interpreted to the electorate by political parties, their leaders and the mass media. Which interpretations define the political issue agenda at any given point in time reflects an ongoing contest among parties to determine the content of the political communication channels to which

TABLE 7   PARTISAN INSTABILITY BY TYPE OF ISSUE
MENTIONED AS MOST IMPORTANT

A. 1974–79   1974–79 Party Identification

Types of issue mentioned 1979	Stable identification	To/from nonidentification	Unstable identification	V	p
	%	%	%		
Economic: mentioned	67	16	18	0.04	NS
+(42%) Not mentioned	65	18	17		
Confederation: mentioned	74	14	13	0.10	0.01
(26%) Not mentioned	63	14	19		
Resource: mentioned	73	14	13	0.05	NS
(10%) Not mentioned	65	17	18		
Social: mentioned	66	15	19	0.02	NS
(4%) Not mentioned	66	17	17		
Miscellaneous: mentioned	69	13	18	0.06	NS
(25%) Not mentioned	65	18	17		

B. 1979–80

Types of issue mentioned 1980	Stable identification	To/from nonidentification	Unstable identification	V	p
	%	%	%		
Economic: mentioned	77	12	12	0.05	NS
(44%) Not mentioned	72	13	15		
Confederation: mentioned	73	12	16	0.03	NS
(12%) Not mentioned	75	13	13		
Resource: mentioned	75	10	15	0.07	0.05
(33%) Not mentioned	74	14	12		
Social: mentioned	53	15	32	0.08	0.01
(2%) Not mentioned	75	12	13		
Miscellaneous: mentioned	75	13	13	0.01	NS
(29%) Not mentioned	74	12	13		

+ Percentage mentioning issue type

voters are exposed. Similar to situations in other contemporary liberal democracies, this contest constitutes a major aspect of inter-party conflict in Canada.[30]

The force of this point becomes apparent when one considers relationships between the electorate's issue concerns and the incidence of partisan movement. Such analyses (table 7) reveal that issue concerns *per se* have at best very weak associations with changes in party identification. In the 1974–79 panel, for example, 34 per cent of those mentioning an economic issue as being the most important in the 1979 election switched their party identification, but 35 per cent of those not doing so also switched. In the 1979–80 panel the comparable figures are 24 per cent and 28 per cent. Neither of these relationships is statistically significant. As a second example, one may consider "confederation" issues (i.e., the complex of issues associated with Quebec, national unity, the constitution, and bilingualism). Citation of one of these issues is negatively associated with changing party identification in the 1974–79 panel ($p \leq 0.01$), but the relationship is not strong

TABLE 8   STABILITY OF PARTY CLOSEST ON MOST
           IMPORTANT ISSUE, 1974-79, 1979-80

A. 1974-79   Party Closest 1974

Party closest 1979	Liberal	PC	NDP	SC	None/D.K.	No Issue
	%	%	%	%	%	%
Liberal	38	12	8	20	20	18
PC	17	57	12	20	31	16
NDP	6	5	57	4	10	4
SC	x	0	0	16	1	0
None/D.K.	15	13	10	4	11	15
No issue	24	13	13	37	27	47
(N =)	(438)	(229)	(98)	(30)	(197)	(339)

$V = 0.31, p \leq 0.001$

B. 1979-80   Party Closest 1979

Party closest 1980	Liberal	PC	NDP	SC	None/D.K.	No Issue
	%	%	%	%	%	%
Liberal	62	13	13	16	24	25
PC	11	58	13	8	24	12
NDP	6	9	53	8	11	6
SC	x	x	1	0	x	x
None/D.K.	7	8	5	25	20	11
No issue	14	11	14	44	22	46
(N =)	(421)	(469)	(189)	(14)	(239)	(418)

$V = 0.33, p \leq 0.001$

x = less than 0.5%

(V=0.10). In the 1979-80 panel the relationship is not significant. More generally, this pattern of weak and/or insignificant relationships characterises all of the analyses summarised in table 7. Concern with particular issues, by itself, has little to do with partisan change.

The evidence in table 7 is consonant, then, with the argument that how issues affect partisanship and changes therein is far from automatic. As argued above, the establishment of linkages between parties and issues is a crucial, if problematic, step in the process by which the latter acquire the force to alter party attachments.[31] Moreover, the potential for perceptions of which party is preferred on an important issue to influence changes in the strength and/or direction of party identification is contingent upon the mutability of these perceptions. Stated simply, if party/issue linkages do not change, then it could hardly be argued that they are able to account for changes in party identification. In this regard the 1974-79 and 1979-80 panels clearly illustrate that changing party/issue links are characteristic of large numbers of Canadian voters. In the former only 38 per cent of those perceiving the Liberals as closest to them on the most important issue in 1974, retained this view five years later (see table 8, panel A).[32] Among Progressive Conservatives and New Democrats the comparable percentage is 57 per cent in both instances. In the latter the picture differs only in degree—many of those believing a given party was closest to them in 1979 failed to do so less than a year later (table 8, panel B). In both panels some of those who abandoned a party as closest to them moved to another party while others decided no party was closest or believed there were no important issues. In sum, it can be noted that only 27 per cent and 36 per cent of those in the 1974–79 and 1979–80 panels respectively consistently maintained that the same party was closest to them. Changing party/issue links are clearly a common occurrence.[33]

Persons who changed their view of which party was closest on the issue designated as most important were considerably more likely than others to alter their party identifications. The association between changing party/issue perceptions and changing partisanship is shown in table 9. Considering the 1974–79 panel 9 per cent (cell *a*) of 1974 Liberal identifiers who judged that the Liberals were closest to them in both 1974 and 1979 changed their party identifications between these two years. In contrast, 49 per cent (cell *g*) of those who perceived this party was closest to them on the most important issue in 1974 but not in 1979 changed their party identification. Of those who judged that the Liberals were not closest to them on the most important issue in either year, fully 67 per cent (cell *i*) switched their party ties. Similar patterns characterise the likelihood of partisan migration of 1979 Liberal identifiers in the 1979–80 panel (table 9), and typify the likelihood of migration for Progressive Conservative and NDP partisans as well (data not shown in tabular form).

PARTY LEADER IMAGES

In contemporary liberal democracies party leader images can play important roles as short-term forces affecting electoral choice. The significance of leader images as forces on the vote in countries such as Australia, Canada and the United States is well recognised,[34] and more recently their importance in other political settings, such as Great Britain has been acknowledged as well.[35] Also, as noted previously, recent studies of Great Britain and the United States have shown that the impact of leader images extends beyond the vote per se and encompasses partisan predispositions.[36] Given the widely acknowledged importance of party leader images in Canadian electoral politics, it is plausible to hypothesise that these images and changes therein will influenece variations in the direction and intensity of party identification in this country.

The several Canadian national election studies as well as monthly public opinion polls provide evidence that both the affective and the cognitive dimensions of leader images vary substantially in the aggregate over time.[37] The election study panel data indicate that leader images also vary at the level of the individual voter (data not shown). Across the 1974–79 panel, for example, 30 per cent of the electorate continued to prefer Mr. Trudeau to his PC and NDP rivals.[38] A further 27 per cent consistently preferred one or both of the other leaders to Trudeau and 2 per cent ranked Trudeau and one or more of the other leaders equally. The remaining 41 per cent shifted their party leader preferences over this time span. Between 1979 and 1980, although the amount of shifting in party leader preferences was less, 29 per cent changed their ranking of Trudeau relative to other leaders. More

TABLE 9   PARTISAN INSTABILITY BY PARTY CLOSEST
ON MOST IMPORTANT ISSUE, 1974-79 AND
1979-80 NATIONAL PANELS, CONTROLLING
FOR PRIOR PARTY IDENTIFICATION

A. 1974 Liberal identifiers

| | | Party Closest 1974 | |
	Liberals closest	No difference/ No issue	Other party closest
Party closest 1979 Liberals closest	$9^+{}_a$	7_b	0_c
No difference/No issue	31_d	32_e	42_f
Other party closest	49_g	71_h	67_i

B. 1979 Liberal identifiers

| | | Party Closest 1979 | |
	Liberals closest	No difference/ No issue	Other party closest
Party closest 1980 Liberals closest	$3^+{}_a$	6_b	6_c
No difference/No issue	9_d	15_e	38_f
Other party closest	29_g	52_h	55_i

+ Cell entries are percentages of respondents with directionally unstable party identifications between 1974-79 and 1979-80 respectively.

generally, across the two panels an average of 33 per cent of the electorate shifted their leader preferences.

The relationship between variations in preferences for the national party leaders and changes in party identification is displayed for Liberal identifiers in table 10. Similar to the situation for changing party/issue linkages, changes in leader preferences are strongly associated with variations in party identification. For example, among 1979 Liberal identifiers who preferred the Liberal leader in both 1979 and 1980, only 4 per cent (cell *a*) abandoned their Liberal partisanship. Among those 1979 Liberals who preferred the Liberal leader in 1979, but the leader of another party in 1980, 47 per cent (cell *g*) declared that they did not identify with the Liberals in the latter year. Again, the patterns of partisan switching among 1974 and 1979 PCs and New Democrats are virtually identical to those shown in table 10. Changing party leader preferences are strongly associated with the likelihood of partisan migration.

ISSUES, LEADERS AND PARTISAN CHANGE

Thus far, we have considered the potential impact of changing party/issue perceptions and party leader images in isolation. Each of the factors appears to be related to changes in party identification. It is possible, however, that one or more of these relationships is spurious. Survey evidence suggests that a sizable number of Canadian voters have an issue basis for their evaluations of party leaders.[39] For such

TABLE 10   PARTISAN INSTABILITY BY RELATIVE PARTY
LEADER PREFERENCE, 1974–79 AND 1979–80
NATIONAL PANELS, CONTROLLING FOR
PRIOR PARTY IDENTIFICATION

A. 1974 Liberal identifiers

		Party Leader Preference 1974		
		Prefer Trudeau	No difference	Prefer other leader
Party leader preference 1979	Prefer Trudeau	9+$_a$	16$_b$	0$_c$
	No difference	43$_d$	33$_e$	53$_f$
	Prefer other leader	62$_g$	62$_h$	73$_i$

B. 1979 Liberal identifiers

		Party Leader Preference 1979		
		Prefer Trudeau	No difference	Prefer other leader
Party leader preference 1980	Prefer Trudeau	4+$_a$	12$_b$	3$_c$
	No difference	21$_d$	33$_e$	6$_f$
	Prefer other leader	47$_g$	60$_h$	50$_i$

+ Cell entries are percentages of respondents with directionally unstable party identifications between
1974–79 and 1979–80 respectively.

persons, changing feelings about party leaders may reflect variations in party/issue
perceptions, with leader images having no independent effect on the direction
and/or strength of partisan ties. In contrast, a number of analysts have noted that
voters may rationalize party preferences in issue terms when in reality these
preferences are dictated by feelings about party leaders or other considerations.[40]
In still other cases, voters may project personally preferred issue stands on to parties
or leaders when feelings about the latter have been generated on non-issue bases.
To account for these various possibilities multivariate analyses are required.

Most simply, one can analyse the likelihood of partisan change in terms of
both feelings about leaders and party/issue perceptions. This reveals that both of
the latter variables are associated independently with variations in party identification over the 1974–79 and 1979–80 panels. Considering 1974 Liberal identifiers
(table 11), only 5 per cent of those who preferred Trudeau to the other party leaders
in 1979, and judged that the Liberals were closest to them on the issue they believed
was most important, had abandoned their Liberal identification by 1979. However,
among those who preferred Trudeau, but thought another party was closest on the
issues, 35 per cent (cell c) switched identifications. More generally, reading the two
panels of table 11 horizontally indicates that when leader preferences are held
constant, variations in party/issue preferences are always associated with the probability of partisan change.

Similarly, controlling for issue perceptions indicates that leader feelings are
significant net of judgements about party/issue linkages. In the 1979–80 panel 13
per cent (cell c) of those who believed that a party other than the Liberals was closest

TABLE 11 *PARTISAN INSTABILITY BY RELATIVE PARTY
LEADER PREFERENCE AND PARTY CLOSEST
ON MOST IMPORTANT ISSUE, 1974-79 AND
1979-80 NATIONAL PANELS, CONTROLLING
FOR PRIOR PARTY IDENTIFICATION*

A. 1974–79

1974 Liberal identifiers		Liberals closest	Party Closest 1979 No difference/ No issue	Other party closest
Party leader preference 1979	Prefer Trudeau	5+$_a$	11$_b$	35$_c$
	No difference	18$_d$	53$_e$	40$_f$
	Prefer other leader	32$_g$	66$_h$	71$_i$

B. 1979–80

1979 Liberal identifiers		Liberals closest	Party Closest 1980 No difference/ No issue	Other party closest
Party leader preference 1980	Prefer Trudeau	2+$_a$	7$_b$	13$_c$
	No difference	13$_d$	23$_e$	38$_f$
	Prefer other leader	17$_g$	54$_h$	62$_i$

+ Cell entries are percentages of respondents with directionally unstable party identifications between 1974–79 and 1979–80 respectively.

to them but preferred the Liberal leader to his PC and NDP counterparts switched their party identifications. Among those preferring one of these other leaders nearly five times as many (62 per cent, cell i) changed identifications. These analyses for Liberal identifiers typify those for 1974 and 1979 PC and NDP partisans (data not shown).

Such relationships between partisan change and party/issue preferences and party leader preferences are suggestive of the importance of short-term issue and leader forces on party identification. A more comprehensive examination of possible leader and issue effects requires that controls be imposed for party identification at earlier points in time. The need for such a control is an assumption shared both by those who conceptualize party identification in retrospective voting terms as well as those who retain more conventional social-psychological definitions.[41]

Regarding the impact of prior partisanship, it can be hypothesised that in the Canadian case this will be conditioned by the consistency of voters' partisan attachments across levels of government. Consonant with the major differences in national and provincial party systems that characterise politics in several provinces, a sizable number of voters (e.g., 26 per cent in 1980) do not identify with the same party at both levels of government. For these "split" identifiers, partisanship is not reinforced across levels of government. Accordingly, the stability of a party identification (at either level) should be less for such persons than for those who have the same identifications in federal and provincial politics.

Suggestive of the possible impact of cross-level consistency on partisan stability, inconsistent identifiers in the 1974–79 and 1979–80 panels were more likely than consistent identifiers to change their partisan attachments (data not shown).[42] In the 1974–79 case, among those with directionally different identifications in 1974, 33 per cent switched their federal partisanship by 1979. Among consistent 1974 identifiers, in contrast, 16 per cent switched (V=0.18, p≤ 0.001). Comparable percentages in the 1979–80 panel are 27 per cent and 10 per cent (V=0.22, p ≤ 0.001). In the context of a multivariate analysis of current party identification, the possible reinforcing effects of holding the same party identification in federal and provincial politics will be investigated by employing a prior party identification x partisan consistency variable.

As Franklin and Jackson have argued, an analysis controlling for the influence of prior party identification should also incorporate possible time-related reinforcement effects on partisanship.[43] As noted earlier, data limitations do not permit us to measure directly the length of time that partisan attachments have been held. Thus, similar to others who have attempted to investigate such effects, we are forced to rely on age as a proxy. It will be recalled that age has a statistically significant, albeit modest, association with the likelihood of changing partisanship over the 1974–79 and 1979–80 panels, and that this relationship remains significant in three of four analyses where controls are imposed for a variety of sociodemographic characteristics (table 5). To incorporate possible time-related reinforcement effects in a model of party identification, an age x prior party identification interaction term will be utilised.

It also is plausible to argue that the effects of the short-term force variables (i.e., party/issue perceptions, party leader preferences) will vary across the electorate according to the extent of exposure to stimuli associated with these variables. Variations in such exposure might be indexed in a variety of ways, e.g., extent of media consumption or political interest. Here, a measure of the latter which incorporates both interest in politics generally and interest in a specific election campaign is used.[44] Earlier work with Canadian data has shown that the impact of leader and issue variables on electoral choice varies with a voter's position on such an interest index.[45] Possible effects on party identification are suggested in that the likelihood of partisan change in the two panels also is associated with political interest—with highly interested respondents being more prone to change (data not shown). For the 1974–79 panel 44 per cent of highly interested persons varied their partisan ties while 33 per cent and 27 per cent of those with moderate or low levels of interest did so (V=0.12, p ≤ 0.001). Comparable figures for the 1979–80 panel are 33 per cent, 25 per cent and 21 per cent respectively (V=0.08, p ≤ 0.001). To capture effects of differential exposure to short-term forces on federal party identification, party leader preference and party/issue perception x political interest interaction terms will be constructed.

In sum, the model of party identification suggested by the above discussion is as follows:

$$PID(t) = a + b1\, PIP + b2\, PLI + b3\, PID(t-1) + b4\, PIP \times PI + b5\, PLI \times PI + b6\, PID(t-1) \times AGE + b7\, PID(t-1) \times PC + u$$

where: a = constant
  PID = strength and direction of party identification
  PIP = party/issue perceptions
  PLI = party leader preference

PI = political interest
AGE = age
PC = consistency of federal/provincial party identifications
u = error term
t = time

In estimating parameters for this model, two considerations must be addressed. First, the dependent variable, party identification at time t, is ordinal (a seven-point scale).[46] This suggests that a statistical technique such as probit rather than ordinary least squares regression be employed.[47] Second, party identification at time t–1 appears on the right-hand side of the equation, thus violating the assumption that predictor variables be uncorrelated with the error term.[48] To deal with this latter problem in conjunction with the ordinal character of the dependent variable, a two-stage probit procedure is indicated.[49] In the first stage party identification at time t–1 is estimated using several sociodemographic variables, parental party identification and prior vote as predictors.[50] The estimated party identification at t–1 then is employed as an instrument in a second-stage probit analysis.

The analysis proceeds in several steps. First, a "main effects" model is estimated using party/issue perceptions, party leader preference and estimated prior party

TABLE 12 *TWO-STAGE PROBIT ANALYSES OF PARTY LEADER AND PARTY/ISSUE EFFECTS ON PARTY IDENTIFICATION, 1974–79 AND 1979–80 PANELS*

| | 1979 Party Identification | | | | | |
| | Liberal | | Progressive Conservative | | NDP | |
A. 1974–79	MLE	MLE/SE	MLE	MLE/SE	MLE	MLE/SE
Constant	1.437	18.056+	1.273	19.006+	0.983	13.696+
1974 Party identification++	0.486	10.156+	0.489	10.621+	0.653	13.151+
1979 Party leader preference	0.016	15.539+	0.018	16.253+	0.013	11.805+
1979 Party/issue preference	0.288	9.885+	0.428	11.935+	0.511	10.345+
Estimated R^2 =	0.544		0.557		0.429	

| | 1980 Party Identification | | | | | |
| | Liberal | | Progressive Conservative | | NDP | |
B. 1979–80	MLE	MLE/SE	MLE	MLE/SE	MLE	MLE/SE
Constant	1.128	14.737+	0.987	14.148+	0.854	12.530+
1979 Party identification++	0.616	15.056+	0.558	13.780+	0.557	12.862+
1980 Party leader preference	0.016	17.493+	0.016	16.956+	0.018	17.970+
1980 Party/issue preference	0.542	13.911+	0.625	14.979+	0.631	12.330+
Estimated R^2 =	0.640		0.603		0.516	

+ $p \leq 0.01$
++ First-stage estimate
MLE = Maximum likelihood estimates of probit parameters
SE = Standard error

identification as predictors. In steps two through four the model is re-estimated incorporating the main effects variables, and the age, partisan consistency and political interest interaction terms, respectively. Finally, the model is estimated once more with the main effects and all interaction variables included. For the models with interaction terms, the significance of these terms is assessed using a difference in chi-square test.[51]

Results for the main effects model are displayed in table 12. In both panels, current party identification is affected by party leader and party/issue preferences as well as by prior party identification. All of these variables have statistically significant effects in each of the six analyses (i.e., predicting the strength and direction of current party identifications for Liberals, Progressive Conservatives and New Democrats in the 1974–79 and 1979–80 panels). In each case the estimated percentage of variance explained is reasonably high—ranging from a low of 42.9 per cent for the NDP (1974–79) to a high of 64 per cent for the Liberals (1979–80).

Results when the interaction terms are added to the equations are mixed (data not shown). The inclusion of a party identification $(t–1)$ × age term produces a statistically significant increment in chi-square in three of six cases (Liberals, 1974–79 and 1979–80; NDP, 1974–79). Similarly, the prior partisanship × partisan consistency term achieves significance in both of the Liberal and one of the NDP (1974–79) analyses, but fails to do so in either of those for the PCs. The political interest terms fare considerably better. Their effects are invariably significant with p values less than 0.001 in four of six cases. Inspection of individual coefficients in these models indicates that the party/issue × interest term is more important than that for the leader preferences—the former is significant in five of six cases, whereas the latter achieves significance in two instances only. Finally, when all of the interaction terms are entered, the resulting increase in chi-square over the main effects model is significant for every analysis except that for the PCs in the 1974–79 panel. Thus, although inclusion of interaction terms does not yield large increments (i.e., 2 per cent or less) in the estimated variance explained net of that generated by the main effects models, the several statistically significant interaction variables suggest complexities in the manner in which short-term leader and issue forces affect party identification and changes therein. Specifying these complexities in greater detail is a task for future research.

PARTISAN CHANGE AND THE CANADIAN POLITICAL CONTEXT

This paper has examined sources of partisan change in contemporary Canada. Similar to recent research in Great Britain and the United States analyses indicate that party identification may be usefully conceptualized as endogenous to the set of short-term forces influencing electoral choice. As such, it is subject to short-term variations in response to changing party leader preferences and changing party preferences on various salient issues. In a polity such as Canada where party leader and party/issue preferences are highly mutable, partisan change can assume large orders of magnitude over relatively restricted time intervals.

Regarding sources of change in these preferences, the longstanding tendency of Canada's major national parties, the Liberals and the Progressive Conservatives, to act as political brokers unencumbered by the strictures imposed by rigid ideologies, and the ability of these parties to avoid the development of strongly group-based party images mean that large numbers of voters in all parts of the country are potential candidates to alter their partisan attachments.[52] Relatedly, it may be argued that such patterns of party competition and the party images they engender have served to diminish possible time-related reinforcement properties of existing partisan ties. The *ceteris paribus* assumptions auxiliary to such reinforcement hypotheses are violated in the Canadian case not by some special properties of the electorate, but rather by the characteristics of the party system that confront voters during successive election campaigns and in the interim between these contests.

This is not to say, however, that the likelihood of variations in party identification is equal over the entire electorate. Rather, the present study, as well as the results of previous inquiries, indicate that voters' susceptibility to short-term forces is partially a function of factors such as levels of exposure to relevant political stimuli and patterns of partisanship across different levels of government.[53]

In sum, the picture of the Canadian electorate sketched in this paper is that of a complex and protean entity. In this regard it would appear to differ only in degree from the portrait of its counterparts in Great Britain and the United States depicted by recent research on partisanship in these countries. In the Canadian case the endogeneity of partisan attachments and the presence of large numbers of voters with moderate to high levels of political interest and/or inconsistent partisan ties in federal and provincial politics means that individual-level partisan change is an ongoing phenomenon—one which is virtually guaranteed to continue given existing patterns of "brokerage" party competition. Whether, at any point in time, this large volume of individual instability will be translated into aggregate-level change is necessarily contingent upon the outcome of this competition in the recent past. As for election results, the conversion of party preferences into electoral outcomes is a multi-step process, and the possibility of cross-cutting partisan change is always present, and even likely given prevailing party strategies. Still, as the most recent (September 1984) national election illustrates,[54] offsetting partisan migrations are not inevitable, and while "plus ça change" would often seem to be the safest bet, it will not always be a winner.

NOTES

1. A. Campbell, G. Gurin, and W.E. Miller, *The Voter Decides* (Evanston, Ill.: Row, Peterson, 1954); A. Campbell, P. Converse, W. Miller and D. Stokes, *The American Voter* (New York: John Wiley, 1960).

2. P. Converse and G. Dupeux, "Politicization of the Electorate in France and the United States," in

Elections and the Political Order, ed. A. Campbell, P. Converse, W. Miller, and D. Stokes (New York: Wiley, 1966).

3. S. Eldersveld and A. Kubota, "Party Identification in India and Japan in the Context of Western Theory and Research" (Paper presented at the Annual Meeting of the Canadian Political Science Association, Montreal,

August 1973); J. Thomassen, "Party Identification as a Cross-National Concept: Its Meaning in the Netherlands," in *Party Identification and Beyond* ed. I. Budge, C. Crewe, and D. Fairlie (New York: John Wiley, 1976); I. Crewe, J. Alt, and B. Särlvik, "Partisan Dealignment in Britain," *British Journal of Political Science* (1977), 121–90; B.E. Cain and J. Ferejohn, "A Comparison of Party Identification in the United States and Great Britain," *Comparative Political Studies* 14 (1981): 31–47; G.B Markus, "The Political Environment and the Dynamics of Public Attitudes: A Panel Study," *American Journal of Political Science* (*AJPS*) 23 (1979): 338–59; L. LeDuc, "The Dynamic Properties of Party Identification: A Four-Nation Comparison," *European Journal of Political Research* 9 (1981): 257–68; L. LeDuc, "Canada: The Politics of Stable Dealignment," in *Electoral Change in Advanced Industrial Democracies* ed. P.A. Beck, R. Dalton, and S. Flanagan (Princeton: Princeton University Press, 1984); B. Sarlvik and I. Crewe, *Decade of Dealignment* (Cambridge: Cambridge University Press, 1983); L. LeDuc, H.D. Clarke, J. Jenson, and J. Pammett, "Partisan Instability in Canada: Evidence from a New Panel Study," *American Political Science Review* (*APSR*) 78 (1984): 470–84.

4. For example, P. Converse and G. Markus, "Plus Ça Change ... the New CPS Election Study Panel,"*APSR* 73 (1979): 32–49; G.B. Markus and P. Converse, "A Dynamic Simultaneous Equation Model of Electoral Change," *APSR* 73 (1979): 1055–70.

5. Campbell et al., *The Voter Decides*; Campbell et al., *The American Voter*.

6. For example, M.P. Fiorina, *Retrospective Voting in American National Elections* (New Haven: Yale University Press, 1981); D.R. Kiewet, *Macroeconomics and Micropolitics* (Chicago: University of Chicago Press, 1983).

7. J.E. Jackson, "Issues, Party Choices, and Presidential Votes," *AJPS* 19 (1975): 161–85.

8. B.E. Cain, "Dynamic and Static Components of Political Support in Britain" *AJPS* 22 (1978): 849–66; Markus and Converse, "A Dynamic Simultaneous Equation Model"; B.I. Page and C.C. Jones, "Reciprocal Effects of Policy Preference, Party Loyalties and the Vote," *APSR* 73 (1979): 1071–89; Fiorina, Retrospective Voting; C.H. Franklin and J.E. Jackson, "The Dynamics of Party Identification," *APSR* 77 (1983): 957–73; J. Alt, "Dealignment and the Dynamics of Partisanship in Britain," in *Electoral Change in Advanced Industrial Societies*, ed. P.A. Beck, R. Dalton, and S. Flanagan (Princeton: Princeton University Press, 1984); H.D. Clarke and M.C. Stewart, "Dealignment of Degree: Partisan Change in Britain, 1974–83," *Journal of Politics* 46 (1984): 689–718.

9. B. Gutek, "On the Accuracy of Retrospective Attitudinal Data," *Public Opinion Quarterly* 42 (1978): 390–401; R. Niemi, R. Katz, and D. Newman, "Reconstructing Past Partisanship: The Failure of the Party Identification Recall Questions," *AJPS* 24 (1980): 633–51.

10. LeDuc et al., "Partisan Instability in Canada."

11. The 1974, 1979 and 1980 Canadian national election and panel studies were funded by grants from the Social Sciences and Humanities Research Council of Canada (principal investigators: Harold D. Clarke, Jane Jenson, Lawrence LeDuc and Jon Pammett). Earlier national election studies funded by the SSHRC's predecessor, the Canada Council, were conducted in 1965 and 1968 by John Meisel and associates. The results of these latter studies are used for comparative purposes in some of the analyses which follow. All of the data sets generated by the several studies are available from the Inter-university Consortium for Political and Social Research. Details concerning technical aspects of the design of the 1974 survey may be found in L. LeDuc, H.D. Clarke, J. Jenson and J. Pammett, "A National Sample Design," *Canadian*

Journal of Political Science (*CJPS*) 7 (1974): 701–708. Those for the 1979 and 1980 surveys are available from the principal investigators upon request. The authors are solely responsible for the analyses and interpretations presented here.

12. Weighted panel Ns are: 1974–79—1353, 1979–80—1770, and 1974–79–80—865. The weighted Ns for the 1974, 1979, and 1980 cross-sectional samples are 2445, 2670 and 1786, respectively.

13. The Canadian political system is characterised by the presence of a sizable percentage of individuals (from 18 to 26 per cent in recent election studies) who maintain directionally different identifications at the federal and provincial levels of government (LeDuc et al., "Partisan Instability in Canada"). Although the phenomenon of multiple party identifications seldom has been investigated, it may be that Canada is unique in having such a substantial number of "split" identifiers. On multiple party identifications in the United States and Australia see M.K. Jennings and R. Niemi, "Party Identification at Multiple Levels of Government," *American Journal of Sociology* and D. Aitkin, *Stability and Change in Australian Politics* (New York: John Wiley, 1977): 44–47. The possible impact of cross-level inconsistency in party identification on partisan instability is considered below.

The sequence of questions used to measure federal party identification is as follows: (a) "Thinking of *federal* politics, do you usually think of yourself as Liberal, Conservative, NDP, Social Credit, or what?" (b)"How strongly [party named] do you feel, very strongly, fairly strongly, or not very strongly?" (c)[If "refused," "don't know," "independent," or "none" in (a)] "Still thinking of *federal* politics, do you generally think of yourself as being a little closer to one of the parties than to the others?" [emphasis in original]. (d)[If "yes"] "Which party is that?" All respondents supplying a party label to questions (a) and (c) were considered to have some degree of party identification.

Persons declining to provide a party label in (a) but providing one in (c) were classified with the 'weak' identifiers in the analyses of strength of party identification. A parallel sequence of questions was asked to measure party identification at the provincial level.

14. In Canada, the term "Independent" does not have wide currency among politicians, political observers, or the general public.

15. For example, Crewe et al., "Partisan Dealignment in Britain," N. Nie, S. Verba, and J. Petrocik, *The Changing American Voter*, enlarged ed. (Cambridge: Harvard University Press, 1979); Särlvik and Crewe, *Decade of Dealignment*; W.H. Flanigan and N.H. Zingale, *Political Behavior of the American Electorate* (Boston: Allyn and Bacon, 1983); Clarke and Stewart, "Dealignment of Degree."

16. Recent evidence indicates that the general weakening of partisan ties in Great Britain documented by Crewe et al. in "Partisan Dealignment in Britain," and by Särlvik and Crewe, *Decade of Dealignment*, continued into the 1980s (Clarke and Stewart, "Dealignment of Degree"). In the United States, however, it appears that the percentage of Independents increased from 1964 to 1978 and then declined slightly (Flanigan and Zingale, *Political Behavior of the American Electorate*, 46).

17. Campbell et al., *The American Voter*; For example, Campbell et al., *Elections and the Political Order*; Budge et al., eds., *Party Identification and Beyond* (New York: John Wiley, 1976); D. Butler and D. Stokes, *Political Change in Britain*, 2d college ed. (New York: St. Martin's Press, 1976); P. Converse, "Of Time and Partisan Stability," *Comparative Political Studies* 2 (1969): 139–71; P. Converse, *The Dynamics of Party Support* (Beverly Hills: Sage Publications, 1976); K. Andersen, *The Creation of a Democratic Majority, 1928–1936* (Chicago: University of Chicago Press, 1979).

18. P. Converse, "Of Time and Partisan Stability"; P. Converse, *The Dynamics of Party Support*.

19. For example, Converse, *The Dynamics of Party Support*, chap. 1.

20. For purposes of this analysis age groups are defined in terms of age of entry into the electorate. Groups identified are those first eligible to vote in 1979, 1968, 1957, 1949, 1940, or 1935 or earlier.

21. It can also be noted that the mean strength of party identification (as computed for the 1974, 1979 and 1980 cross-sectional surveys) varies (monotonically in 1974 and 1979) over the several age groups, with younger persons having weaker identifications. Again, the relationships, although statistically significant, are quite modest; etas for 1974, 1979 and 1980 are 0.10, 0.11 and 0.16 respectively.

22. For a detailed discussion of these issues see, H. Penniman, ed., *Canada at the Polls, 1979 and 1980* (Washington, D.C.: American Enterprise Institute, 1981).

23. Campbell et al., *The American Voter*; Campbell et al., *Elections and the Political Order*.

24. R.D. McKelvey and W. Zavoina, "A Statistical Model for the Analysis of Ordinal Level Dependent Variables," *Journal of Mathematical Sociology* 4 (1975): 103–20.

25. In these analyses party identification is measured as follows: stable identification with the governing party (Liberals 74–79, PCs 79–80)=1, switched from governing party to nonidentification=2, switched from governing party to another party=3. The more general measure of party identification is: stable identification=1; switched to/from nonidentification=2; switched from one party to another=3.
    The predictor variables are measured as follows: age: in years; gender: men=0, women=1; community size: over 500 000=1, 100 000–500 000=2, 10 000–99 999=3, 1 000–9 999=4, rural=5; region/ethnicity—a series of dummy variables as indicated in table 5 with Ontario as the suppressed category. (Region and ethnicity are combined into one variable to obviate potential multicollinearity problems oc-

casioned by the strong correlation between French ethnicity and residence in the province of Quebec); socioeconomic status—the Blishen socioeconomic index of occupations which ranges from 14.41 to 75.32 (B. Blishen and H. McRoberts, "A Revised Socioeconomic Index for Occupations in Canada," *Canadian Review of Sociology and Anthropology* 13 (1976): 71–80.

26. Fiorina, *Retrospective Voting*; Franklin and Jackson, "The Dynamics of Party Identification"; Alt, "Dealignment and the Dynamics of Partisanship"; Clarke and Stewart, "Dealignment of Degree."

27. In each of the three surveys respondents were asked if they had ever identified with another party. Those responding affirmatively were asked: "What was the main thing that made you change?" A maximum of two responses was recorded. Although panel data are decidedly superior for measuring partisan change it is worth noting that large numbers of people in each survey answer that they had changed their party identifications one or more times. The percentages recalling doing so are: 1974—34 per cent, 1979—32 per cent, 1980—38 per cent.

28. H.D. Clarke, J. Jenson, L. LeDuc, and J. Pammett, *Political Choice in Canada* (Toronto: McGraw-Hill Ryerson, 1979); H.D. Clarke, J. Jenson, L. LeDuc, and J. Pammett, *Absent Mandate: The Politics of Discontent in Canada* (Toronto: Gage Publishing, 1984).

29. Clarke et al., *Political Choice in Canada*; Clarke et al., *Absent Mandate*; H.D. Clarke and G. Zuk, "Economics, Politics and Party Popularity" (Paper presented at the Annual Meeting of the Midwest Political Science Association, Chicago, April 1984).

30. It is, however, not the only aspect of such conflict. A second important feature of interparty competition involves the presentation of "attractive" party leader images to the electorate. Again, interparty conflicts re: leader images are not confined to election

campaigns but rather continue throughout inter-election periods. These conflicts are related to the ebb and flow of party popularity (as mentioned, for example, by monthly public opinion polls). For a more detailed exposition of this argument in the Canadian context based on a time-series analysis of such polls see H.D. Clarke, and G. Zuk, "Economics, Politics, and Party Popularity."

31. As Butler and Stokes (*Political Change in Britain*, chap. 13) and others have noted, when thinking about how voters relate themselves to parties on issues, it is possible to distinguish between *position* and *valence* issues. In the case of the former, the electorate is divided on an issue and the key variable is the voter's perception of the relative proximity of his or her stand to those of the parties. In the latter case voters do not disagree on an issue and the significant consideration is the voter's judgement of the relative competence of parties and their leaders to deal with the problems associated with that issue. Regardless of whether an issue is of the position or valence type, however, voters concerned with it must make an assessment of which party is closest to them if it is to have an impact on their partisan attachments. Moreover, in general such assessments may utilise varying time horizons and, for present purposes, it is not necessary to determine if judgements about leaders and issues are retrospective, prospective or contemporaneous.

32. The issue questions utilised were worded as follows: (a)"Now, I would like to ask you some more specific questions about the recent *federal* election. What, in your opinion, was the *most* important issue in that election?" If the respondent mentioned an issue he/she was asked, "Which party is closest to *you* or the issue?" [emphasis in original].

33. It is noteworthy that the issues respondents deemed most important also vary markedly at both the aggregate and individual levels over the three election surveys (Clark et al., *Absent Mandate*, chap. 4).

34. Aitken, *Stability and Change in Australian Politics*; Campbell et al., *The American Voter*; Clarke et al., *Political Choice in Canada*.

35. For example, I. Crewe, "Why the Conservatives Won Labour Lost the British Election," *Public Opinion* 6 (1983): 7–9, 56–60; W. Miller, "There Was No Alternative: The British General Election of 1983," *Strathclyde Papers on Government and Politics* no. 19 (Glasgow: University of Strathclyde, 1984).

36. For example, Page and Jones, "Reciprocal Effects of Policy Preferences"; Fiorina, *Retrospective Voting*; Clarke and Stewart, "Dealignment of Degree."

37. Clarke et al., *Absent Mandate*.

38. Party leader affect is measured using 100-point thermometer scales (Clarke et al., *Political Choice in Canada*, 406–407, 421). Party leader preference is assessed in terms of the relative level of affect for the leaders of the three major parties. The resulting variables for each party leader have three categories: party leader preferred=3, party leader not preferred but tied in level of affect with one or more other leaders=2, party leader not preferred and one or more other leaders have a higher level of affect=1. Comparisons such as these made at the level of the individual respondent obviate potential measurement problems that might arise because respondents could vary in their use of the thermometer "space."

39. Clarke et al., *Political Choice in Canada*, chap. 7; Clarke et al., *Absent Mandate*, chap. 6.

40. For example, R. Brody and B. Page, "The Assessment of Policy Voting," *American Political Science Review* 66 (1972): 450–58.

41. For example, Fiorina (*Retrospective Voting*, chap. 5) conceptualizes party identification in retrospective voting terms, and Markus and Converse ("A Dynamic Simultaneous Equation Model") retain more conventional social-psychological definitions.

42. To avoid a tautological definition of the partisan consistency and partisan change variables (see note 24 above), federal nonidentifiers were omitted from these analyses. For purposes of constructing interaction terms for use in the multivariate analyses of current party identification reported below, such respondents are scored as inconsistent partisans, provided they have a provincial party identification.

43. Franklin and Jackson, "The Dynamics of Party Identification."

44. Respondents stating that they were "very interested" in a specific election and generally follow politics "very closely" were scored 2; those stating that they were at best "slightly interested" in the election and follow politics "not much at all" were scored 0; all others were scored 1.

45. Clarke et al., *Political Choice in Canada*; Clarke et al., *Absent Mandate.*

46. The construction of the party identification variables varied depending upon whether Liberal, Progressive Conservative or NDP identifications were being analysed. For the Liberal analyses the categories were: very strong Liberal=+3, fairly strong Liberal=+2, weak/leaning Liberal=+1, nonidentifier=0, weak/leaning other party= −1, fairly strongly other party= −2, very strong other party= −3. For the PC and NDP analyses the categories were very strong Conservative/NDP=+3, etc.

47. McKelvey and Zavoina, "A Statistical Model for the Analysis of Ordinal Level Dependent Variables."

48. H. Asher, *Causal Modelling*, 2d ed. (Beverly Hills: Sage Publications, 1983).

49. F. Nelson and L. Olson, "Specification and Estimation of a Simultaneous Equation Model with Limited Dependent Variables," *International Economic Review* 19 (1978): 695–709.

50. The sociodemographic variables included age, gender, region/ethnicity and socio-economic status as described in note 16. Parental party identifications were scored according to the respondents' party identifications at time *t*–1 in a panel. Thus, if the respondent was a Liberal identifier, father's party identification was scored very strong Liberal=+3, fairly strong Liberal=+2, weak/leaning Liberal=+1, nonidentifier/do not recall father's identification=0, weak/leaning other party=−1, fairly strong other party=−2, very strong other party=−3. Mother's partisanship was scored in an identical fashion. The questions used to measure parents' party identification were: (a)"When you were growing up, did your father have any particular preference for one of the *federal* political parties here in Canada?" [emphasis in original] (b) [If "yes"] "Which party was that?" (c) "How strongly [party named] was he then?" The questions for mother's partisanship were identical. Prior vote was measured as recalled 1972 vote for the 1974–79 panel and recalled 1974 vote for the 1979–80 panel. Stated vote in 1974 was not used in the latter case because not all of those in the 1979–80 panel were interviewed in 1974.

51. McKelvey and Zavoina, "A Statistical Model for the Analysis of Ordinal Level Dependent Variables," 109–11.

52. Clarke et al., *Political Choice in Canada*, chap. 6; Clarke et al., *Absent Mandate*, chap 1.

53. Clarke et al., *Political Choice in Canada*; Clarke et al., *Absent Mandate.*

54. In this election the Progressive Conservatives achieved a dramatic victory, increasing their popular vote from 33 perc cent in 1980 to 50 per cent in 1984 and their seats from 103 to 211. The Liberals, in contrast, saw their vote total fall from 44 per cent to 28 per cent and their seats decline from 146 to 40. NDP vote and seat totals were relatively stable, moving from 20 per cent to 19 per cent and 32 to 30, respectively.

section

2

IDEOLOGICAL AND SOCIAL
FACTORS

IDEOLOGY AND UNSTABLE PARTY IDENTIFICATION IN CANADA: LIMITED RATIONALITY IN A BROKERAGE PARTY SYSTEM◇

H. MICHAEL STEVENSON

○

The now impressive body of survey research on Canadian national elections provides a powerful defence of arguments for the exceptionality of Canadian politics: the weakness of class and ideological cleavages in a regionally divided society, held together by a system of elite brokerage through political institutions minimally affected by public inputs. The survey evidence suggests that Canadian voting is very little influenced (less so than in most electoral democracies) by socio-economic differences; that region, religion and language or ethnicity rather than class cleavages are the most salient of these generally insignificant effects; that voting is more affected by short-term interest in issues manipulated by parties rather than by enduring ideological orientations rooted in class or other group identities; and that the affective ties to parties are weak in intensity, unstable over time, and inconsistent in federal and provincial contexts, creating "an electorate in which the potential at least for wide electoral swings is actually very high."[1]

Until the landslide reversal of the 1984 federal election, however, the argument was weakened by the paradoxical macro-level persistence of Liberal party dominance in federal elections and government, despite the micro-level instability of partisanship. This paradox spawned the lively debate over the nature of partisanship initiated by Sniderman, Forbes and Melzer, who argued that in Canada as elsewhere party identification played a stabilizing, not a destabilizing role.[2] The interlude of minority Progressive Conservative government in 1979–1980 did little to resolve the paradox of stable Liberal electoral dominance, despite fluctuating party attachments,[3] but the massive Conservative victory of 1984, and the widely erratic polls preceding it, have done so. It can now be taken for granted that (a) the intensity and consistency, as opposed to the sheer frequency, of partisan identification is low in Canada as compared to other countries;[4] (b) vote switching is high for weak partisans, but comparatively high even for strong partisans in Canada,[5] and (c) rapid and substantial shifts in party and electoral fortunes can and do follow from the loose party identifications of Canadian voters. While the quantitative incidence and impact of unstable partisanship is thus clear, the qualitative significance of these shifts is not.

Are such changes, and the decisive impact they have upon who governs, attributable to rootless, anomic, irrational voters, or are they the product of increasingly well-educated strata within the electorate, able to function politically without the psychic and informational ties to parties?[6] Are these shifts attributable, that is, to the random changes of "mood" among voters with no well-defined group or class interests? Are they, alternatively, the result of calculated compromises by members of new groups whose interests are neither aligned with those of the major classes in capitalist society, nor satisfied by the vague platforms of brokerage parties with token commitments to the class-rooted ideologies of yesteryear? Is there disproportionate representation, for example, among unstable partisans of concerns with post-materialist or neo-conservative ideological positions, so that partisan instability provides clues to the fundamental ideological redirection and realignments in Canada as, it is argued, in other advanced capitalist states?[7] Or could these shifts still be attributable to those with a more coherent commitment to conventional class interests, so that we might discern shifts to the Conservative party among ideologically more right-wing members of privileged classes, and shifts from the Liberal party to the New Democratic party, or vice versa, among more left-wing voters "betting" on the best electoral chances of securing their interests? Such shifts might be rooted in ideology but not in class, as a result of the divisions in the new middle class and in the "established" and "non-established" working class.[8]

Such questions relate to fundamental concerns with the democratic quality of Canadian politics, and with the particular political character of recent changes in regime. It is odd, therefore, that while the Canadian literature on party identification has become so dominated by the argument over the incidence of partisan instability, there is no systematic evaluation of the socio-economic or ideological characteristics of those who change their party identification. This is less odd if one considers that the main body of research on Canadian partisan instability accepts the standard model of Canada as a brokerage party system which is exceptionally weakly rooted in class differences and ideological cleavages.[9] Odd, nevertheless, because contributors to the debate over the incidence of partisan instability refer to opposing paradigms of voting behaviour in which qualitative issues of the character of stable as opposed to unstable partisans are of central importance, and because both sides to the debate agree that electoral politics should be more focussed on issues relevant to horizontal, integrative rather than vertical, disintegrative social cleavages.[10]

This study attempts, therefore, to refocus the examination of party identification on these issues. It will ask whether there may not be some relationship between class, ideology and *changes* in partisan identification that the much documented non-existence of such bases to cross-sectional differences in partisanship may have obscured. It will seek to discover, therefore, whether there may not be a significant element of "rationality" in shifting attachments to parties, reflecting individuals' judgements of how well "interests" related to their class and ideological position are satisfied by those parties. It will argue that evidence for such rationality in Canada in the period 1977–1981 is slight but significant; that such evidence is consistent with an interpretation of brokerage politics as a check to class politics rather than as a "natural" function of the marginality and irrationality of public interests; that it suggests a view of recent political changes as a partial breakdown in this mediation of class politics, rather than as a response simply to an increasingly alienated and angry, but politically inchoate or irrational mass public; and that it suggests possibilities for the kinds of progressive electoral change in the future that previous commentators on this subject have wished for but denied.

PARTISANSHIP, IDEOLOGY AND RATIONALITY

The classic theory of party identification, espoused by Sniderman et al., emphasises what might be called system rationality as opposed to individual rationality. The rationale of the political system is the production of political order, and a stable party structure is a functional requirement to that end. Unstable party structures and floating voters threaten political order. Stable party structures, in turn, are a product of elite rationality—a commitment to certain "rules of the game," to bargaining and accommodation, to the pragmatic requirement of "centring" party programs at the modal points in the distribution of public opinion, and so forth—and of emotional rather than intellectual–rational commitments to parties in the mass public, which give elites the necessary room to manoeuvre. The average individual voter in this paradigm has relatively low political involvement, information, and ideological constraint. Where such individuals lack the direction of psychologically ingrained party identification, they become unpredictable "floating voters," whose votes may be affected by a host of factors from personal whim to direct-mail, single-issue campaigning.[11]

Jenson raised a number of serious empirical problems with the Sniderman et al. application of this paradigm to an explanation of the stability of the Canadian party system. As a matter of logic, however, its applicability is not as weak as she implied. Elkins has a point that "regardless of the measure, any absolute level of infidelity (in support of parties) is compatible with the hypothesis that party identification reflects the same kind of phenomenon in Canada and the United States."[12] However, unless one accepts also his attempts to dispose of Jenson's indication that the family transference, intensity and stability of partisanship is low in Canada, his point argues for the relevance of the Michigan model as an explanation of the *instability* rather than stability of the Canadian party system. The instability of party and electoral politics, that is, may be accounted for by weakly rooted partisanship, with long periods of Liberal party dominance reflecting the greater number of strong Liberal partisans and the random shifts of weak partisans, and with interruptions of that pattern associated with the short-term mood swings of these unstable partisans in response to the populist promises of a John Diefenbaker or Brian Mulroney in times of economic decline.[13]

The opposing paradigm of voting behaviour, used by Jenson in defence of the standard version of the instability of Canadian party politics, emphasises in a way exactly opposite to the Michigan model the system irrationality of the party system and the rationality of voters, particularly floating voters. From this perspective, party identification is a rational adaptation to changing political environments and a rational calculus by which voters match limited political information to the expectation that the parties they identify with will enunciate programs consistent with their interests. They seek more information or change party identification when this expectation is not satisfied. The stability of party identification in this perspective "changes depending on the political situation at the time," and "party identification is a stabilizing force only to the extent that the political conditions which voters confront are stable. . . . Any stability which does exist derives from the actions of the parties, not from those of individuals."[14] From this perspective, therefore, the fragility and instability of the political order is a product not of irrational floating voters, but of erratic, opportunistic, or otherwise incoherent parties and party leaders. The floating voter, far from being an irrational disturbance to the stability of the political order is the rational citizen choosing amongst competing party preferences, with more rather than less information about issues than the habitual voter.[15]

These opposing logics of voter rationality are not, however, without internal ambiguity. This is perhaps best expressed in conclusions reached by their proponents concerning the constraints on party strategy. Sniderman et al., attached to a theory that stresses the stability of emotional attachments to party, the gradual evolutionary realignment of partisan attachments to changing socio-economic arrangements, and the irrationality of short-term public shifts in voting and party attachment, suggest that Canadian parties can and should pursue more distinctive and innovative economic and social platforms.[16] Jenson, on the other hand, attached to a theory that emphasises the looseness of party identification and the relative rationality of unstable partisans, suggests that "Canadian parties cannot count on stable followings," that "party strategists must always consider the conditions under which loyalty changes," and that brokerage rather than issue-oriented strategies are the logical response to the weakness of party and class identities.[17]

Peculiarly, therefore, those who emphasise voter irrationality advocate party strategies designed to optimise rational public policy choices, and those who emphasise voter rationality see no possibility for reasonable public mandates being given to governments through elections. The question raised by the proponents of the Michigan theory is why Canadian parties should cease to define themselves within the Downsian logic of vote maximisation, and how such a strategy would avoid the problem of magnifying the impact on electoral outcomes of irrational voters. The question for proponents of the rational voter paradigm is why, particularly in times of crisis, no coherent program defining issues across the vertical divisions of region can be produced by Canadian parties, or why rational voters are so constrained by existing party strategies that they shift with little reliable sense of what a party stands for, rather than withdrawing from the electoral system or seeking out more programmatic, if in the short-run unsuccessful, minor parties.

These paradigmatic differences may, however, be overstated and unnecessary. As Elkins suggested in support of Sniderman et al., party identification may be considered a "standing decision" altered in times of political turmoil by a rational consideration of short-term issues. Shorn of the original Michigan assumptions of voter irrationality, and the psychological depth of attachments to party, this position is more or less indistinguishable from that of Jenson, who is nevertheless correct in her insistence that the onus then lies with a satisfactory account of the short-term forces affecting widespread changes in party identification. She and her colleagues have in fact gone a considerable distance towards providing such an account.[18] Their position, however, remains heavily tied to the assumptions that voter rationality and party rationality are mutually exclusive; that the latter seriously limits the former by raising the costs of information necessary to identifying the best choice among parties which opportunistically shift their positions, and by removing the organisational supports for coherent and enduring ideological perspectives embedded in programmatic party policy.

But on this latter point there is perhaps room for a relaxation of theoretical assumption in light of empirical investigation. Although there are no doubt class and institutional forces which restrict the scope of party program formation, the major parties are not completely devoid of ideological conflict and redefinition.[19] And if short-term changes in leadership and electoral platforms are not devoid of ideological resonance, then the response of unstable partisans to the issues emphasised in election campaigns may not reflect a total absence of class or ideological logic. It is important, at least, to discover empirically the extent to which unstable partisans, who are the most concerned with issues, see those issues in a broader context than the disconnected, media-hyped discourse of electioneering.

The difficulty is that the assumptions embedded in both paradigms have tended to make difficult the investigation of such a question. Survey research in either tradition has tended, that is, not to devote space to questions about class location and ideological orientation on the assumption that these factors have little effect on party attachments and voting. The conclusions that partisan instability and the relatively high salience of issues to the voting of unstable partisans are not linked to class and ideology are therefore empirically weak.[20] Using the "Quality of Life Surveys" we are able to remedy this defect of most election surveys, although our investigation will have to be confined to the nature of changes in party identification, and not to the linked question of changes in voting.

We do not, however, expect any radical discovery of large effects of class and ideology on changing party orientations from this analysis. Any such effects will, nevertheless, tend to resolve the ambiguity in the current arguments for voter rationality, and to strengthen the case for the possibility of making the electoral system more responsive to national rather than regional interests; of restoring a greater measure of genuine debate rather than psychological manipulation to the electoral process. In addition, any such linkages will provide a measure of political understanding to our presently overly psychological understanding of recent electoral shifts in Canada. They will serve, that is, to complement the dominant picture of an electorate responding hopelessly to accumulating frustration and anger at the incompetence and incoherence of government and party leadership. Although much of that picture is valid, it needs to be complemented by a more find-grained picture that overlays the image of frenzied, if stable dealignment with the less visible pattern of shifting, issue-oriented alignments that give political character to electoral changes, and which may presage important realignments of classes and ideology within Canadian parties in the future.

In more concrete terms, we shall argue that changes in partisanship among Canadians between 1977 and 1981 revealed: (1) that those under 35, those with no post-secondary education, and those most dissatisfied with their current economic situation were more likely than the relevant comparison groups to have unstable partisan attachments; (2) that while such evidence is consistent with the argument that unstable partisans responded most to short-run, local and conjunctural issues, unstable partisans in this period were more influenced than stable partisans by class and ideological considerations; and (3) that changing party alignments reflected, therefore, shifting class and ideological constituencies: leftwing voters were significantly more likely than others to shift support among parties, all of which presumably failed generally to satisfy their concerns; that the decline in Liberal party support reflected a loss of lower-class and more left-oriented voters; and that consolidation of Conservative support in this period reflected a concentration of stable support for that party, and of shifting allegiance towards that party, among more privileged and right-wing voters.

SURVEY ANALYSIS

This analysis is based upon the "Quality of Life" (QOL) surveys conducted by the Institute for Social Research, York University, for the Social Change in Canada project.[21] These national sample surveys were conducted in 1977, 1979 and 1981, during a period of major economic and political crisis in Canada. The economic disequilibrium following the 1974 energy crisis led the Trudeau government, elected in that year on a campaign against wage and price controls, to implement such controls in 1975, and to inaugurate major cuts in government spending. Such temporary effects as these measures may have had in restraining the rate of "stagflation" soon subsided, and the economy again lapsed into major recession by 1981. Added to the economic "lean times"[22] was a corresponding political crisis, set in motion by the election in 1976 of the Parti Québécois. The struggle over national unity continued through the defeat of the PQ in the 1981 referendum. And a larger, if less visible struggle over the definition of national economic and social policy in the face of economic crisis led to intensified conflict between the national and provincial governments, widespread changes in the parties controlling provincial governments, the brief defeat of the Trudeau government in 1979, and the intensification of attempts by the next Trudeau government elected in 1980 to enlarge the autonomy of the national economy and the national government.[23]

It is to be expected that these interrelated crises and changes were associated with changes in the social forces of class and ideology, although we do not propose to theorise how new conflicts within and between classes arose and were articulated ideologically. Rather, we shall assume that changes in party political allegiances were conditioned in party by such social forces, and give ex post explanations for the empirical form of the relationships we discover. The empirical investigation will be

AUGUSTANA UNIVERSITY COLLEGE
LIBRARY

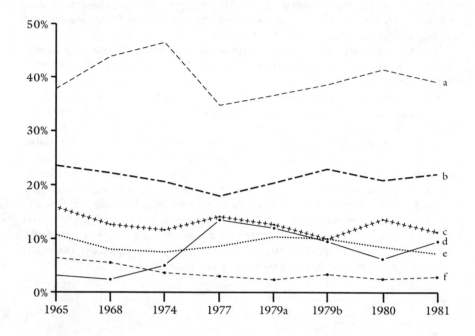

FIGURE 1   *FEDERAL PARTY IDENTIFICATION TRENDS*

Sources: 1965, 1968, 1974, 1979b, 1980 from Canadian National Election Studies; 1977, 1979a, 1981 from Social Change in Canada/Quality of Life Surveys. All surveys achieved at the York University Institute for Social Research, Toronto.

a Liberals
b Conservatives
c New Democrats
d Independent/none
e Don't know/missing
f Other

based primarily upon the changing party identification of a panel of 1665 respondents interviewed in each of the three QOL surveys. Before getting to the panel data, however, it is useful to set the general parameters of changes in partisanship in this period by reference to more representative cross-sectional survey estimates.

As plotted in figure 1, the results of a number of national surveys suggest that after the onset of the post-1974 economic crisis, identification with the Liberal party declined from 45 per cent to 35 per cent by the time of the first QOL survey in 1977, increased imperceptibly if at all before the 1979 election, increased again to 45 per cent before the election and return to power in 1980, and then began to fall off again. As compared to this pattern for Liberal partisanship, Conservative party identification levels fluctuated less: they were not substantially affected by the 1974 crisis, they rose more rapidly than Liberal identification levels after 1977 (from 19 per cent to 25 per cent), and they remained more or less stable between

1980 and 1981 despite the defeat of a Conservative government. This suggests a greater momentum towards increased Conservative identification, since the share of identification with the Liberals was likely exaggerated in 1981 by a halo effect of that party's recent electoral victory. Increasing competition between the two major parties is also suggested by the evidence that the proportion of the population considering themselves independent or unconcerned with party politics declined, and the proportion identified with third parties also declined.

Although these data do not indicate the magnitude of the changes in identification with the two major parties after 1981,[24] they do suggest the pattern of increasing partisan competition and instability up to the massive victory of the Conservative party in 1984. The broad aggregate stability of the structure of party identification in the period we discuss limits, nevertheless, the extent to which we are likely to expose a clear-cut class or ideological bias to changes in partisanship. If, however, there are ideological and class aspects to the more restricted changes before 1981, they may be even more pronounced in data describing the more dramatic changes after that date. Presuming, therefore, that the dynamics of longer-term shifts in party identification will be apparent to some extent in the QOL data, we move to an analysis of the cross-sectional changes in partisanship by region and class, before inquiring into the dynamics of individual changes over time.

The data in tables 1 and 2 reflect the number of operational simplifications of the notions of class and region. Rather than enter into the complexities of measures of social class, we opt for a straightforward classification of occupations into eight categories. The first six of these categories are a condensation of the Porter-Pineo-McRoberts socio-economic classification of occupations for the 1981 census. Using their terms, and the related Statistics Canada codes for occupations grouped by these terms, we categorize full-time employed respondents as follows: (1) self-employed and employed professionals, plus high-level managers; (2) semiprofessionals, technicians, middle management, and farmers; (3) supervisors and foremen/women; (4) skilled clerical, sales and service and skilled crafts and trades; (5) semiskilled clerical, sales and service, and semiskilled manual; (6) unskilled clerical, sales and service, unskilled manual, and farm labourers. The remaining respondents are classified either as (7) houseworkers, or as (8) others, including students, retired persons, and unemployed. Although not the product of a rigorous conceptualization of class, this classification has the virtue of involving a simple operational translation from the occupational codes of Statistics Canada. It also recognises the important conceptual distinctions in class location arising from the degree of control or autonomy in the production process, and the differences in income, security, and organisation associated with skill differentials in the established and non-established labour force.[25] The classification, therefore, isolates meaningful fragments of classes, and does not collapse into other class locations the ambiguous, but politically and economically important categories of household labour and the retired or permanently unemployed. The designation of traditional class categories is, nevertheless, possible, if imprecise: the bourgeoisie being most but not all the respondents in category 1; the petty bourgeoisie, old and new, being mostly in category 2 although some are in category 1, and the working class being in categories 3–6. Our categorization of region amalgamates the Atlantic and prairie provinces, although there are clearly important differences among the provinces in

TABLE 1   POLITICAL PARTY IDENTIFICATION BY REGION, 1977-1981 (In Percentages)

	Liberal	Conservative	New Democratic	Other	Independent	Don't know/ missing	(N)
Atlantic							
1977	35	28	6	1	15	14	(315)
1979	35	29	10	1	13	13	(285)
1981	39	29	9	1	10	10	(283)
Quebec							
1977	46	5	3	6	24	17	(879)
1979	54	8	5	12	8	13	(811)
1981	57	7	5	9	12	10	(782)
Ontario							
1977	35	22	13	0	16	14	(1198)
1979	36	26	13	1	12	13	(1070)
1981	41	27	13	2	9	10	(1091)
Prairies							
1977	26	32	9	3	13	17	(540)
1979	20	38	12	6	9	15	(499)
1981	23	46	11	2	8	11	(482)
British Columbia							
1977	27	16	21	6	11	17	(357)
1979	24	26	28	6	8	8	(314)
1981	23	25	25	4	8	16	(311)
Canada							
1977	35	19	10	3	17	16	(3290)
1979	37	23	12	5	10	13	(2979)
1981	40	25	11	4	9	11	(2948)

Source: 1977-1981 Social Change in Canada surveys, York University Institute for Social Research, Toronto.

TABLE 2   *CLASS DIFFERENCES IN PARTY IDENTIFICATION, 1977–1981 (In Percentages)* *

	Liberal	Conservative	New Democratic	(N)
Professionals/managers				
1977	41	23	12	(220)
1979	40	24	13	(208)
1981	41	31	9	(263)
Small business/ semiprofessional/ middle managers				
1977	43	21	8	(239)
1979	38	28	14	(293)
1981	39	35	13	(293)
Supervisors/foremen				
1977	49	25	8	(135)
1979	38	32	12	(128)
1981	54	24	14	(130)
Skilled workers				
1977	44	20	10	(328)
1979	47	26	15	(331)
1981	45	27	13	(316)
Semiskilled workers				
1977	43	22	13	(352)
1979	46	22	14	(335)
1981	50	24	13	(338)
Unskilled workers				
1977	41	21	16	(268)
1979	42	23	19	(275)
1981	46	26	15	(289)
Houseworkers				
1977	40	25	12	(724)
1979	43	32	11	(562)
1981	49	28	11	(530)
Others				
1977	42	22	11	(484)
1979	39	26	13	(452)
1981	39	27	14	(446)
Total				
1977	42	23	12	(2748)
1979	42	27	14	(2585)
1981	45	28	13	(2605)

+ Percentage of each class identifying with major parties. Percentages do not add up to 100 per cent because calculations exclude those who did not identify with one of the three major parties. Missing Ns were as follows: 1977 (541), 1979 (393), 1981 (343).

these regional blocs that we obscure as a result. Although these operational distortions are regrettable, they are necessary given the relatively low numbers in the panel sample that is the major focus in this article.

As shown in table 1, changes in federal party identification in this period had a definite regional character. The long-remarked bias in electoral outcomes, indicated by regional disproportions in seats won to votes cast for different parties, worked to isolate the federal Liberals from representation in the West.[26] Although the growth in Conservative identification was 6 per cent in the nation as a whole from 1977 to 1981, the equivalent growth was 9 per cent in British Columbia and 14 per cent in the Prairies. Increasing identification with the other opposition party, the NDP, was similarly biased, with a 4 per cent increase in the West as compared to a 1 per cent increase for the country as a whole. Since elsewhere there was almost no change in identification with the opposition parties, it is clear that the increasing party competitiveness in this period was very definitely a regional phenomenon.

As indicated in table 2, changes in partisan alignment also had some class colouration, in addition to the more marked regional character already discussed. The increasing shift to identification with the Conservative party was particularly marked among members of the bourgeoisie and the petty bourgeoisie. As opposed to the 5 per cent overall increase in Conservative party identification in this period, there was an 8 per cent increase in such identification among professionals and managers, and a 14 per cent increase among small businessmen, farmers, middle managers, and technical and semiprofessional workers. Although there were sizeable increases in that party's support within other classes, especially the 7 per cent increase among skilled workers, the bias of upper-class increases in support for the Conservative party is underlined by the consistent and substantial gains in support from the upper two classes registered after the 1980 defeat of the Clark government, as opposed to the reversals in levels of support for superintendents, foremen and houseworkers, and the significantly slower gains after 1979 in Conservative support among the other categories of the working class.

This suggestion of a tendency toward increasing class divisions in the party system is reinforced by data on the changing pattern of support for the Liberal party. Here, there was no change in support from professionals and managers, and less of an erosion of petty bourgeois support than might have been predicted from the rise in the support of this latter class for the Conservatives. There was also no change in Liberal identification among skilled workers, and the notable swings in partisanship among superintendents and foremen is also evident in their support for the Liberals. What most differentiates the changes in Liberal support is the consistent increase among houseworkers and among semiskilled and unskilled workers. The ability of the Liberals to retain or slightly increase their overall level of support in this period, therefore, was attributable to the strengthening of "underclass" identification among these latter categories. This suggests that the emphasis on civil rights and welfare issues in the Liberal government's post-1980 national policy increased class divisions in Canadian political culture by mobilizing support from lower-class fragments protected by those aspects of national policy, and by mobilizing opposition within middle and upper-class fragments which it could be argued were disproportionately responsible for meeting the costs of that protection.

TABLE 3   DIFFERENCES IN CLASS COMPOSITION OF PARTY COALITIONS (In Percentages)

	1977				1979				1981			
	Liberal	Conservative	New Democratic	All	Liberal	Conservative	New Democratic	All	Liberal	Conservative	New Democratic	All
Professional/manager	8	8	9	8	8	7	8	8	9	11	7	10
Small business/semiprofessional/middle manager/farmer	9	8	6	9	10	12	12	11	10	14	12	11
Supervisor/foreman	6	5	3	5	5	6	4	5	6	4	6	5
Skilled worker	12	11	10	12	14	12	14	12	12	12	13	12
Semiskilled worker	13	13	14	13	14	10	14	13	15	11	14	13
Unskilled worker	10	9	13	10	11	10	15	10	11	10	14	13
Houseworker	25	30	28	26	23	26	17	22	22	20	17	20
Others	18	17	17	18	16	17	16	17	15	17	19	17
(N)	(1161)	(622)	(319)	(2748)	(1085)	(693)	(349)	(2585)	(1175)	(723)	(325)	(2605)

These results confirm, therefore, the widely remarked regional bias in partisan shifts during this period and suggest a previously unobserved association between class and partisan realignment. The suggestion should, nevertheless, be qualified. The magnitudes of the changes identified are not large, and our estimates may be sensitive to changes in sampling error and missing data over time. Even though small percentage changes are the difference between winning and losing in electoral politics, one should therefore be cautious about exaggerating any association between class and party alignment. There was no substantial change in this period in the pattern of majority identification with the Liberal party, and the class bias in realignment suggested by changes in the proportion of a given class identifying with the different parties does not substantially alter the heterogeneity of the class constituencies of the major parties. The data in table 3 nevertheless suggest that there was some tendency in this period for the major parties to become more differentiated rather than more similar in the class composition of their respective identification pools. Again, the changes are not large, but they are consistent with the evidence in table 2 for a class dynamic to party politics.

While the proportion of our samples drawn from the upper two class categories increased from 17 per cent to 21 per cent between 1977 and 1981, the proportion of Liberal identifiers who were upper class in these terms barely changed from 17 per cent to 19 per cent; the proportion of NDP identifiers in this category increased from 15 per cent to 19 per cent, making the NDP more like the Liberals in this respect, but the increase for the Conservatives was much more noticeable from 16 per cent to 25 per cent. Similarly, there was increased differentiation of the relative involvement in each party by members of the skilled, semiskilled and unskilled working class. Whereas the proportion of the population in these three lower-class categories increased from 35 per cent to 41 per cent, the proportion of Conservative identifiers in these positions changed not at all from 33 per cent, while the comparable proportion of Liberals grew from 35 to 38 per cent, and that of NDP identifiers from 37 to 41 per cent. Finally, although the proportion of houseworkers declined by 6 per cent overall, the proportion of Liberals in this category moved from slightly below to slightly above the national figure, while that of Conservatives fell 10 per cent from substantially above the national proportion in 1977 to equal it in 1981.

Although there is, therefore, a suggestion of increasing class differentiation in party identification, the small changes identified from tables 2 and 3 in the relative attractiveness of the different parties to individuals in the same class, and in the relative weight of identification within each party by individuals in the different classes, may be attributable to factors other than an increase in the salience of class politics. These changes may reflect an historical change in the perspective of new members of the electorate,[27] such that there is a short-run tendency for new generations of a given class to be more likely to see a given party identified with their interests, without any realignment of older generations. There may, that is, be a "recruitment" effect without the "conversion" implied by realignment, and small recruitment effects may wither over time in the face of experience with opportunistically shifting party organisations. In addition, the short-term class-related changes may have nothing to do with ideologically coherent class interests, but with very short-term, conjunctural issues like the responses to particular policies developed in the face of an economic crisis, or with newly emerging political values and conflicts that have little or no connection to any fundamental conflict of interests between classes.

In order to assess the real significance of the class bias in the changing cross-sectional attraction of parties to individuals so far identified, we have, therefore, to move to the QOL panel data and examine more closely the characteristics of individual changes in partisan identity.[28]

The incidence of partisan shifting in this period as estimated by these panel data is very high. Using responses to the question "Thinking of federal politics, do you usually think of yourself as a Liberal, Conservative, NDP, Social Credit, or what?" we define stable partisans as those who maintain the same party identification in each of the three waves of the QOL survey. All others, including those who did not know or otherwise would not answer the question, are categorized as unstable partisans. Using this definition, the QOL panel data show that 56 per cent of the electorate were unstable partisans between 1977 and 1981, 43 per cent between 1977 and 1979, and 35 per cent between 1979 and 1981. National Election Study estimates for the somewhat longer period 1974–1980 suggest that less than half (41 per cent) of the electorate changed their party identification, with only 35 per cent changing between 1974 and 1979, and only 25 per cent between 1979 and 1980. These differences are primarily a result of different uses of missing data,[29] and no matter what operationalization is used this incidence of partisan shifting is clearly higher than comparable data suggest for the United States and the United Kingdom.[30] What then distinguishes the large number of unstable partisans in the Canadian electorate?

As indicated in table 4, there are proportionately more unstable partisans among younger rather than older Canadians, among the less rather than better educated, among skilled workers as opposed to other occupational groups, and in Quebec as opposed to other provinces. Sixty per cent of those under 40 years old were unstable partisans as opposed to just more than 50 per cent of older respondents. Close to 60 per cent of those who had not completed a high school education were unstable partisans, while high school graduates were typical of the population as a whole, and those with post-secondary education were more likely to be stable partisans. Fifty-nine per cent of skilled workers were unstable as opposed to a very low 44 per cent of supervisors and foremen, and 51 per cent of the professional and managerial upper class. Sixty per cent of Quebeckers were unstable partisans and there were proportionately more unstable partisans in the Atlantic provinces and British Columbia than in Ontario and the Prairies.

Table 4 also shows that more than two-thirds of those identifying with one of the two major parties in 1977 maintained that commitment throughout the period. The high level of partisan instability was disproportionately influenced, therefore, by the greater instability of attachments to the NDP and other minority parties, and by those who had no preliminary attachment to a party. Only 21 of the 296 independents were independent in every wave of the panel, and very few (18 of 204) with missing data failed to answer the party identification question in every wave. There are, that is, very few "pure" independents in this panel, and our all-inclusive operationalization of partisan instability has substantial validity.

TABLE 4   PARTISAN INSTABILITY BY DEMOGRAPHIC
CHARACTERISTICS, 1977 (In Percentages)*

	Unstable	Stable	(N)
Age			
18–29	62.8	37.2	(438)
30–39	57.8	42.2	(398)
40–49	49.8	50.2	(293)
50–59	51.4	48.6	(253)
60+	52.9	47.1	(278)
Total	55.9	44.1	(1660)
Education			
Grade school or less	59.5	40.5	(306)
Some high school	57.7	42.3	(371)
High school graduate	55.2	44.8	(382)
Some university	54.3	45.7	(387)
University graduate	51.9	48.1	(216)
Total	55.9	44.1	(1662)
Region			
Atlantic	56.4	43.6	(202)
Quebec	60.4	39.6	(475)
Ontario	52.3	47.7	(598)
Prairies	53.3	46.7	(210)
British Columbia	58.3	41.7	(180)
Canada	55.9	44.1	(1665)
Federal party affiliation			
Liberal	34.3	65.7	(623)
Conservative	32.4	67.6	(324)
New Democratic	44.1	55.9	(177)
Other	85.0	15.0	(41)
Independent/none	100.0	0.0	(296)
Total valid	49.8	50.2	(1461)
Missing	100.0	0.0	(204)
Occupation			
Professional manager	50.9	49.1	(97)
Semiprofessional/technical/			
farmers	54.7	45.3	(107)
Supervisors/foremen	44.4	55.6	(63)
Skilled workers	59.2	40.8	(179)
Semiskilled workers	55.7	44.3	(185)
Unskilled workers	57.4	42.6	(122)
Houseworkers	57.0	43.0	(547)
Others	57.1	42.9	(261)
Total	56.1	43.8	1561

+ Missing data are excluded unless otherwise noted.

These results suggest the importance of controlling for age and education when investigating the questions of rationality raised here. More recent recruits to the electorate may, in addition to being more likely to shift allegiances among

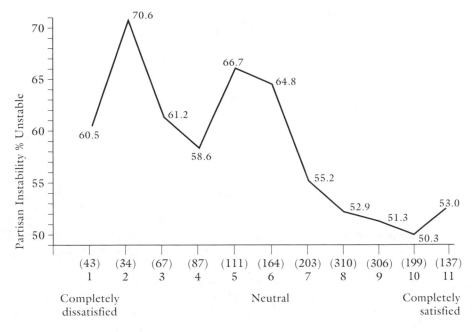

FIGURE 2   *PARTISAN INSTABILITY BY SATISFACTION WITH FINANCIAL SITUATION (%), 1977*

Source: 1977 Social Change in Canada survey, York University Institute for Social Research, Toronto.

parties, be less likely to make such shifts on the basis of information and issues. Likewise, the education effect may suggest the greater irrationality of the less stable partisans. This cannot be assumed, however, and we shall argue in contrast for the greater rationality rather than irrationality of the younger electorate, and for the equivalence in these terms of different educational strata in the population.

What, then, can be said about the reasons for individual changes of party identification? Figure 2 suggests that one important reason is the short-term response to changing economic conditions, that is, a "rational" response to short-term interests as distinct from the more inclusive rationality based on ideologically defined interests that endure over time. Of those who were less than satisfied with their financial situation in 1977, between 60 per cent and 70 per cent changed their party identification in the next five years. Rates of partisan stability were correspondingly higher than average for those satisfied and very satisfied with their financial situation; just more than 50 per cent of those rating their financial situation above the neutral point changed their party identification in this period.

These data can be interpreted as evidence for the importance to partisan instability of short-run, conjunctural responses to economic conditions. Table 5 suggests, however, the imperfection of measures of financial satisfaction as indicators of short-run responses to changing economic conditions, and/or the

TABLE 5   PARTISAN INSTABILITY AND CHANGE IN
LEVELS OF FINANCIAL SATISFACTION (In
Percentages)*

	1977–1979		1979–1981	
	Stable	Unstable	Stable	Unstable
Financial satisfaction				
No change or improved rating	55	44	66	34
Lower rating in later year	59	41	64	36
(N)	(945)	(706)	(1075)	(575)

* Measure computed from subtraction (t_2-t_1) of scores on eleven-point scale of satisfaction with financial situation. All negative scores coded lower rating; all zero or positive scores coded no change or improved rating.

marginal relevance of short-run changes in financial condition to changes in partisanship. Thirty-seven per cent of the panel reported less satisfaction with financial situation in 1979 as compared to their reports in 1977. Forty-one per cent reported less in 1981 than they had reported in 1979. Because of higher measures of unemployment and inflation, one might have expected more than the additional 4 per cent reporting lower rates of financial satisfaction in the latter period. And because this economic deterioration was coupled to electoral changes, one might have expected a particularly strong relationship between declining financial satisfaction and changes in party identification in the latter period.

The evidence in table 5 shows no such relationship. Proportionately fewer of those who reported declining financial satisfaction between 1977 and 1979 changed their party identification as compared to those reporting no or positive change in this period (41 per cent versus 44 per cent), and only 2 per cent more changed parties in the period 1979–1981 (36 per cent versus 34 per cent). Difference scores on our measures of financial satisfaction are, therefore, either too unreliable to indicate declining financial satisfaction, or there is no relationship between short-run changes in financial satisfaction and partisan instability. The meaning of the pattern outlined in figure 2 has probably less to do with evaluations of changing economic conditions (at least not rational evaluations) than with fairly stable differences in satisfaction with financial situation. Those frustrated by standards of living lower than they feel entitled to are more likely to vent that frustration in opposition to ruling parties. This raises the general issue of the value standards by which individuals evaluate objective social circumstances, and in this context we turn to the possible relationships between ideology and partisan instability.

For this purpose we have constructed nine measures of ideological orientation which are summarised in the Appendix. The first five of these measures define the classical left–right political spectrum, touching on questions of the relative powers of labour and capital, the state's role in regulating the economy and its responsibility for assuring standards of social welfare. The last four measures relate to "post-materialist" issues: support for new social movements, social order and commitments to self-actualization or personal security.

The simple correlations of these measures with partisan instability, as indicated in table 6, are all close to zero, and seldom significant, but there is a consistent pattern in the direction of association. The signs of the coefficients suggest, that is, that the more left-wing and the more post-materialist respondents are more likely to shift their party loyalties. Closer inspection of the bivariate distributions (not presented here) indicates an interesting non-linearity obscured by the simple correlation: only those at the extreme "left" ends of the ideological scales are significantly more likely than those elsewhere to change their party identification. As compared to the average of 55 per cent of the panel who changed their party identification, the rate of partisan instability was 64 per cent for those who scored in the top fifteenth percentile of support for social welfare programs, 63 per cent for those who scored in the top fifteenth percentile of support for income redistribution, 59 per cent for those who scored in the top two deciles of support for new social movements, 60 per cent for those who scored in the bottom two deciles of support for social order, and 60 per cent for those who scored in the top fifteenth percentile of commitment to self-actualization. This non-linearity is confirmed by comparison of the zero-order correlations of partisan instability with the ideological scales to the multiple correlations of partisan instability with those scales reformulated as sets of dummy variables describing clusters in the continuous distribution. The multiple R so obtained is regularly larger than the simple correlation, indicating the non-linear effect of greater partisan instability in the extreme left-wings of the ideological spectra.

Table 6 also indicates the importance of age as a variable conditioning a qualitatively different type of partisanship. As indicated here, the effect of class and the traditional left–right ideological orientations on partisan instability is much stronger for *younger* Canadians than for the population as a whole. Younger Canadians (see table 4) are more likely than others to shift their partisanship, but they are also more likely, according to the significant coefficients in table 6, to do so on the basis of class and ideological orientations with lower-class leftist-oriented youth tending toward more unstable and upper-class and right-wing youth more stable attachments.

These results contradict conventional explanations for the greater partisan instability of youth. First, youth are not less rational, more governed by fads, moods or attractive personalities, in their party attachments than those with a longer experience of politics. Rather, youth are more influenced than older voters by considerations of class and ideology when changing their identification with political parties. Second, there is no suggestion that the new politics of post-materialism have superceded the old politics of class as the basis for the ideological alignments of new political generations. As compared to the highly significant effect on changes in party identification of attitudes towards social welfare, income redistribution and foreign investment among younger Canadians, the post-materialist concerns with new social movements, with self-actualization, and (negatively) with political order and personal security have no effect. The one post-materialist issue for which there is a significant effect is the concern with personal security, and in this case the effect is entirely confined to older rather than younger respondents. There is, therefore, little support here for suggestions that debates over new rather than old politics have special importance in the political behaviour of young people.[31]

The results in table 6 also contradict expectations that greater partisan instability among less educated voters results from a lower capacity to link parties

TABLE 6   CORRELATIONS OF PARTISAN STABILITY
(Dummy) WITH CLASS AND IDEOLOGICAL
ORIENTATION (Pearson's r)

Ideological orientation	Full panel	Age		Education	
		Under 30	Over 30	Low	High
Social class	-.03	-.10**	-.02	-.03	-.02
Support for social welfare	-.06**	-.13*	-.02	-.07**	-.00
Support for income redistribution	-.08*	-.15*	-.05	-.07**	-.08**
Support for economic nationalism	-.02	-.15*	.03	-.02	-.10**
Support for state regulation of economy	-.01	-.04	.01	.01	.00
Support for labour rights	-.03	-.06	.00	-.01	-.07
Support for new social movements	-.03	-.06	.00	-.01	-.06
Support for social order	.03	.01	.03	.05	.02
Value self-actualization	-.01	.00	.00	.00	-.02
Value personal security	.07**	.01	.08**	.06*	.11**

$*\ p \leq .001$
$**\ p \leq .01$
$✦\ p \leq .05$

rationally to ideological perspectives. Change in party identification among lower-educated respondents is as likely to be motivated by ideological considerations as is such change among highly educated respondents. There are as many significant coefficients measuring such links in the two subsamples, and there is no difference in the average size of the coefficients. There is, however, a difference in the dimensions of ideology which are salient in affecting changes in party identification among the lower rather than higher educated. It is only the latter for whom issues of foreign investment are salient, and they are more influenced by issues of personal security. Lower-educated respondents, in contrast, are the only ones for whom attitudes towards social welfare are significant in affecting changes in party iden-tification. This suggests that education is more an indicator of social class than of ideological constraint; members of all classes are equally likely to be ideologically constrained in their evaluations of political parties, but the content of left-wing ideology in the lower classes is more rooted in issues of social welfare, as opposed to issues of economic and cultural nationalism in more privileged classes. Both ideological perspectives are left-wing in the sense that they counterpose public or collective interests to individual interests, and they call for state intervention to correct market deficiencies in this regard. A concern with equality and redistribution that is *the* conventional identifying mark of left-wing movements is, however, salient only for members of the lower class.

If education does not, therefore, appear to increase ideological constraint and thereby affect the degree to which partisan instability is affected by ideological deliberation, it remains, nevertheless, interesting to examine ideological constraint by a direct rather than inferred procedure, and to ask again whether unstable voters are less ideologically constrained, and therefore less rational, than stable voters. The data in table 7 show coefficients measuring the relationship between the four ideological measures dealing with traditional questions of social welfare and state regulation in a capitalist society, and the one post-materialistic issue that had the greatest salience in affecting partisan instability among younger voters.

The top half of the matrix in table 7 gives the constraint coefficients for respondents with stable party identification; the bottom half for those with changing party identification. Clearly there is no difference between the levels of constraint for stable as opposed to unstable partisans according to this evidence. For both groups, the measures of ideological constraint suggest highly significant and generally strong relationships (an average correlation of .35 for stable and .33 for unstable partisans) between attitudes on different dimensions of ideology. In general, therefore, there is no evidence here for concerns that unstable partisans think less coherently or rationally about political issues, and, therefore, that the decisive shifts in electoral outcomes are disproportionately influenced by irrational rather than rational voters.

It remains, however, difficult to understand how rational changes of party identification on ideological grounds can be understood in Canada, where the differences between the major parties, and perhaps between all three significant parties, are so minor. Although our analysis so far suggests that more left-wing voters are more likely to shift their loyalty from one party to another, and that ideological differences are associated with partisan instability among young people in particular, it is not clear yet that these shifts represent more than a random change of identification with parties that have little or no salience for these voters, rather than a deliberate selection of parties that are most likely to favour or do least damage to a particular ideological position.

In order to look further into this question, we examine the differences in ideological orientation among the stable constituencies of the major parties, those shifting to the Conservative party in this period, those shifting in and out of the Liberal and/or New Democratic parties but never to the Conservative party, and others shifting among all parties. The isolation of these groups is based upon the assumption that the Conservative party is the most clearly right-wing, the NDP the most left-wing, and that the Liberal party is more at the centre with a history of co-optation of NDP policy proposals, especially in periods of minority government. We hypothesise, therefore, that if there is any ideological rationality to partisan shifting, "converts" to the Conservative party in this period should have been more right-wing than other unstable partisans, and closer to stable Conservative partisans than any others; and that those shifting only between the Liberals and NDP should be closest to the stable NDP partisans and more left-wing than other unstable partisans who identified with the Conservative party at some time in this period but did not convert to it in 1979 or 1981. This latter hypothesis assumes that the most left-wing of the unstable partisans will identify with anything but the most right-wing party, in attempts to secure the best protection of their interests depending on conjunctural changes in party programs and public opinion. It may also be the case, however, that those unstable partisans who did not convert permanently to

TABLE 7   CORRELATIONS AMONG MEASURES OF IDEOLOGY FOR STABLE AND UNSTABLE PARTISANS (Pearson's r)

Unstable	Stable				
	Support for social welfare	Support for income redistribution	Support for economic nationalism	Support for labour rights	Support for new social movements
Support for social welfare	—	.46*	.25**	.40*	.51*
Support for income redistribution	.49*	—	.34*	.39*	.29*
Support for economic nationalism	.28*	.29*	—	.29*	.22*
Support for labour rights	.34*	.31*	.35*	—	.30*
Support for new social movements	.47*	.25*	.21**	.27*	—

* p ≤ .0001
** p ≤ .001

TABLE 8 IDEOLOGICAL DIFFERENCES AMONG PARTISAN TYPES*

		Partisan Type				
	Stable New Democrats	Liberal/New Democratic switchers	All Party switchers	Stable Liberals	Conservative converts	Stable Conservatives
Support for social welfare++	26.8	26.6	26.4	26.2	25.2	24.7
Support for income redistribution++	12.0	11.3	11.2	10.6	10.3	10.3
Support for economic regulation♦	1.2	1.4	1.3	1.5	1.3	1.2
Support for economic nationalism++	10.6	10.0	10.2	9.8	9.7	9.4
Support for labour rights++	12.5	11.4	11.4	11.1	11.0	10.7
Support for new social movements++	15.1	14.8	14.6	14.5	14.3	14.0
Support social order++	10.1	10.6	11.0	10.8	11.0	11.5
Value personal security	0.52	0.48	0.49	0.57	0.53	0.57
Value self-actualization♦	8.5	8.6	8.5	8.7	8.4	8.2
(N)	(106)	(562)	(180)	(408)	(186)	(218)

*Table shows scale averages. Statistical tests were for one-way analysis of variance.
++ $p(F) \leq .001$
♦ $p(F) \leq .05$

the Conservatives in 1979 or move to them in 1981, but who identified with that party in 1977 and/or 1979, may also be more left-wing than stable Liberals, Conservative converts and stable Conservatives rather than being a less ideologically coherent group, spread randomly across the ideologically grounded spectrum of partisanship. This group may, that is, predominantly include relatively left-wing Liberals defecting from the party after right-wing shifts in Liberal government policy between 1974 and 1979, but returning to an identification with the Liberals after the brief interlude of Conservative government.

As indicated in table 8, these arguments have some validity. The left–right ordering of the partisan types at the head of the table is systematically confirmed by the differences in average scores on the ideological scales. The magnitude of the differences between average scores is very slight, but in three-quarters of the tests these differences are so highly significant that it makes sense to treat them as reflecting real differences in ideological orientation within the limits of a hegemonic consensus on most questions of politics and economics in a liberal state.

In every case, those who converted to an identification with the Conservatives in 1979 and stuck to that identification through 1981, or who converted in 1981 when Liberal identification was increasing elsewhere in the population, are more right-wing than any other partisans except the stable Conservative partisans. On all of the questions of "old politics" concerning rights and redistribution in a capitalist society, the Liberal/NDP switchers are more left-wing than all other partisan types except the stable NDP identifiers.[32] The one slight exception to this latter position is the greater support for economic regulation by the all-party switchers as compared to never-Conservative switchers, probably supporting our assumption of a greater proportion of left-wing Liberals in this group who were more likely than other more left-wing citizens to support Liberal government policy on wage and price controls. This assumption about the composition of the all-party switchers is further corroborated by the evidence that these unstable partisans are more left-wing than stable Liberals on all questions of "old politics."

The ideological placement of partisan types is not as clear on questions of "new politics." On questions of support for new social movements the partisan types are arrayed in exactly the same left–right order. These "new politics" cleavages, therefore, do not have counteracting effects on the traditional left–right structure of partisan identities; they simply reinforce it. The ordering is similarly close (with the inversion of stable Liberals and all party switchers) on questions of social order. Differences in the value placed on personal economic security and self-actualization are of much less or no statistical significance, indicating the tenuous character of the conceptualization of post-materialism as a crucial dimension of modern political consciousness. The fact that stable Liberals score highest on self-actualization suggests that self-actualization values are, if anything, more associated with ideological and party commitments to Liberalism than to any more activist or revolutionary political credo unconnected to traditional party politics. And the lower scores on personal security of the left-wing unstable partisans is very weak evidence for the argument that new post-materialist, quality of life concerns motivate new generations of political activists and distance them most from the traditional party system.

This analysis of the ideological differentiation of stable partisans and switchers rests heavily upon the statistical significance of the results in table 8, which is not necessarily, of course, an indication of their substantive significance. The small differences in mean values on the ideological scales might rather be emphasised to suggest the absence of a substantively significant relationship. The small differences in means are, however, no more an automatic indication of the lack of substantive significance than the measure of statistical significance is an indicator to the contrary. Since the distributions on our scales measuring ideological perspectives are not strictly normal, but rather indicate a tendency towards a hegemonic position at the centre, and since the differences in the ideological or programmatic definition of political parties are weak, one does not anticipate large differences in table 8. Small differences may, therefore, be substantively significant. But are they large enough to be really interesting?

The persistent question cannot be definitively answered. One might answer positively on the basis that small mean differences conceal much larger differences in the concentrations of left- and right-wing ideological perspectives among partisan types. If one looks, for example, at those respondents systematically supporting social welfare initiatives (that is, the 18 per cent of the panel calling for much more effort in at least six of the seven policy areas referred to in this scale), they are nearly twice as visible as a proportion of the never-Conservative switchers (23 per cent) as they are of the Conservative converts (12 per cent). The difference is even greater if we look at those systematically supporting income redistribution, that is, the 24 per cent of the panel who strongly agree with at least two of the items in this scale. These strong advocates of income redistribution account for 32 per cent of the respondents in all three partisan types to the left of the stable Liberals, as opposed to 18 per cent in each of the other three partisan types. And the differences are yet larger if we focus on the top deciles of the distributions. Although there is a good deal of ideological heterogeneity in each partisan type, therefore, there are sizeable differences in the concentrations within types of respondents on different ends of the ideological spectrum.

But such elaboration does not resolve the issue. As in so many debates about statistical evidence, where the argument is of the glass half-full or half-empty variety, the evidence produced cannot decide between the two interpretations. In our case, indeed, the argument is less about whether the glass is half-full or half-empty, than about whether in an eight-ounce mix there may be an ounce of liquor with a distinct effect. Clearly, there is nothing close to a dominant effect of class and ideology on partisanship in Canada. Equally clearly, however, the null hypothesis of no such effect, normally assumed in writing on this topic, can be rejected on the evidence in this study. And one is surely entitled on this basis to speculate, if only to prompt more carefully formulated theoretical and empirical analysis, about the broader implications of small but significant class and ideological correlates of changes in partisanship in Canada.

It will be apparent that we have not been concerned in this work with the debate over the stabilizing effect of party identification, but with the corollary arguments in that debate over the rationality of party choice and voting. Rather than looking again at the question of the relationship between party identification and voting (which we cannot in any event do with the QOL data), we have assumed that party identification is a strong if not tautological predictor of vote, and have argued in support of the critics of the Michigan model that changes in party identification and voting are rationally rather than irrationally based. Extending the argument of those critics, we have argued that this rationality is not confined to responses to short-term influences, subject to the unilateral manipulation of political parties, but is grounded in more deeply structured cleavages of class and ideology, which place limits upon party elite manipulation of the electorate.

Using data not generally available in Canadian election surveys, we have, to use the words of Key, "established patterns of movement of party switchers and patterns of stability of the standpatter that lead us to a conception of the voter that is not often propounded. From our analysis, the voter emerges as a person who appraised the actions of government, who has policy preferences and who relates his vote to those appraisals and preferences."[33] In the period 1977–1981, that is, we have argued that the increasing competitiveness of the Conservative party was based upon its disproportionate attraction to voters from more privileged social classes, and to converts with more right-wing ideological leanings. The Liberal party increased its attractiveness to voters from the least privileged classes and benefitted from the switching of more left-leaning voters. The Liberals' hold on the very large number of left-leaning unstable partisans was, however, uncertain. Although our data cannot substantiate the argument, the analysis in this article would suggest that declining Liberal party identification after 1981 followed the deepening economic crisis in the period 1981–1982; that increasing identification in the latter stages of the Trudeau government followed more left-leaning postures on peace, health care, and Charter issues; and that the precipitous drop in support before the 1984 election reflected the ideological turnaround by the party on such issues under the leadership of Turner, coupled with the vague commitment to them by Mulroney and the Conservatives.[34]

These latter remarks indicate a large effect on electoral and party politics of leadership strategy and behaviour, and of short-term changes in political and economic affairs. In this sense, we agree with Jenson's arguments for the instability of the Canadian party system, and for its responsiveness to short-term changes. We have tried, however, to indicate that the response to short-term effects is grounded to a significant extent in class positions and ideological orientations. Among younger Canadians, who are disproportionately unstable partisans, the likelihood of partisan instability increases in non-privileged sectors of the middle and working class, and increases among individuals with more left-wing views on ideological questions. In the population as a whole, unstable partisans who converted to the Conservative party tended to be more right-wing than other unstable partisans; those who shifted in and out of only the Liberals and/or the NDP were more left-wing.

The importance of ideology to party politics in Canada is further underlined by the positioning of stable NDP identifiers, Liberals and Conservatives at the left, centre and right of the ideological spectrum. The minority of stable partisans in the electorate give the party system a measure of ideological character, therefore, and such stability as they engender in electoral politics, pace the Michigan argument, is a stability that has a meaning beyond a purely psychological affection. The Canadian party system, that is, does have an enduring ideological character as defined by the interests of activist party members. The failure of the system to acquire greater stability is, as both sides of the debate on Canadian partisanship agree, a failure of party leadership to articulate more clearly and consistently their programmatic differences. That failure, in turn, reflects the successful electoral position in the stable three-party system of the centre Liberal party through much of this century.

Despite the difficulty therefore facing the left- and right-wing opposition parties with much smaller stable constituencies, our evidence of the greater numbers of the left- rather than right-wing unstable partisans suggests a much greater opportunity for a more coherent left opposition than has hitherto been suggested by brokerage-model political analysis using survey data without adequate measures of ideological orientation. The left-wing leanings of the largest blocs of unstable partisans in the latter days of the Trudeau era confirm the general argument recently popularized by Gwyn and Graham:[35] that the modal consensus in the Canadian political culture lies to the left of classical liberalism's centre. In this clear appreciation of the significance of ideology in Canadian politics, the journalists have significantly improved upon the academic portraits of Canadian politics as devoid of ideological dynamics.

Clearly there are brokerage mechanisms that minimise the influence of ideology, just as there are hegemonic influences which limit the range of ideological variation in the political culture. It is, nevertheless, important to identify the substantive character and the limits of ideological consensus in the Canadian polity. Limited though the distance travelled by this study in that direction may be, it will have served its purpose if it invites some political scientists, and political activists, to re-examine the orthodox "necessity" of a party politics fixed at an un-ideological centre.

APPENDIX: MEASURES OF IDEOLOGICAL ORIENTATION

Nine multiple-item scales were constructed for the QOL panel respondents, using the questions and coding as described below. Except in the cases of support for economic regulations and the two measures developed from the ranking and rating of personal goals, the items included in scales not only satisfy a face relevance to the concepts they measure, but also a factor analysis (not reported here) showing that they define independent dimensions of ideological orientation among respondents.

1. Support for Social Welfare Programs

We would like to know how much effort you think government should put into a number of activities. Please choose the answer which comes closest to your opinion about the effort that should be made in each area: Much less effort (1) less effort (2) about the same effort (3) more effort (4) much more effort (5). Remember that putting more effort into one of these areas would require a shift of money away from other areas or an increase in taxes. How much effort should government put into:

- health and medical care
- creating more jobs
- helping the poor
- building public housing
- education
- helping retired people
- workman's compensation.

The scale was computed for all panel respondents (N=1662) who answered more than half of the items. "Depends" or "don't know," responses were recoded (3), and the scale score was the sum of the scores assigned to each of the items.

2. Support for Increased Income Redistribution

We would like to know whether you strongly disagree (1) disagree (2) neither agree nor disagree (3) agree (4) or strongly agree (5) with the following statements:
- There is too much of a difference between the rich and poor in this country
- The government should provide jobs for Canadians who want to work but cannot find a job
- People with high incomes should pay a greater share of the total income taxes than they do now.

The scale was computed as the sum of scores on each item for all panel respondents (N=1664), with "depends" or "don't know" responses recoded to (3).

3. Support for Economic Regulation

Do you think the government should have the power to:
- stop wages and other incomes from rising
- stop rising prices.

The scale was computed for all respondents who answered each item (N=1450) by summing scores for the responses "no or voluntary restraint" (0) and "Yes" (1).

4. Support for Controls on Foreign Investment

We would like to know whether you strongly disagree (1) disagree (2) neither agree nor disagree (3) agree (4) or strongly agree (5) with the following approaches to dealing with foreign investment in Canada:
- Requirements that make radio and television stations carry a certain amount of Canadian programming
- Requirements that companies which want to start a business in Canada join with a Canadian company in the new business
- Legislation to force the sale of foreign-owned companies to Canadians.

The scale was computed for all respondents who answered at least two of the items (N=1660) by recoding "depends" and "don't know" to (3) and summing the scores for each item.

5. Support for Labour Union Powers

We would like to know whether you strongly disagree (1) disagree (2) neither agree nor disagree (3) agree (4) or strongly agree (5) with the following statements:
- During a strike, management should be prohibited by law from hiring workers to take the place of strikers
- Workers should have positions on the board of directors of the organisations for which they work
- Workers should have the right to refuse to work in conditions which they consider to be unsafe.

The scale was computed for all respondents who answered at least two of the items (N=1656) by recoding "depends" and "don't know" to (3) and summing the scores for each item.

6. Support for New Social Movements

Measure 6 used the same introduction as Measure 1, followed by:
- protecting the rights of native peoples
- eliminating discrimination against women
- protecting the environment
- providing daycare.

The scale was computed in the same way as Measure 1.

7. Support for Measures to Increase Social Order

Measure 7 used the same introduction as Measure 1, followed by:
- crime prevention
- eliminating pornography
- national defence.

The scale was computed in the same way as Measure 1.

8. Priority Value on Personal Security Goals

Respondents were asked to indicate which of 11 goals was *the* most important to them. If any of the following three were mentioned, respondents (N=804) were scored positively on a dummy variable:
- Prosperity: having plenty of money to afford the better things in life
- Economic stability: having a steady, secure income to provide for your basic needs
- Family security: providing love and care for family members.

9. Commitment to Non-Materialist Goals and Self-Actualization

Respondents were asked to rate the importance of each of 11 goals using a four-point scale: "not very important" (1); "fairly important" (2); "very important" (3); and "of utmost importance" (4). This scale was constructed for all respondents

(N=1650) answering more than one of the following items, with "depends" or "don't know" recorded (0):
- Excitement: having a stimulating and active life
- Achievement: having a sense of accomplishment, being successful
- Self Development: being able to improve your skills and abilities.

NOTES

1. Lawrence LeDuc, "Canada: The Politics of Stable Dealignment," in *Electoral Change in Advanced Industrial Democracies* ed. Russell J. Dalton, Scott C. Flanigan and Paul Allen Beck (Princeton: Princeton University Press, 1984), 403.

2. Paul M. Sniderman, H.D. Forbes and Ian Melzer, "Party Loyalty and Electoral Volatility: A Study of the Canadian Party System," *Canadian Journal of Political Science* (*CJPS*) 7 (1974): 266–88.

3. LeDuc, "Canada: The Politics of Stable Dealignment."

4. Jane Jenson, "Party Loyalty in Canada: The Question of Party Identification," *CJPS* 8 (1975): 543–55; Harold D. Clarke, Jane Jenson, Lawrence LeDuc, and Jon H. Pammett, *Political Choice in Canada* (Toronto: McGraw-Hill, 1979), chap. 5, and, by the same authors, *Absent Mandate: The Politics of Discontent in Canada* (Toronto: Gage, 1984), 56–62, 73; LeDuc, H.D. Clarke, J. Jenson, J.H. Pammett, "Partisan Instability in Canada: Evidence from a New Panel Study," *American Political Science Review* 78 (1984): 470–84.

5. Jane Jenson, "Comment: The Filling of Wine Bottles Is Not Easy," *CJPS* 11 (1978): 437–46, and Clarke et al., *Absent Mandate*, 69.

6. See the summary of contending theories of partisan dealignment in the editors' introduction to *Electoral Change*, ed. Dalton et al., 2–23.

7. An excellent summary of this argument is Ronald Inglehart, "The Changing Structure of Political Cleavages in Western Society," in *Electoral Change*, ed. Dalton et al., 25–69.

8. See the emphasis on this issue in Ole Borre, "Critical Electoral Change in Scandinavia," in *Electoral Change* ed. Dalton et al., 355–61.

9. See the concise statement of the nature of the brokerage party system in Clarke et al., *Absent Mandate*, 10–16.

10. Sniderman et al., "Party Loyalty and Electoral Volatility," explicitly attack the disintegrative consequences of the brokerage party system and its failures to produce policy innovation in ways which closely parallel the critique a decade later by Clarke et al. (*Absent Mandate*).

11. The central proposition in the early research on party identification has been expressed as follows: "The more electors are attached by enduring psychological links to political parties ... the more the polity is insured against 'flash parties' and sudden demagogic incursions." See *Party Identification and Beyond*, ed. I. Budge, I. Crewe, and D. Fairlie (Toronto: Wiley, 1976), 3. In these terms, the United States was interpreted as a model of democratic stability, and countries like France, where long-term political and economic changes had not yet produced such stable conditions, were seen to be converging towards such conditions in the postwar era. See Philip Converse, "Of Time and Partisan Stability," *Comparative Political Studies* 2 (1969): 139–71. The dramatic decline in the incidence and intensity of party identification among Americans after 1964 has, however, prompted a substantial critical revision of this perspective. In the United States itself, parties have been seen less as a model for other democratic polities than as a symptom of domestic political troubles, or as

"one component of the malperforming engine of governance in the United States." See E.C. Ladd, *Where Have All the Voters Gone?* (New York: Norton, 1978), xvi. In other advanced capitalist countries, the intensity of party identification has never been as strong as in the heyday of American party democracy, and it has similarly declined. According to P.A. Beck, "party loyalties are more instrumental elsewhere and tend to be less distinguishable from vote choice at any particular time. The rules of the electoral game in these systems—for example, multipartyism, parliamentarism, short and infrequent ballots, even proportional representation and party lists—reduce the need for a separate party loyalty that can remain intact in the face of vote defection. More primordial group loyalties (e.g. to a social class or a religious grouping) instead anchor the voter in the electoral arena, making it difficult for the parties themselves to become objects of psychological identification" (Introduction to Part Four in *Electoral Change*, ed. Dalton et al., 234). In typical hybrid fashion, neither the psychological nor group loyalties are strong in Canada.

12. David J. Elkins, "Party Identification: A Conceptual Analysis," *CJPS* 10 (1978): 423.

13. Elkins's argument is in fact quite different. He sees party identification as constituting a long-term, stabilizing effect upon the vote, with short-term factors like campaign and leadership characteristics influencing the residual vote switching, and a lagged adjustment of partisanship to vote. Jenson properly points out that this formulation evades "the logical requirement, the necessity of stable partisan ties" in the original Michigan theory, and that in this form it tends to be circular and unfalsifiable. It holds where voting stability is observed (long-term forces outweigh short-term) and where voting instability is observed (short-term forces outweigh long-term). According to Jenson, "if the argument is to be theoretically viable it is necessary to provide an independent demonstration, rather than merely an assertion, that short-term forces are the reason for the difference" ("Comment," 441).

14. Jenson, "Party Loyalty in Canada," 544, and "Comment," 443.

15. Documentation of the greater influence of issues on the voting choices of unstable partisans is given in Clarke et al., *Absent Mandate*, 94, 131–33, and in Clarke et al., *Political Choice in Canada*, 346–47.

16. According to Sniderman et al., "if Canadian party loyalty is not weakly rooted and fickle in the way commonly assumed, major parties can advance innovative economic and social policies without courting electoral disaster or the disruption of the party system. At a minimum, we see no evidence of irresistible pressures on the major parties to pursue similarly centrist policies. In short, the textbook theory may be misleading not only about what is the case, but also about what can and what ought to be the case" ("Party Loyalty and Electoral Volatility," 288). This conclusion rests, of course, upon acceptance of the opening conditional clause.

17. Jenson, "Party Loyalty," 553.

18. See the historical detail in M. Janine Brodie and Jane Jenson, *Crisis, Challenge and Change: Party and Class in Canada* (Toronto: Methuen, 1980), and the historical context of recent partisan instability given in Clarke et al., *Absent Mandate*, chap. 1.

19. See, for example, the discussion of the Toronto-based reform movement which worked in the 1960s to reorient the Liberal party under the leadership of Pearson and the policies of Gordon in Christina McCall-Newman, *Grits* (Toronto: Macmillan, 1982), and the discussion of ideologically motivated reform groups within the Conservative party leading up to the selection of Mulroney as party leader in Patrick Martin, Allan Gregg and George Perlin, *Contenders: The Tory Quest for Power* (Scarborough: Prentice-Hall, 1983). Evidence for the ideological distinctiveness of the two major federal parties, and for the influence of ideology on internal party dynamics is contained in H.M. Stevenson, "Ideology and Canadian Party Leadership Selection: No Relationship or Type I Error"

(Toronto: York University, Institute for Social Research, January 1986). For a general history of this topic see William Christian and Colin Campbell, *Political Parties and Ideology in Canada* 2d ed. (Toronto: McGraw-Hill Ryerson, 1983).

20. The 1984 National Election Study has, however, incorporated a great deal more information on class-related questions of ideology and political attitude.

21. Documentation on these surveys is contained in *Social Change in Canada: Technical Documentation* (Toronto: York University Institute for Behavioural Research, June 1984).

22. See the titles and substance of the successive annual reports of the Economic Council of Canada for 1979 to 1982: *Two Cheers for the 1980's, A Climate of Uncertainty, Room for Manoeuvre,* and *Lean Times* (Ottawa: Minister of Supply and Services Canada).

23. These changes are the subject of a growing library of recent political books by Canadian journalists. They include Richard Gwyn, *The Northern Magus* (Toronto: McClelland and Stewart, 1980); Jeffrey Simpson, *Discipline of Power* (Toronto: Personal Library, 1980); McCall-Newman, *Grits*; Robert Sheppard and Michael Valpy, *The National Deal* (Toronto: Fleet Books, 1982); Martin et al., *Contenders*; Graham Fraser, *P.Q.: René Lévesque and the Parti Québécois in Power* (Toronto: Macmillan, 1984); Norman Snider, *The Changing of the Guard* (Toronto: Lester and Orpen Dennys, 1985); Richard Gwyn, *The 49th Paradox* (Toronto: McClelland and Stewart, 1985); and Ron Graham, *One-Eyed Kings* (Toronto: Collins, 1986). This list excludes the less serious, if seriously intended, anthologies of short pieces by such journalists as Alan Fotheringham and Charles Lynch.

24. Our results are confirmed by the spread in vote intentions reported by major polling firms in the spring of 1981, which gave a 15 per cent advantage to the Liberals. In the summer of 1981, however, the advantage shifted so that a year later the Conservatives enjoyed a 10 per cent lead, which grew to more than 20 per cent shortly after Brian Mulroney's election as leader in the summer of 1983. Liberal support then increased until the party was again even with the Conservatives in the spring of 1984. See summary poll data in the *Globe and Mail*, 24 August 1984.

25. See the discussion and references to alternative conceptualizations of class in Michael D. Ornstein, H. Michael Stevenson and A. Paul Williams, "Region, Class and Political Culture in Canada," *CJPS* 13 (1980): 227–72. For the importance of distinctions between established and non-established labour forces, see R. Cox, "Employment, Labour and Future Political Structures," in *Canada Challenged* ed. R. Byers and R.W. Reford (Toronto: Canadian Institute of International Affairs, 1979), 262–92. For the coding details on the component occupational groups in our class categories, see Peter C. Pineo, "Revision of the Pineo-Porter-McRoberts Socio-Economic Classification of Occupations for the 1981 Census" (QSEP Research Report no. 125, McMaster University, Program for Quantitative Studies in Economics and Population, February 1985).

26. See Alan C. Cairns, "The Electoral System and the Party System in Canada, 1921–1965," *CJPS* 1 (1968): 55–80, and D.E. Smith, *The Regional Decline of a National Party: Liberals on the Prairies* (Toronto: University of Toronto Press, 1981).

27. The impact of new voters is difficult to estimate. See the discussion in Clarke et al., *Absent Mandate*, 153–57, where it is argued (without very convincing documentation) that new voters tended disproportionately to support the Liberals, but that this tendency became less noticeable in the 1974, 1979 and 1980 elections.

28. The panel of 1665 respondents is slightly biased by attrition from the original 1977 national sample toward more women, youth, and well-educated respondents and fewer unmarried and Quebec respondents. The panel slightly over-represents identification

with each of the three major parties, and under-represents those with no or unknown partisanship. This suggests that the panel slightly over-represents the "attentive public," and that it should give reliable estimates of partisan shifts and their correlates. More detailed information on the panel sample is available from the author.

29. These differences may also reflect an increase in partisan instability due to the worsening economic crisis of 1981, and the inability of the government to follow through on its 1980 campaign promises of economic recovery. Further, our estimates may be inflated slightly because of the greater length of time between our surveys and actual elections. The overall figure of partisan instability in the national election panel is taken from Clarke et al., *Absent Mandate*, table 3.3, 67, the figures for changes between the 1974 and 1979 elections and the 1979 and 1980 elections from table 3.1, 62. These estimates are apparently based on calculations that exclude missing data on party identification, although there is no clear indication of how missing data were treated apart from the different Ns reported in different tables for the three-wave panel. If we had excluded respondents with "don't know" or missing data on the party identification item from our operationalization of partisan instability, our estimate would have been very close to that of the National Election Study. As shown in table 4 elimination of missing data in the 1977 wave of the panel reduces our estimate from 56 per cent to 50 per cent, and elimination of additional missing data from other waves would bring our estimate closer to 45 per cent. We felt it conceptually more appropriate, however, to include a nonresponse to the question of partisan identity in the measure of partisan instability.

30. See references and data in LeDuc, "Canada: The Politics of Stable Dealignment," and LeDuc et al., "Partisan Instability in Canada."

31. This does not mean that new politics issues are of less interest to younger as opposed to older Canadians, or that younger Canadians are less supportive of new social movements, self-actualization goals, and so forth.

32. The size of the group who confine their changes of partisanship to the Liberal and New Democratic parties is remarkable. The group includes those who shift between the two parties and those who shift to only one of them from "independent" or "don't know" categories. Clarke et al., *Absent Mandate,* table 3.3, indicate that a maximum of 24.8 per cent of their 1974–1980 panel would be in this group if it included all "homing" Liberals and NDP identifiers, all "movers" to the Liberal and New Democratic parties, all non-identifiers, and all third-wave changers. Their estimate would be lower adjusting for the exclusion of conversions to the Conservatives from the last two groups. Our estimates would not be substantially different, however, if we adjusted for the differences in operationalization discussed in note 29.

33. V.O. Key, Jr., *The Responsible Electorate* (New York: Random House, 1968), 58–59.

34. We would expect, that is, to find a much larger group of all-party switchers after the 1984 election and to find, as in our data for the earlier period, a disproportionate number of relatively left-leaning voters in this group. Evidence from the 1984 National Election Study confirms this expectation: "If there was a pattern in the stated attitudes of the two groups of voters, it was that those who abandoned Turner and the Liberal Party for the Conservatives were more 'libertarian' in their outlook than were loyal Liberals" (Barry J. Kay, Steven D. Brown, James E. Curtis, Ronald D. Lambert, and John M. Wilson, "Some Aspects of Electoral Change in 1984," in *Politics: Canada* 6th ed., ed. Paul W. Fox and Graham White [Toronto: McGraw-Hill Ryerson Limited, 1987], 434).

35. Gwyn, *The 49th Paradox,* and Graham, *One-Eyed Kings.*

EXPLAINING THE RELIGIOUS BASIS OF THE CANADIAN PARTISAN IDENTITY: SUCCESS ON THE THIRD TRY*

WILLIAM P. IRVINE

o

The various subtables of table 1 or some variant of them, must be familiar to every teacher and to every student of Canadian voting behaviour. While most of our history books, and certainly all of our current concerns, focus on cultural differences in Canada, all our voting and party identification data suggest that the primary line of political division is between Roman Catholics and non-Catholics. The leftmost tables in the two rows of table 1 indicate that religious differences are approximately three times as strong as ethnic ones, regardless of the index chosen. The percentage difference in Liberal identifiers is 20 across religious categories, but only 6 across the ethnic ones; the phi coefficient is .21 as compared to .06, while Yules Q is .42 as opposed to .13. Nor is this simply an artifact. The same finding shows up for vote as for party identification, for a linguistic dichotomy as for an ethnicity dichotomy, and for undichotomized as for dichotomized variables. Similarly, the religious dichotomy need not be imposed, but emerges quite freely when similar data are analysed with the AID program. Indeed, one need not depend on using dichotomies at all, though the analysis becomes more complex. In each case, however, the basic generalization holds.[1*]

Though strongly grounded statistically, the finding is often treated as a moderately interesting, but strikingly peculiar, houseguest who has overstayed his welcome.[2] While some may take comfort in the belief that he is bound to leave eventually, most of us would like to make him go away now. The reason for our

* Canadian Journal of Political Science 37 (September 1974): 560–63.

+ I should like to express my thanks to the Canadian Council for supporting me in a year of research and analysis, to the University of Essex for providing me with an office and congenial colleagues, and to my assistant, Phillip Wood, for extracting the data from the computer. Customary absolution from responsibility for the interpretations herein is in order for all of these.

TABLE 1 RELIGIOUS AND ETHNIC BASES OF PARTY IDENTIFICATION IN CANADA

					French Canadian			Not French Canadian	
	RC	Not RC		RC	Not RC		RC	Not RC	
Liberal	49	29	1011	43	17	268	56	29	744
Not Liberal	51	71	1709	57	83	368	44	71	1341
	1139	1581	2720	604	31	636	535	1550	2085

Phi = 0.21   Phi = 0.11   Phi = 0.25
Q = 0.42   Q = 0.58   Q = 0.52

					Roman Catholic			Not Roman Catholic	
	FC	Not FC		FC	Not FC		FC	Not FC	
Liberal	42	36	1011	43	56	561	17	29	450
Not Liberal	58	64	1709	57	44	578	83	71	1131
	636	2084	2720	604	535	1139	31	1550	1581

Phi = 0.06   Phi = 0.12   Phi = 0.03
Q = 0.13   Q = –0.25   Q = –0.32

embarrassment is that his presence is difficult to account for. Pure religious conflict has not been dominant in Canadian history. Even the controversy over the Jesuit estates bill had considerable cultural overtones, and few other matters in federal politics could be held to have been primarily religious. It is true that conflict over religious schools has been frequent and recurrent in a number of provinces, but Canadians show considerable propensity to differentiate between levels of government in their partisan loyalties.[3] In any case, one would be hard put to find much appeal to religious sentiment or much prominence given to religious issues in the 1960s when these data were gathered. On the other hand, one could quite easily document appeals on a regional or cultural basis. Why, then, does the religious cleavage persist, rather than giving way to these other cleavages? To return to our analogy, is there any way to make our unwanted guest depart? There are, in fact, at least three strategies to pursue.

The first is to show that the relationship between religion and identification disappears, or is markedly reduced, we have explained away the source of our embarrassment. No doubt collectively, in the course of their teaching, Canadian political scientists concerned with such things have controlled every variable available—and with indifferent results. Certainly one of the most plausible to control is ethnicity itself. This is done in the two rightmost subtables of the first row of table 1. The results suggest, if anything, that the relationship between religion and identification is enhanced by the control. Percentage differences are now of the order of 26 and the Q coefficient is over .50. While the phi declines for the subtable for French Canadians, this is due to the sensitivity of this coefficient to the small number of French-Canadian non-Catholics.

TABLE 2   PHI CORRELATIONS WITH LIBERAL/NON-
LIBERAL DICHOTOMY FOR POTENTIAL LINES
OF CLEAVAGE, BY TYPE OF IDENTIFIER

	Whole population	Type of Identifier	
		Inheritor	Bootstrapper
Roman Catholic/other	0.21	0.32	−0.01
French Canadian/other	0.06	0.17	−0.17
City born/other	0.02	−0.01	0.12
Quebec/other resident	0.07	0.14	−0.08
Centre/periphery resident	0.11	0.14	0.05
White collar/blue collar	0.02	0.02	0.01
Earns over $5000/earns less	0.04	0.03	0.03
Partial correlations for Roman Catholic/ non-Catholic controlling for:			
French Canadians	0.11	0.08	0.14
non French Canadians	0.25	0.32	0.09
Partial correlations for French Canadian/ other controlling for:			
Roman Catholics	−0.12	−0.06	−0.25
non-Catholics	−0.03	0.01	−0.14
city born	0.01	0.16	−0.30
not city born	0.09	0.18	−0.09
Partial correlations for city-born/ not city-born controlling for:			
French Canadians	−0.03	0.00	−0.13
non French Canadians	0.05	0.00	0.15

The two tables just below these indicate that, if any relationship is spurious, it may be the ethnic one. When religion is controlled, French Canadians become less, and not more, Liberal than their English-Canadian coreligionists. Percentage differences are of the order of 13, almost twice what they were before. The Qs have changed from weakly positive to moderately negative. Certainly our first explanatory strategy has failed us, at least with respect to this control. The author is unaware of others that are systematically more successful.

Our second strategy for disposing of an unwanted intruder is to show that the relationship is conceptually spurious, even though it is not statistically spurious. This would mean showing that the religious correlation is made up of a number of discrete elements, none of which is really religious. The explanatory scenarios become more complex. Consider the following. It could be the case that the English and French, the two charter groups, provide the basic cleavage among long-established Canadians, while the old-immigrant/new-immigrant dichotomy is the primary cleavage for the other third of our population. Since French Canadians and new immigrants are primarily Catholic, the fact that both had chosen the same political champion would make it appear that the alliance was religious, though in fact it is not.[4] Similarly, the English and the old immigrants are both primarily non-Roman Catholic. This reasoning leads, statistically, to a more elaborate parcelling out of the Canadian population than is involved in a straightforward search for statistical spuriousness. Unfortunately, it is of no greater success in explaining away religious differences. Nor have I had any better luck in applying similar reasoning to the fact that Roman Catholics usually are paid less than non-Catholics in similar occupations. Whatever the Liberal party is, it is not the party of those inadequately rewarded for the work they do.

The third explanatory strategy is the most theoretically rewarding and the most successful. Using a political socialization model, we find that religious differences persist mainly through the family perpetuating old cleavages. Where family transmission is absent (one-third of Canadians fail to name the party of either parent) or breaks down (some 20 per cent of Canadian identifiers follow neither parent) the religious cleavage is minimal and is overshadowed by cultural and urban/rural differences. The data supporting these generalizations are reported in table 2.

The analysis leading to this table is quite straightforward. The respondents to the 1965 Canadian national survey are divided into two groups. The first, the inheritors, are Liberal identifiers, at least one of whose parents is remembered as being a Liberal supporter. Also included in this group are non-Liberal identifiers (including non-identifiers) neither of whose parents is remembered as being a Liberal supporter. In this case, the parent may be remembered as partisan of some other party, or his commitments may not have been known to the respondent. The second group, bootstrap identifiers, got their identity on their own. They are either Liberals whose parents were not, or non-Liberals whose parents were Liberal. Clearly, reality is more complex than these simple dichotomies, but they are not misleading. Clearly too, correlations within this second group constitute better indices of the bases of electoral cleavage than would correlations based on the population as a whole. The latter are too encumbered with the freight of past political conflicts.

The entries in table 2 are phi coefficients, with negative signs attached where the first mentioned category of the variable is *not* the more Liberal category. This coefficient is more rigorous in the sense of more sensitive to small cell sizes than Q or the percentage difference and hence may constitute a stricter test. In any case, the story would be much the same. Looked at horizontally, we find that religion is much the most powerful differentiating factor among those who have inherited their identifications. Whether it constitutes a cleavage is more open to interpretation. It seems likely that these respondents have inherited both their religious and their partisan loyalties without any necessary felt connection between the two. In the absence of current religious conflicts, they may never learn to make any visceral connection between these two aspects of their identities. Such a failure would explain why Canadians are so little moved on those occasions when the connection could obviously be made—as when the Liberal government appointed an ambassador to the Vatican.

The absence of current religious issues would also account for the failure of our bootstrappers to divide along the traditional lines. Over-all, this groups shows no correlation between the religious and the partisan dichotomies. It seems clear that all of the religious polarization observed with respect to the vote or to identification in Canada is traceable to those who inherit their identities. Similarly, the ability of the religious variable to explain away the bivariate correlation between ethnicity and identity is confined to this group. Among bootstrap identifiers, not only is ethnicity a stronger source of cleavage than religion, but it also survives or is enhanced by the religious control. Indeed, in this subset of respondents, it is ethnicity that overrides the religious correlation. When ethnicity is controlled, we find moderately strong religious correlations of .09 and .14, both in the predicted direction. Even these, however, are insufficiently strong to support a claim that religion is a primary source of cleavage.

Not only is the cultural cleavage strong and enduring (surviving a control for place of birth, the urban/rural dichotomy) but it is reversed from our normal expectations. Among those not simply following their family's lead, the Liberals do relatively badly in their traditional constituency. Underlying the negative phi of .17 is the perhaps more meaningful comparison between the 37 per cent of the 200 French Canadians in our subsample of bootstrappers who identify with the Liberal party and the 57 per cent rate of Liberal support among the non-French. Glancing down the column to the partial correlations, we find that this effect is particularly strong among the urban born. Phi increases to –.30 and the Liberals are some 40 percentage points less successful in attracting new identifications from French Canadians than from the non-French.

Bootstrap identifiers are distinctive also in dividing along urban/rural lines, with Liberal identification being some 12 percentage points higher among the urban born. This line of cleavage survives well the control for ethnicity, though sides are chosen differently depending on one's ethnic background. The Liberals are attracting the English urban-born but the French rural-born. Again, this suggests that, in the absence of family impetus, French-Canadian support for the Liberal party is coming from a vanishing segment of the population. The by now well-documented bureaucratic-reformist image of the Liberal party[5] is successful only in English Canada.

This very brief analysis has thus led to some quite interesting substantive conclusions. Finding the paramountcy of French/non-French and urban/rural cleavages with Liberals doing relatively badly among the French and relatively well among the urban accords quite well with our intuitive sense of what recent Canadian politics has been about. The purpose of examining these findings is not to document our intuitions, but to suggest that it is often wise to be guided by them rather than by our computer output. Those who claim religion as an important cleavage in current Canadian politics would seem to be falling into this trap. Not only does such a claim overlook the absence of issues and organisations focussed on religious lines at the national level, it also attaches excessive weight to issues which may be no more than a memory, if that. The religious cleavage has indeed been shown to have been the man who came to dinner—early in this century or before. Our findings suggest that it is now time to show him the door in generalizing about the current bases of electoral cleavage in Canada.

NOTES

1. Among the numerous studies reporting the impact of religion in Canadian electoral politics are J.A. Laponce, "Postdicting Electoral Cleavages in Canadian Federal Elections, 1949–69," *Canadian Journal of Political Science* (*CJPS*) 5 (1972): 270–86; J. Meisel, "Cleavages, Parties and Values in Canada," (Unpublished paper presented to the Ninth World Congress of the International Political Science Association, Montreal, 1973); R.R. Alford, *Party and Society* (Chicago, 1963), chap. 8; Grace M. Anderson, "Voting Behaviour and the Ethnic-Religious Variable," *Canadian Journal of Economics and Political Science* 32 (1966): 27–37; Lynn McDonald, "Religion and Voting: a Study of the 1968 Canadian Federal Election in Ontario," *Canadian Review of Sociology and Anthropology* 6 (1969): 127–44; and Wallace Gagne and Peter Regenstreif, "Some Aspects of New Democratic Party Urban Support in 1965," *Canadian Journal of Economics and Political Science* 33 (1967): 529–50. The list is not exhaustive.

2. Note the characteristically careful judgements of John Meisel in "Cleavages, Parties and Values in Canada."

3. George Perlin and Patti Peppin, "Variation in Party Support in Federal and Provincial Elections," *CJPS* 4 (1971): 280–86; John Wilson and David Hoffman, "The Liberal Party in Contemporary Ontario Politics," *CJPS* 3 (1970): 171–204.

4. This sort of model is suggested in Peter Regenstreif, *The Diefenbaker Interlude* (Toronto, 1965), 89–94.

5. John Meisel, *Working Papers on Canadian Politics* (Montreal, 1972), chap. 2.

THE REPRODUCTION OF THE RELIGIOUS CLEAVAGE IN CANADIAN ELECTIONS*

RICHARD JOHNSTON

o

Canadians are typically astounded when told that religion is the most powerful predictor of their party preferences. Public policy attitude differences between religious groups are not mirrored by differences between the parties. How can a variable with so little purchase on policy or on voters' imaginations be the driving force of party choice? Irvine appears to have supplied an answer; a family socialization theory of the religious basis of Canadian partisanship.[1] This article will show that Irvine's answer cannot suffice. To persist, a religious cleavage, or any cleavage, must be renewed by forces outside the family.

THE RELIGIOUS CLEAVAGE

In Canadian survey analyses, the sharpest group difference in Liberal and Conservative party preference is between Catholics and Protestants. In some recent elections, notably that of 1972, the religious effect was nearly as great as in the watershed elections of 1917 and 1921.[2] Survey evidence for the power of this religious factor spans three decades.[3] The Catholic–Non-Catholic difference may have declined from 1965 to 1979, according to some survey evidence, but even in its weakened later state, that difference remains the most powerful one in party choice.[+]

* *Canadian Journal of Political Science* 18,1(March 1985): 99–13.
+ Advice from Jean Laponce, Campbell Sharman, Donald Blake, William Irvine, and anonymous referees has contributed greatly to this article. My greatest debt is to Henry Brady. Survey data reported in text and tables are from the various Canadian national election studies by: the 1965 and 1968 studies John Meisel and the 1974 and 1979 studies by Harold Clarke, Jane Jenson, Lawrence LeDuc, and Jon Pammett. National election study data were furnished by the Interuniversity Consortium for Political and Social Research. The census and electoral data are from Donald E. Blake, *Canadian Census and Election Data 1908–1974* (Vancouver: University of British Columbia Data Library, n.d.). None of the above mentioned individuals or institutions bears any responsibility for defects in the final product.

Whatever its exact strength, the Catholic–Non-Catholic difference cannot be resolved into some other cleavage. Class, for example, is only weakly associated with religious preference and controlling for class does not attenuate the religious effect on party preference. The religious effect is not merely a proxy for French–English differences. Indeed, in many recent surveys, English Catholics are more distinct from English non-Catholics than are French Catholics. Similarly, the religious cleavage does not simply stand for differences by country of ancestors or country of birth.[4] As a predictor of party choice, religion stands by itself.

But this social difference between the major parties is not obviously mirrored by differences between those parties in religious policies. The religious disputes that traditionally have divided the major parties, over schooling or property, are ancient and are usually regarded as settled. The religious questions that presently divide Canadians, over abortion for instance, cut across parties. To the extent that such questions divide Liberals from Conservatives, they may do so in the direction opposite to that indicated by each party's religious base. How, then, can a social characteristic with apparently weak to nonexistent implications for contemporary policy drive Canadian party choice?

A PUTATIVE EXPLANATION

An intuitively pleasing answer to this question has been given by Irvine[5] and Irvine and Gold,[6] an answer which seems to have gained widespread acceptance among students of Canadian elections. One key piece of evidence in this account appears as table 1. Among those who have "inherited" their party loyalty, the Catholic–Non-Catholic difference is very wide. Among those who have not inherited a loyalty, the difference is very narrow.[7] This suggests that an archaic cleavage such as the Canadian religious one is maintained by socialization within the family. Choice dominated by influence outside the family, as indicated by "non-inheritor"

TABLE 1   THE RELIGIOUS CLEAVAGE
           AMONG INHERITORS AND
           NONINHERITORS

Party	Denomination		Religious Cleavage
	Catholic	Other	
A. Inheritors			
Liberal	85.0%	46.7%	39.2%
Other	15.0	53.3	
	(353)	(409)	
	$\phi = 0.40$		
B. Noninheritors			
Liberal	52.6%	39.2%	13.4%
Other	47.4	60.8	
	$\phi = 0.13$		

status, fails to respond to the call of religion. Real world social influence helps dissolve the anachronism.

A complementary piece of evidence comes from the only available indicator of respondents' denominational integration: frequency of church attendance. Frequency of attendance ought to affect response to a religious group norm. If some party preference were truly a denominational norm, frequency of church attendance should affect the likelihood of supporting that party. In fact, frequency of attendance hardly affects the width of the Catholic–Non-Catholic difference in party choice. The data thus give little hint of differential exposure to a denominational partisan norm.[8]

At first glance the case seems closed. Almost all of the measurable Catholic–Non-Catholic party difference seems to come from "inheritors." Degree of involvement in organised denominational life, at least as indicated by the one measure available to us, gives no purchase on the cleavage. The survey evidence, properly arranged, seems to mirror the lack of live religious policy differences between the major parties. As Irvine puts it, "The religious cleavage has indeed been shown to have been the man who came to dinner—early in this century or before. Our findings suggest that it is now time to show him the door in generalizing about the current bases of electoral cleavage in Canada."[9] Neat as it seems, however, the story will not wash. The data as presented in table 1 tell a very misleading story about the acquisition of party loyalty, as the next section will show.

PARTY RENEWAL AS A STOCHASTIC PROCESS

Table 1 and interpretations of similar tables by Irvine, and Irvine and Gold, confuse process with outcome. Apparently "inherited" loyalties are treated as the product only of socialization pressures within families. Influence outside the family implicitly works only on loyalties which are not "inherited." Common sense suggests, however, that "inheritors" will typically have experienced extra-family pressures. Conversely, many "non-inheritors" will have experienced socialization pressures in their family of origin.

To see what this implies, leave the religious difference aside for a moment and consider table 2. The table shows rates of transition between parties across generations. For simplicity, the parents' "generation" is represented by respondents' fathers only.[10] For discussion purposed, let:

p_{ij} be an entry in the body of the table, the proportion supporting party j among respondents whose fathers support party i;

$p_{i.}$ be the proportion of fathers who support party i, indicated by the row margin; and

$p_{.i}$ be the proportion of respondents who support party i, indicated by the column margin;

$$\sum_j p_{ij}, \sum_i p_{.i}, \sum p_{i.} = 1;$$

$$0 \leq p_{ij}, p_{i.}, p_{.i} \leq 1$$

Each internal cell entry, p_{ij}, is a "transition rate." Together, the transition rates transform the row, or fathers', margin into the column, or respondents', margin, such that:

$$p._i = \sum_j p_{ij}p_j.$$

These relationships are all by way of definition. Now consider some substantive relationships.

First compare diagonal entries with off-diagonal ones. For convenience, think of any diagonal entry, p_{ii}, as an "inheritance rate" and the off-diagonal entries, p_{ji}, in the same column as p_{ii} as "recruitment rates." Each inheritance rate is much larger than its corresponding recruitment rates. To an extent, this difference may reflect self-directed recall bias.[11] This bias might also reduce the net shift, as measured, from the row margin to the column margin. Even so, the lumping of cases along the diagonal is consistent with a standard observation in socialization research: party loyalty is heritable, if not always inherited.[12]

But no inheritance rate in table 2 exceeds 0.65 and only one exceeds 0.50. The majority of the cases in table 2 lie off the major diagonal, and the bottom right entry on that diagonal, for independent children of independents, hardly indicates partisan inheritance. Altogether, about two-thirds of the respondents in table 2 cannot be said to have inherited a party preference. Yet the relative shares of the parties remain little changed from the fathers' margin to the respondents' margin, a lack of change consistent with the historical record. How does a distribution of party shares remain more or less stable in the face of massive individual-level defection across generations?

The answer begins with the pattern of rates in the body of table 2. Transition rates in the body of table 2 covary directly with proportions on either margin. This covariance is clearest for the column, or respondents', margin. The larger the party, as indicated by $p._i$, the higher its inheritance rate, p_{ii}. Similarly, the larger the party, the higher its recruitment rates, p_{ji}. To an extent, this is only arithmetic, as equation (1) above indicates; the inheritance and recruitment rates, together with the bases for inheritance and recruitment, produce the party's current share. But inheritance and recruitment, rates also correspond to party sizes on the fathers' margin, $p_i.$, and here no arithmetic dependence exists. If transition rates correspond to party sizes in the fathers' generation, the correspondence must be the product of some substantive social or psychological process.

But some large parties appear to win both ways. Not only do they keep relatively large proportions of their own supporters' offspring, but they steal relatively large proportions of smaller parties' supporters' children. Will the large parties simply grow indefinitely, eventually to exclude their rivals?

Nothing of the sort will happen. The exchange process in table 2, if repeated indefinitely, will move party shares asymptotically toward an equilibrium distribution. The actual distribution in equilibrium is determined by the relative values of the *off diagonal* entries in table 2.[13] The logic of the equilibrium process should be quite clear without any algebra. Although a large inheritance rate, p_{ii}, will typically work on a large base, $p_i.$, and thus inheritance rates and bases will compound each other's effect, no such compounding works for recruitment rates. The larger the party, the larger its recruitment rates, p_{ji}, as we have already established. But the larger the average recruitment rate, the smaller typically is the recruitment base. The total recruitment base for party i is $1-p_i.$, by definition. But the larger is $p_j.$, the

TABLE 2 THE INTERGENERATIONAL TRANSMISSION OF PARTY PREFERENCES, 1974

Father's Party	Respondent's Party					
	Liberal	Conservative	New Democratic Party	Social Credit	Other/None	
Liberal	0.652	0.105	0.056	0.026	0.161	0.286
Conservative	0.335	0.398	0.067	0.019	0.182	0.223
New Democratic Party	0.307	0.159	0.409	0.011	0.114	0.034
Social Credit	0.286	0.229	0.171	0.257	0.057	0.014
Other/None	0.422	0.211	0.094	0.030	0.243	0.443
	0.463	0.221	0.089	0.029	0.199	(2562)

$1 = p_1^+ + p_2^+ + p_3^+ + p_4^+ + p_5^+$
$p_1^+ = .652p_1^+ + .335p_2^+ + .307p_3^+ + .286p_4^+ + .422p_5^+$
$p_2^+ = .105p_1^+ + .398p_2^+ + .159p_3^+ + .229p_4^+ + .211p_5^+$
$p_3^+ = .056p_1^+ + .067p_2^+ + .409p_3^+ + .171p_4^+ + .094p_5^+$
$p_4^+ = .026p_1^+ + .019p_2^+ + .011p_3^+ + .257p_4^+ + .030p_5^+$
$p_5^+ = .161p_1^+ + .182p_2^+ + .114p_3^+ + .057p_4^+ + .243p_5^+$

smaller $1-p_i$. must be. At some point, recruitment rate and recruitment base variation will exactly offset each other and the actual volumes (as opposed to the rates) of exchange between each party and the rest of the system will exactly balance. In this situation, party shares will remain stable across generations, even as volumes and rates of individual defection remain about as at present in Canada. Indeed, the historical record suggests that the Canadian system is nearer to an equilibrium than the margins of table 2 suggest.

But reflect for a moment on the simple algebra of equilibrium. If an equilibrium distribution of party shares is to persist, it must do so not through the persistence of individual partisanship across generations, but through the persistence of a particular *pattern of exchange* between parties. The differences between party transition rates maintain the differences in party shares. If for some reason, transition rate differences between two or more parties disappear, so, asymptotically, will the difference in party shares disappear.

Can a process located entirely within a respondent's origin family produce a pattern like that in table 2? I can readily imagine an intrafamily process which would produce large volumes of defection across generations, but this process would still fail to explain important pieces of table 2. Imagine, for example, that a parent emits cues favouring not one party but several. The parent may generally prefer one party to the others, but need not utterly exclude parties other than the normal first preference. Influence on the child may thus be a vector of preference probabilities. Probabilities may be larger for some parties than for others but not necessarily zero for any party. Probabilities may decline as a function of the ideological or social distance between the parent's most preferred party and each of the other parties. Summed across the population, individual parent–child influence vectors could yield a matrix of transition probabilities similar to table 2. But such a family-centred model would fail to account for variation along the diagonal of table 2.

The obvious explanation for the diagonal pattern appeals to forces outside the family. New citizens, in forming party preferences, sample from the cues both inside and outside the family. Having a father who prefers a given party increases the new citizen's likelihood of preferring that party, as compared with a new citizen whose father prefers some other party or no party or all. But the push the new citizen receives from his or her father is no greater, over the random likelihood of preferring the party in question, for the Liberal's child than for anybody else. The relatively high Liberal inheritance rate reflects the distribution of influence outside the family: Liberals are more successful at transmitting their party loyalty not because they are peculiarly dominant models but because they are more likely to have their influence reinforced by factors outside the home. This logic can be extended to variation off the diagonal. Liberal recruitment rates may be higher than those for other parties not because Liberal policies are closest to those preferred by some median voter but because the Liberals are most numerous to begin with.[14]

THE REPRODUCTION OF A POLITICAL CLEAVAGE

The perpetuation of a cleavage follows much the same logic as the maintenance of party size differences in the whole sample. The logic of stochastic processes requires that, if group differences in party shares are to persist across generations,

TABLE 3 DENOMINATIONAL DIFFERENCES IN INTERGENERATIONAL TRANSMISSION, 1974

Father's Party	Respondent's Party					
	Liberal	Conservative	New Democratic Party	Social Credit	Other/None	
A. Non-Catholics						
Liberal	0.599	0.160	0.062	0.007	0.173	0.216
Conservative	0.244	0.512	0.066	0.003	0.175	0.257
New Democratic Party	0.296	0.197	0.394	0.000	0.113	0.050
Social Credit	0.133	0.467	0.267	0.133	0.000	0.011
Other/None	0.253	0.347	0.270	0.118	0.012	0.467
	0.370	0.307	0.108	0.009	0.206	(1421)

TABLE 3 CONTINUED

B. Catholics

Father's Party	Respondent's Party					
	Liberal	Conservative	New Democratic Party	Social Credit	Other/None	
Liberal	0.690	0.066	0.052	0.040	0.153	0.373
Conservative	0.495	0.194	0.068	0.049	0.194	0.181
New Democratic Party	0.353	0.000	0.471	0.059	0.118	0.015
Social Credit	0.400	0.050	0.100	0.350	0.100	0.018
Other/None	0.528	0.127	0.061	0.055	0.229	0.414
	0.578	0.113	0.066	0.053	0.190	(1141)

intergenerational transition rates must differ between the groups in question. To see how this is so, imagine, per contra, that transition rates do not differ between two groups, say, Catholics(c) and non-Catholics(p). If for all i and all j, $p_{ijc} = p_{ijp}$, then in equilibrium $p_{ic} = p_{ip}$. Transition patterns identical between groups would map distributions of party preference also asymptotically identical between groups. If one observed a difference between groups in party preference at the same time as one observed a transition pattern identical between groups, one would have a system out of equilibrium, although presumably tending toward an equilibrium in which party preferences no longer differed between groups in the way originally observed. This argument readily generalizes to differences across more than two groups and to a cleavage structure involving several social characteristics.

The argument is borne out empirically in table 3. Liberal transition rates are sharply higher among Catholics than among non-Catholics, while the opposite is true for Conservatives and the New Democratic party. The religious difference is especially marked in recruitment rates.[15] The transition rate differences in table 3 imply an "equilibrium" religious cleavage no smaller than the one we observe now.[16]

The simplest explanation for transition rate differences between groups for any given party is exactly parallel to the simplest explanation for transition rate differences between parties: group differences in the partisan direction of influence *outside the family*. A Catholic Liberal father is more likely than a non-Catholic Liberal father to pass along his Liberal loyalty because his influence on his offspring is more likely to be reinforced by influence outside the home in the larger Catholic community. Conversely, a Catholic Conservative is less likely than a non-Catholic Conservative to pass his loyalty along, because his influence within the home is relatively unlikely to find extra-family reinforcement. A Catholic child who defects from a party other than the Liberal party or from nonpartisanship is more likely to feel pro-Liberal influence than would a similarly defecting non-Catholic child. In short, the maintenance of a cleavage, even an archaic one, requires the intervention of live social forces outside the family.

DISCUSSION

Party loyalty is certainly heritable in Canada. But the heritability of party loyalty does not help explain the persistence of the religious cleavage in Canadian elections. To understand the persistence of the religious cleavage, or of any aggregate electoral form, we must link to processes outside citizens' families of origin.

What should we find when we get outside the family? In our example, why should Catholics coming of age still face pressures to choose the Liberal party? Four alternatives have recently been suggested by Wald.[17] First, religious denominations are *interest groups* which demand policy concessions in education and other areas. Second, denominations may define the boundaries of *subcultures*. The definition will be sharper the more self contained the group is. Third, a religious group may represent a distinct *ethos*. Fourth, a religious denomination may be a *surrogate* for other, more directly politicized characteristics.

To begin, consider the first two lines of attack. Although we commonly regard the great religious controversies of the past as settled, we may have overestimated the extent to which this is true. In Ontario, for example, access to Catholic schools does not yet completely match that to public schools. Controversy over the remaining differences boils over from time to time.[18] Further, the settlement of this sort of controversy may itself provide the structural basis for the perpetuation of the religious cleavage. The more complete is access to Catholic schools, for example, the more self-contained the Catholic subculture is likely to become. Young Catholics will interact mainly with other Catholics, with further consequences in adulthood for mate selection and family formation. Access to schooling may join other factors in inducing Catholics to cluster geographically. Such geographical clustering will also assist the perpetuation of the subculture.[19]

We may also speculate about the two remaining lines of approach. Is there a distinctive Catholic ethos, for example? To the extent that a specifically religious ethos prevails amongst Catholics, it may work against party preferences as actually revealed. There may, however, be a countervailing *ethnic* ethos amongst Catholics which produces the Catholic–Liberal attachment. Growing up Catholic may produce a distinct view of the ethnic character of the Canadian nationality. To those schooled in the company of other Catholics, Canada will seem perhaps more French and almost certainly less British than may be the case in non-Catholic circles. Such a denominational difference in ethnic viewpoints would reflect the ethnic composition of the religious communities. While many Catholics are of British Isles origins (from Great Britain as well as from Ireland) and many non-Catholics are not of British origin, the ethnic centres of gravity do differ greatly between Catholics and non-Catholics. Although analysis to date[20] indicates that religion is not an individual-level surrogate for ethnicity, denominational membership may still index variation in the ethnicity of individuals' social contexts.

At the moment we are left mainly with speculation. Further analysis of Canadian voting would do well to incorporate the attitude and social background variables implied in this discussion. Beyond this, exploring the religious basis of Canadian party choice begs for contextual variables and analyses.

Finally, we should recognise that analysis of the group basis of the vote still leaves us in a world of probabilities. Some Catholics will become Conservatives, even when the parents in question are Liberals. Many Protestant children of Conservatives become Liberals. The choice of party seems to have an irreducible stochastic component. Individuals evidently sample political stimuli or have political stimuli administered, as it were, somewhat randomly, however constrained the distribution of those stimuli may be by the social settings through which individuals travel. The random component in party choice is no barrier to, and in a sense is the medium for, the reproduction of party alignment.

APPENDIX: THE STATISTICAL SIGNIFICANCE OF THE LOGICALLY IMPOSSIBLE

How can the same data generate tables as apparently contradictory as tables 1 and 3? The answer lies in the algebra of a stochastic process with an implied equilibrium. Recall that the larger a party, as indicated by either the column margin or the row margin, the larger its recruitment rates. But, typically, the larger the recruitment rates the smaller the recruitment bases, as the recruitment bases are simply the proportions loyal to each of the other parties in the system. With large parties recruiting at high rates from small bases and small parties recruiting at small rates from large bases, the system has a built-in equilibrium. In equilibrium, each party will recruit exactly as many new supporters as it loses to other parties.

If a cleavage structure is in equilibrium, the picture just described will hold in each of the subgroups which define the cleavage. Among Catholics, for example, the Liberals will lose just as many supporters as they recruit. But so will the Liberals lose just as many as they recruit among non-Catholics, even though the party's share differs greatly among Catholics and non-Catholics. The equilibrium ratio of recruitment volume to defection volume will thus be 1:1 for the Liberals in each religious group. But this ratio of recruitment to defection is essentially what is picked up in Panel B, for "non-inheritors," of table 1. In equilibrium, no cleavage would appear in the "non-inheritors" group. But the lack of cleavage would not indicate a lack of group difference in extra-family partisan influence. It would reflect only the equilibrium tendency in exchanges between parties. Panel B of table 1 does not give exactly a 1:1 recruitment–defection ratio, of course. This reflects coding divergences between tables 1 and 3 and the fact that the Canadian system is not actually at the equilibrium implied in table 3, but only tending toward it.

Just as simple algebra dictates an apparently weak cleavage amongst "non-inheritors," so does algebra dictate an apparently strong cleavage amongst "inheritors." Recall that the larger the party, the larger will be its inheritance rate. But in contrast to the recruitment case, the larger the inheritance rate, the larger the inheritance base. Inheritance rate and base variation thus compound each other. Panel A of table 1 reflects this compounding. The Liberal share in the Catholic "inheritor" group is large because the large Catholic Liberal inheritance rate has worked on a large base of Liberals in the earlier generation. Conversely, the Liberal share in the non-Catholic "inheritor" group is small because the small non-Catholic Liberal inheritance rate has worked on a small base of earlier-generation Liberals. In large part, then, the cleavage in Panel A of table 1 is produced by the Catholic–Non-Catholic inheritance rate *difference*, a difference produced by influence not inside, but outside origin families.

NOTES

1. W.P. Irvine, "Explaining the Religious Basis of the Canadian Partisan Identity: Success on the Third Try," *Canadian Journal of Political Science* (*CJPS*) 7 (1974): 560–63; and W.P. Irvine and H. Gold, "Do Frozen Cleavages Ever Go Stale? The Bases of the Canadian and Australian Party Systems," *British Journal of Political Science* 10 (1980): 187–218.

2. The census and electoral data are from the Blake file and were analysed by myself. In 1972, a unit increment in the percentage Catholic in a constituency produced a 0.209 point increment in the Liberal share and a 0.386 point decrement in the Conservative share. The 1972 impact on the Conservative vote was the greatest for all elections in the Blake file except 1917. The 1972 impact on the Liberal vote was about average. Estimates are OLS from bivariate regressions. Attempts to separate religious from linguistic effects were bedeviled by multicollinearity; religion almost always dominated language as a predictor, however. On the relative power of religion and language, see also note 4.

3. For the 1950s and 1960s, see J.A. Laponce, "Postdicting Electoral Cleavages in Canadian Federal Elections,

1949–68: Material for a Footnote," *CJPS* 5(1972): 270–86. For 1965, 1968, 1974, and 1979, the generalizations are based on analyses by myself with national election study data. Copies of the analyses are available on request.

4. The statements in this paragraph are based on my own analyses with national election study data and on the following sources: Irvine, "Explaining the Religious Basis"; and H.D. Forbes and P.M. Sniderman, "The Statistical Relation between Religion and the Vote in Canada"(Unpublished manuscript, University of Toronto, 1976). The latter is by far the most subtle account of the Canadian religious cleavage to date.

5. See above, note 1.

6. See above, note 1.

7. I attempted to reproduce the coding scheme of Irvine and Gold, "Frozen Cleavages," but was unable to do so exactly. The minor differences between my estimates and theirs do not affect any conclusions here or below.

8. The empirical statements in this paragraph are based on Irvine and Gold, "Frozen Cleavages," table 1. Their findings with 1974 data are substantially confirmed with data from other years.

9. Irvine, "Explaining the Religious Basis," 563.

10. A "family" party measure would shift estimates in table 1 only slightly, as most respondents impute the same party loyalty to their mothers as to their fathers.

11. On self-directed bias in recall of parents' preferences, see R.G. Niemi, *How Family Members Perceive Each Other* (New Haven: Yale University Press, 1974).

12. Classic sources on political socialization include H.Hyman, *Political Socialization* (Glencoe: Free Press, 1959); R.D. Hess and J.V. Torney, *The Development of Political Attitudes in Children* (Chicago: Aldine, 1976); D. Easton and J. Dennis, *Children in the Political System: Origins of Political Legitimacy* (New York: McGraw-Hill, 1969); and M.K. Jennings and R.G. Niemi, *The*

Political Character of Adolescence (Princeton: Princeton University Press, 1974). For a comparative evidence on the "heritability" of party loyalty see R. Johnston, "Families and the Fate of Party Systems" (Paper presented to the Canadian Political Science Association Annual Meeting, Halifax, 1981).

13. The equilibrium distribution implied in table 2 is 50.3 per cent Liberal, 18.7 per cent Conservative, 10.5 per cent NDP, 3.1 per cent Social Credit, and 16.9 per cent nonpartisan. To calculate the equilibrium, let entries in the equilibrium probability vector, p^*, be p_i^*, with the parties numbered in the row and column order that they appear in table 2. See note to table 2 for equations.

With six equations and five unknowns, solving for p_i^* is straightforward.

The calculations in the preceding paragraph and the argument in the body of the text assume that the intergenerational transmission of party loyalty is some kind of Markov process. Although party loyalty transmission does not meet all of the assumptions of the simplest kind of Markov process, the stationary, first-order, homogeneous-population process, the Markov image is still apt. It is especially so as it dramatises the dependence of equilibrium on interparty exchanges. For simple examples of Markov chains see J.G. Kemeny, J.L. Snell, and G.L. Thompson, *Introduction to Finite Mathematics* 2d ed. (Englewood Cliffs: Prentice-Hall, 1966), 194–201, 271–89. For a more formal exposition see J.G. Kemeny and J. L. Snell, *Finite Markov Chains* (New York: Van Nostrand, 1960).

The bulk of the difference between row and column margins comes from the bloated "other/none" share on the row margin. This probably reflects the large percentage of immigrants in the population. The standing of parties relative to each other differs only a little between margins. The differences that do appear reflect the historical record: third-party growth relative to the major parties.

A more vexing problem with table 2 is the overestimation of the Liberal share. This overestimation is endemic to Canadian national election study surveys and merits investigation.

14. Clearly other factors are at work as well as the simple collective inertia described in the text. The parties' relative standing shifts from the fathers' margin to the respondents' margin, as noted above. This realignment may help explain some of the strength of the NDP inheritance rate in table 2. The strong NDP rate may also reflect relatively intense influence within the family, as conventional wisdom leads us to expect. The difference between the NDP inheritance rate and the random likelihood of becoming a New Democrat is much greater than the corresponding difference for any other party.

15. Within father's party groups, the Catholic–Non-Catholic difference in current Liberal or Conservative preference is always significant. The bulk of the religious difference is mapped by recruitment from the children of nonpartisans. This is so for two reasons: first, the sharp Catholic–Non-Catholic differences in Liberal and Conservative recruitment; and, second, the large proportion of respondents unable to impute a party loyalty to their fathers.

16. The implied "equilibrium" Catholic–Non-Catholic difference is +18.8 for the Liberals and –22.1 for the Conservatives. This implied equilibrium is only notional, of course. Survey evidence, cited in note 3, suggests that the religious cleavage has shrunk since 1965. But the shrinkage itself reflects a contemporary reorientation of political forces. The cleavage that remains is a product of the Catholic–Non-Catholic transition rate differences that endure. The remaining cleavage cannot be simply an artifact of family socialization.

17. K.D. Wald, *Crosses on the Ballot: Patterns of British Voter Alignment Since 1885* (Princeton: Princeton University Press, 1983), chap. 5.

18. At the time of writing, the government of Ontario gave province-wide support to separate schools only through the elementary grades; in some school districts, support extends to grades 9 and 10. In 1971, the Ontario Liberal party campaigned pointedly on full financial support for the Catholic system. Although the disaster which befell the Liberals in the 1971 election deterred them from emphasising the schools issue in more recent elections, partisan differences on the schools issue remained much as before (see the Toronto *Globe and Mail*, 26 November 1983, 11). It may be no accident, then, that the religious cleavage as measured in 1974 is wider in Ontario than in any other province.

On 12 June 1984, the provincial government announced full support for the Catholic system, to begin in September 1985. This may take some of the partisan edge off the issue, although the traditional lines of controversy revealed themselves the moment the announcement of support was made. For immediate comment and a telling editorial, see the Toronto *Globe and Mail*, 13 June 1984.

19. For grades one to ten in Ontario, the ratio of Catholic system enrolment is very close to the whole-population Catholic–Non-Catholic ratio (*Globe and Mail*, 26 November 1983). Novelists are well in advance of political scientists in seeing the social separation of Catholics and non-Catholics. Here, for example, is Marian Engel: "Now I think of it, there was a profound division all along that shore. Tess's church, white board-and-batten with a rounded apse that glimmered like a ghost on summer nights, was bigger than ours. Its churchyard bore witness to many more generations of settlement than ours did. The names were French and Irish. And we didn't know any of the French or the Irish except McCrorys because my father worked with Tess's sometimes; otherwise, Catholics were not available to us. We were like the French and English in Montreal, looming invisibly over each others' shoulders" (*The Glassy Sea* [Toronto: McClelland and Stewart, 1978], 42).

20. See note 4.

COMMENT ON "THE REPRODUCTION OF THE RELIGIOUS CLEAVAGE IN CANADIAN ELECTIONS"◇

WILLIAM P. IRVINE

o

Richard Johnston's article[1] is addressed to an article of mine and to another, co-authored with Haim Gold.[2] It is much more relevant to the former than to the latter, despite the fact that Johnston uses the data from the 1974 National Election Survey on which the Irvine and Gold article was based. The purpose of that article was to discover whether, if at all, a cleavage between two groups is sustained by social processes involving members of those groups. It compared the class cleavage in Australia with the religious cleavage in Canada. Briefly, it found that the class cleavage in Australia was reinforced by interaction with peers within each class group. By contrast, the religious cleavage in Canada was not reinforced by similar interaction (as indexed by frequency of church attendance). Johnston does not comment on that demonstration, and I shall not repeat the argument. It is important to note, however, that there are two different analyses with different objectives.

The earlier note in [the *Canadian Journal of Political Science*] based on 1965 data, also divided the sample into those who apparently had, and those who apparently had not, inherited their partisan identities. Agreed, there may be additional social pressures impinging on inheritors. Though they may have existed, it would be hard to discover their impact. Hence, the strategy in the article was to look for these social pressures among the non-inheritors. Again, as Johnston says, many of these "will have experienced socialization pressures in their family of origin." These pressures may well have to do with ethos or values, but not with strict partisan identity.

The argument in that article was that divisions among non-inheritors would be better indices of the group bases of electoral division. There is always the implicit

◇*Canadian Journal of Political Science* 18, 1 (March 1985): 415–17.

qualifier, "if any such bases exist and if they can be measured." Johnston's article assumes that they do not. Hence, he emphasises the mathematics of random decay of the religious cleavage. He is correct in asserting that the absence of a cleavage among non-inheritors does not *necessarily* prove that religion is no longer relevant. There could be a zero cleavage, but there could also be a positive cleavage (as we do find) and there could even have been a negative correlation. However that may be, there might also have been a cleavage along some new dimension. When one social cleavage is replaced by another, we usually expect that certain definite classes of Catholics (in the Canadian case) will abandon the Liberals while definite segments of the non-Catholic population will come to them. Indeed, this is what the 1974 article found. Among non-inheritors, Liberal identification was more common among those born in large cities than among those from smaller centres, and was relatively *un*common among French Canadians. The preference of Canadians in large cities for the Liberal party was the objective of the Walter Gordon–Keith Davey changes in the party.[3] The relative weakness among French Canadians was due to the rise of the *Parti créditiste*, which did recruit (outside the urban areas, as well) French-Canadian children of Liberal parents or French Canadians who claimed not to know their parents' partisanship. Looking at the results for the whole population obscured these effects. The 1974 article was expressly looking for emergent cleavages, and was not attempting to suggest that the methodology of the search was inherently flawed.

Johnston also concludes from his formal demonstration that there must be extra-familial factors to account for differences in inheritance rates and in recruitment rates. Granted, but what are they? Johnston has some interesting speculations, which are testable with the right kind of data. It may be that recurring controversy over access to Catholic schools is part of the explanation, though one would have to look at this province by province and allow for differential translation from provincial cleavages to federal cleavages in different provinces. It may be that there is a Catholic subculture, but, if so, membership in it is indexed by something other than religious practice. I find most appealing the Johnston hypothesis that religious differences tap differential sympathy for the ethnic character of Canadian nationality. If this were adequately measured (and were correct) Catholic–Non-Catholic differences might disappear under controls for these ethnic viewpoints, as the 1974 article implied.

The discussion in the appendix is correct as far as it goes, but it implies a closed population. In a country like Canada, where immigration since the Second World War has been sizeable from both Catholic and non-Catholic countries, the pool of non-inheritors is constantly replenished. Typically, the parents of immigrants will have remained in their country of origin. Even if they accompanied the respondent, they are rarely in a position to guide his other political choices in Canada. The vast majority of non-inheritors are therefore people who are forming partisan identities for the first time. They are the best guides to the presence of current group cleavages. The results in the 1974 article in [the *Canadian Journal of Political Science*] would not be much changed if rebels from clear family influence were totally excluded.

The conclusion of both the article in [the *Canadian Journal of Political Science*] and the one in the *British Journal of Political Science* was that the persistence of an apparent religious cleavage was due less to religion than to something else, whose nature was open to conjecture, which coincided with religion. The conclusion of Johnston's argument is much the same.

NOTES

1. "The Reproduction of the Religious Cleavage in Canadian Elections," *Canadian Journal of Political Science* (*CJPS*)18 (1985): 99–113.

2. W.P. Irvine, "Explaining the Religious Basis of the Canadian Partisan Identity: Success on the Third Try," *CJPS* 7 (1974): 560–63; and W.P. Irvine and H. Gold, "Do Frozen Cleavages Ever Go Stale? The Bases of the Canadian

and Australian Party Systems," *British Journal of Political Science* 10 (1980): 187–218.

3. On the Walter Gordon–Keith Davey strategy, see Christina McCall-Newman, *Grits* (Toronto: Macmillan, 1982), 42, and Joseph Wearing, *The L-Shaped Party* (Toronto: McGraw-Hill, Ryerson, 1981), 35–36 and 69–73.

THE GEOGRAPHY OF CLASS AND
RELIGION IN CANADIAN ELECTIONS*

RICHARD JOHNSTON

Canadian elections present a multiple paradox. First, the sharpest non-geographic difference in major-party preference is between Catholics and Protestants. Yet religious questions surface rarely in Canadian politics and the policy content of these rare appearances is perverse. Second, class plays a very modest role in differentiating Canadian party preferences, especially in national elections. But there is no reason to assume that objective conflicts of interest between classes are any less in Canada than in the other Anglo-American settler societies. Third, geography plays a major role in party choice. But the logic which seems to account for one party's geographic distribution is directly contradicted by the logic which most readily explains another party's distribution. A fourth paradox lies in the traditional dominance of the system by the Liberal party. Observers commonly attribute this dominance to the Liberal party's unerring capacity to home in on the median voter. In other multiparty systems, however, such a capacity has typically availed centrist parties little; it is usually they who get squeezed. Finally, in many provinces both long-standing alignments of parties and short-term fluctuations in party shares seem only weakly related between federal and provincial elections. From these seeming

* Prepared for the Canadian Political Science Association Annual Meeting, McMaster University, Hamilton, Ontario, 6 June 1987. Earlier versions of this paper were given to the Bay Area Political Behavior Seminar in Berkeley, to the Southern California Political Behavior Seminar (the "running dog") at Lake Arrowhead, to the International Political Science Association Round Table on Political Geography, Maison Française, University of Oxford, Oxford, UK, and to the Western Political Science Association 1987 Annual Meeting, Anaheim, CA. I have benefitted greatly from comments and advice given at each place. My greatest debt is to my colleague, Jean Laponce.

The survey data analysed here were made available by the UBC Data Library and were originally collected by Harold Clarke, Jane Jenson, Lawrence LeDuc, and Jon Pammett. Neither the UBC Data Library, the original collectors, nor any of the groups or individuals mentioned in the first paragraph bear any responsibility for the analyses and interpretation presented here.

paradoxes and incongruities many have concluded that party choice in Canada is idiosyncratic where it is not merely random and that Canadian parties have few real and meaningful roots in the electorate.

These paradoxes can be resolved by reference to a simple model of party choice. I argue that at least two policy dimensions drive voters' evaluation of Canadian parties, such that each party anchors a pole on at least one dimension. On one dimension, union members oppose those outside unions. On the other, Catholics oppose Protestants. Although Catholics are outnumbered in English Canada, they are distributed over the landscape in a tactically efficient way. The geographic differentiation of the major religious blocs forces out strategic choices, by Catholics where their own numbers are weak and by non-Catholics where Catholics are numerically strong. The spatial segregation of Catholics and Protestants is thus a major factor in the very persistence of the religious cleavage. But it also conditions the overall structure of cleavages: as the Catholic percentage increases, the religious cleavage widens and the class cleavage shrinks. The geographic shift in the class and religious cleavages also helps account for the complementary geographic patterns in Liberal and NDP support. The strategic logic which underpins national election results also helps sort out federal–provincial differences. The Canadian party system, far from lacking a social base, is profoundly rooted in tribal loyalties.

THE PROBLEM

THE DATA PATTERN

Tables 1 and 2 give the bases of Canadian party preference in outline. On each of three nongeographic dimensions two groups are distinguished: Catholics and those of no religion; French-speakers and "other language" speakers; and union families and farmers. Three regions are distinguished: the Atlantic provinces, Quebec, and the Western provinces.[1] Data from the 1979 study appear as, on balance, they are fairly representative and correspond to events likely to still to be fresh in most readers' minds.

In table 1, the most important nongeographic contrast is between Catholics and others. For Liberal and Conservative choice, any serious rival to the "Catholic" coefficients is attached to a variable which marks a less important divide in Canadian life. The "farm" coefficient, for instance, is about as large for the Liberals as the Catholic one but where Catholics make up about 45 per cent of the sample, farmers constitute only about 4 per cent. For Conservative choice the "no religion" coefficient rivals that for "Catholic," but those unwilling to admit even a nominal religious affiliation make up only about 6 per cent of the sample. For the New Democratic Party, the Catholic/non-Catholic contrast is of secondary significance. But the NDP is the smallest party in the system. The big battalions in Canadian national elections seem to carry religious banners.

The religious differences cannot be resolved into ethnic differences. While francophones constitute about 60 per cent of all Catholics and are themselves an almost homogeneously Catholic group, the French–English contrast is of no *ceteris paribus* significance in the major-party equations. For NDP choice, that French–English contrast is significant, but pulls against the "Catholic" coefficient. "Other"

TABLE 1   THE SOCIAL BASES OF THE 1979 NATIONAL
ELECTION**

Social Characteristic	Liberal	Conservative	NDP
Catholic	0.123* (0.026)	−0.203* (0.025)	0.068* (0.020)
No Religion	−0.011 (0.043)	−0.208* (0.041)	0.162* (0.032)
French	−0.018 (0.046)	0.015 (0.044)	−0.078+ (0.034)
"Other" Language	0.063+ (0.030)	−0.036 (0.044)	−0.004 (0.022)
Union	−0.023 (0.019)	−0.068* (0.019)	0.092* (0.014)
Farm	−0.118++ (0.048)	0.085+ (0.046)	−0.059+ (0.036)
Atlantic	0.031 (0.036)	−0.005 (0.035)	−0.055+ (0.027)
Quebec	0.191* (0.044)	−0.199* (0.042)	−0.098++ (0.032)
West	−0.152* (0.025)	0.087* (0.024)	0.029 (0.018)
Intercept	0.330* (0.019)	0.518* (0.019)	0.118* (0.014)
Adj. R^2	0.114	0.145	0.063
F	33.39*	45.28*	18.57*

Standard errors in parentheses. One-tailed test.
+ $p < 0.05$
++ $p < 0.01$
* $p < 0.001$
** (OLS Estimation; N = 2346)

language use is about as likely among non-Catholics as among Catholics and is not significantly at issue in Conservative or NDP choice. "Other" language speakers are somewhat more likely than English and French speakers to prefer the Liberals.[2]

Union membership is a factor in Conservative and NDP choice. If union exposure is of only modest importance for Conservative preference, it is absolutely critical for the NDP. The likelihood of choosing the NDP is most sharply differentiated by "no religion," to be sure, but recall that that characteristic is shared by few respondents. In contrast, over 40 per cent of respondents are in union families. Still, one should not exaggerate the significance of the union movement in the overall system of preferences. The party for which union exposure makes the greatest difference is, to repeat, the smallest in the system.

TABLE 2   THE SOCIAL BASES OF PROVINCIAL
ELECTIONS, 1976-79**

Social Characteristic	Liberal	Conservative	NDP
Catholic	0.093* (0.026)	−0.109* (0.024)	0.049++ (0.018)
No Religion	−0.019 (0.043)	−0.167* (0.040)	0.189* (0.033)
French	−0.153* (0.045)	0.006 (0.042)	−0.075+ (0.034)
"Other" Language	0.015 (0.030)	−0.015 (0.028)	−0.005 (0.023)
Union	−0.041+ (0.019)	−0.103* (0.018)	0.118* (0.014)
Farm	−0.021 (0.046)	0.064 (0.043)	−0.046 (0.035)
Atlantic	0.052 (0.035)	0.039 (0.032)	−0.098* (0.026)
Quebec	0.181* (0.043)	−0.313* (0.040)	−0.139++ (0.033)
West	−0.267* (0.024)	0.052* (0.023)	0.144* (0.019)
Intercept	0.349* (0.020)	0.476* (0.018)	0.106* (0.015)
Adj. R^2	0.110	0.163	0.164
F	30.97*	48.46*	48.78*

Standard errors in parentheses. One-tailed test.
+ $p < 0.05$
++ $p < 0.01$
* $p < 0.001$
** (OLS Estimation; N = 2193)

This brings us to geography. Here as with the nongeographic variables, asymmetries emerge among the parties. Liberal support finds three levels: highest in Quebec; middling in the Atlantic provinces and Ontario; and lowest in the West. The Conservative party differences mirror Liberal ones east of the Manitoba–Ontario border: no Ontario–Atlantic difference; and an Ontario–Quebec difference within a percentage point of the Liberal estimate. The Conservative party's Ontario–West contrast is only about half as wide as that for the Liberals, however. NDP support comes almost entirely from west of the Ottawa River. In national elections, the West is no more fertile a source of NDP votes, other things equal, than is Ontario.

The bases of provincial elections, estimated in table 2, resemble those for national choice but with critical differences of emphasis. In the nongeographic realm, Liberal choice remains dominated by religion; NDP choice, by union exposure; and Conservative choice, by both religion and union exposure. But the religious basis of choice seems slightly weaker and the union/nonunion basis, slightly stronger in the provincial context. For the Liberals, a powerful language difference appears, but one which pulls against the Catholic/non-Catholic contrast: the negative sign suggests that the "French" coefficient is dominated by respondents in Quebec. In that province, the Liberal party's role as advocate of ethnic accommodation makes it the virtually unanimous choice of the anglophone minority.[3] That the Liberal party's share among francophones in the province is also large is indicated by the strong positive coefficient on the "Quebec" dummy variable.

The most striking contrast between the provincial and federal estimations lies in the sectional base of the system. Provincial party choice, not surprisingly, is more regionalized than federal choice. For the Liberals, the Quebec–West contrast is especially marked. This reflects the abject weakness of the Liberal party in the West; indeed, the sharpening of the Quebec–West difference comes about in spite of the smaller Liberal share in provincial than in federal choices in Quebec. The Quebec–West contrast is also very sharp for the Conservative provincial choice: the Conservative party does not even contest provincial elections in Quebec. In the West, it is a serious contender in three of the four provinces.[4] The NDP, meanwhile, is a much more distinctively Western party in provincial than in federal politics.

THE POLICY CONUNDRUM

Whatever the differences of detail between federal and provincial elections, each arena is striking for the extent to which the nongeographic bases of its partisanship are at odds with the surface features of party strife. The Catholic/non-Catholic difference is the prime mover of the system. But when religious group differences over questions of faith or morals are engaged, party policy positions, where distinguishable, commonly do not correspond to those group differences. Even if their party is fearful of raising the abortion question, the individual candidates who are most likely to voice the Catholic position are usually Conservatives. The amendments to the Criminal Code which facilitated access to abortion are identified with the Liberal party and, indeed, with the person of Pierre Trudeau. Those same criminal code amendments also eased restrictions on divorce, over the objections of the Catholic hierarchy. It is true that the Liberal party has been a more consistent advocate of public funding of Catholic separate schools than has any other party, at least in Ontario. But even this conformity of party policy distances to the group basis of the vote has its problematic elements: although school finance is pre-eminently a provincial question,[5] the Catholic/non-Catholic difference is sharper for federal than for provincial choice; and the most consistent opponent of such funding, the NDP, excites less aversion among Catholics than among non-Catholics. The incoherence in the domain is perhaps best summarised by the behaviour of the "no religion" coefficients: they tend to follow the "Catholic" pattern directly in spite of the fact that, among the major denominations, Catholics are the most highly mobilized, that nominal Catholics are more likely actually to practise their religion than are nominal non-Catholics.[6] In any case, the economic agenda in Canadian politics is dominated not by religious questions but by linguistic, immigrant/native, and ethnic questions. Yet party-choice differences between language groups are typically weak, as tables 1 and 2 have made clear. Irvine makes a convincing case that the same is true for immigrant/native, and ethic questions.[7]

An economic agenda, meanwhile, receives much more attention than is reflected in the mass base of the system. Popular commentary usually depicts the system as ordered from the NDP on the left to the Conservative party on the right and emphasises economic and social policy in generating the left–right order. Recent work on major-party leadership conventions suggests that this popular commentary is generally on the mark.[8] If observers are unimpressed by differences between the two major parties, the NDP provides a clear economic policy alternative to them. Survey evidence confirms that many Canadian voters themselves rank parties in ways consistent with the simple left–right order.[9] Surveys also indicate that voters' subjective policy emphases are on economic questions, especially on the unemployment/inflation tradeoff.[10] For all that, however, one natural class-related contrast, between those in and those not in union families, is evoked only weakly, and then only for the Conservatives and the NDP.

Class differences in Canadian party choice have excited commentary in inverse ratio to their empirical importance. Earlier literature tended to insist that class was truly a central factor but had just not yet been measured correctly[11] or that class was the real explanation behind the impact of some other characteristic, such as the Catholic/non-Catholic contrast.[12] Few still cling to this view and the empirical weakness of class differences in party preference is now taken as given.[13] The problem has now become the one of explaining that weakness. At present, the most influential explanation seems to be that in Brodie and Jenson[14]: Canadians do not respond to the major parties in class-differentiated ways because those parties do not make class differentiated appeals. The major parties, in effect, rule class questions off the agenda. Instead, they make appeals, mainly in the domain of language-group relations, which split classes and which encourage voters to see the essential boundaries of Canadian life as vertical rather than horizontal.

Brodie and Jenson can be no more than half right. Their characterisation of the major parties' appeals seems faithful to the historical record. But they fail to substantiate why the major parties have made that particular tactical choice and not some other. Although an emphasis on ethnolinguistic or religious questions may help split the working class, so might it split the bourgeois camp. Often, what seems required is a consolidation, not a fragmenting of the bourgeois vote. British Columbia's high-stakes class politics have repeatedly seen fusion strategies on the centre–right.[15] Why is the fusion strategy not similarly appropriate in the federal arena? Is it possible that the major federal parties address questions in the ethnolinguistic and even in the religious domain because such questions are truly important and are forced upon them? Even if one is reluctant to concede the importance of the issues, one must nevertheless ask why such appeals resonate in the mass public. Another way of posing this last question is to ask: why has the NDP been so weak?

Now consider the geographic differences in tables 1 and 2. The geography of the system has been amply documented[16] and nothing in those tables is at odds with our commonplace notions about that geography. But those commonplace notions are incoherent. Two explanations for the geographic structure commonly recur; each is couched mainly in economic terms. On one account, the rough East–West gradients (Quebec aside) in Conservative and Liberal support might seem like a resource-producer/resource-consumer, or centre/periphery, conflict. But the eastern end of the gradient, the Atlantic provinces, is a resource producing, or peripheral, region, much like the West. And Western support for the NDP is difficult to square with that region's support for the party which anchors the other end of the economic policy axis, the Conservative party. The east–west gradients might be read as expressions of rich-region/poor-region conflict. But, again, why does the geographical pattern for the NDP, the most redistributively oriented party, follow the pattern for the Conservative party, the least redistributively oriented one?

Finally, consider the differences between tables 1 and 2. The differences are actually represented as rather smaller than they might have been, as the two single-province parties are not considered. In British Columbia, the Social Credit vote occupies the space that the Conservative party might otherwise control and also overlaps significantly with a proto-Liberal clientele. In Quebec, the Parti Québécois forces provincial choice onto a nationalist–federalist axis unique to that province.[17] In these two provinces, typically, at least half the voters would have to shift their votes to bring federal and provincial outcomes into line with each other.[18] The two provincial parties which account for much of this shift are outside the scope of this paper.

The federal–provincial differences that remain are not trivial and no straightforward explanation for them leaps from the table. The existing literature on federal–provincial electoral relations is similarly bereft of explanations. Much of that literature's emphasis has been on aspects of elections other than those at issue here, on, for instance, whether or not voters consciously "balance" outcomes between arenas.[19] Neither a theory predicting such balancing nor a theory predicting the opposite behaviour would account for the mixed results that tables 1 and 2 actually exhibit.

TOWARD A THEORY OF THE PARTY SYSTEM IN ENGLISH CANADA

The conundrums just outlined can be brought some distance toward resolution by a simple model of strategic choice. The model aims at the weakness of the union/nonunion contrast, at the strength of the Catholic/non-Catholic contrast, and at the anomalies in the geographic pattern.

Although the existence and demographic weight of Quebec gives the model much of its force, the response actually examined is in the other nine provinces. Indeed, the electoral response analysed here could be said to be, to a great extent, specifically to the challenge posed by the usually monolithic behaviour of the Quebec voters I choose to exclude.[20] That exclusion is made for two reasons. One reason is substantive and should be obvious: in many respects Quebec (anglophone as well as francophone) is an electorate apart, even if choices in Quebec must be added to choices elsewhere to produce the total federal result. The other reason is technical. As part of my argument below is couched in terms of the percentage

Catholic in the province, inclusion of Quebec respondents could produce a massive outlier effect, whose real dynamics may not be religious at all, but linguistic. The model has the following elements: a characterisation of how the bases of party choice differ across class and religious contrasts; a consideration of the strategic criteria that constrain the expression of underlying party evaluations in actual behaviour; and the derivation, from these evaluative and strategic elements, of predictions for the geographic structure of the class and religious cleavages.

THE ORDERING OF CANADIAN PARTIES

Assume that voters can rank order parties from most to least preferred. On what basis do they construct their rankings? How many evaluative dimensions characterise that basis? One way to answer these questions is to identify voters' last choices among the parties. If two and only two parties appear as last choices, then those two anchor a single underlying order and the third party must fall in the middle of that order. If more than two parties appear, more than one preference order must be at work.

Elkins found with 1965, 1968, and 1974 evidence that more than one order controlled Canadians' choices. The top row of table 3 confirms that this remained true in 1979.[21] Although the table focusses on the three main parties, the continued existence of Social Credit as a widely reviled but otherwise unfeasible alternative confuses the issue somewhat: Social Credit is the model last choice in the electorate as a whole. Even so, the presence of Social Credit cannot completely obscure the fact that each of the three main parties is the last choice of a significant fraction of the electorate.

If more than one dimension drives choice among the three main parties, what might they be? Most observers agree that, however weak may be the economic and social policy differences among the parties, many Canadian voters order the parties in economic terms, with the NDP on the left and the Conservative party on the right. But this order can never generate last choices for the Liberal party. Table 3 makes clear that many respondents revile the Liberal party above all others. Elkins speculates that Liberal last choice is motivated by a centre–periphery axis.[22] Another possibility is simple adverse retrospective judgement on the quasi-permanent party of government. For the purposes of this paper, however, I propose that many of the Liberal last choices reflect an ethnocultural-cum-religious calculus. If choice is dominated jointly by an economic–social ordering and by an ethnoreligious one, then last-choice frequencies should follow a different pattern across a class contrast than across a religious contrast.

Consider the class contrast first. This contrast should be controlled by the economic–social ordering. Union families should be skewed toward the left, or NDP, pole of the order. Nonunion families should be skewed in the other direction. Whatever the modal last choice in each group, the *difference* between the union and nonunion groups should be sharpest over the polar parties, the Conservatives and the NDP. The Liberals are not particularly at issue here. They may have a significant share of the last preferences in each group but these last preferences should not be expressed for class-specific reasons. To the extent that the forces promoting aversion to the Liberals work at right angles to class interests, the frequency of Liberal last choices should not vary across the class contrast.

TABLE 3   GROUP DIFFERENCES IN PARTY RANKINGS,
1979 ELECTION (Quebec Respondents Excluded)

	Liberal	Conservative	NDP	(N)
A. Least Preferred Party				
All Respondents	16.6%	14.0	31.0	(1361)
Non-Union	15.6%	9.7	37.8	(800)
Union	17.8%	20.2	21.3	(561)
Non-Catholic	18.6%	14.5	31.2	(1088)
Catholic	8.4%	12.3	30.0	(273)
B. Thermometer Rating				
Non-Union	52.5	61.4	42.7	
	(890)	(879)	(845)	
Union	54.1	53.9	53.7	
	(626)	(614)	(608)	
Non-Catholic	52.9	58.7	47.4	
	(1210)	(1191)	(1155)	
Catholic	54.1	56.8	46.8	
	(307)	(302)	(299)	

Now consider an ethnoreligious ordering of the parties and the religious contrast. At present the most obvious issues in this domain concern French–English relations, broadly defined. Also at issue is immigration and the place of the ethnic groups which recent migrations have brought to Canada. Of very great vintage and of more continuing importance than is commonly acknowledged is the whole complex of questions, now mostly symbolic, around the British Connection. Whatever the order's precise content, at one end of it must be the Conservative party, notwithstanding two decades of attempts by its leaders to refashion it into an ethnically neutral vehicle. The other end is anchored by the Liberal party. Its policies may not be obviously more accommodating to French Canadians and to ethnic minorities than are the NDP's but the Liberals have been generally the most successful at actually recruiting voters and activists from the ranks of such groups.

The Catholic/non-Catholic boundary is critical for attitudes in this domain.[23] A Catholic of British ancestry, for example, is likely to come to a much less British sense of the country than would an ethnically identical counterpart who happened to grow up Protestant.[24] In any case, Catholics are numerous even outside Quebec; they provide the numbers to underpin a major cleavage in the alignment of parties. Catholics should be skewed toward the Liberal end of this order. Non-Catholics should tend toward the Conservative end. Once again, any of the three parties can find last place "votes" among both Catholics and non-Catholics. But party selection governed by reasons specific to religious group membership should yield Catholic/non-Catholic last-choice differences mainly for the Conservative and Liberal parties.

The Conservative party occupies a polar position on each evaluative dimension. Because of this compatibility, the movement of individuals or the complementary displacement of aggregate shares, in either direction, between the Liberal party and the NDP could be motivated by either an economic–social or an ethnoreligious calculus. But we can make no such dual imputation for individual movement or for aggregate complementarity between the Liberal and Conservative parties: such shifts must be governed by the economic axis. Conversely, movement or complementarity between the Conservative party and the NDP must be governed by the cultural axis.

In fact, voters can employ both criteria. Where voters distinguish not just the rank order of parties but also the interval-level distances between them, a voter may well discriminate between each pair of parties in terms of the evaluative dimension on which the two parties are further apart. A voter thus might shift the basis of comparison as he or she moves up or down the preference ranking: if the strategic contingency that the voter faces shifts, so may the evaluative criterion that the voter uses to discriminate between the strategically favoured parties. The salience attached to each dimension could also be at issue. Saliences can shift from election to election as issues are raised or dropped. Salience weights can also vary from place to place. As salience weights vary, even a voter whose own weights have not changed may be forced to make a choice over the party pair discriminated by the less important evaluative criterion. The same can be true, *mutatis mutandis* for two otherwise identical voters living in different places. In effect, increasing a dimension's salience is equivalent to lengthening party distances along it. Salience weights may shift from election to election and from place to place.

What then of our expectations for last choices in the non-Quebec electorate? Most are confirmed, according to table 3. The clearest confirmations come for the union/nonunion contrast. For the Conservative party and the NDP the ratios of last choices are about 2:1 in the expected direction. The Liberal party last choice likelihood is, appropriately, unaffected by this contrast. In each group the Liberal party likelihood is the middling one. Note, however, that of the three main parties the NDP remains the modal last choice in each group. Note also that the percentages do not add to 100: in the non-Quebec electorate as a whole, Social Credit is the modal last choice, although NDP last choices slightly outnumber Social Credit ones in the nonunion group. The feeling thermometer evidence corroborates the last choice story. The Conservative and New Democratic parties again make the running in the union/nonunion contrast. Also as before, the NDP remains third (although a close one) in the collective heart of the union group.

The Catholic/non-Catholic contrast provides less satisfactory evidence. Here the availability of Social Credit in the last choice item is especially bothersome. The Liberal party does perform as expected: non-Catholics are about twice as likely as Catholics to give that party as their last choice. Against expectations, the Conservative party share does not move oppositely to the Liberal one; that role falls to the (not directly represented) Social Credit share. In the thermometer evidence, the party feeling differences are as predicted but are always small and statistically insignificant.

Even with the weakness of the Catholic pattern, the preference ranking evidence indicates an opening for the operation of a strategic choice process whose objectives differ across the religious and, more powerfully, across the economic boundaries. But what is the strategic criterion?

THE STRATEGIC CRITERION

Work to date on strategic voting typically takes parties in pairs and identifies as the strategic criterion the vote margin between the more preferred party in the pair and the overall frontrunner. This criterion is conceptually close to the strategic term in expected utility models of voting. There the strategic factor is the voter's expected likelihood that his/her choice between a pair of parties will be decisive for the current election. In merged aggregate–survey analysis, the expected likelihoods are represented by the margins in the overall outcome. The margin may be taken from the previous election,[25] but such information is not always available and even if available may not be relevant to the current election. In merged aggregate–survey analysis, the expected likelihoods are represented by the margins in the current election.[26] It is not clear how exogenous an estimate this really is. Survey items directly on the subjective likelihoods are coloured by wish fulfilment and thus also raise the question of exogeneity.[27]

The best strategic indicator may be the local preponderance of a politically relevant group. Voters may have a sense of that preponderance even if they are unaware of that characteristic's distribution across other locales. Even if they are not aware of the group's local concentration, they may be aware of its effects in the long-term distribution of party shares. The point of our strategic story, in any case, is to help explain aspects of a cleavage structure. It is conceptually satisfying to couch that explanation in terms related to the structure itself. As the most problematic elements in that structure are the strength of the Catholic/non-Catholic difference and the weakness of the union/nonunion cleavage, the local percentage Catholic, the local percentage in unions, or both percentages spring immediately to mind as possible strategic criteria.

This paper will concentrate on the geographic distribution of Catholics. That distribution is much more heterogeneous than is the distribution of union families. This is true even with Quebec excluded from consideration. Where the most unionized province has about twice as many union families as the least unionized province, the extremes for the Catholic percentage have a ratio of about three to one. Moreover, the province-level variance in the percentage Catholic corresponds closely to the east–west gradient we observed above in non-Quebec party preferences. The same cannot be said for the across-province distribution of unionists. The non-Catholic extreme is British Columbia in which about 20 per cent of the population is Catholic. At the other extreme is New Brunswick, in which over 55 per cent of the population is Catholic; about two-thirds of these are francophones. Catholics make up roughly half the populations of Nova Scotia and Newfoundland. Ontario is also about one-third Catholic, while each Prairie province is about 25 per cent Catholic.

Many provinces are sharply differentiated internally. In Newfoundland, a disproportionate share of the Catholic population lives in or near St. John's. In Nova Scotia, New Brunswick, and the three Prairie provinces, Catholics are more numerous in northern than in southern areas. On the Nova Scotia south shore Catholics make up less than 10 per cent of the population. In contrast, Catholics constitute over two-thirds of the population of Cape Breton. Over much of southern New Brunswick, the Catholic percentage is under 20 per cent; in some North Shore ridings, the Catholic share is over 90 per cent. The extremes on the Prairies are not quite as marked but are still notable.

In Ontario, the most heavily Catholic constituencies tend, not surprisingly, to be in the bilingual zones of the north and east. Some constituencies in the Ottawa Valley are over 70 per cent Catholic. Many others in the Valley and along the Northern Ontario Clay Belt are majority Catholic. Outside these areas, the majority Catholic constituencies are in Toronto and Windsor.

What is the proper geographic unit in which to calculate the percentage Catholic? So far, students of strategic voting have assumed that the constituency is the appropriate unit. It is in constituencies, after all, that parliamentary seats are won or lost. But, although the calculus imputed to voters in strategic voting studies is an expected-utility-maximization one, it seems fairly clear that for voters actually to employ such a calculus is, despite its patina of rational action, deeply irrational: most individuals in most ridings will have no effect on the outcome, to a moral certainty.[28] Yet ample evidence has accumulated that voters do behave strategically. But if voters insist on being irrational and on behaving strategically at the constituency level, what is to stop them acting strategically at a higher level of aggregation? In many places voters may not be able to gather constituency-specific information anyway. Media reporting of poll and other information is commonly for the province-wide or for metropolitan area-wide results. Quite apart from information gathering, there remains the question of what the voter imagines him/herself to be doing. Johnston, et al. report that about as many respondents would entertain a second choice to avert the wrong party's forming a government as would do so to defeat the unacceptable party's local candidate.[29] Citizens evidently can participate imaginatively in the election as a *national* event.

This leaves us with several strategic possibilities. This paper will exploit two. One task is to examine the sensitivity of Catholics and non-Catholics and of union and nonunion families to the percentage Catholic in their *province* of residence. The second task is to take the coefficients for provincial-level information and compare them between provincial estimations. To the extent that voters think in terms of who shall form the national government, the percentage Catholic in the province is not the only pertinent information for national elections. Also pertinent is the fact that nearly half the national electorate is Catholic and that, by virtue of that proportion, the liberal party is a force to be reckoned with, as a pole of attraction or aversion, whatever Catholics' local numbers may be. But the national proportion Catholic or the strength of the Liberals in, say, New Brunswick is of little pertinence to *provincial* elections in a province with few Catholics. Where Catholics are greatly outnumbered, non-Catholics can, as it were, control the agenda and divide over class questions. The handful of Catholics may be forced by the electoral system to do likewise. Conversely, where Catholics are locally dominant, the NDP may be squeezed even more efficiently and the class agenda constrained even more tightly than in national elections. In the data analysis to follow, then, the whole-electorate strategic logic should produce larger coefficients on the percentage Catholic in provincial than in federal estimations.

This paper will leave aside what many would regard as the most compelling level of analysis: at the constituency level. Two related considerations move me to concentrate on the provincial and the national results. One is a concern for space. Adding a third constituency level to the analysis would increase the number and scale of tables severalfold. The data analysis in this paper is unwieldy enough as it stands. The second consideration is analytic complexity. It was tempting simply to drop the province level of analysis in favour of the constituency level, but such a move would have been ill advised. If, as I hypothesise, the province is a valid unit for voters' strategic calculations, then the constituency percentage Catholic should not be analysed other than with the province percentage controlled. The positive correlation between the constituency percentage Catholic and the province percentage Catholic[30] could produce a false positive estimate for the effect of the constituency percentage Catholic on some partisan variable. But the failure to control could also produce a false negative. Assume for the sake of argument that the Liberal share shrinks and the NDP share grows as the province's percentage Catholic shrinks. Should the same relationship hold at the constituency level within each province? Not necessarily. If the NDP is the second choice for Catholics, its share might actually grow, not shrink, as a function of the constituency-level percentage Catholic in a province in which the Liberals are not viable.[31]

Confining analysis to the province level and above can lead to misspecification in its own right. We might impute to provinces an effect which is really at some lower level of aggregation. This does not concern me much, at least not for now. The political implications of the findings will remain much the same even if we assign too much of the strategic effect to the province level. If the calculus at the constituency level is subtly different, at least in some provinces, from that at the province level, the province-level estimates may be biased, but the bias is likely to be one of mild attenuation.

EXPECTATIONS FOR GEOGRAPHIC COEFFICIENTS

In this discussion I shall refer to estimations of the following bivariate equation:

$$1. \quad Pr(V_{ij}) = f[\, a + b*RCj + u \,],$$

where $Pr(V_{ij})$ is the likelihood of choosing party i in province j;
RC_j is the proportion Catholic in province j;
u is the error term, which subsumes the influence of unmeasured variables.

In 1. "a" yields the party probability in a province with no Catholics, while "b" gives the probability boost in V_{ij} for a unit increment in the proportion Catholic. Of course a unit increment in a proportion is the entire distance from 0 to 1. Thus "b" gives the shift from a homogeneously non-Catholic to a homogeneously Catholic place.

First consider union (u) and nonunion (nu) estimations. The arguments in the preceding section lead to the following expectations:

Liberal:	$a(u) = a(nu) < 0$
	$b(u) > b(nu) > 0$
Conservative:	$a(u) < a(nu)$
	$b(nu) < 0 < b(u)$
NDP:	$a(u) > a(nu)$
	$b(u) < b(nu) < 0$

Where no Catholics are to be found, I predict no union–nonunion difference in Liberal choice and a low likelihood of Liberal choice in either group. The real action at the intercept involves the Conservative and New Democratic parties: union families should, of course, be more likely than nonunion families to vote NDP and less likely to vote Conservative.

As the proportion Catholic grows, union and nonunion families alike should become more likely to vote Liberal. But I predict that union families should rally to the Liberal fold at a faster clip. In both groups some voters will move strategically, to both the Liberals and the Conservatives, for ethnocultural reasons. But where the Liberals' major rival is likely to be the Conservative party, union families will have an additional, economic incentive to move to the Liberal; hence the differential prediction for the Liberal "b"s.

In Conservative party choice, as the proportion Catholic grows, union and nonunion families should move in opposite directions. Some union families will move to the Conservative party; all of this movement must be for ethnocultural reasons. Some nonunion families will leave the Conservative fold to join the Liberals; these would be families which strictly prefer the Liberal party but which vote Conservative for economic reasons where the small percentage Catholic places the Liberal party in a strategically weak position. The net effect of these movements should be to compress the class cleavage in Conservative choice as Catholic preponderance grows.

As the proportion Catholic grows, the NDP should shrink in both union and nonunion groups. But it should shrink more quickly in union families. To see why this follows, think in terms of shrinkage, rather than growth, in the proportion Catholic. As the Catholic share shrinks, voters who might strictly prefer the Liberal party must move elsewhere. Nonunion voters will split between the NDP and the Conservatives; according to the model, nonunion voters who move to the NDP must do so for ethnocultural reasons. Union voters who leave other parties can do so only to move to the NDP. Thus, the class difference in NDP is allowed to expand, as is the NDP's total share, as the proportion Catholic shrinks.

Now turn to the Catholic/non-Catholic contrast:

Liberal:	$a(c) = a(nc) < 0$
	$b(c) > b(nc) > 0$
Conservative:	$a(c) < a(nc)$
	$b(c) < 0 < b(nc)$
NDP:	$a(c) < a(nc)$
	$b(c) < b(nc) < 0$

The intercept in this case has a slightly odd meaning: it refers to the Catholic/non-Catholic difference in a place where no Catholics live. Think of it as the behaviour of the one Catholic in an otherwise non-Catholic milieu. Keep in mind also that in no province does the proportion Catholic actually touch zero. As before, the Liberal party prediction is for no group difference at the intercept and a small Liberal share in each group. For the Conservatives, Catholics should be less likely than non-Catholics to prefer the Conservatives in a homogeneously Catholic place. Catholics should be more likely than non-Catholics to prefer the NDP.

The Liberal share should grow in both religious groups as the Catholic proportion grows. On the non-Catholic side, this should reflect movement among union families to the Liberals to avert Conservative victories. Such rallying among union families should also be part of the story on the Catholic side. But among Catholics the growth in the Liberal share also reflects the rallying of voters who elsewhere defect to the Conservatives to defeat the NDP or to the NDP to defeat the Conservatives but who, given the chance, strictly prefer to support the polar ethnocultural party, the Liberals. The summarily greater attraction of the Liberal party for Catholics, then, produces a differential prediction for the "b"s. By implication, the religious cleavage in Liberal choice should widen as the proportion Catholic grows.

The cleavage should also widen in Conservative choice. Among Catholics, the prediction is for a steeply negative coefficient as growth in their numbers strips away any need for its nonunion families to vote Conservative to defeat the NDP. Among non-Catholics, in contrast, growth in the provincial proportion Catholic should make the Conservative share grow, mainly as some union families rally to the Tories for ethnocultural reasons.

For the NDP, the religious cleavage at the intercept should evaporate as the Catholic proportion grows. Among non-Catholics the NDP share should shrink as union members shift to the Conservatives to defeat the ethnoculturally unacceptable Liberals. Among Catholics the coefficient should reflect both ethnocultural and economic motives, primarily as Catholic union families move to defeat the Conservatives, the party which is polar on both evaluative dimensions. This compounding of motives in one group but not the other should produce a greater decrement, as a function of the proportion Catholic, among Catholics themselves than among non-Catholics.

Finally, the coefficients ("b") on the percentage Catholic should have greater absolute values in provincial than in federal estimations. This expectation reflects the logic set out at the end of the last section: in provincial elections the absence of the national strategic criterion frees party choice to respond very sharply to the provincial criterion; in national elections, the impact of each province's criterion is constrained by the demographic weight of Catholic voters in the country as a whole.[32]

ESTIMATION

On balance, the estimations are kind to our hypotheses, but glaring exceptions exist. The cleavage structure does prove sensitive to the local preponderance of Catholics although not always in the predicted ways.[33]

In the federal union/nonunion analysis, the only party fully consistent with out intercept expectations is the NDP. Nonunion families are significantly less likely than union ones to support the NDP in homogeneously non-Catholic places. For some reason, neither of the other parties mirrors the NDP convincingly. The Conservatives do better among nonunion families than among union ones, but the difference is small and neither intercept is significantly different from zero. The Liberals are weak in both groups, of course, but seem weaker in the nonunion than in the union group.

Evidence for the "b"s is also only partly consistent with expectations. The general story is one of Liberal growth and Conservative shrinkage with increases in the proportion Catholic. Contrary to prediction is the near identity between union and nonunion families in the Liberal growth. More important for my argument is the pattern for Conservative coefficients. I had predicted that the nonunion coefficient would be negative. The estimated coefficient is negative but is not significantly different from zero. The union coefficient is contrary to prediction and is altogether mystifying. As the percentage Catholic grows, union families flee the Conservatives at a fairly brisk clip; why such families should be especially prone to shun the party where elsewhere they have a nontrivial likelihood of supporting it seems rather odd, as does a widening of the class difference as the Liberals displace the NDP. NDP coefficients, in contrast, continue to be well behaved. As predicted, the geographic coefficient is more steeply negative in the union group than in the nonunion group.

All things considered, estimates in the religious domain are more consistent with expectations than is true in the economic realm. Conservative and NDP intercepts are distributed as they should be, although only for the latter is the Catholic/non-Catholic difference of much note. At the intercept, Catholics are a bit more likely than non-Catholics to vote Liberal, although the dominant message is that where Catholics are few and far between the Liberal party is very weak in each religious group.

As the proportion Catholic grows, the Liberals gain at the expense of the NDP, roughly as expected. Contrary to prediction the Liberal growth rate is essentially identical between the groups. Consistent with prediction, the NDP geographic coefficient is markedly greater among Catholics than among non-Catholics. The Conservative share hardly responds at all in either group.

Provincial Catholic/non-Catholic estimations yield much the same story as in federal estimations. All NDP coefficients are better behaved than are virtually any coefficients for the other two parties: the NDP exhibits a clear class differentiation at the intercept, but this difference evaporates as the Catholic proportion grows. For the Conservatives, intercepts do not differ between groups. Non-union respondents are unresponsive to the percentage Catholic, while union respondents become less likely, as in federal elections, to vote Conservative as the percentage Catholic increases (the provincial union coefficient is of borderline significance but is larger than in the federal estimation). Once again, union families are more likely than nonunion families to vote Liberal but Liberal choice is highly unlikely at the intercept in either group. Both economic groups are very responsive to the percentage Catholic; this is as expected. Contrary to expectation, the nonunion coefficient is rather larger than the union one.

In the Catholic/non-Catholic provincial estimations, the NDP coefficients emerge yet again as the best behaved. Catholics are much more likely to vote NDP

TABLE 4   *THE GEOGRAPHICAL SENSITIVITY OF RELIGIOUS AND ECONOMIC GROUPS IN THE 1979 NATIONAL ELECTION (Probit Estimation; Quebec Excluded)*

	Liberal	Conservative	NDP
A. Union Contrast			
1. Non-Union (N = 1068)			
Proportion Catholic	2.79♦	–0.39	–1.87♦♦
	(0.47)	(0.41)	(0.56)
Constant	–1.51♦	0.13	–0.56♦♦
	(0.17)	(0.15)	(0.19)
–2ln(L)	37.92♦	0.95	11.40♦
% Correct	70.0	53.3	88.3
2. Union (N = 708)			
Proportion Catholic	2.58♦	–1.17♦	–2.34♦
	(0.59)	(0.57)	(0.62)
Constant	–1.30♦	0.02	0.08
	(0.21)	(0.20)	(0.21)
–2ln(L)	19.76♦	4.16+	14.49♦
% Correct	63.8	64.4	75.7
B. Religious Contrast			
1. Non-Catholic (N = 1261)			
Proportion Catholic	2.27♦	0.22	–1.85♦♦
	(0.45)	(0.40)	(0.48)
Constant	–1.39♦	–0.09	–0.40♦
	(0.16)	(0.14)	(0.16)
–2ln(L)	26.22♦	0.30	14.80♦
% Correct	73.4	48.9	83.9
2. Catholic (N = 515)			
Proportion Catholic	2.23♦	–0.82	–3.72♦♦
	(0.66)	(0.69)	(0.86)
Constant	–1.00♦	–0.19	0.44
	(0.25)	(0.26)	(0.31)
–2ln(L)	11.53♦	2.41	20.50♦
% Correct	58.8	69.1	81.7

Standard errors in parentheses. One-tailed test.
+ p < 0.05
++ p < 0.01
♦ p < 0.001

at the intercept and flee the party at a faster clip; each finding is as we predict. Catholics are also more likely than non-Catholics to vote Liberal at the intercept, but again neither group indicates a very high likelihood of doing so. Both groups

TABLE 5   *THE GEOGRAPHICAL SENSITIVITY OF RELIGIOUS AND ECONOMIC GROUPS IN PROVINCIAL ELECTIONS, 1976–79 (Probit Estimation; Non-Voters Excluded)*

	Liberal	Conservative (excluding Quebec and BC)	NDP (excl. Quebec)
A. Union Contrast			
1. Non-Union	(N = 899)		(N = 1004)
Proportion Catholic	3.71✦	−0.50	−3.08✢
	(0.59)	(0.48)	(0.55)
Constant	−1.95✦	0.14	−0.11
	(0.23)	(0.18)	(0.18)
−2ln(L)	42.94✦	1.07	32.31✦
% Correct	70.2	49.8	84.3
2. Union	(N = 553)		(N = 682)
Proportion Catholic	2.78✦	−1.39	−5.64✦
	(0.88)	(0.89)	(0.68)
Constant	−1.46✦	0.13	1.30✦
	(0.33)	(0.33)	(0.22)
−2ln(L)	9.96✢	2.49	78.03✦
% Correct	63.3	64.9	73.3
B. Religious Contrast			
1. Non-Catholic	(N = 994)		(N = 1200)
Proportion Catholic	3.67✦	−0.42	−3.55✦
	(0.66)	(0.52)	(0.47)
Constant	−1.95✦	0.07	0.29
	(0.24)	(0.19)	(0.15)
−2ln(L)	34.19✦	0.65	58.67✦
% Correct	72.0	53.0	78.3
2. Catholic	(N = 458)		(N = 486)
Proportion Catholic	2.38✦	−0.54	−7.17✦
	(0.77)	(0.78)	(1.10)
Constant	−1.22✦	−0.17	1.64✦
	(0.31)	(0.31)	(0.38)
−2ln(L)	9.70✦	0.48	57.54✦
% Correct	61.7	64.9	82.1

Standard errors in parentheses. One-tailed test.
✢ $p < 0.05$
✢✢ $p < 0.01$
✦ $p < 0.001$

rally to the Liberals as the Catholic proportion grows, but, contrary to expectation again, non-Catholics do so more quickly than Catholics do.

TABLE 6   *ESTIMATED CLEAVAGE WIDTHS BY*
PERCENTAGE CATHOLIC IN FEDERAL AND
PROVINCIAL ELECTIONS, 1976-79

Percent Catholic	Union — Non-Union		Catholic — Non-Catholic	
	Federal	Provincial	Federal	Provincial
A. Liberal Party				
15	+4	+7	+10	+11
25	+4	+7	+12	+11
35	+4	+5	+14	+10
45	+4	+3	+15	+6
55	+4	−1	+15	+1
B. Conservative Party				
15	−9	−6	−10	−10
25	−20	−10	−14	−10
35	−15	−12	−18	−11
45	−18	−15	−21	−11
55	−20	−18	−25	−12
C. New Democratic Party				
15	+19	+39	+20	+30
25	+15	+27	+12	+17
35	+12	+13	+4	+2
45	+9	+4	0	−4
55	+5	0	−3	−4

Entry is the estimated party-share differences between the indicated groups.

Table 6 attempts to extract the implications of all this for the cleavage structure. Entries in the table span the plausible range of proportions Catholic and are derived from the coefficients in tables 4 and 5. Note that increases and decreases in estimated cleavage widths are rarely linear.

First consider the union/nonunion basis of the system. For the Liberals, class differences are simply not much of a factor and shift commensurately little over the landscape. The Conservative and NDP stories are dramatically different. For the Conservative party, frankly, the story makes little sense. That the class cleavage should widen as the Catholic proportion grows seems counter-intuitive and is at odds with other, more sensible aspects of the cleavage structure. But NDP shifts are exactly as expected: as the proportion Catholic grows, the cleavage shrinks to a nullity. Indeed it is estimated even to reverse itself; beyond some point the little band of NDP brothers becomes exclusively non-Catholic. For the NDP, the union/nonunion difference is geographically more sensitive in provincial than in federal elections, just as we expect.

The religious-cleavage picture is, if anything, more dramatic and seems plausible in all of its parts. For the Liberals and Conservatives the most interesting story is in federal voting. In that arena the cleavage widens as the proportion Catholic increases. In provincial elections the cleavage width behaves differently

TABLE 7 ESTIMATED PARTY SHARE GAINS/LOSSES BY PERCENTAGE CATHOLIC IN FEDERAL AND PROVINCIAL ELECTIONS, 1976–79

	Union	Non-Union	Catholic	Non-Catholic
A. Liberal Party				
Federal	+37	+37	+34	+29
Provincial	+38	+46	+35	+45
B. Conservative Party				
Federal	–17	–6	–12	+3
Provincial	–21	–9	–8	–6
C. New Democratic Party				
Federal	–28	–14	–40	–17
Provincial	–63	–24	–70	–36

Entry is estimated party share difference in the indicated group between 55 per cent and 15 per cent Catholic locales.

than in federal elections and differently between the two parties. The cleavage shrinks to a nullity for the Liberals and remains stable for the Conservatives. For the NDP, the cleavage widens as the percentage Catholic shrinks. The NDP thus takes on something of the Liberal party's ethnoreligious identity as the Liberal party itself disappears. Keep in mind, however, that the groups in question become a less critical electoral asset as their own numbers shrink.

Although not always in ways that we expected, one major expectation that we brought into the exercise is roundly confirmed: the cleavage structure shifts as a function of the proportion Catholic in the province. The axes of evaluation rotate, as it were, according to the strategic significance of Roman Catholics, a group whose membership is differentially distributed over the landscape. The behaviour of the class cleavage in Conservative choice runs against the grain, however. I am not sure that I believe this finding yet.[34] But until we can lay it aside, our geographic picture although impressively powerful, is still not entirely coherent.

What, finally, of federal–provincial differences in the sensitivity of party shares to the proportion Catholic? Table 7 takes estimates from tables 4 and 5 and makes them speak to this question. The entry is the difference between the minimum and maximum hypothetical "provinces," one with 15 per cent Catholic and the other with 55 per cent Catholic. The larger the absolute value of the entry in table 7, the more sensitive the vote share is. For Liberal and NDP estimated shares, the expectation is confirmed without exception. For the Conservatives the picture is more equivocal: for union and nonunion group sensitivities, the prediction is borne out, but only by a trivial amount; for religious group sensitivities it is not appropriate even to make this sort of comparison. The real story for the Conservative party is that its share is generally less sensitive overall to the proportion Catholic than is either the Liberal or the NDP share. But where a party's share is fairly sensitive to the proportion Catholic, then that sensitivity seems substantially greater for provincial than for federal choice.

CONCLUSIONS AND SOME SPECULATIONS

The initial intuition that geography plays a major role in sustaining the religious cleavage and in constraining the union/nonunion difference, a proxy for a class cleavage, has been handsomely confirmed, even if not always in the precise ways that we anticipated. Part of the geographic story is that Catholics, much more than union families, are distributed unevenly over the landscape. This allows them to control the electoral agenda, so to speak, where their numbers are relatively large. Where Catholics are numerous, class, or union/nonunion, differences are suppressed. But where Catholics are few, class differences, at least in NDP voting, can flourish. This pattern is especially marked in provincial elections. And the logic which underpins strategic choice at each level (to the extent that it does) helps account for what might otherwise be mystifying differences between the levels.

The conditional nature of the class cleavage suggests that the observers who claimed that class truly was empirically important may have been right, in a way, all along. They erred, however, in searching for better indicators of the class positions of individuals. Instead they should have sought indicators of *circumstances that inhibit or facilitate* class differences in the vote. Where circumstances permit, class, or its union/nonunion proxy, is the dominant force in party preference. The key circumstance, however, is not one that is easily manipulated. The rather monolithic response, where they can assert themselves, of Catholics to the party system is a social fact which Conservatives and New Democrats have always had to confront.

It should also be confronted by observers of the Canadian party system, as should the power of class differences where Catholics are numerically weak. The key stylized fact in the conventional wisdom is that the system lacks a social base. On this view the very predominance of the religious cleavage is the exception that proves the rule: how seriously is one to take a cleavage so obviously at odds with the surface features of party conflict? If this paper is any guide, the Catholic/non-Catholic cleavage corresponds to a major divide in Canadian life. Here the emphasis has been on the spatial structure of the Catholic community. But a full and proper exploration of the institutional and ideological characteristics of Canadian Catholics may well reveal them to be a distinct subcommunity, even if Catholics are not often that much more conscious than are non-Catholics of their corporate character. To the extent that Catholics are a real subcommunity, especially with something of a territorial base, then the Liberal party may also have something of a territorial and social base, in the Catholic parts of English Canada as well as in French Canada. Liberal dominance of Canadian elections in this century may not have been the card trick that the conventional wisdom[35] asserts it to have been.

Liberal success may not be a card trick, but it may nevertheless contain the seeds of its own undoing. Liberal strength rests not on the party's middle position on the economic axis of party evaluation. Rather it rests on the party's polar position on the cultural axis. If either or both of the other parties can credibly leapfrog the Liberal party or if Liberal governments ever succeed in making Canada an ethnically truly neutral polity, then the party's fate may be sealed. The Liberal party must also hope that Tory backbenchers define what the Conservative party is better than do frontbenchers and the leader. Liberals must also hope that the NDP remains repellent to Catholics. On this paper's evidence, such a hope may be futile: if Catholics can live with the NDP where they are a religious minority, perhaps they might also rally to the NDP where their coreligionists are numerous.

APPENDIX

This appendix addresses three facets of the estimation strategy: the use of probit to estimate sensitivity of party choice to the proportion of Catholic; the use of separate union/nonunion and Catholic/non-Catholic estimations; and the exclusion of other variables from the estimation.

PROBIT

Choice of this technique is driven by a concern to avoid a specific methological artifact: a floor effect. Recall that two parties tend to disappear from view at one or the other end of the landscape, the NDP in the East and the Liberals in the West. Group differences in support for a party are almost certain to be smaller where the party is weak than where it is strong. This may reflect the fact that there is simply less variance to push around in the former place than in the latter. Probit is not prey to such floor effects, as it assumes from the outset that the slope of a relationship will vary over the range of the independent variable. Thus any difference actually found between groups' coefficients will not be an artifact of the inevitable compression of group differences that comes with the shrinkage in a party's overall share. Note, however, that geographic coefficients identical between groups are compatible in a probit setup with geographic shifts in the cleavage width. Such shifts would most likely be floor effects, however.

GROUP CONTRASTS

In principle, group differences in sensitivity to the proportion Catholic could have been recovered other than by simple comparison of all Catholics with all non-Catholics and of all unionists with all nonunionists. At one extreme would be to mount a whole-sample estimation with a saturated main and interaction effects design. Unfortunately, the multicollinearity among several of the key variables would be too great to allow us to make much sense of the estimates. A compromise might be to divide the sample in two and use interaction terms to capture the other group difference. For example, the sample could be divided between Catholics and non-Catholics and interaction terms used to capture the union/nonunion difference within each religious group. This would require fewer terms in each estimation, but would still present intractable multicollinearity problems. At the other extreme from the whole-sample design would be to break the sample in four, with each group defined jointly by a religious and an economic category. But where Quebec respondents are excluded, this takes us into small sample sizes, especially for the Catholic subgroups. In the end, it seemed best to make two separate contrasts. Aside from being simple, this design also lets us look directly at the dynamics of each cleavage.

EXCLUSION OF CONTROL VARIABLES

Geographic-effects estimations are commonly criticized in terms of specification error. What is represented as an effect from the proportion Catholic may really be from other, excluded variables. For an example of this sort of claim, see the Kelley and McAllister critique of Miller.[36] Obvious candidates for inclusion are the dummy variables of tables 1 and 2.

With this critique in mind, every estimation in tables 4 and 5 was rerun with every variable from tables 1 and 2 whose inclusion was possible. Obviously, "Quebec" could never appear, "Catholic" could not appear in the religious group estimations, and "union" could not appear in the class estimations. Other variables were dropped one or more times. As examples, "French" could not appear in non-Catholic estimations and "no religion" could not appear in Catholic estimations.

Tabular presentation of the full estimations would take several pages. Interested readers may request copies of the estimations from the author. The basic story is that coefficients on the proportion Catholic are almost always attenuated, as we should expect. But so, modestly, are coefficients on the regional dummy variables. In a significant minority of the cases, coefficients which appear significant in the truncated estimations fail to attain significance by even the most forgiving criterion in the full estimations. Conservative party coefficients which are commonly null in the truncated estimation sometimes emerge as significant in the full estimation, but in ways which are difficult to interpret. For the Liberals and the NDP, however, the modal pattern is for religious-proportion coefficients to remain significant, even if attenuated.

There remains the question of what constitutes a fair test of the geographic coefficient. Does entering dummy variables, some of which are regional, up the stakes unduly? Multicollinearity does become a problem, specifically because the percentage Catholic orders the regions in a way which actually makes sense of the regional pattern in tables 1 and 2. But the regional dummy variables also bring all the specific historical and other circumstances of each region to bear on the estimation. Given the collinearity between them and the religious-proportion coefficient in the context of errors in variables, the regional dummies may suck off more than their "fair share" of apparent effect. It may be all the more striking, then, that the proportion-Catholic variable continues to be as important as it does.

NOTES

1. Respondents score one on "Catholic" if they are Roman or Ukrainian Catholics and zero otherwise. A respondent must refuse a religious affiliation to score one on the "no religion" variable. Although it used to make sense to distinguish among Protestant denominations, analyses not reported here suggest that such differences no long exist. [J. Wilson, "Politics and Social Class in Canada: The Case of Waterloo South," *Canadian Journal of Political Science (CJPS)* 1 (1968): 288–309; J.A. Laponce, "Ethnicity, Religion, and Politics in Canada: A Comparative Analysis of Survey and Census Data," in *Quantitative Ecological Analysis in the Social Sciences*, ed. M. Dogan and S. Rokkan (Cambridge, Mass.: MIT Press, 1969.]

The emphasis in the "French" dummy is with *current exposure* to French language use, to active membership in the community of francophones. Thus, those who now speak French at home are classed as French but not those who once spoke French but no longer do. Those who also speak English as well as French are classed as French. The "other language" variable is intended to tap not so much language use itself as cultural distance from the charter groups. Thus, *any* use of a language other than English or French, whether alone or in combination with either official language or with both and whether at present or only in childhood suffices to have the respondent score one on the "other language" variable.

"Union" refers to the respondent and his/her family. Union membership exerts more leverage on party choice than does any measure of class, subjective or objective. I am comfortable in using "union" here as a surrogate for a class measure as the Canadian union movement is committed, at least formally, to a class analysis of Canadian life and to the New Democratic Party as the political expression of its class interests [G. Horowitz, *Canadian Labour in Politics* (Toronto: University of Toronto Press, 1968).] even if the NDP itself commonly avoids a class analysis in its electoral appeals. [G. Teeple, " 'Liberals in a hurry': Socialism and the CCF-NDP," in *Capitalism and the National Questions in Canada*, ed. G. Teeple (Toronto: University of Toronto Press, 1972).] I do not differentiate by kind of union or by whether or not the family's local is affiliated with the NDP. But see K. Archer, "The Failure of the New Democratic Party: Unions, Unionists, and Politics in Canada," *CJPS* 18 (1985): 353–66. As my argument develops, the union movement and the Roman Catholic Church will emerge as the rival organisational building blocks of the Canadian party system.

The regional dummy variables follow convention. Each Atlantic province has too few respondents for comfortable estimation, even though important political differences within the region exist. The same considerations apply to the western provinces. The geographical dummies give the difference between the indicated region and Ontario.

2. More refined analyses, not reported in tabular form here, reveal that the two ethnic groups which stand out as one-sidedly Liberal are also one-sidedly Catholic: French and Italian Canadians. Non-Christian groups, notably Jews and immigrants of Third-World origin, also tend to be strongly Liberal.

Otherwise, religion cuts through ethnic groups. Among those of British Isles origin, for instance, the difference is as sharp as in the population as a whole; indeed, the Catholic/non-Catholic difference has often been sharper within the British group than is the difference between British Protestants and non-British Catholics. The differences within the British group are not merely between the Irish and the rest. About two-thirds of those who identify themselves as of Irish origin are Protestant. On this see also D.H. Akenson, *The Irish in Ontario: A Study in Rural History* (Montreal: McGill-Queen's University Press, 1984). Within the Irish-Canadian community the religious difference in party preference is very sharp. A substantial fraction of Scottish and English Canadians are Catholic and here too the religious cleavage is very clear. The Catholic/non-Catholic distinction also runs through many of the other ethnic elements ins the Canadian mosaic and never fails to divide a group politically. Immigrants are divided by religion as much as natives: not only are the Catholic/non-Catholic proportions much the same in the immigrant as in the native group but so is the Catholic/non-Catholic difference in party preference.

3. Support for the Parti Québécois, not analysed here, is concomitantly homogeneously francophone.

4. Note that the Conservative coefficient for "West" is smaller in provincial than in federal estimations. In part, this reflects the party's greater strength in Ontario in provincial than in federal elections. It also reflects the fact that the reverse was true in this period in the

West. The Conservative party, at least by that name, is all but extinct in British Columbia provincial politics. In Saskatchewan at the time of the survey the party was only part way through its climb out of organisational and electoral nullity.

5. This is not entirely true, but even here the situation is equivocal. The *Manitoba Act* (1870) gives the federal government a watching brief over separate schools in that province and controversy over Manitoba schools was intense in the 1890s. The controversy was initiated by a Liberal government which sought to restrict support for the schools. The national Liberal party supported its provincial counterpart against the hierarchy of the Church and against the Conservative government in Ottawa, which brought down a remedial bill under the terms of the *Manitoba Act.* All the while, Liberal electoral support in the Catholic community appears to have been building!
   On the other side of the ledger, the Laurier Liberal government inserted separate-school clauses into the *Alberta* and *Saskatchewan Acts* (1905) over the opposition of the Conservatives and of some English-Canadian Liberals. The Minister of the Interior and author of the government's open-door immigration policy, Clifford Sifton, resigned over the matter. And in latter Manitoba politics, the further extinction of separate school rights was associated with the Conservative government of Sir Rodmond Roblin. See P. Crunican, *Priests and Politicians: Manitoba Schools and the Election of 1896* (Toronto: University of Toronto Press, 1974); and M.R. Lupul, *The Roman Catholic Church and the North-West School Questions; A Study in Church–State Relations in Western Canada 1875–1905* (Toronto: University of Toronto Press, 1974).

6. And the persistence of the Catholic/non-Catholic cleavage cannot be explained away by reference to "socialization," as attempted by W.P. Irvine, "Explaining the Religious Basis of the Canadian Partisan Identity: Success on the Third Try," *CJPS* 7 (1974): 560–63; and W.P. Irvine and

H. Gold, "Do Frozen Cleavages Ever Go Stale? The Bases of the Canadian and Australian Party Systems," *British Journal of Political Science* 10 (1980): 187–218. See R. Johnston, "The Reproduction of the Religious Cleavage in Canadian Elections," *CJPS* 18 (1985): 99–113.

7. On ethnic (defined here as country of ancestry) differences, see above, note 2.

8. D.E. Blake, "Division and Cohesion among Canadian Party Activists," in *Party Democracy: The Politics of National Conventions,* ed. G.C. Perlin (Toronto: Prentice-Hall, 1987); R. Johnston, "The Ideological Structure of Opinion on Policy," in *Party Democracy,* ed. G.C. Perlin.

9. D.J. Elkins, "The Structure of Provincial Party Systems," in *Small Worlds: Provinces and Parties in Canadian Political Life* by D.J. Elkins and R. Simeon (Toronto: Methuen, 1980).

10. R. Johnston, *Public Opinion and Public Policy in Canada: Questions of Confidence* (Toronto: University of Toronto Press, 1986).

11. See for instance, N.H. Chi "Class Cleavage," in *Political Parties in Canada,* ed. C. Winn and J. McMenemy (Toronto: McGraw-Hill Ryerson, 1976).

12. Wilson, "Politics and Social Class in Canada."

13. For a review of the work on the class cleavage, see M.J. Brodie and J. Jenson, *Crisis, Challenge, and Change: Party and Class in Canada* (Toronto: Methuen, 1980), chap. 1. For a summary of two decades of estimates for the cleavage, see Archer, "The Failure of the New Democratic Party."

14. Brodie and Jenson, *Crisis, Challenge, and Change.*

15. A.C. Cairns and D. Wong, "Socialism, Federalism, and the B.C. Party Systems 1933–1983," in *Party Politics in Canada* 5th ed., ed. H.G. Thorburn (Scarborough: Prentice-Hall, 1985).

16. See D.E. Blake, "The Measurement of Regionalism in Canadian Voting Patterns," *CJPS* 5 (1972): 55–81; Elkins

and Simeon, *Small Worlds*, M.A. Schwartz, *Politics and Territory: The Sociology of Regional Persistence in Canada* (Montreal: McGill-Queen's University Press, 1974).

17. Well, almost unique. Alberta elections also frequently turn on federal–provincial relations. Although few Albertans see themselves as other than Canadians (Johnston, *Public Opinion and Public Policy*), their collective response to anti-Ottawa appeals tends to be overwhelming [T. Levesque and K. Norrie, "Overwhelming Majorities in the Legislature of Alberta," *CJPS* 12 (1979): 451–70.] Survey evidence gathered during the 1980–81 constitutional crisis indicates that Alberta and Quebec subsamples were more intensely divided than were subsamples in any other province; elsewhere, evaluations of federal and provincial governments remained strongly positively correlated (Johnston, *Public Opinion and Public Policy*.)

18. R. Johnston, "Federal and Provincial Voting: Contemporary Patterns and Historical Evolution," in *Small Worlds* by Elkins and Simeon.

19. For a review of the arguments and an empirical account see Johnston, "Federal and Provincial Voting."

20. It does not matter for my argument that popular vote majorities in Quebec are not always overwhelming. What is critical is that Quebec's distributions in the real currency of the parliamentary market, seats, have almost always been one-sided.

21. The last-choice item follows a second-choice item which refers to "the recent election." The last-choice item is: "Which of the federal parties would you least want to vote for?"
Ideally, we would like to characterise the full three-party ranking, but any attempt to do so would be dogged by what might be called revealed-preference problems. Does the vote actually cast indicate the sincere first preference or the strategically motivated second preference? In the absence of a direct question on the matter, side information is necessary to tease out the

answer. The second-choice item ("If, for some reason, you had been unable to vote for the federal party that you most preferred in the recent election, which other federal party would you have voted for?") talks of the first preference and might seem to allow for the possibility that the vote actually cast was strategic. But the item then casts the strategic choice as an hypothetical, which probably leads the voter toward an alternative to the actual vote, where that alternative might still be the real first preference. Use of the vote, the second preference, and the last preference to spin out the preference ranking may be possible but would require more validation work than time permits at this writing. The last choice question, notwithstanding the Social Credit option, has the virtue of being fairly unambiguous (even so, I suspect that many respondents fold strategic perceptions into the last choice item). Feeling thermometers give some idea of the full ranking and are employed in table 3 but yield rather flabby evidence.

22. Elkins, "The Structure of Provincial Party Systems."

23. Johnston, *Public Opinion and Public Policy.*

24. Two further comments are in order here. First, older voters may remember specifically religious characterisations of the nationality. Catholic conceptions of the nationality used to dominate debate in French Canada, of course [M. Brunet, "Trois dominantes de la pensée canadienne-française: l'agriculturisme, l'anti-étatisme, et le messianisme," in *La présence anglaise et les Canadiens: études sur l'histoire et la pensée de deux Canadas* by Brunet (Montreal: Beauchemin, 1964).] English Canadians commonly saw the country as essentially Protestant. As C. Berger remarks in "The True North Strong and Free," in *Nationalism in Canada*, ed. P. Russell (Toronto: University of Toronto Press, 1966): "A whole series of desirable national characteristics were derived from Canada's northern location. It was implied that northern peoples expressed their hard individualism in an individualistic religion, stripped of the

gorgeous luxuries congenial to southern Catholicism. The climate, said Parkin, imparts 'a puritan turn of mind which gives moral strenuousness.' " (p. 10; Parkin quotation from *The Great Dominion, Studies of Canada*, p. 216). C.J. Houston and W.J. Smyth in *The Sash Canada Wore: A Historical Geography of the Orange Order in Canada* (Toronto: University of Toronto Press, 1980) remind us that the Orange Order was remarkably polyethnic; its test of admission was religious. For an example of the continuing importance of religion as a badge of ethnic identity, see O. Macfarlane, "Stations of the Heart," *Saturday Night* 102, 4 (April 1987): 44–50.

Second, my argument ignores attitudes on the undoubtedly critical axis of Canadian–American relations. I neglect such attitudes here as I suspect that, these days, they lack an ethnoreligious base. In earlier decades, feelings about the British connection were probably inversely related to feelings about the United States and Canadians of British ancestry and Protestant religion probably anchored the anti-American pole of sentiment. This is implied by the Conservatives' historic position as the most anti-American party. Today ethnoreligious positions on the matter seem thoroughly confused and the Conservative party is now the most *pro*-American party. For party differences over Canadian–American relations see Blake, "Division and Cohesion among Canadian Party Activists." For the structure of sentiment on the issue within each party see Johnston, "The Ideological Structure of Opinion on Policy."

25. D.S. Spafford, "Electoral Systems and Voters' Behaviour," *Comparative Politics* 5 (1972): 129–34.

26. B.E. Cain, "Strategic Voting in Britain," *American Journal of Political Science* (*AJPS*) 22 (1978): 639–55; J.H. Black, "The Multicandidate Calculus of Voting: Application to Canadian Federal Elections" *AJPS* 22 (1978): 609–38.

27. L.M. Bartels, "Expectations and Preferences in Presidential Nominating Campaigns," *American Political Science Review* (*APSR*) 79 (1985): 804–15; H.E. Brady and R. Johnston, "Conventions vs Primaries: A Canadian–American Comparison," in *Party Democracy*, ed. Perlin.

28. P.E. Meehl, "The Selfish Voter Paradox and the Thrown-away Vote Argument," *APSR* 71 (1977): 11–30.

29. R. Johnston, D.J. Elkins, and D.E. Blake, "Strategic Voting: Individual Reasoning and Collective Consequences," (Paper prepared for delivery at the 1980 Annual Meeting of the American Political Science Association, Washington, D.C., 1980).

30. The correlation between the constituency-level and the province-level percentage Catholic hovers around 0.45.

31. The example in the text draws on estimations yet to be reported.

32. Strictly speaking, strategic arguments produce nonmonotonic predictions. If, for example, the Catholic share is so massive that a Conservative victory is very unlikely, then a unionist might just as well stay with the NDP. One can multiply examples like this for each group and party. As it happens, however, the actual distribution of Catholics across the provinces other than Quebec never produces a hegemonic Liberal stronghold. Growth in the Catholic proportion never gets beyond making the party competitive in a province taken as a whole, although there are some constituencies even outside Quebec where the Catholic proportion is overwhelming.

33. In Liberal and Conservative provincial estimations, British Columbia respondents are dropped. To all intents and purposes, neither party seriously contests provincial elections in that province. The weakness of the Liberals is perfectly consistent with my general argument and so a case might be made for keeping BC respondents in the Liberal estimation. A party's inability or unwillingness to offer candidates is mute, anticipatory testimony to the power of the strategic logic. Even so, prudence seemed to dictate dropping

provincial subsamples where the party failed to offer a choice. Doing so avoids an outlier effect, although a different kind of one from that presented by the Quebec subsample. The weakness of the Conservatives in BC is counterindicated by the model. It helps my case that the Social Credit party has many affinities with the Conservative party. But those affinities should not be pushed too far. Although the Liberal elements in the Social Credit coalition have declined in importance, some still remain.

34. In an earlier version of this paper, in which the party variables were derived from identifications rather than from the votes and in which the estimation strategy differed subtly from the one

here, the class basis of Conservative choice mirrored that for NDP choice almost perfectly.

35. See, for instance, P. Regenstreif, *The Diefenbaker Interlude: Parties and Voting in Canada* (Toronto: Longmans, 1965); H.D. Clarke, J. Jenson, L. LeDuc, and J.H. Pammett, *Absent Mandate: The Politics of Discontent in Canada* (Toronto: Gage, 1984).

36. J. Kelley and I. McAllister, "Social Context and Electoral Behavior in Britain," *AJPS* 29 (1985): 564–86; W.L. Miller, "Social Class and Party Choice in England: A New Analysis," *British Journal of Political Science* 8 (1978): 257–84.

section

3

CLASS AND VOTING

CLASS VOTING AND CLASS CONSCIOUSNESS IN CANADA[◇]

JON H. PAMMETT

ɔ

The relationship (or rather the absence of a relationship) between measures of individual location in the social class structure and voting in Canada has been a major puzzle for Canadian social science. Why, in an industrialized country, with the majority of the workforce making its living from employment, and with wide differentials in the standard of that living, have substantial social class differences not emerged in the public's choice of political parties? Was it because of the societal preoccupation with questions of national integration? Or did the elites running the political parties refuse to espouse class-relevant appeals? Did the problem lie with other institutions, like trade unions, whose bargaining strategies were more concerned with the financial security of their own members than the advancement of class interest? Or perhaps the reason was cultural—Canadians in general were not concerned to make a social class analysis of their society, or were so oriented toward the middle class as to obviate any recognition of class conflict.

Examinations of the relationships between social structure and voting traditionally begin with the Alford Index of class voting which subtracts the percentage of nonmanual workers voting for parties of the left from the percentage of manual workers doing so. Using Gallup Poll data, and considering the Liberals and the CCF/NDP as leftist parties, Alford found the mean class voting score for Canada to be +8 for the 1952–62 period, well below the index values for Britain, Australia, and the United States.[1] Subsequent applications of the Alford Index have identified various parties, or combinations of parties, as the appropriate left-wing alternatives, but have still found the amount of class voting to be low.[2] The index reaches its highest point when Social Credit is considered to be a left-wing party;[3] however, the reasoning used to classify that party as left-wing is controversial[4] and may be difficult to justify on the grounds of its recent ideology or policies.[5] In addition, the

◇ *Canadian Review of Sociology and Anthropology* 24, 2 (1987): 269–90.

virtual disappearance of Social Credit in recent elections makes its placing of rather marginal importance.

The 1979 National Election Study was used to calculate the relationships between the commonly used measures of social structure and voting.[6] With regard to the Alford Index, in no case is it over +10, regardless of whether farmers are considered manual or nonmanual workers, and regardless of which parties are considered to be left-wing. However it is calculated, this class voting index is low in Canada compared to Britain, where it was +27 in 1979 and had been much higher in previous years.[7] The correlation of income with voting in 1979 produces a small relationship (V=.05), as does the Blishen score of social status (V=.06).[8]

The relationship between standard categories of occupation and voting is displayed in table 1, which ranks the groupings in terms of the percentage voting NDP in 1979. Those in unskilled labour occupations give the highest amount of support to the NDP. Second in terms of NDP voting comes skilled labour, but the difference between this and some other occupational groups is not large. In addition, these two labour groups do give substantially less support to the Conservative party than the others. From the perspective of a class voting pattern, however, the position of the semiskilled category among those giving below-average support to the NDP is disconcerting, as is the low level of support for that party among clerical/sales employees, since such employees are a borderline category in class analysis[9] and are sometimes considered to be members of the working class in objective class rankings.[10] Overall, the Liberals captured the votes of a plurality of the occupational categories involving manual workers in 1979, and its degree of labour support resembled that from the professions and business.

Revisionist interpretations of the class/vote connection have resulted from dissatisfaction with the performance of the variables displayed above, and have gone in several directions.[11] We have already noted how political parties have been re-considered as proper recipients of left-wing votes.[12] In addition, some analysts have looked within the broad national picture at the situation in certain provinces like B.C.,[13] certain constituencies like Waterloo South,[14] and certain historical time points like wartime Winnipeg,[15] finding in each case a higher than average degree

TABLE 1   *VOTE OF OCCUPATIONAL GROUPS, 1979 (%)*

	NDP	PC	Lib
Unskilled labour	25	28	40
Skilled labour	19	30	45
Small business	18	37	42
Large business/managerial	17	34	46
Semiskilled labour	15	36	43
Semiprofessional	14	49	36
Professional	13	40	44
Farm	13	56	29
Clerical/sales	12	38	49

V = .11
N = 2115

of social class voting. In another approach, efforts have been made to define and measure social class structure from a Marxist or neo-Marxist perspective, as in the work inspired by Erik Olin Wright. These new class categories in Canadian research have not noticeably improved the correlations with partisanship and voting[16] but have produced some connections with political ideology.[17]

The most important alternate way of looking at the class–vote relationship has been premised on the limited nature of opportunities for such voting. Sometimes, this has been stated very generally, as in Schwartz's comment that "class-based voting exists; it is class-based parties that are missing."[18] Brodie and Jenson argue that elites of all political parties tend to avoid class issues and class polarization.[19] Empirical work on the party images held by the public has persuaded some analysts that voters are prepared for (and even desirous of) a politics of class, if only the parties would respond.[20] In other work, it is shown that among voters who know the "correct" positions of the parties on a left–right dimension (i.e., place the NDP to the left of the Liberals) class voting is higher,[21] and if measures of the voters' subjective perceptions of the party positions are used, class voting rises.[22] Finally, it has been shown that in areas of NDP strength, where the party is more electorally viable and votes less likely to be shifted to other less-preferred parties for strategic reasons, class voting is higher, though class effects even there are "not overwhelming."[23]

It is significant that one direction not regularly taken in the empirical or theoretical examination of class and vote has been a move from the objective to the subjective dimensions of class. This involves more than the simple substitution of the standard subjective class variable for objective variables like occupation or income, or the examination of party image data. Rather, it is important that attention be paid to the concepts of class formation and class consciousness or identification in examining the problem of the low levels of class voting in Canada. To explain the lack of correspondence between class structure and voting choice we must explicitly attend to class formation and consciousness in order to develop persuasive arguments about present and possible future behaviour of voters and parties.

Class formation, in normal Marxist formulations, is the transition from a class-in-itself to a class-for-itself.[24] Classes exist, in the objective sense, in terms of the structure of social relations entered into by individuals. While the class structure may thus determine the "class interests" of individuals, class formation "refers to the formation of organized collectivities within that class structure on the basis of the interests shaped by that class structure."[25] And class consciousness, to cite Wright again, is "the realization by subordinate classes that it is necessary to transform the class structure if there are to be any basic changes in their capacities to act, and the realization by dominant classes that the reproduction of their power depends upon the reproduction of the class structure."[26] If class can meaningfully shape political (in this case, electoral) behaviour, it needs to be supported by organisational structures and to be accompanied by conscious feelings that it is the appropriate vehicle for that behaviour. Without such consciousness any consensus on appropriate goals and instrumental organisations is unlikely to exist.

Nevertheless, if classes are to be formed and people to be conscious of their class interests, the relative importance of the organisations and the terms used to characterise the classes must still be established. In both traditional Marxist and

Social Democratic thought, the agents for class formation have been the party and the trade union. As for the vocabulary of class, it may be argued that terminology like "working class," "class struggle," "class conflict," and even "class" itself, is not often used in the political discourse in a country like Canada. If this is true, it is not clear what agreed-on terminology could be substituted to organise the formation of classes and generate consciousness, and it is difficult to see how a common class consciousness could arise without an implicit consensus on a lexicon.

If a "pocketbook vote" is a vote determined by individual self-interest and calculated by the electoral outcome most likely to bring this about, the class vote is most logically considered an indirect pocketbook vote. It interposes, between the individual interest and the voting choice, a calculation of group interest, and presupposes an identification of the individual with the group. In such a class-voting model, individuals must be conscious of class as an entity (however defined), identify with it, and determine which electoral choice would be most likely to advance that group interest, assuming indirect individual benefit through direct class benefit. This class-voting model can be distinguished from more general "sociotropic" models, in which a judgement is made about the electoral outcome most likely to bring about an improvement in the whole society, thereby benefiting everyone. Class formation, and class identification or consciousness, are important preconditions for the existence of a class-voting situation, as opposed to either direct pocketbook or sociotropic voting.

With these considerations in mind, this paper will examine various explanations for the low levels of class voting. These explanations can be roughly divided into those we might call Cultural/Attitudinal and those which are Elite/Institutional. Explanations of the former sort hold the low level of class consciousness responsible for the lack of class formation, while the latter hold the lack of class formation responsible for the low level of class consciousness. The former thus proposes cultural attitudes or ideology as the causative agents, while the latter identifies elite behaviour as the reason. Choosing between these alternate approaches has often been a matter of the researcher's personal ideology.[27] However, my argument is that a choice between them, at least on the grounds of empirical evidence, is currently impossible, since the variables used to test them are not measured in the same analytical dimension. Institutional and individual behaviour are both relevant to the class-voting questions.

CULTURAL/ATTITUDINAL HYPOTHESES

1. The low level of class consciousness in Canada has made class politics irrelevant and class voting unimportant.
2. The identification with class which does exist is predominantly with the middle class, which also makes class politics irrelevant as it creates little demand for a working-class alternative.
3. Class consciousness is highly variable over time, and this instability inhibits class formation from taking place.
4. The lack of correspondence between occupation and class identification inhibits class voting from taking place.

ELITE/INSTITUTIONAL HYPOTHESES

5. Potentially structuring institutions, especially unions, have not developed class issues or educated their members or other members of the working class.
6. The lack of class parties, especially of major status, has meant that the institutional mechanisms for class politics are absent. Class formation and class consciousness are not encouraged and developed.

This listing by no means exhausts the hypotheses about low class voting in Canada. It ignores, for example, the traditional argument that class issues in Canadian politics have been pre-empted by issues of national integration.[28] This explanation properly belongs in both the Cultural and Elite categories used above, since the impetus for this situation can be seen as coming from either the society at large, or from elite manipulation of the political agenda. While one cannot ignore elite and mass public concern for issues of national unity, French–English relations, language, intergovernmental relations, regional autonomy, and other related formulations of problems of Canadian integration, at no time since opinion polling began in Canada have such issues been ranked by public majorities as the most important facing the country.[29] Economic problems have been the overwhelming public response to such questionnaire items. In the years immediately prior to the Quebec Referendum, for example, the average number of Canadians citing integration problems in answer to the Gallup Most Important Problem question was less than 10 per cent (versus over 70 per cent mentioning economic problems). While the elite agenda has certainly given more attention to integration issues than such levels of public concern might warrant, economic issues have certainly not been downplayed in Canada, particularly during election campaigns. That these economic issues have not been discussed by elites, or interpreted by the public, in class terms is another point entirely.[30] That situation can be, in its turn, interpreted as evidence of elite manipulation or cultural norms.

HYPOTHESIS ONE: THE LOW LEVEL OF CLASS CONSCIOUSNESS

Only a minority of Canadians (42 per cent in 1979) think spontaneously of themselves as belonging to a social class.[31] When forced to make a class choice (by the question wording "Well, if you had to make a choice....") and then asked several other questions about the nature of class relations, 54 per cent of the sample report feeling "pretty close" to their own class, while 33 per cent do not. When asked whether there is "bound to be some conflict between classes," Canadians split down the middle—46.5 per cent feel that this is a true statement, while 46.2 per cent think that classes "can get along together without conflict." In either case, half of Canadians feel that politics are not concerned with relations between classes, one-quarter that they help classes get along, and another quarter that they make things worse. Finally, about half of the Canadian citizenry feel that one class gets too much and/or pays too much in terms of societal benefits or costs.

While some of the closed-ended questions just cited reveal that about half of the electorate is willing to discuss class relations in a conflictual context, the low

TABLE 2   CHARACTERISTICS OF PEOPLE IN
OWN OR OTHER CLASSES (%)

Class Defined in Terms of	Own Class	Other Classes
Income	41	53
Occupation	60	26
Education	5	12
Possessions	8	22
Personal characteristics	41	21
	N = 2108	N = 1910

Note: In tables 2, 3, 4 percentages are of cases. Multiple responses permitted. Other responses and denials of difference omitted.

levels of spontaneous class identification support the hypothesis that class consciousness in Canada is weak.[32] The 1979 National Election Study dataset permits a unique elaboration on this analysis, in that it contains a special sequence of open-ended questions which ask about the "kinds of people" who are in one's own class and in other classes. In Britain, where class alignments are relatively strong and stable compared to Canada, occupation is predominant in descriptions of who belongs to classes.[33] People within British classes are defined in terms of what they do, indicating if not necessarily a Marxist awareness of exploitation and relations to the means of production, at least an awareness of society's occupational structure. Without such awareness, it is difficult to see how class formation could occur.

Table 2 shows the dominant content of Canadian perceptions of class membership. In defining their own class, 60 per cent of respondents used an occupational definition, while just over 40 per cent referred to a particular level of income, and a group of similar size referred to personal qualities (honesty, niceness, etc.). There is some basis for thinking that people judge the social class they consider to be "like them" according to the kinds of jobs they do, and only to a lesser extent according to the amount of money made or the kinds of possessions attained. When it comes to other social classes, however, income was twice as important as occupation in identifying who these other people might be, and a more sizeable group thought about the possessions other classes enjoyed.[34] To the extent that a meaningful class analysis of society depends, at the very least, on identifying particular groups with different places in the social structure from "one's own," Canadians generally are disinclined to define such a group in terms of their occupations. Instead, they feel that society contains a substantial number of individuals who make more money than they do, or receive other benefits for which they did not work, and at times feel that this is unjust. It is not what the other classes do that is important—it is just how much they have.

Table 3 shows the items mentioned by those who felt a social class received undue benefits. Those most frequently mentioned were government services (primarily welfare-related) and tax breaks. While the second of these relates, at least in part, to popular perceptions of how the rich can evade proportional taxation, the first directly indicates middle-class resentment of those who are poorer benefiting from the welfare system. These grievances about other people receiving more than they deserve may possibly indicate some potential for class formation at the upper

TABLE 3   UNDESERVED BENEFITS
           RECEIVED BY OTHER
           CLASSES (%)

	% Mentioning
Government services	39
Tax benefits	34
Financial benefits	24
Possessions	13
Political power	12
Jobs	4
Legal benefits	3
Education	1
Other	4
	N = 1257

end of the class structure (with a resulting potential impact on the lower part of the structure). However, it is doubtful that these responses indicate deep-rooted discontent with the social class structure. Categories which might indicate such deeper feeling are present in table 3, namely beliefs that other classes are in differential positions of political power and can structure the system to their benefit, and feelings that other classes benefit from preferable jobs, but these categories are distinctly less populated than many of the others.

The public's analysis of the class system may be indicated by answers to a final question in the open-ended sequence reviewed. In this case, those who believed either that one class received too much in the way of benefits, or paid too much in the way of costs (just over half the sample) were asked the reasons for this. Table 4 reports the results. By far the most popular culprit for class inequality is the tax system, with a majority feeling that other people are being favoured by the revenue department. This feeling is, however, so generalized that we cannot conclude that only rich capitalists with tax shelters are implied. The fact, for example, that many of the poor pay lower rates and amounts of tax is also resented by the middle class, and the tax advantages to the married and to families with children are resented by

TABLE 4   REASONS FOR CLASS
           INEQUALITIES (%)

	% Mentioning
The taxation system	58
Political power	18
The welfare system	14
Class structure	13
Financial differences	12
It's the way of the world	7
Population distribution	5
Government	5
Injustice in general	3
Group behaviour	1
	N = 1380

TABLE 5   THE CANADIAN SUBJECTIVE
CLASS STRUCTURE, 1979 (%)

	Spontaneous	Forced Choice
Upper Class	.2	.5
Upper middle class	5.5	9.9
Middle class	25.3	53.7
Working class	10.1	32.6
Lower class	.8	3.2
Does not think of class	58.3	+
	N = 2605	N = 2388

+ Refusals and Don't Knows omitted.

the single. As with table 3, we may assert that those mentioning "unequal political power" and the class structure itself are most likely to sustain a conflictual structural analysis of social class. However, it bears repeating that some of the resentment comes from the feeling that the poor have been the favoured ones through their ability to get "something for nothing" from government programs and services.

HYPOTHESIS TWO: THE MIDDLE-CLASS NATURE
OF CLASS IDENTIFICATION

The predominantly middle-class nature of Canadian subjective class identification may be noted from table 5. When a forced choice by the rest of the sample is added to those spontaneously offering a class identification, over half of Canadians are middle-class identifiers. In such a forced-choice situation, about one-third of Canadians identify with the working class.

While working-class identification is limited in Canada, such a choice can be related to objective class variables. The TauBeta of spontaneous class identification and income is .34, and the mean of the identification categories on the Blishen score divided into four quartiles is 3.5 (out of 4) for the upper-middle class, 2.8 for the middle class and 2.2 for the working class. The relationship between spontaneously

TABLE 6   OCCUPATION AND CLASS SELF-
IDENTIFICATION, 1979 (%)

Occupation	Spontaneously Identifying with Working Class	With any Spontaneous Identification
Professional	1	65
Semiprofessional	17	56
Big business/managerial	7	54
Small business	26	48
Clerical/sales	18	46
Skilled labour	42	42
Semiskilled labour	54	47
Unskilled labour	45	37
Farmers	27	29
	N = 712	

TABLE 7   *CLASS CONSCIOUSNESS AND*
          BELIEFS IN INEVITABILITY OF
          CLASS CONFLICT, 1974-79 (%)

A. Class Consciousness over 5 Years

Keeps thinking in terms of class	28
Starts thinking in terms of class	16
Stops thinking in terms of class	18
Never thinks in terms of class	39

$N = 1265$
$Phi = .32$

B. Inevitability of Class Conflict over 5 Years

Continues to believe it	30
Starts believing it	18
Stops believing it	23
Never believes it	29

$N = 1208$
$Phi = .17$

chosen social class consciousness and occupation is shown in table 6. Only manual labour occupations contain large numbers of working class identifiers, although about a quarter of small business persons and farmers and a fifth of clerical/sales personnel feel themselves to be working class. Overall, however, when a simple manual/nonmanual split is made in the population, the manual occupations are more likely to have a middle- or upper-middle class identification than a working-class consciousness (52 per cent versus 48 per cent) and furthermore, only 43 per cent of manual workers have any spontaneous class consciousness at all.

Using several questions from the 1979 survey to determine the potential constituency of those making a full class analysis of society, a group of people was identified who: 1. spontaneously thought in terms of class; 2. felt that class conflict was inevitable in society; 3. could identify a class which benefits unduly; and 4. cited a class which pays too much. This group of about 200 people (8 per cent of the sample) is slightly more middle class in identification than the total, more likely to think the middle class pays an undue amount, and more likely to think politics hurt rather than help class relations. Several "degrees" of class awareness were used in alternate analyses, and the results were much the same. Any search for a militant working class on which to base Canadian class voting is doomed to be restricted to a small group of people.

Furthermore, the search would reveal a satisfied group of people.[35] When questioned about their degree of satisfaction with the material side of their lives, 62 per cent of those identifying with the working class declared themselves at least "fairly" satisfied with the material standard of living. This satisfaction level is not as high as that of the middle- and upper-middle-class identifiers; 81 per cent of that group is at least "fairly" satisfied with the material side of their lives. Nevertheless, the working-class satisfaction level is reasonably high, and furthermore there is no indication that those who are dissatisfied among the working class are any more likely to have a class consciousness.

HYPOTHESIS THREE: VARIABILITY IN CLASS CONSCIOUSNESS OVER TIME

One contributing element to the overall weakness of Canadian class consciousness may be its tendency to fluctuate over time. The instability of spontaneous feelings of class consciousness makes class politics harder to sustain and discourages elites from a commitment to class rhetoric or education. We can use the 1974–1979 National Election Study panel to investigate the stability or variation within class consciousness.

Panel A of table 7 shows that feelings of class consciousness in Canada are indeed unstable. Over the 1974–79 period, only 28 per cent of Canadians spontaneously maintained the opinion that they belonged to a social class. Even this figure is somewhat misleading, since of that group of people who continued to be conscious of class, less than two-thirds (63 per cent) considered themselves members of the same class at the two points in time. In particular, the percentage with a consistent working-class identification is exactly the same as that percentage moving from working- to middle-class consciousness over the five years (12 per cent of those with a class identification at the two times). Overall, then, only 3 per cent of Canadians maintain a spontaneous working-class identification over a five-year period. Panel B of table 7 also indicates that less than one-third of the population maintains a belief over five years that conflict is inevitable between the classes.[36]

HYPOTHESES FOUR: THE INTERACTION OF SUBJECTIVE AND OBJECTIVE CLASS MEASURES

The nature of class voting in Canada can be examined in detail by employing both the variable of spontaneous class identification already examined and the objective class variable of occupation. We have already seen that the two are only moderately related (table 6). Table 8 shows us that the presence or absence of class consciousness relates much more substantially to Liberal and Conservative voting than to support for the NDP. Thus, of those Canadians with a feeling of class consciousness, 47 per cent voted Liberal in 1979, while of those without such a feeling, 45 per cent voted Progressive Conservative.

The negative association of class consciousness and Conservative voting holds across all the occupational categories displayed in table 8. For the Liberals, however, the situation is much more variable; it is mainly in the professional, semiprofessional, clerical/sales and farm groups that the class conscious are more likely to vote Liberal. There is very little difference in the subjective class basis of Liberal support in the small and large business categories, and in two of the three labour categories the relationship is actually reversed. In particular, among unskilled labour, the class conscious tend less to support the Liberals and the Conservatives, and more to support the NDP and Social Credit. With NDP voting, class consciousness appears most important in the three labour categories, although it is also interesting to note that those who are conscious of class in the big business/managerial occupations are twice as likely to vote NDP as those who are not.

TABLE 8 CLASS CONSCIOUSNESS, OCCUPATION, AND VOTE, 1979 (%)

		Occupation								
		Total Sample		Professional		Semiprofessional		Big Business		Small Business	
Class Consciousness:		Yes	No	Yes	No	Yes	No	Yes	No	Yes	No
1979 Vote	Lib	47	38	48	38	46	28	48	43	43	41
	PC	32	45	35	44	38	57	26	45	34	41
	NDP	17	15	13	14	15	14	22	10	19	18
	SC	4	2	3	3	1	1	4	2	4	0
		V = .13		V = .10		V = .19		V = .22		V = .16	
		N = 2044		N = 578		N = 285		N = 150		N = 214	

		Clerical/Sales		Skilled Labour		Semiskilled Labour		Unskilled Labour		Farm	
		Yes	No	Yes	No	Yes	No	Yes	No	Yes	No
1979 Vote	Lib	57	43	49	45	41	44	36	43	46	16
	PC	31	44	22	34	28	44	21	31	49	62
	NDP	12	12	25	14	22	9	30	22	0	22
	SC	1	2	4	7	10	3	14	3	5	0
		V = .16		V = .19		V = .25		V = .23		V = .44	
		N = 265		N = 140		N = 148		N = 152		N = 58	

TABLE 9   VOTING BEHAVIOUR OF OBJECTIVE AND
SUBJECTIVE CLASS GROUPS, 1979

Class Group	Vote in 1979				% of Electorate
	Lib	PC	NDP	SC	
Nonmanual occupation, with spontaneous middle-class identification+	49%	37	13	2	22
Nonmanual occupation, with spontaneous working-class identification++	45%	22	31	2	3
Nonmanual occupation, no spontaneous identification	37%	48	14	1	28
Manual occupation, with spontaneous middle-class identification	42%	29	21	8	8
Manual occupation, with spontaneous working-class identification	44%	28	21	7	8
Manual occupation, no spontaneous identification	40%	40	16	4	26
Farm occupations excluded from table					5

+ Middle-class identification includes upper and upper-middle class categories.
++ Working-class identification includes lower class category.

Before concluding that it is necessarily working-class consciousness that is important to NDP (or Liberal) support, table 9 presents some confounding evidence. It shows that working-class identification supports the propensity to vote NDP only within nonmanual occupations, such as those managerial types we noted in table 8. And intriguing as this finding is, we should not fail to note that only 3 per cent of the total sample falls into such a situation of "reverse class consciousness," with almost half voting Liberal. When it comes to those with manual occupations, simply having a class consciousness makes a person somewhat more likely to vote NDP (21 per cent versus 16 per cent) but it makes no difference at all whether that identification is with middle class or working class.

Table 9 reveals a weak relationship between both subjective and objective class variables and voting in Canada that may be contrasted usefully with an identical analysis undertaken on the British Election Study of 1979.[37] Even though class/vote relationships have declined in Britain since the mid-1960s, Robertson shows substantial differences in support for the Labour Party between those manual workers who see themselves spontaneously as working class and those who do not, and between those who are or are not manual workers regardless of class self-identity. In Canada it makes only a moderate amount of difference to NDP support whether a person is a manual worker or not (table 1), a very small amount of difference whether a person is conscious of class or not (table 8), and any difference at all whether a person has a working-class identification or not only in the case of one sparsely inhabited category (table 9).

HYPOTHESIS FIVE: THE UNION LINK

The connection of the NDP with organised labour, through the endorsement of the party by the Canadian Labour Congress and the direct affiliation with it by a number of union locals, has been a mixed blessing for the party. On the one hand, the financial and campaign help from labour has been important. On the other, the fact that Canadian unions have been primarily interested in the material advancement of their own members has meant that unions are perceived as special interest groups rather than the vanguard for the working class and society's exploited in general. Thus, the NDP has become identified with only one part, the more prosperous part, of the working class. This has made it difficult for either unions or party to act as agents of class formation, and to work to raise class consciousness, since the interests of nonunionized workers do not necessarily coincide with those of the unionized.

TABLE 10   SOCIAL CLASS IDENTIFICATION AND UNION MEMBERSHIP, 1979 (%)

Class Identification	Union Family	Nonunion Family
Upper or upper middle class	11	16
Middle class	64	57
Working or lower class	25	27
	N = 500	N = 573

It can be argued, however, that the union link has brought the NDP some votes, or at least has solidified existing patterns. In 1979, for example, those survey respondents who were either union members, or had a union member in their family, voted NDP at a 21 per cent rate, while in contrast, of those without a union connection, only 11 per cent supported the NDP. Isolating those respondents from families with more than one union member, the proportion voting NDP rises to 24 per cent. And in a detailed analysis of members from those union locals affiliating with the NDP, Archer reports that 30 per cent voted for the party in the 1979 Federal election.[38] However, the percentage of union members belonging to locals affiliating with the NDP is low and declining—by 1981 it was only 8 per cent of Canadian unionists.[39]

Most tellingly for any potential role of unions as agents of class politics, the modest link of union membership with NDP voting described above does not emerge from a working-class consciousness of union members. While those with a family union member tend more to have a class consciousness than those from nonunion families (49 per cent versus 41 per cent), this is more likely to be a middle-class identification than a working class one (table 10). To the extent that the behaviour of union elites can be inferred from the member attitudes, few efforts at working-class consciousness raising appear to exist.

The degree of connection of unions with working-class consciousness does vary somewhat with the type of union concerned (table 11). Members of international unions are less likely to declare that they belong to a social class, but those

TABLE 11 CHARACTERISTICS OF UNION TYPES (%)

Types of Unions	With Class Consciousness	Working Class Consciousness	Voting NDP	
International	41	35	26	N = 134
National	54	23	20	N = 233
Federations	62	3	13	N = 65

who do so are more likely to choose the working class as their own. The international unions (which at the time of the study included the United Auto Workers, a union most supportive of the NDP) are more likely to be industrial unions. Canadian unions, more likely to be in the public sector and to be organisations of nonmanual workers, have been less outspoken in support of the NDP. Federations, like teachers' and other professional organisations, and farmers' organisations, have a particular clientele; while their members are quite conscious of social class, they are virtually unanimous that they belong to the middle classes, and they support the NDP at a lower than average level (though not as low as one might expect if they identified the NDP as a working-class party).

HYPOTHESIS SIX: THE LACK OF CLASS PARTIES

In direct opposition to the view that the Canadian public desires a class politics not provided by parties,[40] the reverse has also been maintained, that whereas the Canadian public may not yet be ready for class politics, there are class parties which will be ready for the public when that time eventually comes.[41] To the extent that these arguments are based on judgements about party elite behaviour, they are not amenable to testing with individual level data. Chi's argument cited above, however, is based on an assessment of the support base of the party, and the judgement that NDP support comes disproportionately from the working class. By employing the federal party identification measure[42] from the 1979 National Election Study we can examine the question "Of what kinds of people are the parties composed?" If the party clienteles look different on objective or subjective class dimensions, we might be more willing to make inferences about class formation and the parties' potential willingness to act as agents of class consciousness raising. In the former case, they might be more likely to act to reinforce a distinctive base of support.

Table 12 provides some limited evidence that the NDP, and particularly Social Credit, have more credibility as parties with working-class support bases than do the Liberals and the Conservatives. The difference shows up most clearly with the occupational characteristics of the party identifiers. By this measure, almost half (46 per cent) of Social Credit support is from the three manual labour categories, and just over a third (34 per cent) of identifiers with the New Democrats have manual labour jobs. When it comes to class consciousness, while the levels of such feeling among supporters of three of the four parties are much the same (with the Conservatives 10 per cent lower, in line with the earlier findings of table 8), the class conscious among NDP and Socred supporters are twice as likely to identify with the working class as are Conservative and Liberal partisans.

TABLE 12   *COMPOSITION OF PARTY SUPPORT, 1979*

	Liberals	Progressive Conservatives	New Democrats	Social Credit
Income: % of high or moderately high income families				
	59	56	56	46
Blishen score: % with Blishen score above the mean				
	51	48	40	18
Occupation:				
Professional	30%	32%	20%	26%
Semiprofessional	13	19	13	7
Big business/manager	8	6	8	7
Small business	10	11	13	4
Clerical/sales	15	12	11	6
Skilled labour	8 ⎫	4 ⎫	10 ⎫	11 ⎫
Semiskilled labour	7 ⎬ 21	6 ⎬ 16	10 ⎬ 34	22 ⎬ 46
Unskilled labour	6 ⎭	6 ⎭	14 ⎭	13 ⎭
Farm	2	5	3	3
Class consciousness: % with class consciousness				
	48	38	48	51
% of class conscious with working-class identification				
	22	21	40	41

While this analysis of table 12 has pointed out the differences between the parties, and noted that the composition of support for the NDP and Social Credit was somewhat different on some class variables, a fair assessment of the evidence must indicate that those two parties do not really have working-class support bases, and hence cannot realistically be called "working-class parties." In particular, the NDP consists of only one-third holders of manual occupations, and less than 20 per cent of its supporters are spontaneous working-class identifiers (40 per cent of the 48 per cent of NDP identifiers who have a spontaneous class consciousness). Therefore, while one might conclude that the NDP is slightly more working class than the Liberals and Conservatives with regard to its support, overall it resembles the middle-class parties.

CONCLUSION

The analyses in this paper support the hypotheses advanced to explain the low levels of class voting in Canada. Hypotheses resting on the low levels of class consciousness, and its middle-class nature, have clear evidence in their support. Those believing that unions and political parties have not reflected class formation or attempted to enhance class consciousness in the electorate are also justified. The disjunctions between the levels of analysis that measure the important variables in these competing explanations make it impossible, however, to test them against each other in a multivariate model. We can measure many individual attitudinal variables, but our consideration of party and union behaviour was restricted to looking at member attitudes and social characteristics.[43]

The Cultural/Attitudinal hypotheses examined say that Canadian society is not class conscious, and that these societal attitudes prevent elites from acting to promote class politics, or at least make it tactically unsound for them to do so. The argument, then, is that individual attitudes cause a lack of elite action, a proposition virtually impossible to test, even if data from candid elite interviews were available. The Elite/Institutional hypotheses have the reverse problem, in that they posit that the lack of elite action causes a particular set of individual attitudes to at least sustain itself. As thus formulated, such a proposition is as difficult to deal with as the previous one. Both involve cross-level inference, and would require much more synthetic datasets, containing matched individual and aggregate variables, than are currently available. The negative character of all these arguments—concerning attitudes *not* possessed, elite actions *not* engaged in, adds to the difficulties of empirically examining the relative plausibility of the arguments.

It is best, then, to regard the two lines of argument as interactive and equally plausible, rather than as alternatives between which to choose. The fact that individual attitudes are as they are, and that elite actions or inactions are consistent with them, combine to keep class politics in Canada relatively irrelevant, along with class voting resulting from class politics. With this perspective in mind, we can evaluate whether increases in class politics and class voting could come about from increased class consciousness on the part of the mass public, or increased class formation on the part of elites and institutions.

What are the possibilities for a rise in class consciousness in the mass public, that could lead to class formation? Probably low, given the current public disinclination to think in terms of class conflict. Even if the realization of place in the class structure were to develop further, a parallel rise in feeling that class conflict is inevitable must exist for a class struggle interpretation to be widely held. Patterns in the rest of the world give little encouragement that these feelings might develop from example, since social class connections with party support seem to be declining all over the industrialized world.[44] Canada would seem an unlikely place for a countertrend to appear.

And what are the possibilities for a rise in class formation by left-wing political parties, leading to elite attempts to create more working-class consciousness in the public? A number of dilemmas face any working-class party or socialist party attempting to act this way, and the NDP has been caught in these dilemmas for much of its existence.[45] NDP elites have tended primarily to move to broaden support by diluting ideology rather than by broadening class consciousness in the electorate.

Given prevailing public attitudes which perceive other social classes primarily in terms of consumption levels rather than structural characteristics (table 2) the appeal of a Canadian socialist party has been based on enhanced distribution of benefits to have-not sectors of society. Given the prevailing public acceptance of "restraint" arguments in the 1980s, this appeal would be difficult to expand. The NDP could attempt to broaden the basis of class definition by extending it to sex, ethnicity or region, but this could weaken the link to the economic structure and make it less likely that an agreed-on lexicon for class analysis would emerge.[46]

Another possibility would be to broaden the arguments for socialism from the realm of the consumption of material goods into areas of lifestyle—quality of life, freedom, leisure, freedom from violence, etc.[47] Again, however, this would tend to weaken the overt class link.

Another possibility, following the American or British example, would be an attempt at class formation on the part of a middle-class party, rather than a working-class one. If the Progressive Conservatives were to pursue policies of attacking the consensus on universal social programs, for example, they might raise an opposing group consciousness which would approximate that of the working class without using the vocabulary of class. The flexibility of partisanship in Canada[48] could allow a realignment on the basis of such distributional issues if the issues were sufficiently crucial and sustained. It seems highly unlikely that the Canadian Progressive Conservative party would pursue such a right-wing ideological program, however, and even if it did this might not raise class consciousness in the electorate, given that this has not happened in the United States and Britain despite Republican and Conservative party behaviour.

The combined weakness of class formation and class consciousness or identification in Canada makes the likelihood of a class-voting increase remote at the present time. Without these key links, a class voting model of indirect self-interested voting is not a promising avenue for the analysis of Canadian voting behaviour. Canadian voting seems much more sociotropic, with the parties identifying broad national problems with the economy, translating them into general election issues like inflation, unemployment, the state of the currency and the extent of the deficit, and the electorate rendering an overall judgement about which party might be most likely (or least likely) to improve the total picture. Under such circumstances, the electorate makes few connections between personal financial circumstances or relations of exploitation in the economic structure and these vast national problems. Without those connections, however, class voting cannot develop.

NOTES

1. R. Alford, *Party and Society* (Chicago: Rand-McNally, 1963), 102.

2. M.A. Schwartz, "Canadian Voting Behavior" in *Electoral Behavior* ed. R. Rose (New York: Free Press, 1974), 543–618; H.D. Clarke, J. Jenson, L. LeDuc, and J. Pammett, *Political Choice in Canada* (Toronto: McGraw-Hill Ryerson, 1979); R.D. Lambert and A.A. Hunter, "Social Stratification, Voting Behaviour and the Images of Federal Political Parties," *Canadian Review of Sociology and Anthropology* (*CRSA*) 16 (1979): 287–304.

3. R. Ogmundson, "Party Class Images and the Class Vote in Canada,"

American Sociological Review 40 (1975): 506–12; J.F. Myles, "Differences in the Canadian and American Class Vote: Fact or Pseudofact?" *American Journal of Sociology* 84 (1979): 1232–37; J.F. Myles and D. Forcese, "Voting and Class Politics in Canada and the United States," *Comparative Social Research* 4 (1981): 3–31.

4. R. Ogmundson, "On the Measurement of Party Class Positions: The Case of the Canadian Federal Parties," *CRSA* 12 (1975): 565–76.

5. M. Stein, *The Dynamics of Right Wing Protest: A Political Analysis of Social*

Credit in Quebec (Toronto: University of Toronto Press, 1973).

6. The 1979 National Election Study is based on a national probability sample of 2744 respondents. 1295 of these respondents were interviewed at the time of the 1974 election as well, and form a 1974–79 panel which will be used later in the paper. For more details about the study, see H.D. Clarke, J. Jenson, L. LeDuc, and J. Pammett, *Absent Mandate: The Politics of Discontent in Canada* (Toronto: Gage, 1984).

7. B. Sarlvik and I. Crewe, *Decade of Dealignment* (Cambridge: Cambridge University Press, 1983).

8. The measure is developed in B.R. Blishen and H. McRoberts, "A Revised Socioeconomic Index for Occupations in Canada," *CRSA* 12 (1976): 71–79.

9. E.O. Wright, *Classes* (London: Verso, 1985).

10. D. Butler and D. Stokes, *Political Change in Britain* 1st ed. (London: Macmillan, 1969); see discussions in R.F. Hamilton, *Class and Politics in the United States* (New York: Wiley, 1972) and in D. Robertson, *Class and the British Electorate* (Oxford: Basil Blackwell, 1984).

11. R.J. Brym, "Trend Report: Anglo-Canadian Sociology," *Current Sociology* 34 (1986): 1–152.

12. Myles, "Differences in the Canadian and American Class Vote."

13. D. Blake, *Two Political Worlds: Parties and Voting in British Columbia* (Vancouver: U.B.C. Press, 1985).

14. J. Wilson, "Politics and Social Class in Canada: The Case of Waterloo South," *Canadian Journal of Political Science* (*CJPS*) 1 (1968): 288–309.

15. N. Wiseman and K.W. Taylor, "Ethnic versus Class Voting: The Case of Winnipeg, 1945," *CJPS* 7 (1974): 314–28.

16. A.P.M. Williams, D. Bates, M.D. Ornstein, and H.M. Stevenson, "Class Ideology and Partisanship in Canada" (Paper presented at CPSA meetings, Saskatoon, 1979); J.F. Zipp and J. Smith, "A Structural Analysis of Class

Voting," *Social Forces* 60 (1982): 738–59.

17. M.D. Ornstein, H.M. Stevenson, and A.P. Williams, "Region, Class and Political Culture in Canada," *CJPS* 13 (1980): 227–71; W. Johnston and M.D. Ornstein, "Class, Work and Politics," *CRSA* 19 (1982): 196–214.

18. Schwartz, "Canadian Voting Behavior," 589.

19. M.J. Brodie and J. Jenson, *Crisis, Challenge and Change: Party and Class in Canada* (Toronto: Methuen, 1980).

20. R. Ogmundson, "Mass-Elite Linkages and Class Issues in Canada," *CRSA* 13 (1976): 1–12; J.F. Zipp, "Left-Right Dimensions of Canadian Federal Party Identification: A Discriminant Analysis," *CJPS* 11 (1978): 251–78; R. Ogmundson, "Liberal Ideology and the Study of Voting Behaviour," *CRSA* 17 (1980): 45–54.

21. B. Erickson, "Region, Knowledge and Class Voting in Canada," *Canadian Journal of Sociology* 6 (1981): 121–44.

22. R. Ogmundson and M. Ng, "On the Inference of Voter Motivation: A Comparison of the Subjective Class Vote in Canada and the United Kingdom," *Canadian Journal of Sociology* 7 (1982): 41–59.

23. Zipp and Smith, "A Structural Analysis of Class Voting," 753.

24. A. Przeworski, "Proletariat Into a Class: The Process of Class Formation from Karl Kautsky's *The Class Struggle* to Recent Controversies," *Politics and Society* 7 (1977): 343–401.

25. Wright, *Classes*, 9–10.

26. Ibid., 28.

27. For one exchange see E.M. Schreiber, "Class Awareness and Class Voting in Canada: A Reconsideration of the Ogmundson Thesis," *CRSA* 17 (1980): 37–44 and Ogmundson, "Liberal Ideology and the Study of Voting Behaviour."

28. Alford, *Party and Society*; J. Porter, *The Vertical Mosaic* (Toronto: University of Toronto Press, 1965); Brodie and Jenson, *Crisis, Challenge and Change*.

29. Clarke et al., *Absent Mandate*; J.H. Pammett, "Inflation, Unemployment and Integration," in *The Integration Question: Political Economy and Public Policy in Canada and North America*, ed. J.H. Pammett and B.W. Tomlin (Toronto: Addison-Wesley, 1984).

30. Schreiber, "Class Awareness and Class Voting in Canada"; Ogmundson, "Liberal Ideology and the Study of Voting Behaviour"; Clarke et al., *Absent Mandate*.

31. The question used in the spontaneous class consciousness variable reads: "One hears a lot about different social classes. Do you ever think of yourself as belonging to a social class?" Respondents answering "Yes" were asked "Which of the following social classes would you say you were in: upper class, upper-middle class, middle class, working class or lower class?"

32. M.P. Marchak, *Ideological Perspectives on Canada* (Toronto: McGraw-Hill Ryerson, 1975); Schreiber, "Class Awareness and Class Voting in Canada"; A.A. Hunter, *Class Tells: On Social Inequality in Canada* (Toronto: Butterworths, 1981).

33. D. Butler and D. Stokes, *Political Change in Britain* 2d ed. (London: Macmillan, 1974), 70.

34. In their 1970 Toronto sample, Grabb and Lambert reported that responses to the question "What do you think are the differences between social classes?" contained "surprisingly few respondents who referred specifically to occupation ($N = 59$ [out of a sample of 3218])" (E.G. Grabb and R.D. Lambert, "The Subjective Meanings of Social Class Among Canadians," *Canadian Journal of Sociology* 7 [1982]: 297–307.)

35. Note that the measure being discussed here is satisfaction with material well-being not with job. On the latter, see J.W. Rinehart, "Contradictions of Work-Related Attitudes and Behaviour: an Interpretation," *CRSA* 15 (1978): 1–15.

36. Social mobility itself may also be measured with these data. One-quarter of the sample moved in five years between quartiles of the Blishen scale,

although the TauBeta between the two time points is .77. More of this movement is upward than downward; however, social mobility is not associated with any diminution of class feeling. The upwardly mobile tend less to think that any class pays or gets too much of the costs or benefits of society. The downwardly mobile have not changed their class identification appreciably (the upwardly mobile are somewhat more likely to have upgraded theirs), nor do they tend to see the inevitability of class conflict or to feel closer to members of their class. They are more likely to think that politics has nothing to do with class conflict, and they are more likely to have voted Liberal than any other group (though they are also more likely to have voted NDP than those who stayed in their social place).

37. Robertson, *Class and the British Electorate*, 84.

38. K. Archer, "The Failure of the New Democratic Party: Unions, Unionists, and Politics in Canada," *CJPS* 18 (1985): 353–66.

39. Ibid., 361.

40. Schwartz, "Canadian Voting Behavior"; Ogmundson, "Mass-Elite Linkages"; Ogmundson, "Liberal Ideology and the Study of Voting Behaviour."

41. N.H. Chi, "Class Voting in Canadian Politics" in *The Canadian Political Process* ed. O. Kruhlak et al., 2d ed. (Toronto: Holt, Rinehart and Winston, 1973), 226–47.

42. For an outline of the party identification measure see Clarke et al., *Political Choice in Canada*, 412. Note that, in the analysis reported in this paper, the "leaners" (those who declined party identification in the initial question but who responded positively to a follow-up asking if they felt "a little closer" to one of the parties) are not included.

43. In an effort to sort out the predictive power of the attitudinal variables employed in the paper, a series of multiple regression analyses were run to determine the most significant, "class related" predictors of 1979 vote for

each party. The variables employed were: Class identification (middle or working); occupational type (manual or nonmanual); union membership; level of material satisfaction; having a class consciousness in both 1974 and 1979, or not; believing in the inevitability of class conflict in 1974 and 1979, or not.

The class variables taken together have weak predictive power in explaining vote for the three parties. The multiple *R* for all predictor variables is .18 for Liberal voting, .19 for Conservative voting, and .20 for NDP voting. Thus, less than 5 per cent of the variance in the vote for any of the parties can be explained by considering the whole set of class-related variables available to us in the dataset.

NDP voting, in contrast, is best predicted by an institutional factor, the presence of union membership, either in the respondent or in the immediate family. This variable emerges from stepwise regressions no matter what set of class-relevant predictors is employed, and indicates the relative importance to the party of the union link, even though, as we have seen, such a link may

not appear in itself very strong. The second significant predictor of voting for the NDP is attitudinal, the feeling that class conflict is inevitable over time, indicating at least some element of support for the party that accepts a conflictual class analysis.

44. R.J. Dalton, S.C. Flanagan and P.A. Beck, *Electoral Change in Advanced Industrial Democracies* (Princeton: Princeton University Press, 1984).

45. L. Zakuta, *A Protest Movement Becalmed* (Toronto: University of Toronto Press, 1964); W. Young, *The Anatomy of a Party* (Toronto: University of Toronto Press, 1969); Brodie and Jenson, *Crisis, Challenge and Change.*

46. Przeworski, "Proletariat Into a Class."

47. Wright, *Classes.*

48. Clarke et al., *Political Choice in Canada*; L. LeDuc, H.D. Clarke, J. Jenson and J. Pammett, "Partisan Volatility in Canada: Evidence from a New Panel Study," *American Political Science Review* 78 (1984): 470–84.

SOCIAL CLASS, LEFT/RIGHT POLITICAL ORIENTATIONS, AND SUBJECTIVE CLASS VOTING IN PROVINCIAL AND FEDERAL ELECTIONS[◇]

RONALD D. LAMBERT, JAMES E. CURTIS,
STEVEN D. BROWN AND BARRY J. KAY

o

INTRODUCTION

Since Alford and later, the Lenskis, presented evidence on how Canadians were much less likely than citizens of other western, industrialized nations to vote for political parties ostensibly orientated to their own social classes, researchers have subjected this finding to a variety of tests.[1] Among the more provocative studies dealing with this phenomenon have been those reported by Ogmundson.[2] Using data on the 1965 federal election, he showed that the strength of the relationship between people's social class and their federal party vote depended largely on whether researchers defined the social class orientations of political parties in terms of experts' opinions or in terms of what the voters themselves thought. The strength of the relationship was the greatest when the presumed class interests of political parties were defined by the voters themselves. This procedure allowed Ogmundson and Ng[3] to account for much of the discrepancy between the levels of class voting observed in Canada and the United Kingdom as measured by expert opinion.[4] It would appear, therefore, that the comparatively low level of class voting in Canada using experts' opinions is at least partially attributable to greater disagreement between experts' and voters' ideas about the class orientations of Canadian parties. Our calculations of class voting in this paper rely on the subjective class voting (SCV) procedure of asking respondents themselves to judge political parties' class orientations.

◇ *Canadian Review of Sociology and Anthropology* 24, 4 (1987): 526–49.

The analyses reported here depart in a number of important respects from previous research on the SCV. First, we analysed class voting at the federal level *within provinces*, where frequencies permitted, using data from the 1984 Canadian National Election Study of CNES[5] This allowed us to test predictions about which provinces should manifest the highest and the lowest levels of subjective class voting in individual-level data. Second, the scale measuring the class orientations of the parties in the 1984 CNES was defined in terms of "for the lower social classes" vs. "for the higher social classes," whereas the 1965 and 1968 CNES studies, which have been widely utilised in earlier studies of the class vote, used a scale whose end points were labelled "for the working class" vs. "for the middle class." The change was introduced in the 1984 CNES to test the assumption that class conflict, if it is perceived, is more likely to be between the lower and upper social classes, instead of between the lower and middle social classes.[6] Third, the 1985 CNES asked respondents to rate their respective provincial parties, as well as the federal parties, on the social class scale. We were able, therefore, to test for provincial class voting within provinces and across provinces. Fourth, our approach was multivariate. We were interested in the combined and relative effects of the traditional set of "objective" social class measures (income, occupation and education) on respondents' voting behaviour.[7] Fifth, we coded each of the social class measures into as many levels as frequencies permitted, instead of treating them as dichotomies as Ogmundson and Lambert and Hunter did.[8] This permitted us to inspect the pattern of effects associated with each predictor for any apparent departures from linearity. As well, the measurement of parties' class orientations was retained as a seven-point scale rather than dichotomizing it as in previous research. Finally, we distinguished between the so-called "objective" social class indicators, on the one hand, and social psychological indicators of class identification and class beliefs, on the other, as predictors of class voting. We treated respondents' social class self-placements and their left/right political orientations as intervening variables standing between their "objective" social class and the subjective class vote. We were interested in exploring the extent to which these social psychological variables 1. might interpret any objective social class effects, and 2. might magnify the estimates of the extent of class voting.

The foregoing analyses were repeated using respondents' beliefs about how they thought they would vote if a "provincial [federal] general election were being held today. . . . " These analyses of what might be called SCV *intentions* were undertaken because the comparisons between class voting at the two political levels did not cover the same time frame. The voting questions asked respondents about a federal election that had occurred only a few months before the interviews, and about provincial elections that had occurred as much as three years earlier.

WORKING HYPOTHESES

The purpose of our analyses is to test predictions about interprovincial and provincial vs. federal differences in SCV. Our point of departure is the proposition that appeals to parochial interests by federal parties, coupled with regional variations in the party system across Canada, typically override appeals to class interests as determinants of the vote. The analyses addressed three kinds of questions. First, is class voting stronger provincially than federally? Second, are the effects of social class on voting behaviour more pronounced in some provinces than in others, and does the pattern of interprovincial differences make sense in light of what we know about party politics in the provinces? And, third, how significant are intervening social psychological variables in explaining the presence of SCV?

DIFFERENCES BETWEEN PROVINCIAL AND FEDERAL LEVELS OF CLASS VOTING

The meaning and appeal of each of the federal parties vary greatly across the country, reflecting the different preoccupations of Canadians with questions of region, language and ethnicity. Indeed, the parties shape their platforms and campaigns to appeal to these regionally based priorities. The net effect of regionally oriented politics should, therefore, work to suppress the level of class voting when the latter is measured overall and with respect to federal politics. We expected higher levels of class voting at the provincial level than at the federal level within provinces.

DIFFERENCES IN CLASS VOTING BETWEEN PROVINCES

Brym and Wilson have provided two reasonable rationales for predicting patterns of provincial differences in SCV.[9] For Brym, class voting is conceptualized at the aggregate level, in terms of the proportion of the electorate voting for the NDP, rather than at the individual level. He has shown that most of the interprovincial differences in the levels of support for the NDP are attributable to the relative power of the working class in the different provinces.[10] Brym indexed the strength of the working class in each province according to 1. the proportion of the population that belongs to labour unions and co-operatives and 2. per capita income. His analyses showed that union and co-operative membership explained more of the inter-provincial differences than did per capita income.[11] We have therefore used the former criterion to order the provinces in terms of predicted class voting. The highest level of class voting should occur in Saskatchewan, intermediate levels in Manitoba, British Columbia and Alberta, and the lowest levels in the remaining provinces. Brym's hypothesis would seem to offer little basis for predicting different patterns in SCV at the provincial and federal levels in so far as his explanatory variables do not differ between the two levels of government. Presumably we would have to look elsewhere for an explanation of any such differences.

Wilson's hypothesis is cast in terms of provincial political cultures and the economic conditions which produce them.[12] He distinguished

> three rather different points on a time scale of economic, social, and political development: preindustrial or beginning industrial society, industrializing society, and advanced industrial society ... [N]ot only will there be important and perhaps fundamental differences between the dominant social and political institutions at different points on the scale—due to the very different needs and interests of the society which

each point represents—but the leading political beliefs and values at each point are likely to vary substantially as well.[13]

The structure of the party system in each province was used to categorize the four Atlantic provinces at the underdeveloped stage vs. Quebec, Ontario, Manitoba and British Columbia at the transitional stage vs. Alberta and Saskatchewan at the developed stage.

Wilson argued that people's political participation and the character of their support for political parties reflect the different stages in the development of their societies. Thus, "social class is a more important political cleavage in an advanced system while religious affiliation is more significant in an underdeveloped system. ..."[14] In his view, roughly the same kind of party system prevails at the two levels of government within provinces.[15] On the basis of Wilson's theory, we were led to predict the strongest relationship between the measures of social class and the class orientations of the parties for which people voted in Saskatchewan and Alberta.[16] The weakest relationships should appear in the four Atlantic provinces, with British Columbia, Manitoba, Ontario and Quebec falling somewhere between the two extremes.

The principal differences between the Brym and Wilson predictions seem to lie in their rankings of Alberta and Quebec. On the basis of his 1974 article, Wilson would have relatively more class voting taking place in Alberta and Quebec than Brym does. However, Wilson has had second thoughts and has "downgraded" these two provinces on the basis of what he has observed since 1974.[17] In the latter case, there is little to choose between Brym's and Wilson's overall rank orders, although the dynamics accounting for them may well differ.

EXPLAINING THE CLASS VOTE

Broadly speaking, there are two ways of explaining how social class affects people's voting behaviour. In the first, social class—as income, occupation and education—is seen to structure people's opportunities by defining their positions within systems of social interaction. It is not assumed that people need to reflect upon their social class as a precondition for class-based activities. The second perspective on the problem presupposes that reflexive thinking about social class forges the necessary links between the objective circumstances of people's lives and their behaviour. In this view, it is necessary to develop a social psychology of these intervening processes to understand fully the direction of people's behaviour.

To explain the vote in the second approach, we must conceive of subjective social class and various other social psychological factors as intervening variables located between social class and the voting decision. We used social class self-placement and left/right political orientations to explore, first, their independent effects on class voting, and second, the extent to which they mediated the effects of (objective) social class on class voting. We expected that people who think of themselves in specifically class terms would more likely translate their class memberships into class votes. Moreover, we expected self-defined leftists more than rightists to vote for parties which they perceived to favour the lower social classes.[18]

TABLE 1 OBJECTIVE SOCIAL CLASS INDICATORS & PROVINCIAL LEVEL SUBJECTIVE CLASS VOTING (MCA)**

Analysis of:	Atlantic			Quebec			Ontario			Manitoba		
Grand Mean =	4.21			4.06			4.23			4.02		
	N	Unadj.	Adj.	N	Unadj.	Adj.	N	Unadj.	Adj.	N	Unadj.	Adj.
Education												
Elem. & some hi	76	.04	.15	151	-.08	-.02	224	.02	.12	50	-.06	-.14
Hi graduate	33	-.13	-.11	133	.04	.05	112	-.23	-.20	27	.32	.24
Post-hi	24	-.01	.05	142	.05	.05	114	.23	.21	36	.09	.19
Univ. graduate	22	.09	-.43	65	.00	-.16	85	-.05	-.33	33	-.26	-.19
e/b =			.05/.14			.04/.06			.10/.14			.15/.15
F =		0.63			0.39			2.88+			0.84	
Income												
Less than $10K	62	-.27	-.27	176	-.15	-.18	184	-.25	-.33	62	-.10	-.08
$10–20K	28	-.31	-.31	109	-.15	-.14	115	.08	.15	36	.34	.30
$20–30K	17	.31	.37	94	.13	.14	94	.00	.05	20	-.48	-.57
$30–50K	21	.25	.20	51	.12	.14	75	.38	.43	19	.16	.18
$50K+	3	—	—	22	.43	.46	18	.17	.26	6	—	—
DK; Refused	23	.53	.54	39	.39	.40	50	.08	.03	4	—	—
e/b =			.24/.25			.15/.16			.14/.18			.20/.22
F =		1.69			2.02			2.68+			1.30	
Occupation												
Hi white collar	28	.36	.41	106	.10	.02	138	.26	.24	44	-.12	-.04
Lo white collar	20	-.19	-.19	85	-.08	-.07	102	-.37	-.38	24	.39	.34
Hi blue collar	53	-.03	-.06	128	.06	.04	146	-.11	-.25	44	-.21	-.22
Lo blue collar	21	-.20	-.13	38	-.25	-.24	39	.28	.31	8	—	—
Farmer	2	—	—	18	.08	.06	15	.29	.34	8	—	—
Homemaker	30	-.04	-.08	116	-.03	.06	95	.04	.27	18	.07	-.02
e/b =			.13/.14			.08/.06			.16/.19			.19/.17
F =		0.35			0.37			3.59++			0.75	
Variance Explained =		7.9%			2.8%			6.3%			9.2%	

TABLE 1 CONTINUED

Analysis of:	Saskatchewan			Alberta			B.C.			National		
Grand Mean =	3.57			4.39			3.91			4.12		
	N	Unadj.	Adj.	N	Unadj.	Adj.	N	Unadj.	Adj.	N	Unadj.	Adj.
Education												
Elem. & some hi	74	-.32	-.23	41	.31	.25	55	-.26	-.11	708	-.02	.05
Hi graduate	27	.48	.62	40	.13	.23	56	.16	.29	465	-.01	.02
Post-hi	45	.23	.25	47	-.19	-.23	61	.30	.11	499	.10	.11
Univ. graduate	20	.01	-.50	21	-.41	-.42	30	-.43	-.56	291	-.11	-.33
e/b =		.21/.25			.20/.21			.16/.16			.05/.10	
F =		3.18*			1.68			1.70			4.90**	
Income												
Less than $10K	71	.16	.19	44	-.14	-.06	82	-.30	-.42	713	-.21	-.24
$10–20K	37	-.33	-.32	38	-.36	-.44	33	.07	.06	419	-.06	-.06
$20–30K	24	-.10	-.16	23	.13	.12	26	.07	.17	322	.07	.09
$30–50K	21	.35	.32	20	-.10	-.07	35	-.18	-.08	259	.17	.21
$50K+	5	—	—	5	—	—	14	1.82	2.07	78	.63	.69
DK; Refused	8	—	—	19	.86	.81	12	.13	.13	172	.34	.34
e/b =		.21/.21			.29/.29			.31/.35			.15/.17	
F =		1.33			2.46+			4.55*			9.25*	

TABLE 1 CONTINUED

Analysis of:	Saskatchewan			Alberta			B.C.			National		
	N	Unadj.	Adj.	N	Unadj.	Adj.	N	Unadj.	Adj.	N	Unadj.	Adj.
Grand Mean =	3.57			4.39			3.91			4.12		
Occupation												
Hi white collar	32	.50	.63	41	-.25	-.02	56	-.02	.02	476	.13	.12
Lo white collar	14	.14	-.08	32	.33	.14	36	.31	.28	345	-.07	-.08
Hi blue collar	20	-.60	-.59	22	.12	.21	45	.08	-.29	495	-.02	-.09
Lo blue collar	9	—	—	11	-.07	-.28	17	-.86	-.78	155	-.12	-.10
Farmer	46	-.20	-.09	18	.33	.19	2	—	—	95	.10	.04
Homemaker	44	.17	-.02	26	-.31	-.34	45	-.07	.23	397	-.04	.07
e/b =		.24/.24			.21/.16			.19/.21			.06/.06	
F =		1.32			0.64			1.83			1.33	
Variance Explained =		13.7%			14.9%			16.1%			3.1%	

Significance levels:
+ p < .05
++ p < .01
** p < .001
** Scores are deviations (plus or minus) from the appropriate grand mean. Unadj. = deviations unadjusted for other variables in the table; Adj. = deviations adjusted or controlled for other variables. National weights used for Atlantic provinces and for national analyses; provincial weights used for individual provinces.

DATA SOURCE AND MEASUREMENTS

The 1984 Canadian National Election Study employed a multi-stage, stratified cluster sample of the electorate, with systematic oversampling of the less populous provinces.[19] The raw sample of 3377 respondents was weighted (N = 3380) to make it nationally representative for analyses involving more than one province. For the analyses within single provinces, we employed provincial weights in order 1. to make each sample provincially representative and 2. to exploit the larger number of respondents who were interviewed in the smaller provinces, but which would not be available using the national weights.

We created two *party class orientation* variables by asking respondents to rate each of the federal parties and each of the provincial parties in their respective provinces on the seven-point "for the lower social classes" vs. "for the higher social classes" scale; and then we assigned the appropriate ratings given by each person to the parties for which he or she reported voting at each level.[20] Parallel versions of these variables were also constructed in terms of respondents' federal and provincial voting intentions.

The five predictor variables included the three measures of socio-economic status traditionally employed in SCV studies—occupation, income and education. As noted, however, we utilised more detailed codes than in the previous studies, as follows: *education* (some high school or less, high school graduate, some post high school, university graduate); *income* (total 1983 pre-tax income less than $10 000/year, $10–20 000, $20–30 000, $30–50 000, $50 000+, don't know and refused; *occupation* (professional, owner, manager, executive; sales, clerical; skilled labour; unskilled labour; farmer; homemaker). The social psychological predictor variables were: *subjective social class* (upper class, upper-middle class; middle class; working class, lower class);[21] and *left/right political orientation* (left-of-centre, centre, right-of-centre, no answer and don't know).[22] *Province* was also used as a control variable in supplementary analyses of the combined Atlantic provinces and for the national analyses of SCV, at both the federal and provincial levels.

Our analyses employed Multiple Classification Analysis (MCA) and various measures of association.[23] In MCA, we adopted the convention of not reporting estimates for a category on a dependent variable where there were fewer than ten cases.

FINDINGS

RESULTS FOR THE OBJECTIVE SOCIAL CLASS VARIABLES

Table 1 reports on the levels of class voting for *provincial* parties in each of the provinces, as well as in the combined Atlantic provinces and nationally.[24] The strongest relationship between social class and SCV appeared in British Columbia (16.1 per cent variance explained), Alberta (14.9 per cent), and Saskatchewan (13.7 per cent), while the lowest amounts occurred in Quebec (2.8 per cent), and Ontario (6.3 per cent). The total explained variance was 7.9 per cent in the four Atlantic provinces. Nationally, only 3.1 per cent of provincial SCV was explained by the three social class measures.

TABLE 2 OBJECTIVE SOCIAL CLASS INDICATORS AND FEDERAL LEVEL SUBJECTIVE CLASS VOTING (MCA)**

Analysis of:	Atlantic			Quebec			Ontario			Manitoba		
	N	Unadj.	Adj.	N	Unadj.	Adj.	N	Unadj.	Adj.	N	Unadj.	Adj.
Grand Mean =	4.26			4.32			4.40			4.12		
Education												
Elem. & some hi	80	.13	.17	161	-.16	-.11	275	.02	.09	53	-.27	-.30
Hi graduate	39	-.16	-.17	138	.26	.27	141	-.04	-.03	31	.26	.21
Post-hi	37	-.33	-.31	158	-.17	-.16	186	.05	.06	46	.20	.23
Univ. graduate	29	.28	.14	62	.27	.08	112	-.08	-.29	38	-.07	-.03
e/b =			.15/.14			.15/.13			.03/.09			.17/.17
F =		1.10			2.94+			1.44			1.42	
Income												
Less than $10K	75	-.12	-.11	217	-.19	-.20	283	-.03	-.08	73	-.07	-.05
$10-20K	35	-.17	-.15	104	.03	.04	145	-.15	-.11	36	.13	.15
$20-30K	16	.15	.23	83	.07	.09	111	.04	.08	22	-.27	-.44
$30-50K	28	.17	.16	51	.41	.45	88	.32	.35	24	.16	.22
$50K+	4	—	—	20	.21	.18	21	-.02	.01	6	—	—
DK; Refused	26	.17	.09	45	.14	.12	67	-.01	-.02	7	—	—
e/b =			.13/.12			.14/.15			.09/.10			.11/.16
F =		0.40			1.74			1.26			0.75	
Occupation												
Hi white collar	34	.11	-.03	110	.09	-.02	189	.17	.21	51	-.02	-.05
Lo white collar	23	-.11	.02	74	.12	.08	149	-.18	-.16	27	.38	.36
Hi blue collar	65	.04	.02	135	-.12	-.14	184	-.08	-.17	50	-.20	-.14
Lo blue collar	24	-.55	-.50	61	-.06	.00	56	-.11	-.11	12	-.33	-.33
Farmer	3	—	—	17	.13	.05	16	.43	.42	8	—	—
Homemaker	35	.27	.33	122	.00	.12	122	.08	.13	21	.22	.18
e/b =			.17/.16			.07/.07			.10/.13			.17/.15
F =		0.89			0.48			1.85			0.65	
Variance Explained =		5.9%			4.3%			2.4%			6.9%	

TABLE 2 CONTINUED

Analysis of:	Saskatchewan			Alberta			B.C.			National		
Grand Mean =	3.74			4.41			4.23			4.31		
	N	Unadj.	Adj.	N	Unadj.	Adj.	N	Unadj.	Adj.	N	Unadj.	Adj.
Education												
Elem. & some hi	82	-.17	-.08	47	.09	.10	62	-.21	-.18	811	-.05	.00
Hi graduate	29	.53	.48	44	-.09	-.04	69	.01	-.03	536	.07	.08
Post-hi	41	.02	.04	65	-.12	-.10	82	.12	.08	668	-.04	-.02
Univ. graduate	22	-.13	-.42	30	.25	.12	35	.08	.19	346	.08	-.08
$e/b =$		.16/.17			.11/.08			.08/.08			.04/.04	
$F =$		1.34			0.32			0.40			0.91	
Income												
Less than $10K	78	-.14	-.31	73	-.24	-.20	103	-.29	-.31	964	-.14	-.16
$10–20K	34	-.05	.09	35	.17	.15	47	.10	.09	469	-.03	-.01
$20–30K	28	-.05	.12	30	.09	.06	31	.41	.44	349	.09	.11
$30–50K	19	.08	.13	23	.11	.02	35	-.01	.01	287	.24	.26
$50K+	8	—	—	4	—	—	15	.99	.99	82	.37	.38
DK; Refused	7	—	—	21	.22	.28	16	-.13	-.09	212	.10	.08
$e/b =$		.19/.26			.17/.15			.22/.23			.10/.11	
$F =$		1.97			0.70			2.24+			4.94*	

TABLE 2 CONTINUED

Analysis of:	Saskatchewan			Alberta			B.C.			National		
Grand Mean =	3.74			4.41			4.23			4.31		
	N	Unadj.	Adj.	N	Unadj.	Adj.	N	Unadj.	Adj.	N	Unadj.	Adj.
Occupation												
Hi white collar	33	.18	.20	49	.23	.17	70	-.08	-.22	580	.11	.07
Lo white collar	12	.50	.40	46	-.22	-.19	51	.22	.18	427	-.02	-.02
Hi blue collar	21	-.31	-.54	29	.11	.14	60	.16	.08	592	-.04	-.07
Lo blue collar	13	-.21	-.10	12	.01	.00	19	-.34	-.25	214	-.17	-.13
Farmer	45	-.20	-.34	19	.00	-.11	2	—	—	96	-.02	-.05
Homemaker	49	.13	.34	31	-.13	-.06	46	-.20	.10	454	.01	.11
e/b =			.15/.22			.15/.12			.12/.12			.06/.06
F =		1.37			0.44			0.61			1.34	
Variance Explained =		10.3%			4.9%			6.5%			1.5%	

Significance levels:
+p < .05
++p < .01
✦p < .001
✦✦See footnote to table 1.

Income proved to be the most important of the three social class predictors in the national analysis. The effects were quite regular across income levels, with and without controls ($F = 9.25$; $p < .001$). As respondents' reported income went up, so did their tendency to vote for provincial parties perceived by them to favour the higher social classes. The adjusted mean scores for the lowest and the highest income levels were 3.88 and 4.81, respectively. The pattern of effects for education demonstrates the desirability of employing more than a binary split on this variable. Its effects were significant ($F = 4.90$; $p < .01$) and somewhat curvilinear. The adjusted effect for respondents who had obtained a degree was 3.79, compared to 4.23 for respondents who had progressed beyond high school but stopped short of a degree. A curvilinear relationship, or course, departs from the idea of subjective class voting, which supposes a linear relationship. The effect for occupation was not statistically significant.[25]

In view of the curvilinear relationship between education and the perceived class orientation of the parties for which respondents voted, we extracted some additional descriptive statistics for respondents who had obtained university degrees. Among these people, 91 voted for the federal Liberals and rated it 4.28 on the scale "for the lower social classes" vs. "for the higher social classes" (standard deviation = 1.04). The mean rating that the 202 Conservative voters gave their party was 5.05 (sd = 0.94), and that the 72 New Democratic voters gave the NDP was 2.72 (sd = 1.05). Comparing these figures with those for the electorate in general (see note 20), we see that university-educated respondents who reported voting Liberal or NDP believed these parties were more lower class orientated, while those who said they voted Conservative believed their party was more higher class orientated.[26] The net effect of these differences, then, was to produce a curvilinear education effect, with somewhat greater levels of self-professed lower class voting among the most educated respondents than among those with intermediate levels of education.

The effects of the three social class measures were more spotty and irregular in the provincial level analyses (see the other columns of table 1). As can be seen, all three predictors showed significant relationships with SCV in Ontario. Outside Ontario, however, income was a significant predictor only in British Columbia and Alberta, education only in Saskatchewan, and occupation in no other province.

Table 2 parallels the preceding table by summarising the results for federal level SCV. Comparing these two tables, first, it is clear that the total explained variance was higher for provincial class voting than for federal class voting in every comparison, save Quebec. In British Columbia, for example, R-squared was 6.5 per cent federally vs. 16.1 per cent provincially. In the case of Quebec, the exception to the rule, the figures were only 2.8 per cent for provincial SCV and 4.3 per cent for federal SCV.

In the national analysis, income was the only social class variable that reached significance ($F = 4.94$; $p < .001$). Although the adjusted mean scores were all around the midpoint, the higher respondents' incomes, the more they reported voting for parties perceived as biased in favour of the higher social classes. In the provincial analyses of federal SCV, income was a significant predictor only in British Columbia ($F = 2.24$; $p < .05$); although the pattern was less regular than in the national analysis, the adjusted mean scores for the lowest and highest income categories were 3.92 and 5.22, respectively.

RESULTS FOR THE SOCIAL PSYCHOLOGICAL INTERVENING VARIABLES

We added subjective social class and left/right orientations to the three objective social class measures as predictors in tables 3 and 4. This time, the latter variables were treated as control variables. As expected, we explained much more variance in the extended analyses compared to the analyses in which the intervening variables were omitted. By themselves, the three objective measures of social class explained 9.2 per cent of the variance in provincial SCV in Manitoba, 13.7 per cent in Saskatchewan and 16.1 per cent in British Columbia (see table 1). Adding the social psychological variables increased these figures to 22.9 per cent in Manitoba, 24.1 per cent in Saskatchewan, and 23.7 per cent in British Columbia (table 3). For federal politics, the figures rose from 6.9 per cent to 20.4 per cent in Manitoba; 10.3 to 23.3 per cent in Saskatchewan and 6.5 to 19.4 per cent in British Columbia (comparing tables 2 and 4).

Comparisons of tables 3 and 4 also show that the total explained variance in the federal SCV was less than for the provincial SCV in Ontario, Manitoba, Alberta and British Columbia, as well as nationally. The difference was less than a percentage point in Saskatchewan. In Quebec and the Atlantic provinces, however, the extended set of predictors explained more variance in federal SCV than in provincial SCV.

The *betas* in table 3 demonstrate that left/right orientation was a more substantial predictor of provincial SCV than was subjective social class in all comparisons. The *F*-tests show that left/right orientation was a statistically significant predictor in each of the analyses, except for the combined Atlantic provinces. In every case where the effect was significant, left-wingers were most likely to vote for a party biased toward the lower social classes, and right-wingers were most likely to vote for a party biased toward the higher social classes. The table also shows the interesting finding that those respondents who did not report their left/right orientations tended to place their subjective votes in the centre–right region, except in Quebec.[27]

In contrast with the left/right orientation variable, subjective social class achieved statistical significance only in Ontario, British Columbia and nationally (table 3). In these three instances, the expected pattern of effects was produced, with working class respondents supporting parties oriented to their social class and upper class respondents voting for parties oriented to their social class.[28]

The *betas* in table 4 show that the left/right self-rating was clearly a more important predictor than subjective social class for federal SCV in all provinces except Quebec, where these two variables had similar effects. In Manitoba, the *beta* for the left/right variable was .39, compared to .12 for subjective social class. The comparable figures were .36 vs. .18 in Saskatchewan and .30 vs. .18 in British Columbia. The *F*-tests show statistically significant effects for left/right orientation in all analyses except those for Atlantic Canada and Alberta. Moreover, this predictor showed the expected pattern of effects wherever it was significant. Once again, respondents who produced missing values on the left/right scale were generally in the centre–right region of SCV. Subjective social class was a significant predictor in Quebec, Ontario, British Columbia and nationally; and its effects were patterned as expected.

TABLE 3   SUBJECTIVE SOCIAL CLASS, LEFT/RIGHT POLITICAL ORIENTATIONS, AND PROVINCIAL LEVEL SUBJECTIVE CLASS VOTING, WITH CONTROLS (MCA)**

Analysis of:	Atlantic			Quebec			Ontario			Manitoba		
Grand Mean =	4.20			4.05			4.23			4.03		
	N	Unadj.	Adj.	N	Unadj.	Adj.	N	Unadj.	Adj.	N	Unadj.	Adj.
Subjective Social Class												
Upper	10	.28	.23	51	.03	-.03	53	.28	.34	12	-.48	-.07
Middle	64	.11	.10	330	.07	.06	245	.27	.25	77	.16	.01
Lower	73	-.13	-.12	100	-.24	-.20	223	-.36	-.36	53	-.13	.00
e/b =			.09/.08			.09/.08			.21/.21			.16/.02
F =		0.40			1.46			10.30*			0.02	
Left/Right Self-Rating												
Left	14	-.21	-.04	62	-.35	-.30	65	-1.03	-.99	20	-1.27	-1.34
Centre	32	.20	.22	102	.15	.12	158	-.16	-.14	33	.29	.33
Right	28	.29	.17	138	.26	.24	140	.49	.41	44	.12	.05
Missing values	73	-.16	-.15	179	-.17	-.15	159	.14	.18	45	.23	.30
e/b =			.14/.12			.17/.15			.31/.29			.40/.43
F =		0.58			3.53+			16.40*			6.46*	
Controls												
Education:												
e/b =			.04/.16			.05/.03			.11/.15			.15/.20
F =		0.74			0.07			3.70++			1.18	
Income:												
e/b =			.23/.23			.14/.11			.15/.16			.20/.17
F =		1.24			0.93			2.32+			0.83	
Occupation:												
e/b =			.13/.12			.07/.08			.16/.19			.18/.17
F =		0.22			0.63			3.91++			0.78	
Variance Explained =		9.0%			5.4%			19.1%			22.9%	

TABLE 3 CONTINUED

Analysis of:	Saskatchewan			Alberta			B.C.			National		
Grand Mean =	3.57			4.38			3.90			4.11		
	N	Unadj.	Adj.	N	Unadj.	Adj.	N	Unadj.	Adj.	N	Unadj.	Adj.
Subjective Social Class												
Upper	6	—	—	11	-.29	-.20	16	1.38	.76	176	.26	.21
Middle	76	.13	.10	81	.01	.03	95	.18	.19	1040	.14	.12
Lower	82	-.17	-.12	56	.04	-.01	87	-.45	-.35	704	-.27	-.23
e/b =		.14/.09			.06/.05			.30/.20			.14/.12	
F =		0.57			0.15			3.62*			12.33*	
Left/Right Self-Rating												
Left	30	-1.01	-1.01	12	-1.11	-1.03	31	-1.14	-.83	244	-.84	-.78
Centre	41	.34	.32	37	-.13	-.04	50	-.07	-.01	488	.00	.00
Right	35	.16	.15	60	.10	.09	54	.71	.35	536	.37	.31
Missing values	59	.18	.21	38	.32	.22	63	.02	.12	651	.01	.04
e/b =		.32/.32			.28/.25			.34/.22			.25/.22	
F =		6.13*			2.79+			3.08+			33.08*	
Controls												
Education:												
e/b =		.21/.20			.19/.16			.14/.13			.04/.08	
F =		2.28			0.99			1.04			2.94+	
Income:												
e/b =		.21/.23			.30/.28			.31/.24			.14/.12	
F =		1.72			2.31			1.79			4.98+	
Occupation:												
e/b =		.24/.19			.21/.28			.16/.12			.05/.04	
F =		1.06			0.79			0.58			0.52	
Variance Explained =		24.1%			20.6%			23.7%			9.3%	

Significance levels: +p < .05; ++p < .01; *p < .001
** See footnote to table 1.

TABLE 4   SUBJECTIVE SOCIAL CLASS, LEFT/RIGHT POLITICAL ORIENTATIONS, AND FEDERAL LEVEL SUBJECTIVE CLASS VOTING, WITH CONTROLS (MCA)*

Analysis of:	Atlantic			Quebec			Ontario			Manitoba		
	N	Unadj.	Adj.	N	Unadj.	Adj.	N	Unadj.	Adj.	N	Unadj.	Adj.
Grand Mean =	4.28			4.31			4.41			4.17		
Subjective Social Class												
Upper	14	.16	-.08	60	.29	.32	75	.21	.23	13	-.57	-.34
Middle	87	.01	.02	348	.10	.08	342	.13	.12	86	.27	.13
Lower	78	-.04	-.01	103	-.51	-.47	277	-.22	-.21	64	-.25	-.11
e/b =		.04/.02			.19/.18			.13/.12			.23/.12	
F =		0.04			7.66*			4.31**			0.97	
Left/Right Self-Rating												
Left	18	-.39	-.45	61	-.59	-.51	90	-.53	-.57	21	-1.23	-1.31
Centre	40	-.49	-.46	106	.22	.18	203	-.16	-.16	36	.24	.18
Right	34	.36	.34	150	.24	.22	186	.39	.36	50	.21	.21
Missing Values	87	.17	.18	195	-.12	-.10	215	.03	.08	57	.13	.19
e/b =		.23/.23			.20/.18			.21/.21			.37/.39	
F =		2.74			5.10**			10.25*			6.73*	
Controls												
Education:												
e/b =		.16/.14			.14/.13			.04/.11			.12/.18	
F =		1.03			2.84*			1.90			1.06	
Income:												
e/b =		.12/.10			.13/.08			.09/.10			.10/.08	
F =		0.32			0.60			1.27			0.20	
Occupation:												
e/b =		.19/.19			.08/.05			.11/.12			.15/.14	
F =		1.21			0.22			1.88			0.58	
Variance Explained =		11.7%			9.7%			8.2%			20.4%	

TABLE 4 CONTINUED

Analysis of:	Saskatchewan			Alberta			B.C.			National		
Grand Mean =	3.73			4.41			4.22			4.32		
	N	Unadj.	Adj.	N	Unadj.	Adj.	N	Unadj.	Adj.	N	Unadj.	Adj.
Subjective Social Class												
Upper	6	—	—	13	-.26	-.41	20	.73	.34	226	.26	.21
Middle	74	.18	.30	106	-.04	-.06	125	.26	.22	1272	.12	.11
Lower	90	-.19	-.26	67	.12	.17	99	-.47	-.34	817	-.26	-.23
e/b =		.14/.18			.09/.13			.26/.18			.14/.12	
F =		2.55			1.10			3.47*			14.82*	
Left/Right Self-Rating												
Left	29	-1.22	-1.20	15	-.26	-.36	35	-1.12	-1.16	286	-.68	-.67
Centre	46	.16	.27	37	-.11	-.22	61	.22	.14	574	-.02	-.03
Right	36	.42	.33	86	.10	.16	66	.45	.30	660	.32	.27
Missing Values	60	.21	.18	48	.00	-.01	82	-.05	.14	794	.00	.03
e/b =		.37/.36			.09/.15			.32/.30			.21/.20	
F =		7.35*			1.21			6.96*			31.11*	
Controls												
Education:												
e/b =		.17/.13			.12/.06			.09/.10			.03/.04	
F =		0.78			0.18			0.64			0.91	
Income:												
e/b =		.19/.26			.16/.17			.23/.21			.10/.09	
F =		1.84			0.86			1.85			3.47++	
Occupation:												
e/b =		.15/.18			.14/.15			.12/.10			.06/.04	
F =		0.93			0.60			0.46			0.82	
Variance Explained =		23.3%			7.7%			19.4%			6.8%	

Significance levels: *p <.05; **p < .01; *p < .001
** See footnote to table 1.

A rough indication of how much of the class effects was mediated by the two intervening variables may be obtained by calculating the difference in explained variance attributable to the three objective social class indicators with and without the intervening variables. This was accomplished by summing the squared *betas* for the three class measures when the intervening variables were not used and doing likewise for the analyses when these variables were used. Our main interest was in the analyses for provinces where there was a substantial social class effect to be explained, in the neighbourhood of 10 per cent or more. In the case of *provincial* level SCV, 53.6 per cent of the social class effect in British Columbia was mediated by subjective social class and left/right orientation. The comparable figures for Saskatchewan and Alberta were 21.4 and 11.3 per cent, respectively. The figure for SCV at the *federal* level was 19.3 per cent for Saskatchewan.[29]

RESULTS OF USING SUBJECTIVE CLASS VOTING INTENTIONS AS THE DEPENDENT VARIABLE

To circumvent the problems of recall associated with respondents' reports of how they voted in the last provincial election, and to place the provincial and federal votes on the same temporal footing, we repeated all of the above analyses using respondents' voting intentions "if an election were held today" to create the SCV measure. Overall, the pattern of findings remained intact. In general, we explained less variance in respondents' hypothetical votes than in their reported provincial and federal votes.

Consistent with what we have previously observed, *provincial* SCV intentions were most pronounced in British Columbia (table not shown). In that province, 18 per cent of the total variance in provincial SCV intentions was explained by the three objective social class variables combined; this figure climbed to 29.5 per cent when the two subjective predictors were added to the equation. Left/right orientation was clearly more important than subjective social class as a predictor. Income was the most important of the three objective social class variables, whether the consciousness measures were included in the analysis or not. The variance explained in provincial SCV intentions by income, education and occupation together was less than 10 per cent in all of the other analyses. Apart from British Columbia, the set of three objective and two subjective measures accounted for 19.4 per cent of the variance in provincial SCV intentions in Ontario, 21.8 per cent in Manitoba, and 20.5 per cent in Saskatchewan. The figures were 6.8 per cent for the Atlantic provinces, 9.2 per cent for Quebec, and 10.9 per cent for Alberta. Less then 10 per cent of the variance in *federal* SCV intentions was explained by the three objective social class measures. The extended set of predictors pushed these figures to highs of 19.3 per cent in Manitoba, 16.2 per cent in British Columbia, and 15.1 per cent in Saskatchewan.

DISCUSSION & CONCLUSIONS

We will briefly summarise the answers to the three questions with which we began this paper. The prediction that SCV would be higher in provincial elections than in the federal election was generally borne out. Our reasoning was that non-class factors would be more likely to override class factors as determinants of voting behaviour in federal politics. The one exception to this pattern occurred in Quebec where there was more subjective class voting federally than provincially. Although it is tempting to engage in some post hoc speculation about the greater importance of nationalist issues in the 1981 Quebec provincial election (which followed the 1980 referendum in that province) compared to the 1984 federal election, it is more appropriate to emphasise the low levels of class voting in both elections.

Notwithstanding these differences in the overall levels of provincial and federal class voting, we are impressed with the substantial correlations between the class orientations of the parties for which respondents reported voting at the two levels of government. If respondents voted for provincial parties which they believed to favour the lower social classes, they tended to do the same thing at the federal level. In saying this, we are mindful of the fact that these correlations by themselves do not mean that respondents support provincial and federal parties biased in favour of their own social classes.

The data at our disposal did not permit a critical test between the broad interpretations of the social sources in SCV that we might entertain. These are illustrated in the debate of a few years ago between Schreiber and Ogmundson.[30] Schreiber contended that different levels of SCV are attributable to voter preferences, and Ogmundson claimed that they are the products of party and elite tactics. For our part, we would be surprised if both processes were not at work in producing the kinds of patterns present in cross-sectional, individual-level survey data. On the assumption that the party systems and elites are relatively discrete provincially and federally, we might see the correlations between respondents' definitions of the class orientations of the parties for which they voted at the two levels as at least consistent with Schreiber's proposition that class voting tells us more about the electorate than it does about the elites.[31] At the same time, it needs to be said that there was little evidence of greater left/right polarization in provinces supporting high levels of class voting than in provinces characterised by low levels of class voting. We single this variable out because it was the most striking predictor in the array of variables considered here. The disjuncture between voters' thinking and their votes seemed to occur around the ballot box, and this would point to party effects.

Starting with ideas about the relative strength of the NDP and the working class in the different provinces, as well as the level of each province's economic and political development, we checked, next, for interprovincial differences in class voting. The results of the analyses of provincial SCV using the extended set of five predictors revealed that the provinces can be grouped into roughly two categories. The highest level of provincial SCV occurred in Saskatchewan, followed closely by British Columbia, Manitoba, Alberta, and Ontario. The spread in the amount of variance between Saskatchewan and Ontario was only five percentage points. The lowest level of provincial SCV appeared in Quebec, followed by the Atlantic provinces. The provinces also seemed to fall into two categories when we looked at federal SCV. This time, however, relatively high levels of class voting were confined to Saskatchewan, followed by Manitoba and British Columbia, a spread of slightly less than four percentage points in variance explained. The lowest level of federal SCV was found in Alberta, followed by Ontario, Quebec, and Atlantic Canada, in ascending order.

Brym and Wilson, it will be recalled, provided predictions about the (rough) rank order of the provinces on the basis of processes said to be productive of class voting.[32] Brym focussed on the strength of the working class, while Wilson emphasised the level of socio-economic development in each of the provinces. Our analyses have addressed the "output" side of these processes, that is, the relative amounts of class voting in the different provinces, rather than the "input" side, which provides the rationales for their hypotheses. In general, the pattern of interprovincial differences in SCV accords rather well with Brym's prediction and with Wilson's revised prediction. Although our analyses did not address the specifics of their respective explanations, it will presumably be necessary to draw upon different factors to account for the generally higher levels of provincial than federal SCV. In moving from one level of government to the other, there were some shifts in the ranking of individual provinces. Alberta, for example, showed more provincial SCV than federal SCV. The explanation will likely be found in the functioning of the party system at the two levels of government.

Finally, we distinguished between the three objective measures of social class (occupation, income and education), and the two social psychological variables (subjective social class and left/right political orientation) in terms of their proximity to the dependent variable—subjective class voting. As expected, the two subjective predictors greatly improved our ability to explain SCV beyond what we could do with the three objective measures alone. In addition, a substantial portion of the effects associated with the objective variables was mediated by the subjective variables. Overall, and especially in provinces high in SCV, left/right orientation was clearly the most important predictor of SCV. Income, among the objective predictors, appeared to be the most important.

Since we believe our results have some important implications for how class voting can best be studied in further work, we will conclude with some comments on this point. First, it is important to recall that the disciplines of political science and sociology, share "joint custody" for this area of study. Not surprisingly, political scientists have been more interested in voting behaviour than in social class which they use to explain voting. Sociologists, on the other hand, have had an overriding interest in social class and social stratification. The electoral system and voting behaviour have little intrinsic appeal for them. They have been more inclined to examine the array of effects associated with social class as a means of understanding the workings of the social class system. One of these effects is voting choice. In short, students of social class fit class voting into theories of social class, not into theories of voting. A consequence of this curious division of intellectual labour, from our point of view, has been an exceedingly truncated view of voting behaviour within sociology.

Political scientists know that voting behaviour is the product of a number of major variables, such as leader and party images, policy issues and party identification.[33] These variables, in turn, are understood to be the products of still other antecedent variables, including, but not limited to, social class. Social class may affect voter choice either indirectly through these intervening variables, or directly. Seen from a political science perspective, the question is not whether there is or is not a class vote, but under what circumstances the electoral effects of social class variables are most or least likely to appear.

Sociologists can make a major contribution to the answer to this question if they join the issue directly. Our results suggest that class voting is most pronounced in political systems in which political life is cast in explicitly class terms, as in British Columbia.[34] It appears to be minimized in systems in which the substance and rhetoric of politics is cast more in non-class terms, as in Quebec. In addition, appeals to regional, ethnic, and other loyalties are more likely to displace social class in federal politics. Thus, class voting is more likely to occur at the provincial level than at the federal level, and in some provinces more than others. However, since society is not static, we can anticipate changes in the level of class voting in the future, depending on shifts in the bases of social conflict. In Quebec, for example, class voting may become more pronounced in the future if the recent upsurge in NDP popularity in the polls translates itself into votes and if it persists. The short ascendance of the Créditistes in the 1960s and 1970s, however, not to mention the short-lived rise of the Progressive Conservatives under Diefenbaker and, perhaps, Mulroney, counsels skepticism. In any event, our understanding of class voting should benefit from a more sustained attempt to marry theories of social class and the vote.

NOTES

1. Robert A. Alford, *Party and Society* (Chicago: University of Chicago, 1963); Alford, "Class Voting in the Anglo-American Political Systems" in *Party Systems and Voter Alignments: Cross-National Perspectives*, ed. S.M. Lipset and S. Rokkan (New York: Free Press, 1967), chap 1. Gerhard Lenski and Jean Lenski, *Human Societies* (New York: McGraw-Hill, 1970), 362.

2. Rick Ogmundson, "On the Use of Party Image Variables to Measure the Political Distinctiveness of a Class Vote: The Canadian Case," *Canadian Journal of Sociology* (*CJS*) 1, 2 (1975): 169–77; Ogmundson, "Party Class Images and the Class Vote in Canada," *American Sociological Review* 40, 4 (1975): 506–12; Ogmundson, "On the Measurement of Party Class Positions: The Case of Canadian Federal Political Parties," *Canadian Review of Sociology and Anthropology* (*CRSA*) 12 (1975): 565–76; Ogmundson, "Mass-Elite Linkages and Class Issues in Canada" *CRSA* 13, 1 (1976): 1–12; Rick Ogmundson and Mary Ng, "On the Inference of Voter Motivation: A Comparison of the Subjective Class Vote in Canada and the United

Kingdom," *CJS* 7 (1982): 41–59. See also Harold D. Clarke, Jane Jenson, Lawrence LeDuc and Jon H. Pammett, *Political Choice in Canada* (Toronto: McGraw-Hill Ryerson, 1979), 107–19; Ronald D. Lambert and Alfred A. Hunter, "Social Stratification, Voting Behaviour, and the Images of Canadian Federal Political Parties," *CRSA* 16, 3 (1979): 287–304; John F. Myles, "Differences in the Canadian and American Class Vote: Fact or Pseudofact?" *American Journal of Sociology* 84, 5 (1979): 1232–37; E. M. Schreiber, "Class Awareness and Class Voting in Canada: A Reconsideration of the Ogmundson Thesis," *CRSA* 17, 1 (1980): 37–44; Bonnie H. Erickson, "Region, Knowledge, and Class Voting in Canada," *CJS* 6, 2 (1981): 121–44; John F. Myles and Dennis Forcese, "Voting and Class Politics in Canada and the United States," *Comparative Social Research* 4 (1981): 3–31; Alfred A. Hunter, "On Class, Status and Voting in Canada," *CJS* 7, 1 (1982): 19–39; John F. Zipp and Joel Smith, "A Structural Analysis of Class Voting," *Social Forces* 60 (1982): 738–59; Linda Gerber, "The Federal Election of 1968: Social Class Composition and Party

Support in the Electoral Districts of Ontario," *CRSA* 23, 1 (1986): 118–35.

3. Ogmundson and Ng, "On the Influence of Voter Motivation," 49.

4. Myles, "Differences in the Canadian and American Class Vote"; Myles and Forcese, "Voting and Class Politics."

5. Ronald D. Lambert, Steven D. Brown, James E. Curtis, Barry J. Kay, and John M. Wilson, *The 1984 Canadian National Election Study Codebook* (Waterloo, February 1986).

6. The 1984 CNES also asked respondents to rate the three major federal parties, but not their respective provincial parties, on the traditional "for the working class" vs. "for the middle class" scale.

7. The concept of social class is used throughout this paper to refer to differences in occupational status, income levels, educational status and subjective class placement because these are the referents for the concept in the subjective class voting literature to which our analyses are addressed. We acknowledge that there are competing views about the appropriate referents for the concept, especially the Marxist definition. Our focus on provincial level analyses, and the consequences of this for small *N*s for capitalists, precluded a detailed look at the effects of Marxist class categories.

8. Ogmundson, "On the Use of Party Image Variables"; Ogmundson, "Party Class Images and the Class Vote." Lambert and Hunter, "Social Stratification, Voting Behaviour, and the Images of Canadian Federal Political Parties."

9. Robert J. Brym, "An Introduction to the Regional Question in Canada" in *Regionalism in Canada*, ed. R. Brym (Toronto: Irwin, 1986), 1–45; Robert J. Brym, "Incorporation versus Power Models of Working Class Radicalism: with Special Reference to North America," *CJS* 11, 3 (1986): 227–51; John M. Wilson, "The Canadian Political Cultures: towards a Redefinition of the 1974 Nature of the Canadian Political System," *Canadian Journal of Political Science* (*CJPS*) 7, 3 (1974): 438–83.

10. Cf. Gerber, "The Federal Election of 1968"; Brym, "Incorporation versus Power Models of Working Class Radicalism," 233.

11. Brym, "Incorporation versus Power Models of Working Class Radicalism," 235.

12. Wilson, "The Canadian Political Cultures."

13. Ibid., 455.

14. Ibid., 475.

15. Ibid., 457.

16. Ibid., 474.

17. Wilson reports that he had trouble classifying Alberta in his 1974 article and that he no longer regards this province as fully developed (Wilson, personal communication to R. D. Lambert, 4 March 1987). Quebec is "still very much in the early 'industrializing' stage," in his opinion, while British Columbia and Manitoba have evolved into two-party systems since 1974.

18. Cf. Paul Stevenson, "Class and Left-wing Radicalism," *CRSA* 14, 3 (1977): 269–84; Jean A. Laponce, *Left and Right: The Topography of Political Perceptions* (Toronto: University of Toronto Press, 1981).

19. Lambert et al., *The 1984 Canadian National Election Study Codebook*.

20. The rating questions for this scale were as follows:

Some people believe that political parties favour particular social classes over other social classes. Here is a scale for describing each of the federal parties. [Show Card] The closer to "1," the more the party favours the lower social classes, and the closer to "7," the more a party favours the higher social classes. Where would you place the federal Liberal party on this scale? Where would you place the federal Progressive Conservative Party? Where would you place the federal NDP?

Now I would like to ask you about the provincial political parties here in [Name Province]. First, how much does the provincial Liberal party favour the

[Respondents in all provinces except Quebec were then asked about the provincial Progressive Conservatives and the provincial NDP; respondents in Alberta and British Columbia were asked about the provincial Social Credit; and respondents in Quebec were asked about the Union Nationale, the Parti Québécois and the Créditistes.]

The mean ratings for the three federal parties on this scale, with their standard deviations in parentheses, were as follows: Liberals = 4.96 (1.34), Progressive Conservatives = 4.93 (1.26), and New Democrats 2.98 (1.37). The correlations between the ratings of the parties voted for at the provincial and federal levels were highly significant in all provinces except Prince Edward Island. The correlation was highest in New Brunswick ($r = .724$) and Saskatchewan ($r = .719$), and lowest in Prince Edward Island ($r = .242$) and Quebec ($R = .403$).

21. Respondents were first asked the following question: "One hears a lot about different social classes. Do you ever think of yourself as belonging to a social class?" Those who answered "yes" were then asked: "Which of the following social classes would you say you were in? [Show Card]—upper class, upper-middle class, middle class, working class or lower class?" Those who answered "no" or "don't know" on the screener question were asked the following: "Well, if you had to make a choice, which of these social classes would you say you were in? [Show card and read above options]" We defined subjective social class in terms of both the voluntary and forced choice questions in order to preserve cases.

22. Respondents were first asked the following:
    Sometimes in Canada people use the labels "left" or "left-wing" and "right" or "right-wing" to describe political parties, politicians and political ideas. I'm going to ask you what these terms mean to you. If either or both of them don't really have any meaning for you, please say so.

Regardless of their answers to the preceding questions, all respondents were then asked the following:
    For the next few questions I would like you to use this scale which goes from left to right, with "1" being the most to the left and "7" being the most to the right. [Show Card] When you think of your own political opinions, where would you put yourself on this scale?
Answers were coded so that 1 to 3 = 1; 4 = 2; 5 to 7 = 3; no answer and don't know = 4. When the left/right scale was used as a predictor in the MCA, missing values were retained as a separate category rather than declared missing. The implication of this strategy is that the left/right variable combined two sets of distinctions: whether a respondent was "on" or "off" the scale and, in the former event, where on the scale. This should be borne in mind in interpreting the results for the left/right variable. See Ronald D. Lambert, James E. Curtis, Steven D. Brown and Barry J. Kay "In Search of Left/Right Beliefs in the Canadian Electorate" *CJPS* 19, 3 (1986): 541–63 for their analyses of respondents' answers to the definitional questions.

23. MCA is like multiple regression with dummy variables [F. Andrews, J. Morgan, J. Sonquist and L. Klem, *Multiple Classification Analysis* (Ann Arbor: Institute of Social Research, University of Michigan, 1973)]. This technique is used to examine the relationship between a single predictor or independent variable (e.g., education, in this study) and a dependent variable (i.e., the perceived class bias of the parties for which respondents reported voting), or the relationship between each of a set of predictors and the dependent variable, holding the effects of the remaining predictors constant. The analysis yields an overall mean score on the dependent variable and a *deviation* from the overall mean score for each category of each predictor variable. Adding or subtracting a deviation score to or from the overall mean score produces a mean score for the category in question. The procedure also yields *eta* and *beta* coefficients. These figures squared provide a

rough indication of the proportion of the total variance in the dependent variable that is accounted for by each predictor variable 1. without controls (*eta*) and 2. with controls (*beta*) on the other predictors.

24. Since it might be argued that the analyses are "over-controlled" for social class, with the effects of income, occupation, and education upon SCV controlled for each other, we have also provided the unadjusted means on the dependent variable for each category of the three social class indicators. This permits the reader to inspect the effects for each social class measure before the effects of other measures have been partialled out. The unadjusted figures and the *eta* values are also conceptually closer to the zero-order comparisons reported in Ogmundson, "Party Class Images and the Class Vote in Canada"; and Lambert and Hunter, "Social Stratification, Voting Behaviour, and the Images of Canadian Federal Political Parties."

25. Having included homemakers as an occupational stratum, we wondered about the contribution of gender to the pattern of findings presented here because most homemakers are women. We therefore deleted homemakers (as well as the few farmers) from the occupational measure and added a separate gender predictor in supplementary analyses for provincial SCV nationally, and in Saskatchewan, Manitoba and British Columbia combined. Gender was not a significant predictor in any of these analyses.

26. Lambert et al., "In Search of Left/Right Beliefs in the Canadian Electorate," 561.

27. The strength of the relationships between left/right political orientation and SCV piqued our interest in the distribution of left/right scores across country. We wondered, first, whether voters in provinces with high levels of provincial SCV tended to be more left-oriented than voters in provinces with low levels of SCV; second, whether people who voted for the NDP in provinces with high levels of SCV tended to be more left-oriented than

people who voted for the same party inprovinces where SCV was low; and, third, whether people who voted for a party other than the NDP in provinces with high levels of SCV tended to be more right wing than people who voted for a party other than the NDP in provinces where SCV was low. Briefly, our analyses showed that there was no more of a tilt to the left or to the right in provinces characterised by high SCV as opposed to low SCV. Interprovincial differences in the amount of SCV appeared not to have their origins in differences in the degree of ideological polarization within provinces.

28. We inserted a union membership measure into some supplementary analyses as an intervening variable, standing between the three objective social class measures and SCV. The effects for this measure were statistically significant for provincial SCV nationally ($F = 8.03$; $p < .001$) and for federal SCV ($F = 8.47$; $p < .001$). In both analyses, respondents who were union members and whose families included another union member were most likely to vote for parties perceived to favour the lower social classes. These people were followed by respondents who were union members in families where no one else was a member; and they in turn were followed by respondents who were non-members but where a family member belonged to a union. Respondents who were not union members and who came from families in which no one else was a member were most likely to favour parties oriented to the higher social classes.

29. In analyses that we have had to delete from this paper because of space limitations we replicated, for 1984, the analyses that we reported in Ogmundson, "On the Use of Party Image Variables"; Ogmundson, "Party Class Images and the Class Vote in Canada" for the 1965 CNES and in Lambert and Hunter, "Social Stratification, Voting Behaviour, and the Images of Canadian Federal Political Parties" for the 1968 CNES. The results were roughly consistent across years. The highest level of class voting in 1984, as in 1965 and

1968, occurred for subjective class membership. However, class voting was somewhat lower in 1984 than in either of the two previous studies. The table summarising these findings is available from the authors on request.

30. Schreiber, "Class Awareness and Class Voting in Canada"; and Rick Ogmundson, "Liberal Ideology and the Study of Voting Behaviour," *CRSA* 17, 1 (1980): 45–54.

31. Cf. Benjamin Ginsberg, *The Captive Public: How Mass Opinion Promotes*

State Power (New York: Basic Books, 1986).

32. Brym, "An Introduction to the Regional Question in Canada"; Brym, "Incorporation versus Power Models of Working Class Radicalism"; Wilson, "The Canadian Political Cultures."

33. Clarke et al., *Political Choice in Canada.*

34. But cf. Donald E. Blake, *Two Political Worlds: Parties and Voting in British Columbia* (Vancouver: U.B.C. Press, 1985), chap. 5.

THE FAILURE OF THE NEW DEMOCRATIC PARTY: UNIONS, UNIONISTS, AND POLITICS IN CANADA*

KEITH ARCHER

o

In 1961 the recently formed Canadian Labour Congress (CLC) joined with the Co-operative Commonwealth Federation (CCF), farm organisations and other "liberally minded Canadians" to form the New Democratic Party (NDP).[1] Billed as the Canadian counterpart to the British Labour Party,[2] the NDP was welcomed enthusiastically by the CLC as the political arm of labour, representing the first challenge in the post-First World War period by a united working class movement[3] to the Liberal and Progressive Conservative parties.[4] Despite the initial euphoria, and the apparently new-found enthusiasm of organised labour in Canada for direct political action, the electoral fortunes of the NDP have not been significantly better than those of its organisational predecessor, the CCF.

The NDP's poor electoral performance appears to be quite anomalous given the importance often ascribed to labour union–party linkages for parties of the left. For example, Duverger has argued that the inclusion of the working class in political conflict is a function of the propensity of trade unions to become involved in mobilizing their members in a tightly organised, mass-based political party: "Here perhaps we touch upon one of the deep-seated reasons which have led all Anglo-Saxon Socialist parties to organise themselves on a Trade Union basis; it alone could put at their disposal sufficient strength for the takeoff."[5]

Although Barnes basically agreed with Duverger's analysis, he took the argument a step further, suggesting that what was true of working class organisations in structuring political debate was applicable to all groups in society:

> No idea has ever made much headway without an organization behind it. . . . While small organizations and movements may have thrived on the ideological enthusiasm of their members alone, it is difficult to

make a big impact without organizing large numbers of people. . . . It is probably that organizational ties to parties, trade unions, and other associations are more important than ideology in imposing constraints on mass belief systems. . . . The institutional structure of the polity is crucial not only for an understanding of the relationship between ideology and the outputs of the system; it is also critical for the survival of particular ideologies.[6]

Thus, according to Barnes, political discourse is conditioned by organisations imposing the terms of a particular debate upon their members and society as a whole.

This notion gained further support from Sartori, who noted that:

What we are really investigating via class behaviour, is the impact of an organizational variable: *The influence of party and trade union control.* Class conditions are only a facilitating condition. To put it bluntly, it is not the "objective" class (class conditions) that creates the party, but the party that creates the "subjective" class (class consciousness). More carefully put, wherever parties reflect social classes, this signifies more about the party end than about the class end of the interaction. . . . [L]arge collectivities become class structured only if they are class persuaded; and the most likely and apt "persuader" is the party (or the union) playing on class appeal.[7]

This note will examine in detail the nature and effects of union linkages with the NDP. We will demonstrate that the union–party linkage (as measured by rates of union local affiliation with the NDP) is very weak in Canada. Furthermore, we will show that where that linkage is present (that is, when union locals affiliate with the NDP), *individual* union members are more likely to identify with and vote for the NDP, and to view politics in class-based terms, than are individuals whose union locals do not affiliate. Thus, our analysis will differ from previous studies in that we will differentiate between, on the one hand, individuals and their family members who belong to union locals which affiliate with the NDP, and, on the other hand, those who do not. Before doing so, however, it will be useful to discuss briefly our reasons for expecting union local affiliation with the NDP to increase levels of support for the party to a greater extent than simple union membership.

Robert Dahl has identified several ways in which a group can exert influence on its members (or, more generally, in which A can influence B).[8] He terms the three types of influence control by training, persuasion, and inducement. Control by training exists when A receives B's co-operation as a consequence of cues or signals which A has given B. Influence through persuasion exists when A convinces B to co-operate either through "rational" or "manipulative" use of evidence and argument. A influences B to co-operate through inducement either when the benefits to B of co-operation increase (for example, B receives some desired good, such as promotion), or alternatively, the costs of not co-operating increase (for example, A exerts a severe sanction if B does not co-operate). Dahl notes that the most desirable (that is, least costly) form of influence is control by training, which is a product of prior persuasion and/or inducement.

Although each of these methods may be used by trade unions to influence their members to support the NDP, some may be more successful than others. For example, union leaders can preach the benefits of supporting the NDP to the union rank and file in an effort to persuade them to support the party. Indeed, this is the strategy increasingly being followed by the CLC under the leadership of Dennis McDermott. It was most clearly exemplified by the adoption of a "parallel political campaign" run on behalf of the NDP during the 1979 and 1980 federal elections.

In addition, union locals may attempt to persuade their membership to support the party by formally affiliating. Through affiliation, a union local is explicitly telling its membership that the NDP is the party of organised labour, and deserves the support of members of that local. It also is an attempt to "control by training" since the local is providing a signal or cue to the rank and file.

Influence through inducement, on the other hand, is much more difficult for unions to exert. Since the ballot is a secret one the union cannot induce co-operation because it has no way of determining whether and/or how individual members voted. On the other hand, a union may be able to induce individuals to work for the party either by providing rewards for party work (such as prestige) or by sanctioning those who refuse to do so.

In sum, trade unions have several methods by which they can influence their members to support the NDP. The least expensive method is through some form of control by training. In the sense in which it is used here, control by training is the end product of a process of adult political socialization, with the trade union acting as the socialization agent.

In the Canadian case, the most salient cue given by unions trying to influence their members is local union affiliation with the party. Local union leaders are signalling their members that they strongly approve of the party. If the union as a group influences its individual members, that influence should be strongest in such settings; certainly it should be stronger than in union settings in which an approving signal is *not* being given. We will test this assumption below.

To date, very little empirical research has been conducted on the union basis of partisan support in Canada. For example, none of the major reports of the Canadian national election studies features unions in their analyses.[9] In the few studies which have examined the effect of union membership on voting, no distinction is made between individuals belonging to unions affiliated with the NDP and those not affiliated. The assumption appears to be that all Canadian unionists should be equally inclined to support the party. For example, Miller presents data which illustrate that twice as many union as nonunion members (28 per cent versus 14 per cent) voted for the NDP in 1968, compared to the 1963 figures of 21 and 11 per cent, respectively; while Chi and Perlin suggest that in 1968, 30.9 per cent of union members compared to 11.6 per cent of nonunion members voted for the NDP.[10] For 1965 the corresponding figures are 26.9 per cent and 14.9 per cent. Similarly, in a 1971 study of the determinants of party preference among workers in four Ontario communities, Keddy found that 35 per cent of union members were "consistent" NDP supporters, whereas only 8 per cent of nonunionists consistently supported the NDP.[11]

The finding that approximately 30 per cent of unionists support the NDP is at odds with our own analysis of union members' support for the NDP during the period 1965 to 1979. In particular, we examined percentage vote for the NDP among union families as opposed to nonunion families in each of the 1965, 1968, 1974 and 1979 Canadian national election studies.[12] Beginning with 1965, percentage vote for the NDP among union members was 22.8, 19.5, 18.4 and 21.5 per cent for each of the four studies, respectively, whereas for nonunion members, the corresponding figures are 13.5, 8.9, 8.8 and 11.5 per cent respectively. Thus, approximately 20 per cent of union members voted for the NDP in each of the four elections, a figure approximately twice that obtained from nonunion members. Since these data are very stable across time, and are consistent with our expectations, given aggregate rates of support for the NDP, we feel they are a reliable indicator for support for the NDP among the union and the nonunion groups. Indeed, these data call into question the validity of the data reported by both Miller and by Chi and Perlin, especially since the latter report that their data also are from the 1968 national election study. Chi and Perlin note that the 1968 data are weighted to account for the underrepresentation of the NDP vote in the election study, but they neglect to report the criteria used for the weighting. (The 1968 national election study does not contain a standard "national weight" variable.) We can surmise that their weighting technique had the effect of differentially affecting the weight of union members as opposed to nonunion members, and thereby created an artificially strong relationship. Miller's data, on the other hand, were obtained from an NDP monthly periodical *The New Democrat*, and he provides no other reference to the manner in which the data were compiled.

Whereas Chi and Perlin's, and presumably Miller's, data were from national election studies, Keddy's paper reports data gathered in four Ontario communities, and may be confounded by a "constituency" effect. For example, Zipp found support for the NDP to be greatest in constituencies in which the party is a viable (that is, electable) alternative to the Liberals and Progressive Conservatives.[13] We will present evidence below which supports this finding. Thus, it might be presumed that Keddy sampled an unrepresentative population, constituencies that were NDP strongholds (for example, Sudbury).

To reiterate, the data suggests that union members are more likely to support the NDP than are nonunion members, although at rates substantially below those reported in the literature. In the remainder of the note, we will examine the extent to which union local affiliation with the NDP affects the propensity of individuals to support the NDP and to think about politics in class-based terms.

DATA ANALYSIS

Using data from the 1979 Canadian National Election Study[14] and from the files of the NDP,[15] this section examines the extent to which union affiliation with the NDP affects both the political attitudes and behaviour of union members. The expectation is that members of union locals affiliated with the NDP will exhibit attitudinal and behavioural characteristics that differ from those of either nonunion members or members of non-NDP affiliated locals. Specifically, we hypothesise that union status[16] acts as an important independent variable affecting an individual's class awareness and ideological self-image: perception of the NDP, its leaders and

TABLE 1   UNIONS AFFILIATED WITH THE NDP AND THE
MEMBERSHIP OF AFFILIATED UNIONS AS A
PERCENTAGE OF TOTAL UNION MEMBERSHIP,
1961-1981

Year+	Number of Affiliated Locals++	Members of Affiliated Locals (000s)	Total Union Membership◆ (000s)	Percentage Union Members Affiliated
1961	278	71	1423	4.99
1962	612	186	1449	12.86
1963	689	218	1493	14.60
1964	683	216	1589	13.61
1965	642	223	1736	12.82
1966	680	247	1921	12.86
1968	729	247	2010	12.29
1969	764	256	2075	12.33
1970	792	266	2173	12.25
1971	759	273	2231	12.23
1972	790	272	2388	11.37
1973	796	277	2591	10.71
1974	754	283	2732	10.36
1975	765	274	2884	9.49
1976	737	263	3042	8.63
1977	747	278	3149	8.82
1978	739	280	3278	8.55
1979	745	295	3397	8.67
1980	758	297	3487	8.53
1981	765	296	3617	8.20

+ The date at which the information on affiliation was compiled was changed from December 31 to January 1, between 1966 and 1968 so that these data are continuous even though there appears not to be data for 1967. Since the data on total union membership was compiled as of January 1, for the period 1961 to 1966 we have used the figures listed for the subsequent year. From 1971 to 1978 the information on union affiliation to the NDP is as of April 1. For 1979 and 1980, it is as of July 31 and for 1981 it is as of August 31.
++ Source: NDP files.
◆ Source: Canada, Labour Canada, Directory of Labour Organizations in Canada, 1982.

local candidates; direction of party identifications; perception of issues and, ultimately, vote. In short, union status has both a direct effect on vote and an indirect effect, acting through variables which previous research has shown to be important determinants of voting.[17]

Before examining the effect of union affiliation on support for the NDP, it is instructive to examine briefly aggregate rates of union local affiliation with the party. Although considerable concern had been voiced with the CCF that the affiliated trade unions would dominate the party's convention and control the direction of party policies, it is abundantly clear some 20 years after the formation of the NDP that those fears were groundless.[18] The data in table 1 indicate that not only have affiliated unions not dominated the party through overwhelming affiliation, their rate of affiliation has failed even to keep pace with the rate of growth of union membership. Other than during the first year and one-half there has been little growth in the number of locals affiliated with the party. These have remained

TABLE 2 PARTY IDENTIFICATION AND VOTE IN 1979 BY
UNION STATUS (Row Percentages)*

Panel A: Party Identification

| | Party Identification | | | |
Union Status	Liberal	Conservative	NDP	N
Nonunion member	44.8	34.9	9.5	(1376)
Member of nonaffiliated union	45.2	23.2	17.5	(908)
Member of affiliated union	39.8	22.5	32.6	(127)
N	(1076)	(719)	(331)	
p < .001				

Panel B: Vote in 1979 Federal Election

	Vote			
Nonunion member	42.2	43.1	11.5	(1221)
Member of nonaffiliated union	41.8	31.9	20.0	(812)
Member of affiliated union	40.4	28.6	29.9	(110)
N	(899)	(817)	(336)	
p < .001				

* Row percentages sum to less than 100 because other parties were included in the analysis.
Nonidentifiers and nonvoters were excluded.

relatively constant at approximately 750. During the same period, the number of members belonging to affiliated locals increased by 50 per cent from approximately 200 000 to 300 000. Total union membership, however, increased from roughly one and one-half million to over three and one-half million, an increase of approximately 150 per cent, during this same period. Thus, the percentage of union members affiliated with NDP locals actually declined during the 20-year period from an initially low level of 12.9 per cent to an even lower 8.2 per cent.

In table 2 we examine the effect of union affiliation with the NDP on levels of identification with and vote for the Liberal, Progressive Conservative, and New Democratic parties. The data suggest that union–party affiliation has a moderate positive effect on rates of support for the NDP. For instance, in 1979 fully 32 per cent of members of NDP affiliated locals identified with the NDP, compared to 17.5 per cent of non-NDP affiliated union members, and 9.5 per cent of nonunion members, respectively (see Panel A). Data on reported vote in 1979 (Panel B) reveal similar patterns. For example, 30 per cent of union members belonging to NDP-affiliated locals reported voting for the NDP in 1979, compared to 20 per cent of unionists whose locals were not affiliated with the party. The corresponding figure for nonunion members was 11.5 per cent. Recalling our earlier analysis, which found that in 1979, 21.5 per cent of all unionists voted for the NDP, the decision of union locals to affiliate with the party appears to produce a significant increase in party support.

Also important for an understanding of Canadian politics is the finding in table 2 that support for the Liberal party is greater than for the NDP even among

TABLE 3 *PARTY IDENTIFICATION AND VOTE IN 1979 BY UNION STATUS (UAW and USWA Union Members Only: Row Percentages)**

Panel A: Party Identification

| | Party Identification | | | |
Union Status	Liberal	Conservative	NDP	N
Member of nonaffiliated union	48.6	23.9	15.7	(19)
Member of affiliated union	34.2	28.0	34.2	(51)
N	(27)	(19)	(21)	

Panel B: Vote in 1979 Federal Election

	Vote			
Member of nonaffiliated union	41.8	30.5	27.7	(17)
Member of affiliated union	34.6	30.3	35.1	(43)
N	(22)	(18)	(20)	

* Row percentages sum to less than 100 because other parties were included in the analysis. Nonidentifiers and nonvoters were excluded.

members of NDP-affiliated union locals. Fully 40 per cent of the latter identify with the Liberal party compared to 32.6 per cent with the NDP. The difference between rates of identification with the Liberal and New Democratic parties is substantially less among members of affiliated locals (7.2 per cent) than among members of nonaffiliated locals (27.2 per cent). In this regard, affiliation with the party may provide an important "cue" to the union rank and file. Nonetheless, the NDP's lack of electoral success can be attributed in part to the inability of union locals either to deliver more votes to, or to stimulate higher rates of affiliation with the party.

Historically, union support for the CCF–NDP has come disproportionately from industrial unions, especially from the United Automobile Workers (UAW) and the United Steel Workers of America (USWA). Indeed, 71 of the 127 members (56 per cent) of affiliated union locals in the sample belong to either the UAW or the USWA.[19] Thus, one might argue that the effects of affiliation presented in table 2 are spurious, the real causal factor being industrial as opposed to craft unionism. To test this hypothesis, we isolated UAW and USWA union members to examine whether union local affiliation to the NDP is positively related to support for the NDP among otherwise similar individuals. The findings, presented in table 3, are consistent with those in table 2. Of those UAW–USWA unionists who belong to union locals not affiliated with the NDP, 16 per cent identified with the party, whereas 34 per cent of their counterparts who belonged to NDP-affiliated locals identified with the party. In addition, 28 per cent of nonaffiliated UAW–USWA union members voted for the NDP in 1979, compared to 35 per cent who belonged to affiliated locals.

One might also hypothesise that NDP supporters come from constituencies in which the NDP is stronger. To test this hypothesis, we included a measure of the relative constituency strength of the NDP as a contextual variable. The result of the analysis, including an additional control for region of residence, is presented in

TABLE 4   *PERCENTAGE NDP IDENTIFICATION AND VOTE BY UNION STATUS, CONTROLLING FOR REGION AND LEVEL OF CONSTITUENCY SUPPORT FOR THE NDP+*

Panel A: Per Cent NDP Identification

NDP Constituency Support   Per Cent NDP Identification

Union Status	Atlantic and Quebec		Ontario		West	
1. NDP polled 0–15%						
nonunion	5.1%	(388)	6.6%	(150)	4.9%	(144)
nonaffiliated union	8.5	(317)	10.3	(60)	4.7	(47)
affiliated union	0	(3)	0	(4)	0	(0)
2. NDP polled 15.1–25%						
nonunion	2.2	(71)	13.9	(208)	14.6	(73)
nonaffiliated union	19.1	(64)	21.4	(99)	17.5	(48)
affiliated union	0	(0)	26.9	(32)	0	(7)
3. NDP polled over 25%						
nonunion	10.5	(10)	15.2	(134)	19.3	(155)
nonaffiliated union	3.9	(13)	22.6	(90)	38.0	(139)
affiliated union	0	(1)	41.0	(51)	48.9	(21)

Panel B: Per Cent NDP Vote

Per Cent NDP Vote

	Atlantic and Quebec		Ontario		West	
1. NDP polled 0–15%						
nonunion	4.2%	(341)	7.2%	(138)	5.2%	(116)
nonaffiliated union	8.7	(282)	15.0	(53)	5.1	(43)
affiliated union	0	(3)	0	(2)	0	(0)
2. NDP polled 15.1–25%						
nonunion	4.5	(58)	16.3	(189)	22.4	(65)
nonaffiliated union	21.2	(55)	18.6	(94)	19.5	(43)
affiliated union	0	(0)	24.0	(31)	0	(5)
3. NDP polled over 25%						
nonunion	33.3	(8)	22.3	(125)	21.6	(143)
nonaffiliated union	19.1	(11)	29.6	(79)	46.2	(125)
affiliated union	0	(0)	34.7	(46)	54.7	(15)

+The data on constituency support for the NDP were taken from the results of the 1979 federal election as reported in Canada. *Report of the Chief Electoral Officer* (1979).

table 4. Three features of this table warrant specific comment. First, the distribution of members of NDP-affiliated locals is very uneven across the regions. In Quebec and the Atlantic provinces, the total number of members of unions affiliated with the NDP in the sample is four. The corresponding figures for Ontario and the West are 87 and 28, respectively.[20] These figures approximate the distribution of members of affiliated unions in the Canadian population, where in 1979 the proportion of affiliated union members by region was 4.6, 76 and 19.4 per cent for

Quebec–Atlantic, Ontario and the West.[21] Second, the data illustrate a perceptible relationship between the constituency support for the NDP and the rate at which members of all groups support the party. For example, in Ontario, 6.6 per cent of nonunion members who lived in constituencies in which the NDP did very poorly in 1979 (0–15 per cent of the vote) identified with the party, as compared to 13.9 per cent of their nonunion member counterparts residing in constituencies where the NDP did substantially better (15.1–25 per cent), and 15.2 per cent among nonunion members in constituencies in which the NDP polled very well (over 25 per cent).

Third (and most important for the thesis advanced here), in each instance where there were more than a handful of cases, members of affiliated union locals identified with the NDP at higher levels than did those of their non-NDP-affiliated union member counterparts. For instance, in Ontario constituencies in which the NDP received 15–25 per cent of the vote in 1979, 26.9 per cent of members of affiliated union locals identified with the NDP, compared to 21.4 and 13.9 per cent of the non-NDP-affiliated, and nonunion members, respectively. Likewise, fully 41 per cent of NDP-affiliated union members in Ontario constituencies in which the NDP was very strong identified with the party, almost twice the rate of union members whose locals were not affiliated with the NDP (22.6 per cent). A similar pattern can be discerned among residents of the four western provinces. In constituencies in which the NDP is strong, members of NDP-affiliated locals were more likely to identify with the NDP (48.9 per cent) than were either non-NDP-affiliated union members (38.0 per cent) or nonmembers (19.3 per cent).

The data on vote for the NDP, presented in Panel B of table 4, reveal a similar pattern—members of NDP-affiliated locals are more inclined to vote for the NDP than are their nonaffiliated counterparts, controlling for the constituency strength of the party. Again, in each instance for which there are more than a few cases, the trends are in the anticipated direction.

We also examined whether local union affiliation with the NDP affected perceptions of the leader Ed Broadbent, the NDP generally, and the local NDP candidate; and whether it influenced the likelihood that individuals thought about politics in class-based terms (data not shown). The data indicated that members of NDP-affiliated locals had more positive evaluations of the NDP, its leader and local candidates; were more likely to see themselves as members of the working class; and had a more "leftist" self-image than did union members whose local was not affiliated with the NDP.

Taken together, these data lend considerable support to the argument that the decision of union locals to affiliate with the NDP has an important independent effect in mobilizing members of that local to support the party.

SUMMARY AND CONCLUSION

This note has examined the extent to which local union affiliates with the NDP influence the attitudes and voting behaviour of their members. Analysis revealed that only a small, and declining, proportion of union members in Canada belong to locals affiliated with the NDP. Contrary to the popular belief that a strong link exists between organised labour and the NDP,[22] we found the link—as measured by rates of affiliation—to be very weak. The data also revealed that when the link was present, it clearly had a positive effect on levels of NDP support. For example, membership in an NDP-affiliated local was found to be positively related to identification with and vote for the party, and this relationship persisted after controlling for the constituency strength of the party and the type of union to which an individual belonged. Thus, union–party affiliation appears to provide an important "cue" to behaviour.

With respect to election outcomes, it is important to note that members of NDP-affiliated locals were more likely to support the Liberal than the New Democratic party. Although the difference between levels of support for the Liberals and NDP among union members narrowed considerably when the local was affiliated with the NDP, the Liberal party has been able to maintain substantial support even among the latter individuals. That finding notwithstanding, it would appear that increased union affiliation with the NDP is one way the party could increase its electoral support.

NOTES

1. Stanley Knowles, *The New Party* (Toronto: McClelland and Stewart, 1961); Gad Horowitz, *Canadian Labour in Politics* (Toronto: University of Toronto Press, 1968), 198–233; and Desmond Morton, *NDP: Social Democracy in Canada* 2d ed. (Toronto: Hackett, 1977), 19–32

2. As the National Committee for a New Party stated, "a central organization like the Canadian Labour Congress, which itself is made up almost entirely of affiliated organizations, will not be affiliated to the new party as a Congress. Individual trade unions each make their own democratic decision whether to affiliate to the party or not. If they decide in favour, they will be affiliated to the CLC for economic purposes and to the party for political purposes. It is important to keep the two functions separate. The Congress and the new party will undoubtedly have a very friendly relationship with each other, but in all probability there will be no formal ties between them. This is the situation in Great Britain and other democratic countries" (quoted in Horowitz, *Canadian Labour*, 242). For a reiteration of this position once the NDP had been established, see the

lead editorial in the official journal of the CLC, *Canadian Labour* 6 (September 1961), on the occasion of the NDP's founding convention.

3. The merger of the American Federation of Labor (AFL) and the Congress of Industrial Organizations (CIO) in the United States in 1955 opened the way for a merger of their Canadian counterparts, the Trades and Labor Congress and the Canadian Congress of Labour, respectively. The latter organisations merged in 1956 to create the CLC which, as of 1982, represented 57.6 per cent of organised labour in Canada (Labour Canada, *Directory of Labour Organizations in Canada, 1982* [Ottawa], 19). For a more detailed discussion of the TLC/CCL merger see Horowitz, *Canadian Labour*, chap. 5. It should be noted that the description of the CLC as a united working class movement is necessarily a relative one. It is obvious from the above that fully 42.4 per cent of union members in Canada belong to unions not affiliated with the CLC. A disproportionate share of these unionists reside in the province of Quebec, in which many of the union federations are affiliated with the Confédération des syndicats nationaux

(CSN), Confédération des syndicats democratiques (CSD), and Confédération des syndicats canadiens (CSC). Thus, a more accurate description may be a united English-speaking working class movement.

4. See, for instance, *Canadian Labour 6* (September 1961).

5. Maurice Duverger, *Political Parties*, trans. Barbara and Robert North (New York: Wiley, 1967), 227.

6. Samuel Barnes, "Ideology and the Organization of Conflict," *Journal of Politics* 28 (1966): 522–30.

7. Giovanni Sartori, "From the Sociology of Politics to Political Sociology," in *Politics and the Social Sciences* ed. Seymour Martin Lipset (New York: Oxford University Press, 1969), 84–85 (emphasis in original).

8. Robert Dahl, *Modern Political Analysis* 3d ed. (Englewood Cliffs: Prentice-Hall, 1976), 44–53.

9. John Meisel, *Working Papers on Canadian Politics* (McGill-Queen's University Press, 1972); Harold Clarke, Jane Jenson, Lawrence LeDuc and Jon Pammett, *Political Choice in Canada* (Toronto: McGraw-Hill Ryerson, 1979).

10. Richard Miller and Fraser Isbester, eds., *Canadian Labour in Transition* (Scarborough: Prentice-Hall, 1970), 231; and N. H. Chi and George C. Perlin, "The New Democratic Party: A Party in Transition," in *Party Politics in Canada* 4th ed., ed. Hugh G. Thorburn (Scarborough: Prentice-Hall, 1979), 179.

11. V. Keddy, "Class Identification and Party Preference among Manual Workers: The Influence of Community, Union Membership and Kinship," *Canadian Review of Sociology and Anthropology* 17 (1980): 31.

12. When we examined union members instead of union families, the results of the analysis were essentially identical within sampling error.

13. John Zipp, "Social Class and Canadian Federal Electoral Behaviour: A Reconsideration and Elaboration" (Unpublished PhD diss., Duke University, 1978).

14. Data from the 1979 Canadian National Election Study were provided by the ICPSR. The data were originally collected by Harold Clarke, Jane Jenson, Lawrence LeDuc and Jon Pammett. Neither the ICPSR nor the original collectors of the data bear any responsibility for the analyses or interpretations presented here.

15. Annual reports on local union affiliation with the NDP covering the period from 1961 to 1981 were made available by the federal office of the NDP, which bears no responsibility for the interpretations presented here.

16. Union status has been operationally defined as a trichotomous variable, including nonunion members; union members who belong to union locals not affiliated with the NDP; and union members who belong to NDP affiliated locals. An individual is considered to be a union member if he or she, personally, or a family member, belongs to a union. Similarly, an NDP-affiliated union member is one who personally belongs to an affiliated union local or is part of a family, one of whose members belongs to an affiliated local. In cases in which an individual belongs to a nonaffiliated union and a family member belongs to an affiliated union, the individual is considered to be part of an NDP-affiliated family unit.

The 1979 National Election Study included information on individuals' and family members' union affiliation. In those cases for which the union was not specified (such as "other international union"), we referred to the original interview schedules to obtain the name of the specific union. Unfortunately, respondents were not questioned on the union local to which they belonged and, thus, most individuals did not supply that information. In those cases, determination of whether an individual belonged to an NDP-affiliated local was as follows. First, we determined whether any locals of the individual's union were affiliated to the NDP in the respondent's province. If not, he or she was deemed a member of a nonaffiliated union. If there were locals of the individual's union affiliated to the NDP within the province, we examined whether this was the case within the individual's constituency. Thus, for example, if 1. an individual belonged to the UAW, 2. lived in Windsor–Walkerville, and 3. it was determined that a UAW local in Windsor affiliated with the party in 1979, the individual was coded as a member of an affiliated union. The distribution of locals affiliated with the NDP—over two-thirds are located in Ontario, and throughout the country they tend to cluster in larger urban areas—make this procedure less tentative than might initially appear to be the case. The distribution of cases on the union status variable (57.6 per cent nonunion, 37.4 per cent members of nonaffiliated unions, and 5.0 per cent members of affiliated unions) corresponds relatively closely to the distribution in the public: 30.5 per cent of the civilian labour force were union members in 1980 (Labour Canada, Directory, 18) and 8 per cent of union members belonged to NDP-affiliated unions (see table 1). Copies of the interview schedules were made available by Harold Clarke.

17. See, for instance, Clarke, Jenson, LeDuc and Pammett, *Political Choice in Canada*, 517–22.

18. For a discussion of the fear of labour domination once organisational links were established between the party and unions, see Horowitz, *Canadian Labour*, 140–50.

19. This is consistent with the aggregate proportion of union local affiliation in Canada. In 1979, 404 of the 745 affiliated locals (54 per cent) were either UAW or USWA locals, which together comprise 59 per cent of affiliated unionists (NDP files).

20. The number of members of NDP-affiliated unions in the sample by region is: Quebec and Atlantic region, 4; Ontario, 95; and the West, 30; summing to 129.

21. Data from NDP files, 1979.

22. Gary Teeple, "'Liberals in a Hurry': Socialism and the CCF-NDP," in *Capitalism and the National Question in Canada*, ed. Gary Teeple (Toronto: University of Toronto Press, 1972), 245.

section 4

THE ECONOMY AND VOTING

o

THE ECONOMY AND POLITICAL SUPPORT: THE CANADIAN CASE

KRISTEN MONROE
LYNDA ERICKSON

o

How important are economic conditions in determining political support? Is voting a simple referendum on economic outcomes? Or must voters perceive critical party differences over economic policy before the economy has a political impact? Although these questions have received considerable attention in the last decade, analysts have nonetheless overlooked an important national system which could offer rich opportunities for theoretical insight: the Canadian one.[1] With a disciplined party system, the Canadian parliamentary system is highly executive-dominated and has formed no coalition governments since World War I. Executive-sponsored economic policies traditionally prevail in the Canadian legislature, with responsibility for the creation and passage of such policies clearly resting with the party in power.[2] This means the Canadian voter can more reasonably assign blame (or reward) for economic policies and conditions than can the voter in the more frequently examined American system, where power to shape economic policy is shared between the president and an independent Congress, often controlled by the opposition party.

Further, the Canadian party system presents the voter with an interesting configuration of comparative economic policy choices. The two major parties, the Liberals and the Progressive Conservatives, widely believed to offer little that is different in economic policy, locate themselves at the centre of the political spectrum in a relationship that Downs originally suggested would encourage voters to respond primarily to the performance of the incumbent party.[3]

At the same time, the New Democratic Party, strong in certain provinces, attracts a sufficient portion of the national vote to consider it a possible alternative for expressing discontent with the two centrist parties.[4] This allows us to test another Downsian assumption that public perceptions of party differences are

TABLE 1   *POLITICO-ECONOMIC VIEWS AND VOTING*

Prior Questions	Findings

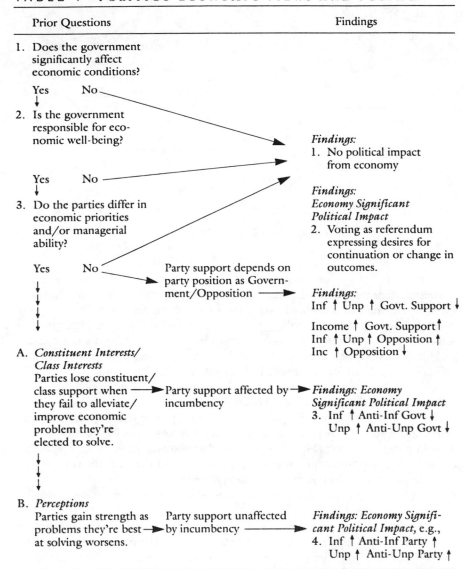

1. Does the government significantly affect economic conditions?

Yes   No

2. Is the government responsible for economic well-being?

Yes   No

3. Do the parties differ in economic priorities and/or managerial ability?

Yes   No

Party support depends on party position as Government/Opposition ⟶

A. *Constituent Interests/ Class Interests*
Parties lose constituent/ class support when ⟶ they fail to alleviate/ improve economic problem they're elected to solve.

Party support affected by ⟶ incumbency

B. *Perceptions*
Parties gain strength as problems they're best ⟶ at solving worsens.

Party support unaffected by incumbency ⟶

Findings:
1. No political impact from economy

Findings:
Economy Significant Political Impact
2. Voting as referendum expressing desires for continuation or change in outcomes.

Findings:
Inf ↑ Unp ↑ Govt. Support ↓

Income ↑ Govt. Support↑
Inf ↑ Unp ↑ Opposition ↑
Inc ↑ Opposition ↓

Findings: Economy Significant Political Impact
3. Inf ↑ Anti-Inf Govt ↓
Unp ↑ Anti-Unp Govt ↓

Findings: Economy Significant Political Impact, e.g.,
4. Inf ↑ Anti-Inf Party ↑
Unp ↑ Anti-Unp Party ↑

critical in determining how economic conditions influence political support.[5] The Canadian system thus allows us 1. to test whether voting is a simple referendum on economic conditions; 2. to ascertain whether perceived party differences on economic policy are critical politically; and 3. if they are, to discover what kind of impact they have on mass political support. This paper addresses these questions via an economic analysis of Canadian party and government support between 1954 and 1979.

POLITICAL SUPPORT: A REFERENDUM ON OUTPUTS OR A CHOICE AMONG POLICY ALTERNATIVES

The logic behind our examination is as follows. Three factors in the voters' calculus will mediate the economy's effect on voting or public opinion measures of political support: 1. voters' beliefs about government control over economic conditions or outcomes; 2. voters' views on government responsibility for domestic economic well-being; and 3. voters' beliefs concerning party differences on economic priorities or managerial ability. The effects of the first two factors are straightforward: voters who believe the government cannot determine economic outcomes (for reasons beyond its control), or who believe government does not and should not determine economic well-being, will quite reasonably not be influenced by the economy when they vote. The effects of the third factor are more problematic. From the literature, we derive four possible outcomes.

The first outcome suggests that voters who find the parties identical on economic policy priorities and abilities will cast their votes on the basis of non-economic factors, e.g., foreign policy issues or personality. Thus, the economy will have little or no political impact (outcome 1 in table 1).

A second scenario suggests that identical parties make voting a referendum on economic policies. This view assumes the public believes domestic economic conditions result from policies which either party could and would pursue equally well. The vote choice thus is designed to send a message to the government to continue or discontinue its economic policy. Under this scenario, the economic influence on support should be the same regardless of which party holds office. The critical dependent variable to consider is Government and Opposition support, rather than party support. In terms of specific findings, we should expect a deteriorating economy to hurt any governing party. Inflation and unemployment therefore will be negatively related to Government popularity, regardless of the particular party forming the government. Conversely, income should be positively related to Government popularity. Patterns of Opposition popularity should reflect the reverse picture (outcome 2 in table 1). This logic is found in Downs's original economic theory of voting and is tested in some form by virtually every analyst in the field.[6]

Our third and fourth outcomes describe situations when the parties are believed to differ on their policies. Here the logic involves even more attention to complex empirical reality and to the distinction between short-term and long-term voter behaviour. Both outcomes originate in the assumption that voting is a choice between parties believed to differ significantly in their economic policy priorities and/or managerial abilities. Parties to the right of centre are said to be perceived as more concerned with lowering inflation, while parties to the left are more concerned with lowering unemployment.[7] The difficulty concerns the next step in the process. Here analysts tend to divide into those who stress perceptions versus those who stress constituent or class interests.

The class or constituency adherents argue that because voting is essentially a group phenomenon, it is therefore critical to examine policy responses of the groups which support a specific party.[8] The key is group expectations, expectations which make voters more angered by failures from such a party than from parties which actually may do far less for them but which had never been expected to help in the first place.[9] Party support should be strongly affected by incumbency under this scenario, with parties being blamed or rewarded for economic conditions but only when in a position to actually make economic policy—i.e., only when they form the Government. In terms of specific findings, this means that while in office, an anti-inflation government should suffer more from high inflation than a party taking no stand on inflation, or a party whose platform makes inflation a low priority. Conversely, a government elected to alleviate unemployment should be blamed more for unemployment. When in Opposition, an anti-inflationary party should benefit from inflation and an anti-unemployment party from unemployment.[10] Or noneconomic factors might become more important (outcome 3 in table 1).

The perceptionists disagree, arguing that when voters choose between anti-unemployment or anti-inflationary parties, they are selecting different economic strategies, based on their perceptions and beliefs about which political party has the greater commitment and/or ability to alleviate a problem.[11] This reasoning results in high unemployment's helping parties who are believed to be more committed to decreasing unemployment, and high inflation's evoking a similar response that turns voters toward the anti-inflationary party.[12] Whether that party holds office is not crucial. The main consideration here for voters is their perception of long-term party preferences and abilities. What this logic suggests for our test is that, in the short term, inflation should help a Canadian party believed to be anti-inflationary, and unemployment should turn voters toward a Canadian party which makes alleviating unemployment a central goal (outcome 4 in table 1).

GOVERNMENT RESPONSIBILITY FOR ECONOMIC CONDITIONS

Following the logic summarised in table 1, our first task was to determine public beliefs concerning governmental responsibility for economic conditions. This determination is particularly important in Canada, where several factors limit the federal government's control of economic conditions and, as a result, may limit public assignment of blame or reward for economic conditions. First, the federal system in Canada has become increasingly decentralized, especially in the 1960s and 1970s, as the provincial governments' share of government expenditures expanded and some provinces began to devise independent economic strategies based on resource development and control.[13] Second, the Canadian economy is highly vulnerable to external factors, especially events occurring in the American economy. This fact has often been emphasised and used by government leaders to excuse apparent failures in government economic policy.

How do Canadians view these constraints on the government? Data on Canadian politico-economic attitudes are available from two main sources: the Canadian Institute for Public Opinion (CIPO), a Gallup affiliate,[14] and the Canadian National Election Studies, which were conducted following the 1974 and 1979 elections.[15] The evidence concerning Canadians' beliefs about their federal government's capacity to control the domestic economy is limited, sporadic, and calls

TABLE 2   *CANADIANS' VIEWS OF GOVERNMENT RESPONSIBILITY FOR ECONOMIC CONDITIONS*

CIPO December 1969: Do you think enough is being done in Canada to prevent inflation or do you think more could be done?	More could be done	Enough is being done	Don't know
	71%	10%	19%
CIPO June 1974: In view of world-wide inflationary trends, do you think there is anything the Federal Government can do to control inflation in Canada?	Yes	No	Don't know
	69%	15%	16%

Canadian National Election Study, 1974: This is a list of some things for which governments in Canada are responsible. For each one, I would like your opinion about whether the federal government in Ottawa or the provincial government here in (province) is more important in dealing with it. The economy ———	Federal Government	Provincial Government	Both Equally Responsible
	71%	7%	22%

Canadian National Election Study, 1979: Thinking now about the federal government generally, not a particular party government, I would like to read you a list of things people have said the federal government should consider doing...tell me whether you think the government should or should not be doing these things: Make sure that everyone who wants to work has an opportunity to do so ———	Should do	Should not do	Don't know
	93%	5%	2%
Insure that inflation is kept under control———	95%	2%	2%

for cautious interpretation; nonetheless, this evidence does suggest that Canadians hold the government responsible for the economy's performance[16] (see table 2).

It would seem that 1. most Canadians believe their government has substantial control over the domestic economy; 2. Canadians locate this power at the federal

TABLE 3   CANADIANS' BELIEFS ABOUT PARTY
           DIFFERENCES

CIPO January 1969: Do you think there is a real difference between the federal Liberal and Conservative parties or are they much the same?	Real difference	Much the same	Can't say
	19%	71%	10%

CIPO August 1974: Do you or do you not think there is any really important difference between the Liberal and Conservative parties?	Yes differ	Do not differ	Don't know
and Conservative parties?	53%	32%	15%
Between the NDP and Liberal parties?	67%	17%	17%
Between the Conservative and NDP parties?	64%	17%	19%

level; and 3. inflation and unemployment are considered to be a federal government responsibility.

PUBLIC VIEWS ON PARTY DIFFERENCES

The second step in our analysis of the effects of the economy was to examine the available evidence concerning public beliefs on party differences in economic policies. Traditional wisdom on Canada holds that competition for the centre of the political spectrum has led both Liberals and Conservatives to blur their differences even more than is true of major parties in most other liberal democratic systems.[17] But recent work by Johnston, based on reported voting patterns in the 1979 and 1980 elections, argues that Canadian voters may find greater macroeconomic policy differences between the two major parties than do academic observers.[18]

Although still sketchy, Canadian data on public perceptions of party differences are more extensive than those on the federal government's capacity to control economic conditions. In a 1969 CIPO survey, 71 per cent of the respondents thought the federal Liberal and Conservative parties were "much the same" (see table 3). A similar CIPO question in August 1974 asked respondents if they thought there was any "really important difference" between those parties. This time the percentage who said there was a difference between the Liberals and Conservatives was substantially higher, at 53 per cent. However, when these same respondents were asked to compare those parties with the NDP, the percentage who saw a difference between the Liberals and the NDP was 67 per cent and between the Conservatives and the NDP was 64 per cent. These figures suggest that general differences between the major parties are not as striking as those between either major party and the NDP.

TABLE 4   CANADIANS' BELIEFS ABOUT PARTY
DIFFERENCES ON THE ECONOMY

CIPO April 1967:	Liberals	Conservatives	NDP	Don't know
Will you tell me which party you associate with each one of the following:				
Would make the country prosperous ———	25%	13%	11%	45%
Which federal party do you think can do a better job of handling				
inflation ———	27%	13%	10%	47%
unemployment ———	24%	13%	11%	48%
CIPO December 1971:				
Looking ahead for the next few years, which federal party do you think would do the best job of handling inflation				
problems ———	25%	15%	14%	42%
unemployment ———	24%	15%	17%	40%
CIPO June 1972:				
Which federal party do you think can best handle the problem				
of unemployment ———	24%	20%	10%	43%
inflation ———	25%	18%	7%	47%
	Better	**Worse**	**Same**	**Don't know**
CIPO March 1978:				
If we had a Conservative government in Ottawa rather than a Liberal government, do you think the financial and economic situation in this country would be better, worse, or about the same as it				
is now ———	17%	10%	66%	8%
an NDP government ———	14%	30%	39%	18%

More direct evidence on economic policy differences between the parties comes from other CIPO surveys (see table 4). Four times between April 1967 and November 1981 respondents were asked to indicate which federal party they thought would do the best job in bringing prosperity and/or handling inflation and unemployment. For every question, more than 40 per cent of the respondents—by far the largest single group—replied they didn't know or couldn't say. There is certainly not the left–right distinction between the parties that is apparent in the United States and Britain.[19] In Canada, the percentage believing the Liberals can best handle inflation corresponds closely to the percentage believing Liberals can best handle unemployment.

In a later survey in March 1978 the CIPO asked respondents about the potential for economic change with a new government. Sixty-six per cent said that with the Conservatives in power the situation would be about the same. Only 39 per cent said that with the NDP in power the situation would be the same. The surprisingly high proportion of respondents uncertain on these questions indicating party difference, the absence of left–right distinctions and the tendency for respondents to say the economic situation would be the same if the Conservatives were substituted for the Liberals suggest that Canadians find few economic differences between their main parties.

POLITICAL IMPORTANCE OF PERCEIVED PARTY DIFFERENCES

What political consequences result from the fact that Canadians find few economic differences between the two major parties? Time series data on party support provide some answers to this question. The possibilities outlined in table 1 suggest that, in the absence of party differences, party support 1. may reflect no economic influence, or 2. may constitute a referendum on policy outcomes. When voters do see party differences, party support 3. may be strongly affected by incumbency and reflect class or constituent interests, or 4. may be less affected by incumbency and primarily reflect public perceptions concerning long-term party priorities and abilities.

Our political data consist of quarterly responses to CIPO polls taken between March 1954 and September 1979. These polls asked: "If a federal election were held today, which party's candidate do you think you would favour?"[20] The initial observations for each quarter include the percentage of respondents who indicated they would vote for the Liberals, the Conservatives, the NDP, and the percentage of respondents who indicated they were undecided about which party they would choose.[21] Support for the Government and Opposition was constructed by using the appropriate party support figures for the party currently forming the Government or Opposition[22] (see appendix A).

To test these various propositions concerning the effects of the economy, we developed the following statistical models.

$$1. \quad PS = \alpha + B_1 UMP + B_2 \Delta RPI + B_3 INF + \in$$

where:

PS =   political support, indicated by the quarterly responses to the CIPO polls on vote intention for the particular parties,

α =   a constant;

UMP =   the unemployment rate during the quarter;

Δ RPI = the change in real personal income per capita during the quarter
($RPI_t - RPI_{t-1}$);

INF = inflation, as based on the change in the Implicit Price Index
during the quarter;

$\in$ = an error term.

A second model adds a political variable (POLI) to measure the impact of political events that are independent of economic factors, but which may rally support to whichever party is governing. (See appendix B for details on the construction of the political proxy variable and data sources and operationalization of the economic predictors.)

This gives:

2. $\quad PS = \alpha + B_1 UMP + B_2 \Delta RPI + B_3 INF + B_4 POLI + \in$

where all other variables are as described above. A variant on the income variable, defined as levels of real personal income, was also substituted in all equations. This variable (MI) was used not to test for income's political impact, as it is frequently used, since the close relationship between inflation and levels of real income produces multicollinearity; rather, we utilised it to detect the political importance of the money illusion, the belief that more dollars are better, regardless of their buying power.

This general model can be used to measure the economy's political influence by substituting support for the Government, the Official Opposition Party, and the Liberal, the Conservative, and the New Democratic Parties as the dependent variable. By analysing the dependent variable as the percentage of undecided voters (DK), rather than as support for a particular party, the basic model can also be used to detect the economy's importance for the inordinately large number of undecided voters.[23]

Because of autocorrelation inherent in times series, an autoregressive model was used to test the independent effects of the predictors. This procedure—the Cochrane-Orcutt Search procedure—calculates the first order serial correlation coefficient (rho) and allows for it when calculating the beta coefficients.[24] Unfortunately, this procedure lessens the reliability of the R^2 as an estimator of the total explained variance since the value of rho is included in its calculation.[25] Comparing the values of R^2 across equations is statistically valid only if the rhos for the compared equations are the same or statistically quite close. (See appendix C for the zero-order correlations between all economic and political variables.)

Since our earlier findings suggested that Canadians find few party differences on economic policies between the two major parties, we expected one of two outcomes: 1. a lack of economic influence on major party support, but some economic impact on NDP support, or 2. major party support heavily dependent on incumbency, with voting a referendum on economic conditions. In the second case, unemployment and inflation would be inversely related to support for the party forming the Government and positively related to support for the Opposition party. Income would have a positive effect on the governing party's support and a negative impact on the Opposition party.

TABLE 5   DETERMINANTS OF GOVERNMENT POPULARITY 1954–1979

EQ	Constant	MI	Economic Variables ΔRPI	Economic Variables UMP	INFL	Political Variable POLI	R²	Test Statistics d.w.	Test Statistics N	Test Statistics Rho
1**	36.1	-.01 (1.23)		.68 (.87)	-.43 (.67)		.53	2.04	102	.70
2**	32.5		.01 (.23)	.54 (.69)	-.46 (.64)		.52	2.05	102	.74
3**	37.0	-.01 (1.29)		.45 (.60)	-.59 (.94)	3.72* (2.71)	.56	2.05	102	.74
4**	33.9		.001 (.28)	.28 (.35)	-.73 (1.05)	3.69* (2.68)	.56	1.97	102	.70
5◆	47.0	-.00 (.80)		.47 (.54)	-.64 (.87)		.47	1.96	102	.69
6◆	44.7		.029 (.63)	.27 (.33)	-.54 (.68)		.47	2.12	102	.68
7◆	47.5	-.00 (.79)		.33 (.39)	-.74 (1.01)	2.29 (1.42)	.48	2.11	102	.69
8◆	45.4		.024 (.51)	.12 (.15)	-.69 (.86)	2.23 (1.37)	.48	2.08	102	.67

Because of autocorrelation in the series all tables were calculated using the Cochrane–Orcutt procedure as described in K.J. White, "A General Program for Econometric Methods Shazam." *Econometrica* (June 1978): 239–40. T-ratios are in brackets. Coefficients are nonstandardized throughout tables 5–11.
* Significant to .01
** Undecided respondents included.
◆ Undecided respondents excluded.

TABLE 6   DETERMINANTS OF OPPOSITION POPULARITY 1954–1979

EQ	Constant	Economic Variables				Political Variable	R²	Test Statistics		
		MI	ΔRPI	UMP	INFL	POLI		d.w.	N	Rho
1+	22.1	-.00 (.72)		.91 (1.33)	.09 (.14)		.49	2.16	102	.65
2+	21.4		-.03 (.23)	.71 (.69)	-.18 (.64)		.49	2.18	102	.66
3+	22.2	-.00 (.72)		.87 (1.27)	.05 (.07)	.82 (.60)	.49	2.17	102	.64
4+	21.6		-.03 (.73)	.67 (1.01)	-.25 (.36)	.90 (.66)	.49	2.18	102	.66
5++	28.2	.00 (.11)		.70 (.85)	.04 (.05)		.52	2.19	102	.70
6++	28.5		-.02 (.39)	.78 (1.01)	-.09 (.12)		.52	2.17	102	.69
7++	28.2	.00 (.12)		.72 (.86)	-.06 (.09)	-.42 (.31)	.52	2.18	102	.70
8++	28.4		-.02 (.36)	.80 (1.02)	-.06 (.08)	-.42 (.27)	.52	2.17	102	.69

+ Undecided respondents included.
++ Undecided respondents excluded.

FINDINGS

Do fluctuations in party support act as a referendum on economic outcomes, as Downs suggested and as many politicians and scholars believe?[26] No. A close look at tables 5 and 6, summarising predictors of Government and Opposition support, shows that only the political variable is significant. The evidence does not suggest that economic fluctuations affect support for either the governing or the opposition party. These findings thus do not confirm the Downsian referendum scenario suggesting that political support is a simple response to economic conditions, with good times rallying the public behind the incumbent party and bad times causing the public to indicate their desire for a change in economic conditions by supporting the Opposition. Rather, they suggest that when the public finds no significant economic differences between the parties, then noneconomic factors will be critical.

To ensure that our null findings reflected the electorates' political preferences, rather than the methodology we employed, we also performed a number of other tests with our data. First, to allow for multicollinearity between the money illusion variable and inflation ($r = .77$), we not only employed the autoregressive model described earlier, but we also tested each of these variables separately with the unemployment variable. Second, we computed a change variable for our measures of inflation ($INF_t - INF_{t-1}$) and unemployment ($UMP_t - UMP_{t-1}$) and tested all models using the predictors. Third, to allow for a lagged public response to economic conditions, we examined various lag models concentrating on 3 to 6 month lags.[27] Finally, to allow for temporal shifts in the economy's impact of Government popularity between the 1960s and the 1970s, in particular an increase in the economy's political impact during the economic malaise of the 1970s, we examined the post-1970 period separately.[28] None of these tests affected our substantive findings. Economic variables were not related to Canadian support for either the Government or the Official Opposition in the direction predicted by the referendum hypothesis.

What if these findings are an artifact of analysing a time series which includes both Liberal and Conservative parties in one series? It is possible that the purely political components of party support might be enough to cancel out independent economic influences. To allow for this possibility, we analysed as separate time series party support for both major parties throughout the time period and then controlled for incumbency by analysing the Liberals' support only when they formed the Government and the Conservatives' support only when in Opposition.[29] This procedure ensures that we do not miss more subtle public attitudes on party policy differences and enables us to examine the perceptionist and the constituent and/or class-interests theories.

What do these alternate approaches suggest for Canada? If we assume—if only for the purposes of argument—that Canadian parties fit the traditional left/right continuum, with Liberals to the left and Conservatives to the right, then we should expect the Liberals to be seen as the anti-unemployment party and the Conservatives as the anti-inflation party. According to the class/constituent interest theorists, this means Liberals should be harmed by unemployment, and the Conservatives by inflation, while they form the government. If the perceptionists are correct, however, neither of these will occur. The perceptionists argue that incumbency is not critical and therefore Liberal Party support throughout the entire period should follow the same pattern: it will increase as increasing unemployment turns voters toward the anti-unemployment party. Similarly, for the perceptionists, increasing inflation will turn voters toward the anti-inflationary Conservative Party throughout the entire period.

Is either of these theories substantiated by our data? To the extent that our results are affected by incumbency, the patterns are not those predicted by the class and constituent/interest theorists. That is, party support is not more sensitive to economic fluctuations when that party forms the Government than when it is in Opposition, as the class/constituent interest theorists argue. The class/constituent interest theory suggests that unemployment should hurt Liberal Government support; it does not (see equations 5–8 of table 7). (Analysis of support for the Conservative Government, while based on only 25 observations, a sample too small to provide a reliable statistical test of this theory, also suggested that inflation had no significant political effect on Conservative Government popularity.)

The perceptionist theory suggests that throughout the entire period unemployment should turn voters toward the Liberals; the evidence does not support this suggestion. The perceptionist view also argues that inflation should turn voters toward the Conservatives. Again, our data do not support this view (see equations 1–4 of tables 7 and 8, respectively).

An interesting anomaly occurs for the Conservatives, however. Examining support for the Conservative party throughout the entire time period, we find a positive relationship between Conservative party popularity and unemployment, something which supports the general referendum theory insofar as the Opposition Conservatives might gain from economic deterioration which occurs under a Liberal Government. Yet when we examine support for the Conservative party looking only at those periods when it is in Opposition, precisely when both our class/constituent interest theorists and the perceptionist theorists suggest the relationship should be even stronger because incumbency would not "tar" the Conservatives with any responsibility for unemployment, the coefficient for unemployment drops substantially and is no longer significant (see table 8).

Since our survey evidence in table 4 suggested that Canadians judge the Liberal party slightly better at handling both inflation (27 per cent) and unemployment (24 per cent) and since many analysts of Canadian parties have argued that Canadian parties do not fit the traditional left–right distinction, we also examined our results to determine whether the Liberal party might be the party whose support responds more closely to economic conditions. But this was not the case. As we noted earlier, the R^2 is not a reliable measure of total explained variance in an autoregressive model, except when the first-order serial correlation coefficients (rho) are statistically equal, in which case the R^2 can then be used as a relative test of explained variance. This situation occurred here. Despite similar Rho's, the R^2 for Liberal party support ranged from .42 to .46 while Conservative support ranged from .69 to .71.

TABLE 7 DETERMINANTS OF LIBERAL PARTY POPULARITY 1954–1979

EQ	Constant	Economic Variables				Political Variable	R²	Test Statistics		Rho
		MI	ΔRPI	UMP	INFL	POLI		d.w.	N	
Throughout the series:										
1+	40.5	.001		-1.29	-.30	1.81	.42	1.99	102	.60
		(.30)		(1.88)	(.45)	(1.25)				
2+	40.9		.006	-1.21	-.21	1.80◆◆	.42	2.01	102	.61
			(.13)	(1.91)	(.29)	(2.64)				
3++	50.6	.005		-1.71◆	-.41	.20	.46	2.05	102	.62
		(1.10)		(2.18)	(.54)	(.12)				
4++	52.3		.035	-1.41	.04	.16	.46	2.08	102	.64
			(.74)	(1.87)	(.05)	(.10)				
In government:										
5+	40.3	-.005		-.08	-.57	3.72◆	.42	1.94	76	.55
		(.95)		(.09)	(1.36)	(2.07)				
6+	39.1		.009	-.65	-.72	4.00◆	.42	1.96	76	.64
			(1.06)	(.95)	(1.75)	(2.26)				
7++	50.1	-.004		.11	-.76	2.36	.32	1.99	76	.49
		(.73)		(.12)	(1.58)	(1.18)				
8++	49.3		.006	-.37	-.87	2.58	.32	2.00	76	.51
			(.65)	(.56)	(1.88)	(1.31)				

+ Undecided respondents included.
++ Undecided respondents excluded.
◆ Significant to .05
◆◆ Significant to .01

TABLE 8 DETERMINANTS OF CONSERVATIVE PARTY POPULARITY 1954–1979

EQ	Constant	Economic Variables			INFL	Political Variable POLI	R^2	Test Statistics		
		MI	ΔRPI	UMP				d.w.	N	Rho
Throughout the series:										
1+	16.9	-.006 (1.11)		2.35♦ (2.71)	-.10 (.15)	2.06♦ (2.35)	.71	2.10	102	.79
2+	13.2		.010 (.26)	2.26♦ (2.48)	-.14 (.19)	1.90 (1.34)	.70	2.16	102	.81
3++	22.4	-.004 (.79)		2.68♦ (2.63)	-.18 (.24)	.90 (.54)	.69	2.15	102	.76
4++	19.7		.002 (.05)	2.53♦ (2.43)	-.18 (.21)	.74 (.44)	.69	2.17	102	.79
In opposition:										
5+	21.1	-.002 (.32)		.52 (.69)	.32 (.81)	1.23 (.74)	.28	2.02	76	.49
6+	20.8		.007 (.92)	.35 (.65)	.24 (.63)	1.32 (.81)	.28	2.02	76	.50
7++	25.5	.002 (.27)		.66 (.69)	.30 (.64)	.17 (.09)	.34	2.03	76	.53
8++	25.8		.005 (.58)	.83 (1.21)	.29 (.63)	.14 (.07)	.34	2.02	76	.53

+ Undecided respondents included.
++ Undecided respondents excluded.
♦ Significant to .01

Given all of this, we return to our original conclusion: economic policy differences between the parties play an important mediating role in the economy's impact on political support. One last test appeared to offer further support for this position. While few Canadians found economic differences between the Liberal and Conservative parties, a clear majority saw policy differences between the two centrist parties and the NDP (see table 3). According to our theory, NDP support should therefore be more strongly related to economic fluctuations.

Our findings suggest the economy does have a more significant effect on NDP support. Results in table 9 indicate a significant relationship between NDP popularity and economic conditions, but not as predicted by traditional models of left–right voting patterns. As in our other models we allowed for the political importance of the money illusion effect (M1) by examining both levels and changes of real personal income. Using absolute levels of real personal income to detect the impact of the money illusion, both income and unemployment have a significant effect on NDP popularity. But the patterns are not as expected. Support for the NDP increases as personal income and employment rise, suggesting the NDP's social welfare programs may be viewed as luxury goods reserved for times of economic prosperity.

Using changes in personal income as the income measure, however, the unemployment effect declines considerably and is no longer significant. Similarly, the personal-income effect is no longer statistically reliable, making it difficult to arrive at definitive conclusions on the relative importance of different economic predictors.

The results on inflation are even more difficult to ferret out. When undecided voters are included in the calculations of party popularity, the impact of inflation is significant; when they are omitted from the calculus, inflation has no political impact. Since inflation was considerably higher in Canada during the 1970s than during the early period of our series (1954 to 1969), we needed to determine whether our findings might be a period effect.[30] In work on Britain, the US and Germany, Hibbs suggested voters may eventually adjust to higher price levels and that analysts need to allow for this in their attempts to measure inflation's full political impact.[31] (A 10 per cent inflation rate in 1974, for example, simply would not carry the same political costs as in 1954.) This suggests a possible systemic change. In fact, two possible systemic changes may affect patterns of NDP support: 1. shifts in public attitudes to inflation, and 2. decreased public concern with social welfare as a result of passage of broader welfare provisions. Journalistic work on English party support suggests that once political systems pass reasonably extensive welfare programs, social democratic parties become viewed as luxuries to be supported during economic prosperity.[32] Once welfare-state provisions are built into the politico-economic system, economic downturn may simply turn voters to more traditional, lower-spending centrist parties.[33] We needed to allow for both of these possible systemic changes in our analysis of NDP support (see table 9).

To test for both these factors, we examined NDP support during two distinct time periods: 1. 1950–1969, and 2. 1970–1979, before and after a number of major welfare state provisions were expanded and after the patterns of Canadian inflation shifted.[34] Table 10 presents these findings. When we analysed the pre- and post-1970 periods separately, the inflation effect disappears. Now only unemployment is statistically significant, in four out of eight equations (see table 10).

What do these findings mean? The results in tables 9 and 10 suggest the economy has a greater political influence on NDP support than on support for the centrist parties.[35] Given the general direction of the economic influence, however, the NDP's appeal does not seem to increase with unemployment, as traditional analysis of left-wing party support has suggested. Our tentative interpretation of this finding is that NDP popularity resides primarily in its social welfare policies on issues such as pensions and national health, and not as a party believed to offer viable policies for increased employment. Given that the Canadian national unemployment insurance system (originally instituted in 1940) provides at least some safety net for the unemployed, many voters may believe NDP policies are now inappropriate solutions for unemployment in a capitalist economy; as a result, when unemployment increases, their partisan support may go elsewhere. This interpretation is intriguing but cannot be definitive without more extensive survey evidence on NDP support.

It is also likely, of course, that yet a further systemic factor is at work here. Since the NDP remains a third party nationally, their influence on policy may generally be perceived as a voice advocating social programs which the major parties then co-opt. To the extent that this is true, these findings thus offer support for the old pluralist argument that healthy political parties in a two-party system can effectively co-opt a third party, socialist or otherwise.

Taken as a whole, then, analysis of the economy's influence for Canadian political parties suggests that perceived differences on economic policies are important mediating factors in the economy's influence on party support. Public perceptions of differences on economic priorities may be necessary before the economy will play a role in support for parties or the Government. Where the public sees few economic policy differences between the parties, the economy's impact on support for major parties will be limited. Analysis of support for social democratic parties, offering distinct politico-economic alternatives, is more likely to uncover patterns of economic voting than is analysis of support for centrist parties.

ECONOMIC INFLUENCES ON UNDECIDED VOTERS

One last question intrigued us. In a system such as Canada's, in which the major parties are believed to offer few policy differences, and in which the Social Democratic party's policies may be too easily co-opted to make the party truly competitive, is it possible that economic dissatisfaction will take the form of refusal to support any party? Both Arcelus and Meltzer and Rosenstone suggest that the economy's political influence in the US works by affecting participation rates rather than through determining actual vote choice. Does this phenomenon occur in Canada?[36] To answer this, we concluded our analysis by examining the economy's impact on fluctuations in the undecided voters.

TABLE 9 DETERMINANTS OF NDP POPULARITY 1954–1979

EQ	Constant	Economic Variables				Political Variable	Test Statistics			
		MI	ΔRPI	UMP	INFL	POLI	R^2	d.w.	N	Rho
1+	11.7	.008♦ (4.17)		-.99♦ (3.66)	.41 (.98)	-.23 (.28)	.50	1.95	102	.32
2+	11.7		.014 (.26)	-.36 (1.05)	1.02♦ (2.48)	-.22 (.03)	.45	2.07	102	.54
3++	12.1	.010♦ (3.70)		-1.06♦ (2.51)	.58 (1.22)	.63 (.63)	.62	1.89	102	.53
4++	15.5		-.002 (.55)	-.33 (.58)	.64 (1.25)	-.30 (.30)	.60	1.98	102	.74

+ Undecided respondents included.
++ Undecided respondents excluded.
♦ Significant to .01

TABLE 10 DETERMINANTS OF NDP POPULARITY, CONTROLLING FOR SYSTEMIC CHANGES

EQ	Constant	MI	Economic Variables			Political Variable	R²	Test Statistics		
			ΔRPI	UMP	INFL	POLI		d.w.	N	Rho
Period: 1954–1969										
1+	15.3		.045 (.94)	-1.22** (2.68)	-.29 (.44)	.73 (.63)	.49	1.85	63	.49
2++	19.5		.034 (.63)	-1.45* (2.16)	.21 (.27)	.39 (.27)	.61	1.75	63	.64
3+	15.2	.001 (.22)		-1.25** (2.66)	-.24 (.37)	.74 (.63)	.48	1.84	63	.49
4++	23.7	-.009 (1.34)		-1.19 (1.46)	-.25 (.36)	1.05 (.75)	.61	1.73	63	.78
Period: 1970–1979						*1967–1979*				
5+	18.5		-.42 (1.34)	-.88** (2.41)	.38 (.85)	.01 (.01)	.22	1.94	39	.12
6++	21.8		-.04 (1.18)	-.67 (1.25)	.11 (.19)	.51 (.39)	.17	1.83	39	.31
7+	16.2	.001 (.24)		-.84 (1.67)	.54 (.99)	.02 (.02)	.18	1.92	39	.12
8++	18.4	.004 (.70)		-.84 (1.21)	.30 (.45)	-.61 (.50)	.15	1.81	39	.35

+ Undecided respondents included.
++ Undecided respondents excluded.
* Significant at .05
** Significant at .01

Our task here was to determine whether the high levels of undecided respondents (up to 35 per cent) indicate economic dissatisfaction, with the undecided voters moving into and out of the political system as a result of economic concerns. Since the number of undecided voters declines considerably in response to election campaigns and an impending election, we reformulated our political variable (POLI) to include election periods. POLI thus was modified to add a + 1 in any quarter when there was an election (see appendix B). This reformulated model allows us to detect whether the undecided Canadian voters are apolitical actors who form political party loyalties only once a real electoral choice approaches, or whether their lack of party commitment indicates economically founded political alienation. The results in table 11 suggest the former is the case: undecided Canadian voters align as a result of approaching elections, and not because of economic discontent.

Neither unemployment nor inflation affects fluctuations in levels of undecided voters; the impact of personal income, significant in one of the equations, is not in the predicted direction. The lack of effect from most of the economic variables and the apparent perverse direction of the one significant income predictor, plus the remarkable robustness of the POLI variable ($B = 6.87$ and 7.06, each significant at the .01 per cent confidence level), suggest voter apathy rather than economic dissatisfaction and explain the large changes in percentages of undecided voters.

CONCLUSION

Our analysis of economic influences on Canadian political support yields several findings of interest to both Canadian specialists and political economists. Canadians seemingly believe their federal government has both the capacity and the responsibility to ensure economic well-being. Locating a clearly established centre of responsibility for economic conditions led us to expect Canadians would blame and reward the governing party for economic fluctuations. This did not occur, however, since the expected link between responsibility and blame appears to be limited in the Canadian case by a widespread belief that there are few critical party differences in either macroeconomic priorities or in managerial ability. This factor suggests that perceived party differences are an important mediating link in the process by which the economy influences political support in Canada.

More importantly, our findings from a parliamentary system with two disciplined centrist political parties, plus a distinct social democratic alternative, suggest several conclusions concerning the nature of the economy's political impact. First, mass public support is not simply a referendum on economic outcomes. The public does not signal its desire for a shift in economic policies simply by voting for the opposition. Rather, a public sense that there are party differences on economic policies or management is part of the process by which the economy affects support for the government. Second, in countries where the public sees a strong overlap in party priorities and capabilities, the economy's impact on centrist parties will be limited. This may account for the lack of consistent findings in much of the earlier work in this area, particularly theoretical work based on the American case, where the public believes policy differences exist but are slight and where there is no viable third-party alternative.[37] Third, public support for a

TABLE 11 *THE EFFECT OF ECONOMIC AND NONECONOMIC VARIABLES ON UNDECIDED VOTERS*

EQ	Constant	MI	Economic Variables		INFL	Political Variable POLI	R²	Test Statistics		
			ΔRPI	UMP				d.w.	N	Rho
1	18.4	.010* (2.34)		-.15 (.27)	-.29 (.33)	-6.87* (4.65)	.37	2.06	102	.31
2	21.1		.025 (.47)	.42 (.75)	.97 (1.24)	-7.06* (4.62)	.34	2.08	102	.38

* Significant to .01

noncentrist party believed to offer distinct economic alternatives will be influenced by economic considerations. The economic bases of such support, however, may be affected by passage of the party's economic programs insofar as the institutionalization of those programs diffuses the party's potential as a vehicle for expressing economic discontent.

Finally, there is no evidence suggesting Canadian voters express discontent with economic conditions by moving into the undecided category, behaviour which might indicate alienation from the two-party centrist system as a whole.

APPENDIX A: PATTERNS OF POLITICAL SUPPORT 1954–1979

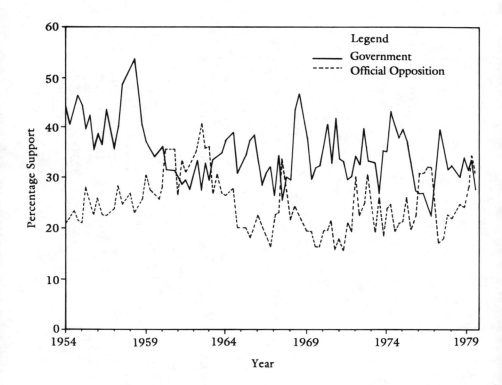

APPENDIX B: VARIABLE CONSTRUCTION AND DATA SOURCES

UNEMPLOYMENT RATE[38]

In 1975 the method of collecting unemployment statistics was changed in Canada. Changes were made in the content of the surveys designed to measure labour force participation and unemployment, in the questionnaire design and in the definition of unemployment. The definition of what constitutes unemployment became more stringent; the age of those considered eligible for labour force participation was raised from 14 to 15; the sample frame for the surveys was designed using the 1971 Census data instead of the 1961 Census, and the later Census was used to revise the weights employed to produce national estimates. For a more detailed discussion of these changes, see Statistics Canada, *Conceptual, Definitional and Methodological Changes in the Labour Force Survey* (71-00-506). Statistics Canada subsequently revised earlier unemployment estimates from 1966 to 1974 to make them compatible with the new series. Since the revised series is more closely tied to the actual size of the population at the time, we used the revised series of our estimates of unemployment from 1966 to 1974.

INFLATION

$$\left[\frac{\text{Implicit}^{39} \text{ Price Index}_t - \text{Implicit Price Index}_{t-1}}{\text{Implicit Price Index}_t} \right] \ 100$$

CHANGES IN REAL PERSONAL INCOME. MONEY ILLUSION

Both of these predictors are based on government series for personal income, where

$$\text{Personal Income} = \left[\frac{\text{Per Capita Personal Income for Quarter}}{\text{Implicit Price Index}^{40}} \right] \ 100$$

This calculation forms the money illusion predictor. For ΔRPI the personal income variable was a first difference variable calculated using seasonally adjusted real per capita income.

POLITICAL PROXY VARIABLE

A change of Prime Minister, a change in Government, and periods of national political crises seen as a potential threat to the regime or political community were identified as times when political support will rally round the party forming the government, regardless of economic conditions. Accordingly, we constructed our political proxy variable as a dummy variable which took the value of 1 for:

a) The six months following a change of Prime Minister or a change in government;
b) the FLQ crisis in 1970;
c) the six months following the election of the separatist Parti Québécois in Quebec;
d) surveys when an election occurred.[41]

This variable corresponds to the rally variable developed originally by Mueller and utilised by most analysts of US presidential popularity with one exception: it omits wars, since Canada has not directly participated as an antagonist in any foreign war since the Korean war.[42]

APPENDIX C: ZERO-ORDER CORRELATIONS

The zero-order correlations with support for the government and official opposition are presented below:

ECONOMIC VARIABLES

Popularity	MI	ΔRPI	Unemp	Infl
Government+	−.36 (p = .00)	−.07 (p = .23)	−.16 (p = .06)	−.17 (p = .05)
Government++	−.22 (p = .01)	−.02 (p = .42)	−.12 (p = .11)	−.11 (p = .14)
Official Opposition	−.17 (p = .05)	−.19 (p = .03)	.27 (p = .00)	−.16 (p = .14)
Official Opposition++	−.03 (p = .37)	−.16 (p = .03)	.35 (p = .00)	−.11 (p = .14)

+ undecided respondents included
++ undecided respondents excluded

NOTES

1. See, for example: Morris Fiorina, *Retrospective Voting in American National Elections* (New Haven: Yale University Press, 1981); Douglas A. Hibbs, Jr., "Political Parties and Macroeconomic Policy," *American Political Science Review (APSR)* 71 (1977): 1467–87; Douglas A. Hibbs, Jr., "On Demand for Economic Outcomes: Macroeconomic Performance and Mass Political Support in the United States, Great Britain and Germany," *Journal of Politics* 44 (1982): 426–62; D. R. Kinder and D. R. Kiewiet, "Sociotropic Politics: The American Case," *British Journal of Political Science* 11 (1981): 129–61; D. R. Kiewiet, *Macroeconomics and Micropolitics: The Electoral Effects of Economic Issues* (Chicago: University of Chicago Press, 1983); Gerald H. Kramer, "Short-Term Economic Fluctuations in the U.S. Voting Behavior, 1896–1964," *APSR* 65 (1971): 131–43, for research on the United States; L. Jonung and E. Wadensjo, "The Effects of Unemployment, Inflation and Real Income Growth on Government Popularity in Sweden," *Scandinavian Journal of Economics* 81 (1979): 343–53, or Martin Paldam and F. Schneider, "The Macroeconomic Aspects of Government and Opposition Popularity in Denmark, 1957–1978," *Nationalokonomish Tidslcrift* (1980), 118, for work on parliamentary systems; or Kristen R. Monroe, "Economic Analysis of Electoral Behavior: A Critical Review," *Political Behavior* 9 (1979): 137–43; Kristen R. Monroe, *Presidential Popularity and the Economy* (New York: Praeger, 1984), for an overview of the literature in this area. Some excellent work on the general nature of Canadian support does exist. The most recent is by Harold D. Clarke, Allan Kornberg, and Marianne C. Stewart, "Parliament and Political Support in Canada," *APSR* 78 (1984): 452–69. Work by Lawrence LeDuc, Harold D. Clarke, Jane Jenson, and Jon H. Pammett, "Partisan Instability in Canada: Evidence from a New Pane

Study," *APSR* 78 (1984): 470–84, presents a three-wave panel study of party identification in Canada. In none of these pieces, however, is the focus on economic components of party support.

2. Even in periods of minority government, the governing party can usually rely on sufficient minority party support to avoid major compromises on important economic policies. In only one period of minority government, from 1972 to 1974, did the opposition seem to play a major role in compromising the policies of the party in power. But even this example of opposition influence on government policy has been questioned in William P. Irvine, "An Overview of the 1974 Federal Election in Canada" in *Canada at the Polls: The General Election of 1974*, ed. Howard R. Penniman (Washington, D.C.: American Enterprise Institute for Policy Research, 1975).

3. Anthony Downs, *An Economic Theory of Democracy* (New York: Harper & Row, 1957); Rick Ogmundson, "On the Measurement of Party Class Positions: The Case of Canadian Federal Political Parties," *Canadian Review of Sociology and Anthropology* 12 (1975): 169–78. Of the two parties, the Liberals so consistently formed the government that the system was at times described as one-party dominant, by Hugh Thorburn, "Interpretations of the Canadian Party System," in *Party Politics in Canada* 4th ed., ed. Hugh Throburn (Scarborough: Prentice-Hall, 1979). From 1921 to 1979, the Liberals held power for 48 of the 58 years, winning 13 of 19 elections. The ambivalent position of the Conservative Party on the political spectrum is illustrated in their official name: the Progressive Conservative Party of Canada. During the last years in our time series, elements in the Conservative Party attempted to make it more of a right-wing alternative. In Parliament as well, the party leadership became critical of the Liberals' use of state intervention, including state ownership, in their economic strategy. But this difference between the parties, if apparent, came at best only at the end of the time period covered in our study, and is not evident in our data on Canadians' perceptions of party differences (see tables 3 and 4).

4. Originally founded in the Depression as the socialist Cooperative Commonwealth Federation (CCF), this party moderated its socialist stance during the Cold War and the prosperity of the 1950s, but was nonetheless unable to stem a gradual decline in its popularity. In an effort to change its national image and create a closer alliance with organised labour, the party reorganised and officially formed the New Democratic Party (NDP) in August 1961. Since the CCF and NDP are thus essentially the same party in different organisational guise, we will treat them as one party.

Another minor party, the Social Credit, is a populist party which also originated in the Depression. It has attracted about half the proportion of the popular vote gained by the CCF/NDP, averaging less than 5 per cent in all but two of the national elections of the period. Because its national support is so low—virtually nonexistent in the polls—we omitted the Social Credit party from our analysis.

5. Downs, of course, is concerned with the general benefits received from government. We have simply applied his theory specifically to economic considerations.

6. Downs, *An Economic Theory of Democracy.* Compare Hibbs, "Political Parties and Macroeconomic Policy"; Hibbs, "On Demand for Economic Outcomes", or Monroe, *Presidential Popularity,* for a review.

7. Jonung and Wadensjo, "The Effects of Unemployment Inflation, and Real Income Growth"; J. J. Rosa and D. Amson, "Conditions économique et élections: une analyse politico-économetrique (1920–1973)," *Revue française de science politique* 26 (1976): 1107–24; Hibbs, "On Demand for Economic Outcomes"; Friedrich Schneider, "Different (Income) Classes and Presidential Popularity: An Empirical Analysis," *Munich Social Science Review* 2 (1978): 53–69.

8. See Hibbs, "On Demand for Economic Outcomes" or Schneider, "Different (Income) Classes."

9. See James Kuklinski and D. M. West, "Economic Expectations and Voting Behavior in United States House and Senate Elections," *APSR* 75 (1981): 436–47.

10. Since the primary factor in this model is voter response to the government, the economy's political effect on Opposition parties should depend partly on whether the system has two parties. In a two-party system, support for the Opposition should be the obverse of government popularity.

11. For example, Kristen R. Monroe and Maurice Levi, "Economic Expectations, Economic Uncertainty and Presidential Popularity" in *The Political Process and Economic Change*, ed. K. R. Monroe (New York: Agathon, 1983); or Martin Paldam, "A Preliminary Survey of the Theories and Findings on Vote and Popularity Functions" *European Journal of Political Research* 9 (1981): 181–99.

12. See Paldam and Schneider, "Macroeconomic Aspects of Government," on Danish support; M. Lewis-Beck and P. Bellucci, "Economic Influences on Legislative Elections in Multiparty Systems: France and Italy," *Political Behavior* 4 (1982): 93–107, or French and Italian party voting; on Monroe, *Presidential Popularity*, for a review.

13. Richard Simeon, "Intergovernmental Relations and the Challenges to Canadian Federalism," *Canadian Public Administration* 23 (1980): 14–32; John Richards and Larry Pratt, *Prairie Capitalism: Power and Influence in the New West* (Toronto: McClelland and Stewart, 1979).

14. The Gallup Poll results come from news releases of the CIPO. Questions on parties' handling of the economy and governmental responsibility for the economy were posed irregularly between April 1967 and March 1978.

15. Data from the National Election Studies were made available by the ICPSR. They were originally collected by Harold Clarke, Jane Jenson, Lawrence LeDuc, and Jon Pammett. For information concerning the sampling method used see Clarke et al., *Political Choice in Canada* (Toronto: McGraw-Hill Ryerson, 1979).

16. Unfortunately, data on public perceptions of responsibility for the economy are available only for the last decade in our time series. Another further limitation involved in using these questions concerns the extent to which asking whether more could be done to hold down inflation, create jobs, or increase social welfare will always elicit widespread assent. Given this, we decided to adopt a cautious interpretation of the responses' significance.

17. William P. Irvine, "The Canadian Voter," in *Canada at the Polls, 1979 and 1980: A Study of the General Elections*, ed. Howard R. Penniman (Washington, D.C.: American Enterprise Institute for Policy Research, 1980).

18. Richard Johnston, "Economic Factors in Recent Canadian Elections" (Paper presented at the Canadian Political Science Association Annual Meeting, Vancouver, B.C., 1983). Johnston's conclusions are based primarily on the difference in employed and unemployed respondents' voting patterns between 1979 and 1980. Unfortunately, the surveys on which he had to rely did not ask the same question with respect to unemployment in 1979 and 1980.

19. See Hibbs, "On Demand for Economic Outcomes"; or Schneider, "Different (Income) Classes and Presidential Popularity."

20. For a discussion of how well these poll data predict voting see Lawrence LeDuc, "The Measurement of Public Opinion" in *Canada at the Polls*, ed. Penniman. In general, the relationship between CIPO predictions of party support and the actual party percentages won in elections is quite close.

21. Data source is the Canadian Institute of Public Opinion. The Gallup Poll CIPO 235–429A (machine-readable files), Roper edition. Toronto, Ontario: Canadian Gallup Poll Ltd. (producer); The Roper Center (distributor), 1954–1979; 99 data files (logical records vary) and accompanying codebooks. Election

months and missing surveys pose problems for time series analysis. During election months a number of surveys were usually conducted asking Canadians for which party they would vote. For those quarters, we averaged the results to give us one set of figures on party support. For missing surveys—that is, those third-quarter months for which no surveys were taken—we used the survey data taken in the month following for our observation; if there were no survey that month, we used the month prior as our quarterly observation. So, for example, if there were no March survey for a particular year, we would use the April survey for our observation for the first quarter. If there were no April survey, we would use the February survey for our first quarter observation. If no surveys from either the month preceding or after our quarterly month were available, then no data for that quarter were recorded. Only nine quarterly records were missing as a result of these procedures. These missing quarters were estimated by averaging the prior and subsequent quarterly data.

22. We calculated Government, Opposition, and party support variables, both including and excluding undecided respondents in our denominator. In part, this is because the large number of undecided respondents suggests "Don't Know" responses should not be ignored. We were also aware, however, that party shares of the decided vote are substantively important. We have therefore analysed our data set using both calculations as the denominator. That is, first we analysed the percentage of total respondents indicating support for the Liberals, the Conservatives and the NDP, including the undecided voters in our denominator, and next we calculated party supporters as a percentage of respondents who expressed support for any party, omitting the undecided voters from the denominator.

23. Canadian surveys frequently report large percentages of respondents who are undecided about their voting preferences. These percentages occasionally are higher than the percentages expressing support for any one of the political parties. Since the percentages of undecided

respondents are always lower in preelection surveys, this suggests approaching elections cause shifts in popular response to parties. While this means interelection polls are not as directly analagous to election results as they should be if we are to use them as surrogates for election results, the movement between elections of large numbers of undecided voters into and out of the ranks of party supporters offers a unique opportunity to determine the extent to which economic fluctuations may motivate such movements; that is, movement of respondents into the undecided category may suggest a tempering of support for the parties in response to economic conditions. It also may indicate a broader form of systemic support, insofar as being an "undecided" voter indicates refusal to support any of the political parties.

24. See K. J. White, "A General Program for Econometric Methods. Shazam," *Econometrica* (June 1978), 239–40.

25. The general form of the first-order autoregressive model used is:

$$Y = Xb + e$$

and

$$e = pe_{(t-1)} + v$$

where:

p is the autoregressive parameter rho;
v is the new independent disturbance.
R^2 output is based on the v disturbance, not the e disturbance term.

26. Cf. John Mueller, *War, Presidents and Public Opinion* (New York: Wiley, 1973); or W. L. Miller and M. Mackie, "The Electoral Cycle and the Asymmetry of Conditions and Political Popularity," *Political Studies* 21 (1973): 263–79.

27. Three to six month lags are the ones found most frequently in the literature. See Helmut Norpoth and T. Yantek, "Macroeconomic Conditions and Fluctuations of Presidential Popularity: The Question of Lagged Effects," *American Journal of Political Science* 27 (1983): 785–807, for a review.

28. See Hibbs, "On Demand for Economic Outcomes," for evidence of shifts in the degree of the economy's political impact.

29. We performed similar tests on the brief period of Conservative Government and Liberal Opposition but decided that the small number of observations made results from standard parametric tests unreliable.

30. The mean quarterly inflation rate in our data from the period 1954 to 1969 was .51; for the period 1970 to 1979 it was 1.75.

31. See Hibbs, "On Demand for Economic Outcomes," for a review of this literature.

32. R. W. Apple, Jr., in "The Welfare State Was a Boon to Mrs. Thatcher," *New York Times* (12 June 1983), sec. 4C, p. E2 suggests that hard times hurt leftist parties, especially in societies where extensive welfare benefits already exist.

33. Many of the NDP programs, such as national health insurance and comprehensive unemployment programs, which effectively expanded the social welfare infrastructure, were adopted in Canada by governments during good economic times.

34. Slight variants on these periods were also analysed; substantive results were the same.

35. We also examined the effect of economic variables on the combined percentage of NDP supporters and undecided respondents. The results, however, were not improved.

36. Francisco Arcelus and Allan H. Meltzer, "The Effect of Aggregate Economic Conditions on Congressional Elections," *APSR* 79 (1975): 1232–39; S. J. Rosenstone, "Economic Adversity and Voter Turnout," *American Journal of Political Science* 26 (1982): 25–46.

37. More than one specialist has suggested the contemporary literature may under report the inconsistency of findings in this area, making it risky to draw conclusions from cumulative evidence in the literature. Paldam writes:

> Two biases operate in the natural processes of selection on the market for scientific papers. There is a bias for clear significant results over unstable insignificant ones; this bias already operates at the supply side (inside every one of us). Second, once a certain coefficient is established, people are reluctant to present results with "wrong signs"; and regression techniques are well known to be flexible. Hence one may doubt that such cumulative evidence may always converge towards the true relation. Perhaps the convergence may occasionally be towards something which is not only *better* than, but even a bit *different* from, the true relation (Paldam, "A Preliminary Survey," 197).

For a more detailed discussion of the extent to which different findings on the economy's political impact results from mere methodological shifts, see Gebhard Kirchgassner, "Rationality, Causality, and the Relation between Economic Conditions and the Popularity of Parties" (Paper presented at the International Seminar on Macroeconomics, Perugia, 1984).

38. Seasonally adjusted unemployment estimate for the last month in each quarter. Data from Statistics Canada, Old Labour Force Survey; 1954–1966, and New Labour Force Survey: 1966–1979.

39. Implicit Price Index for last month of quarter t (based on seasonally adjusted data), 1971 = 100. The implicit price index was used to calculate the measure of the inflation because this index reflects both pure price changes and changing expenditure patterns within and between major groups in the country. For a description of this index see Statistics Canada, *Canadian Price Index: Revisions, Concepts and Procedures* (62–546).

40. Based on the Implicit Price Index for the last month of the quarter.

41. This was utilised only in models estimating the economy's support on undecided voters.

42. Mueller, *War, Presidents and Public Opinion*; analysts, e.g., Henry Kenski, "The Impact of Economic Conditions on Presidential Popularity," *Journal of Politics* 39 (1977): 764–73; Monroe, *Presidential Popularity*.

INFLATION, UNEMPLOYMENT AND CANADIAN FEDERAL VOTING BEHAVIOUR◇

KEITH ARCHER
MARQUIS JOHNSON

How important is economic performance in affecting voting behaviour and election outcomes in Canada? What perspectives do voters bring to bear in evaluating economic performance: are evaluations based on their personal economic well-being or on the health of the economy as a whole? What type of linkage exists between individuals' economic concerns and their support for the political parties: do Canadians turn to one party when they are concerned about inflation, and another when unemployment preoccupies them?

We explore these questions by examining the electoral importance of inflation and unemployment in Canadian elections between 1974 and 1984.[1] We argue that Canadians think the government should ensure full employment and price stability, but this attitude often is not expressed in electoral choice. The importance of the issues of inflation and unemployment is highly variable in the period under study, judgements about their importance are based mainly on sociotropic considerations,[2] and the linkage between issues and parties is very unstable. We conclude by speculating on the causes of partisan-issue instability.

ECONOMIC ISSUES AND VOTING BEHAVIOUR

Research on the importance of economic issues in determining the outcome of Canadian federal elections is decidedly inconclusive. For example, early work on Canadian political behaviour by Regenstrief and Meisel found that the issue of unemployment was important in the 1962 and 1963 federal elections, whereas "economic" issues were the second most important (after majority government) in

◇ *Canadian Journal of Political Science* 21, 3 (September 1988): 569–84.

the 1968 federal election.[3] Furthermore, within the rubric of economic issues, inflation was found to be most important, followed by housing and unemployment.

More recent analyses based upon National Election Studies have ascribed a lesser importance to issues generally and economic issues in particular, while focussing on the broader context of political choice, including partisan attachments and evaluations of party leaders. For example, in their study of the 1974 federal election, Clarke, Jenson, LeDuc and Pammett found that inflation was by far the dominant issue of the campaign.[4] However, the overall effect of this issue on the election outcome was mitigated because most partisans viewed their own party as closest to them on the issue. In subsequent analyses, Clarke et al. found that the salience of inflation declined by the time of the 1979 election, and also that those mentioning economic issues (which included references to inflation) or unemployment as most important to them were more likely than not to remain with "their" party rather than to switch allegiance. However, it should also be noted that among those who changed their party choice between 1974 and 1979, the majority of those mentioning the economy or unemployment as the most important issues switched to the Conservatives.[5] For 1980, the relative importance of economic issues declined again, as did the gap separating the percentage who thought the Liberal or Conservative parties closest to themselves.[6]

In contrast to the findings from individual-level analyses that no issues (including economic issues) had a large effect on election outcomes between 1974 and 1980, several recent aggregate-level studies have found a discernible effect. For example, using aggregate economic and electoral data for Canadian elections from 1930 to 1979, Happy examined the effect of changes in unemployment, inflation and income on percentage vote for the incumbent party. The data, disaggregated to the provincial level to increase the number of cases, suggested that income and inflation were significant predictors of party support. In addition, unemployment was found not to have a significant effect on incumbency voting.[7]

This finding was not corroborated by Monroe and Erickson in their analysis of support for the major parties between 1954 and 1979. Also using measures of inflation, unemployment and income as independent variables, Monroe and Erickson found that all three were unrelated to support for the government or opposition, or for the Liberal party. Increases in levels of unemployment, on the other hand, were positively related to support for the Conservative party, and negatively related to levels of New Democratic party support. Monroe and Erickson note that these findings are inconsistent with the "characteristic bias" of parties of the right and left, respectively, in which the former are assumed to favour price stability and the latter full employment. Rather, according to Monroe and Erickson, the weak effect of economic variables overall follows from the non-ideological "broker" nature of Canada's major parties; the somewhat stronger effect for the NDP reflects its greater emphasis on economic policy.[8]

In contrast to the above, Johnston's analysis indicated that both unemployment and inflation have considerable currency in explaining political attitudes and behaviour in Canada whereas personal income has a marginal effect. For example, he found a strong negative effect of unemployment on approval ratings of the prime minister's performance, particularly in the Pearson–Trudeau era, and a strong effect of unemployment and inflation on confidence in the federal government, with unemployment being somewhat more important. Furthermore, he notes that in the short term Canadians are more sensitive to changes in unemployment than inflation, but with an underlying permanent bias against inflation. Although not specifically concerned with measuring the partisan effects of changes in the macroeconomy, he argues nonetheless that growth or stagnation have important implications for citizen orientations:

> Expectations seem routinely pessimistic, but exert no force on policy emphasis: if the inflation rate is currently high ... one is likely to want the government to deal with inflation now; if the unemployment rate is currently high, then that indicator should be the one attacked. ... [T]he myopia ... leads ... to sacrificing choices between inflation and unemployment. ...[9]

In the Canadian pholitical system, where parties tend not to have stable and identifiable issue positions over time, the importance of inflation or unemployment to election outcomes will depend on their visibility, but also on the willingness and ability of the parties to attach their fortunes to those issues, as opposed to other issues or more general leader and party evaluations. Furthermore, we expect that the parties have considerable latitude in claiming issues as their "own." The following analysis brings to bear on these hypotheses survey data collected over a 10-year period.

DATA ANALYSIS

Preliminary analysis and previous research led us to focus our analyses on sociotropic rather than egocentric economic voting. For example, in the most detailed study of this issue in Canada to date, Clarke and Kornberg found that egocentric economic experiences had virtually no effect on levels of incumbent government support, and a weak effect on sociotropic judgements. The latter, however, strongly influenced the level of support for incumbent governments.[10]

We wished to verify their finding that personal experiences with unemployment and inflation had little impact on the importance ascribed to these issues during elections. Unfortunately, data from the National Election Studies do not allow for a comprehensive and systematic cross-time examination of egocentric economic voting in Canada. Particularly problematic are data relating to inflation. The 1984 National Election Study was the first to include a question probing the respondents' personal experience with inflation.[11] Respondents were asked whether their personal income had kept ahead of inflation or fallen behind, and to what extent. We examined whether those who perceived a decline in their real income were more likely to cite inflation as important in deciding how to vote than were those who did not perceive such a decline. The data, although limited in scope, suggest that past personal experiences exerted almost no independent effect on the perceptions of the electoral importance of inflation (see table 1, panel B). For example, of those respondents who reported that their personal income kept ahead of increases in the cost of living, 1.8 per cent cited inflation as an important issue, compared to 3.3 per cent of those who indicated their personal income had fallen behind a lot.

TABLE 1   *EGOCENTRIC EFFECT OF ECONOMIC*
PERFORMANCE ON ISSUE MENTIONS, 1974–1984

	Percentage	(N)
A. Percentage mentioning unemployment as an important election issue		
1974 Employment type		
Not in workforce	3.6	(1019)
Unemployed	4.9	(36)
Never employed	5.0	(20)
Employed	4.8	(1370)
1979 Not in workforce	11.9	(979)
Unemployed	16.8	(57)
Never employed	5.9	(19)
Employed	11.3	(1616)
1980 Unemployed in the year preceding election?		
Yes	3.8	(180)
No	3.1	(1598)
1984 Laid off or looking for work in the past ___ years?		
a. past 5 years?		
Yes	38.1	(1069)
No	35.5	(2311)
b. past 1 year?		
Yes	39.7	(633)
No	35.5	(2747)
How concerned are you that you might be laid off?		
Very	45.2	(267)
Quite	37.0	(183)
A little	34.2	(349)
Not at all	32.9	(1046)
B. Percentage mentioning inflation as an important election issue		
1984 Over the past five years has your personal income kept ahead of increases in the cost of living, stayed the same or fallen behind some or a lot?		
Kept ahead	1.8	(459)
Stayed same	1.9	(1345)
Behind some	3.3	(926)
Behind a lot	3.3	(492)

The importance of personal experiences with unemployment can be measured much more extensively using data from the National Election Studies. Panel A of table 1 reports findings for each election from 1974 to 1984. For 1974, when unemployment was not an important issue nationally, there was no statistically significant difference in the likelihood of mentioning this issue among the several employment types. For 1979, unemployment seemed to affect the likelihood of mentioning this issue, although the very small number of cases (N = 57) leads us to interpret these results cautiously unless verified in other instances. Data from 1980 do not substantiate the hypothesis that personal experiences with unemployment lead to greater mentions of this issue—there is no significant difference in unemployment mentions between those who had been unemployed in the year preceding the election (3.8 per cent) and those who had not (3.1 per cent). A similar finding was evident when we examined the experience of unemployment in 1984. Among those who personally had been laid off or were looking for work in the five years preceding the election, 38.1 per cent mentioned unemployment as an important election issue, only marginally higher than the 35.5 per cent who cited unemployment despite having no personal experience with it in the previous five years. This pattern of only a marginal difference in the likelihood of citing unemployment between those who did or did not experience it remained when we examined experience during the past year.

It also is interesting to note that although retrospective egocentric economic evaluations appear to have little political effect, prospective evaluations may be more important. Among those who were very concerned that they might be laid off, 45.2 per cent cited this as an important issue, compared to 37.0, 34.2 and 32.9 per cent, respectively, who were quite, a little or not at all concerned with being laid off. However, the very high proportion of respondents who were only a little or not at all concerned personally with being laid off but cited unemployment as the first or second most important issue in an election, together with the relatively large proportion of respondents with these characteristics, leads us to conclude that most of the economic voting which takes place is sociotropic in nature. Given the relatively weak or mixed evidence for egocentric economic voting, the remainder of our analysis is based on aggregate economic performance and sociotropic evaluations.[12]

The Canadian economy of the past two decades has been highly volatile. Inflation increased from approximately 3 per cent in 1971 to over 11 per cent in 1974. It remained high but relatively stable between 1974 and 1980, rose to approximately 13 per cent in 1981, then declined precipitously to about 4 per cent in 1984. The rate of unemployment in contrast, was relatively low and declining prior to the 1974 election, was higher but stable during 1979 and 1980, and increased dramatically prior to the 1984 election.[13] The general finding that governments are more often penalized for poor economic performance than rewarded for improvements[14] leads us to expect inflation to dominate the 1974 election, unemployment to dominate the 1984 election, and for them to be about equally important in the 1979 and 1980 elections.

Given the relatively poor and highly volatile performance of the Canadian economy during the past two decades, and the tendency of Canadians to think that the government is at least partially responsible for economic performance,[15] how important are economic issues in federal elections? Beginning with the 1974 National Election Study, respondents were asked the two most important issues to them personally in deciding how to vote. When examining the four election studies between 1974 and 1984, we found a significant variability in issue mentions over time. In 1974 more than 40 per cent of respondents mentioned inflation as important, and in 1984 almost 40 per cent mentioned unemployment. Except for these two instances, neither issue was mentioned by more than 15 per cent of the respondents, and in 1979 and 1980 mentions of both were dominated by the issues of Quebec separatism and energy pricing.[16]

Although the preceding analysis suggests that economic performance may affect voting behaviour, especially during periods of dramatic change in the economy, these data overstate the influence of economic variables. Previous research has shown that the major determinants of voting in Canada—partisanship, candidate evaluations and attitudes toward issues—are reciprocally related in two-way causal sequences.[17] That is, partisan self-image and evaluation of party leaders may affect the issues which voters see as most important, and the party closest to them on that issue. Thus, even if economic issues are salient and are linked to parties, if the a priori distribution of partisan support does not change because of the issue, its effect on electoral outcomes is minimal. Since the salience of the inflation and unemployment issues was greatest in the 1974 and 1984 federal elections, we will focus our analysis on those two elections.

In attempting to examine the independent effect of issues, we must hold constant prior partisan attachments. However, there are very complex methodological issues involved in doing so. If partisanship was stable in Canada, we would be tempted to use present partisan attachments as the long-term control. However, for a substantial proportion of the electorate, partisan attachments are likely to move with the vote.[18] The typical solution to this problem, both in Canada[19] and in the United States,[20] is to use vote in the previous election as an indicator of long-term partisan effects, and that is the strategy which we adopt.[21]

The analysis of the importance of economic issues controlling for party attachments and attitudes towards party leaders appears in table 2 for 1974 data and table 3 for 1984 data. Each table can be read as the unfolding of a set of Chinese boxes, with each subsequent box or panel of the table eliminating those who voted for reasons other than economic issues. Thus, the first number in each table is the total weighted sample in the survey, and the last number is the percentage of respondents, and by implication the proportion of the electorate, who based their vote for the various parties on the issue under investigation.

Table 2 examines the effect of inflation on voting in the 1974 federal election. The 1974 National Election Study contains a weighted national sample of 2445 cases. Of those, 44 per cent cited inflation as the issue of greatest or second greatest importance in the election. For our purposes, this represents the upper limit in the effect of the inflation issue during that campaign. We assume, in other words, that if respondents do not report that inflation was an important issue to them, it could not affect their voting patterns. Panel A-2 of table 2 illustrates that slightly more than one-third of the respondents thought inflation was important and perceived one of the parties as being closer to them on this issue than were the other parties. Panel A-3 suggests that approximately one-quarter (27.6 per cent) of the respondents actually reported voting for the party that was closest to them on inflation. This latter group of respondents meets the minimal requirements for issue voting—the issue to them is salient, it is linked to a party and they vote in a way which is consistent with their attitudes on this issue. The remaining 72.4 per cent of the electorate did not meet these minimalist criteria and therefore are considered to have voted for other reasons.

In panel B of table 2 we control for the effect of long-term attachment to a political party. The assumption underlying this analysis is that some voters have a very long-term psychological attachment to a political party that can extend

TABLE 2   *EFFECT OF INFLATION ON VOTING BEHAVIOUR, 1974*

	Percentage	(N)
Total weighted sample	100.0	(2445)
A. General		
1. Mentioned inflation as first or second most important issue	44.3	(1083)
2. Saw a party as being closest to them on inflation	34.3	(838)
3. Voted for the party closest to them on inflation	27.6	(676)
B. Controlling for party attachment		
4. Vote in 1972 and 1974 federal elections		
a. same party (standpatters)	18.5	(453)
b. different parties (switchers)	5.3	(129)
c. eligible but did not vote in 1972 (transients)	1.8	(43)
d. not eligible in 1972 (new voters)	1.8	(43)
5. If voted same party in 1972 and 1974, always voted same party?		
a. yes	11.9	(292)
b. no	6.4	(156)
Total inflation vote due to party	11.9	(292)
Total inflation vote not due to party	15.2	(371)
C. Controlling for party and attitudes towards party leaders		
6. Evaluation of leader of party voted for exceeds second most liked leader by 20 points or more (100-point scale)	4.7	(115)
Evaluation of leader of party voted for does not exceed most liked leader by 20 points (inflation voters)	10.5	(256)
D. Direction of vote of inflation voters		
Liberal	4.0	(96)
Progressive Conservative	4.9	(119)
New Democrat	1.7	(41)

throughout their lifetime, or even across generations in a family.[22] Although voters whose attachment to a political party has been very stable over time may mention an issue as being important in their voting decision when asked to do so, we remain skeptical that this issue has had a determining effect for them. Rather, we interpret the direction of causality in such cases to extend from party attachment to issue perceptions.

The data in panel B of table 2 illustrate that for a sizeable proportion of those who meet the minimalist criteria for inflation voting, party attachment impinged upon those perceptions. In panel B-4, the electorate is divided into four groups— those who voted the same in 1972 and 1974 (standpatters); those who voted for different parties (switchers); those who could have voted in 1972 but chose not to, but did vote in 1974 (transients); and those who came of voting age between 1972 and 1974 (new voters).[23] Those who voted for different parties in the two elections, transient voters and new voters, are largely immune from long-term partisan ties—certainly it could be argued that if they purport to identify with a party, their identification was produced by their feelings about the inflation issue. Among those who voted for the same party in both elections, on the other hand, a long-term partisan effect is not so readily dismissed. In panel B-5 we distinguished between those who not only voted for the same party in 1972 and 1974, but had *always* voted for that party, and those who at some point in the past had voted differently. The votes of the former group are determined by a long-term attachment to a party, whereas the latter are grouped with switchers, transients and new voters from B-4 to form the inflation voters after controlling for the effects of party. On the basis of this analysis, we conclude that 15.2 per cent of the electorate in 1974 based their vote on inflation, controlling for the effects of party attachment.

In panel C of table 2 we include the additional control of leader evaluations. This analysis is premised on the assumption that some voters may base their voting choice on their feelings toward a party leader. However, through the processes of persuasion or projection voters may perceive their position on an issue to be consistent with that of one's party or its leader. If that is the case, then we would be more accurate in ascribing primary influence to the leader upon whom the issue position is based rather than to the issue itself.

As with the party attachment variable, we wished to incorporate a relatively stringent test of the effect of leadership on political choice. Using 100-point feeling thermometer scores, we identified feelings toward the leader of the party voted for in 1974, and the feelings toward the most popular of the other party leaders. The latter scores were subtracted from the former, producing a leader preference score ranging from −100 to +100. Negative scores result when the respondents feel more positively towards the leader of a party for whom they did not vote than toward "their" leader. Positive scores indicate a preference for their own party's leader. We assume that leadership predominates when there is a strong preference for the leader of one's own party. Since the standard deviation for the leader evaluation scores tends to approximate 20 points, we operationally defined strong leader preference as a 20-point leader advantage over the next most popular leader.[24] The data indicate that almost one-third of the inflation voters whose behaviour could not be explained by party attachment had a very strong preference for the leader of the party for which they voted, the vast majority of whom voted Liberal. After taking into account the effect of party and leader, the data indicate that 10.5 per cent of the electorate cast their ballots in 1974 on the basis of the inflation issue. By that measure, and we should reiterate that our methodology has ensured the maximum possible importance for this issue, we could conclude that the issue of inflation was important to a substantial number of Canadians in casting their ballots in 1974.

To determine the effect of this issue at the aggregate level (that is, in examining whether it affected the election outcome), it is necessary to examine the partisan distribution of support among inflation voters. For the issue to be important in this context, the distribution of opinion must be skewed in favour of one of the parties.[25] As the data in panel D illustrate, this last criterion was not met. No party was favoured by a majority of those classified as inflation voters. Indeed, despite

TABLE 3 EFFECT OF UNEMPLOYMENT ON VOTING
BEHAVIOUR, 1984

	Percentage	(N)
Total weighted sample	100.0	(3380)
A. *General*		
1. Mentioned unemployment as first or second most important issue	36.3	(1227)
2. Saw a party as being closest to them on unemployment	25.1	(847)
3. Voted for the party closest to them on unemployment	19.7	(667)
B. *Controlling for party attachment*		
4. Vote in 1980 and 1984 federal elections		
a. same party (standpatters)	10.2	(344)
b. different parties (switchers)	5.3	(178)
c. eligible, but did not vote in 1980 (transients)	2.0	(68)
d. not eligible in 1980 (new voters)	2.0	(69)
5. If voted same party in 1980 and 1984, always close to same party?		
a. yes	7.1	(240)
b. no	3.0	(101)
Total unemployment vote due to party	7.1	(240)
Total unemployment vote not due to party	12.3	(416)
C. *Controlling for party and attitudes towards party leaders*		
6. Evaluation of leader of party voted for exceeds second most liked leader by 20 points or more (100-point scale)	2.9	(98)
Evaluation of leader of party voted for does not exceed most liked leader by 20 points (unemployment voters)	9.4	(318)
D. *Direction of vote of unemployment voters*		
Liberal	0.8	(29)
Progressive Conservative	7.2	(242)
New Democrat	1.4	(47)

being the government party during the period of spiralling inflation, the Liberals received a level of support on this issue almost equivalent to that of the official opposition. Overall, the inflation issue had a marginal effect on the distribution of partisan support in the 1974 national election.

Turning to the effect of unemployment on the 1984 federal election, we note that on first blush this issue—while salient relative to other issues of the day—was not as salient as the issue of inflation in 1974 (see table 3). Panel A-1 illustrates that slightly more than one-third of the electorate viewed unemployment as the first or second most important issue in the election. Approximately one in four respondents saw a party as being closest to them on this issue, and about one in five respondents voted for that party.

In panel B of table 3 we controlled for the effect of party attachment. Those who voted for the party closest to them on unemployment were less likely than their 1974 counterparts to vote for the same party as in the preceding election. Approximately one-half of them did so in 1984, whereas two-thirds had this characteristic in 1974 (that is, panel B-4-a divided by panel A-3). This is an important initial indication that the effect of unemployment in 1984 was greater than that of inflation in 1974—those who voted according to this issue were less prone to stable patterns of behaviour.

As with the analysis for 1974, we wished to eliminate those who were very stable supporters of their party since we attribute their behaviour to long-term identification with the party. The latter respondents are identified in panel B-5-a, and the data suggest that 12.3 per cent of the electorate voted on the basis of the unemployment issue, controlling for the effects of party attachment.[26] The effect ascribed to party attachment among unemployment voters is substantially less in 1984 (7.1 per cent) than it was among inflation voters in 1974 (11.9 per cent).

In panel C of table 3 we control for party and attitudes toward party leaders. Using the same methodology as described for table 2-C, leadership evaluations reduced by a further 2.9 per cent the overall proportion of unemployment voters, again a lesser effect than that measured in 1974 (4.7 per cent). This analysis suggests that 9.4 per cent of the 1984 electorate based their vote on the issue of unemployment, controlling for the effects of party attachment and leader evaluations, a proportion similar to the 10.5 per cent of inflation voters in 1974.

Although the unemployment issue in 1984 had a similar effect at the individual level as inflation in 1974, the skew in distribution of partisan support on unemployment meant that it had a dramatically different result on the election outcome. As panel D illustrates, 7.2 per cent of the electorate cast their ballots for the Conservative party on the basis of the unemployment issue, independent of their attachment to parties and feelings toward party leaders. The Liberal party, in contrast, was able to attract less than 1 per cent of the electorate on the basis of this issue. Although research on other advanced industrial democracies might lead us to expect that the most left-wing party, the New Democrats, would benefit disproportionately from high rates of unemployment, in fact their gain was modest and very similar to the support received on account of the inflation issue in 1974.

SUMMARY AND CONCLUSION

A considerable body of research is emerging which suggests that economic issues are becoming more important to election outcomes in advanced industrial democracies. To date, evidence of this trend for Canada is mixed. Little support for the importance of economic issues in survey data contrasts with the mixed results of aggregate data. We wished to examine the electoral effect of economic issues by measuring the change in performance and the reported importance of economic issues in the context of national elections.

Since the data suggested that egocentric evaluations had little effect on reports of issue performance, we focussed on sociotropic evaluations. When examining the Canadian economy during the past two decades, two periods stood out as particularly volatile—the rate of inflation soared in the years preceding the 1974 election, and unemployment skyrocketed in the period leading up to the 1984 election. Prior to 1974 both inflation and unemployment were at relatively low levels but increasing, whereas between 1974 and 1981 both were at relatively high levels and stable or increasing marginally.

Dramatic increases in inflation prior to 1974 gave high salience to this issue, but no party was able to use it to capture large numbers of supporters of the other parties. Despite being the incumbent party, the Liberals were not held responsible for inflation. The strong positive evaluations of Trudeau suggest that the leader was able to overcome any potential disenchantment among Liberals over this issue. The relative stability of high inflation and unemployment in 1979 and 1980 significantly detracted from the salience of these issues. Political debate in 1979 and 1980 was focussed more on issues of national unity and energy policy (with its regional overtones) than on stagflation. By 1984, however, the rate of unemployment had increased dramatically, as had its salience. Unlike 1974, however, high unemployment was linked to the incumbent Liberals and favoured the Conservatives at the expense of the Liberals and, to a lesser extent, the New Democrats.

The key to understanding the importance of economic issues in elections lies not only in their "objective" condition, but also in the ability of parties to link themselves successfully with the majority view. Neither rapid deterioration in performance, as with inflation in 1974, nor stable poor performance, as with both inflation and unemployment in 1979 and 1980, is a sufficient condition for influencing the outcome of elections. In all three cases, although economic performance may have had some effect, its importance was at the margins, superseded by more highly salient issues, prior partisan attachments or evaluations, both positive and negative, or party leaders. The election of 1984, in contrast, illustrates that economic performance can be an issue of significant importance. The data also suggest an asymmetry in the importance of economic improvement and deterioration. For example, inflation in 1984 had declined to levels not seen in more than a decade, yet few respondents were prepared to credit the incumbent party for that performance, whereas almost half thought the surge in unemployment was politically significant. A relatively popular incumbent leader, such as Pierre Trudeau in 1974, can overcome the potential negative effects of poor economic performance. However, an unpopular leader, such as John Turner in 1984, can further penalize an incumbent party by not counterbalancing a potentially harmful issue effect. In either case, the issue does not stand alone.

The data also suggest that voters do not have stable attitudes toward the party best able to deal with economic issues. Perceptions that conservative or right-wing parties have a characteristic bias toward decreasing inflation and liberal or left-wing parties aim first at reducing unemployment seem to hold little currency in evaluations of Canada's major parties. Neither the Liberal party nor the Progressive Conservative party enjoyed an advantage regarding the inflation issue in 1974, and the Conservatives were overwhelming favourites on the "left" issue of unemployment in 1984. Issues matter in Canadian elections, but the parties have considerable latitude in giving issues the proper "spin." Their success in controlling the spin depends to a large extent on more general attitudes toward the parties and toward the party leaders, further underscoring the interrelatedness of the attitudinal determinants of voting in Canada.

NOTES

1. The principal investigators for the 1974, 1979 and 1980 national election and panel studies were Harold Clarke, Jane Jenson, Lawrence LeDuc and Jon Pammett; the 1984 data were collected by Ronald Lambert, Steven Brown, James Curtis, Barry Kay and John Wilson. The data were made available by the ICPSR, and neither the Consortium nor the principal investigators is responsible for analyses or interpretations presented herein.

2. For a discussion of the distinction between egocentric and sociotropic judgements, see Roderick Kiewiet, *Macroeconomics and Micropolitics* (Chicago: University of Chicago Press, 1983), 5–26.

3. Peter Regenstrief, *The Diefenbaker Interlude* (Toronto: Longman's, 1965), 50; John Meisel, *Working Papers on Canadian Politics* (Montreal: McGill-Queen's University Press, 1972), 14–22, and tables 4–6 in Appendix.

4. Harold Clarke, Jane Jenson, Lawrence LeDuc and Jon Pammett, *Political Choice in Canada* (Toronto: McGraw-Hill Ryerson, 1979), 246, especially figure 8.1.

5. Harold Clarke, Jane Jenson, Lawrence LeDuc and Jon Pammett, "Voting Behaviour and the Outcome of the 1979 Federal Election: The Impact of Leaders and Issues," *Canadian Journal of Political Science (CJPS)* 15 (1982): 548, especially table 11.

6. Harold Clarke, Jane Jenson, Lawrence LeDuc and Jon Pammett, *Absent Mandate: The Politics of Discontent in Canada* (Toronto: Gage, 1984), 90.

7. J. R. Happy, "Voter Sensitivity to Economic Conditions: A Canadian–American Comparison," *Comparative Politics* 19 (1986): 54. However, Happy notes that this latter finding is a "serious anomaly" and suggests that the model requires fuller specification to include a measure of partisanship among others (see his note 23).

8. Kristen Monroe and Lynda Erickson, "The Economy and Political Support: The Case of Canada," *Journal of Politics* 48 (1986): 629–40. Further analysis by Erickson, however, suggests that the effect of economic performance on NDP support may be less than initially estimated. See Lynda Erickson, "CCF-NDP Popularity and the Economy," *CJPS* 21 (1988): 99–116.

9. Richard Johnston, *Public Opinion and Public Policy in Canada*, Research Studies for the Royal Commission on the Economic Union and Development Prospects for Canada, vol. 35 (Toronto: University of Toronto Press for Supply and Services Canada, 1986), 138.

10. Harold Clarke and Allan Kornberg, "Public Reactions to Performance and Political Support in Contemporary Democracies: The Case of Canada" (Working paper no. 3: Duke University Program in International Political Economy, October, 1986), especially 17–18 and figure 2.

11. The 1974 National Election Study included the following question: "How much were you personally affected by inflation over the past year or so, a great deal, some or not much at all?" However, this question was asked only of those who did *not* specifically mention inflation as personally important in the election. Since we are concerned with examining whether reported personal experience with inflation leads to more mentions of inflation, this variable is inappropriate for our purposes.

12. Our findings that egocentric economic conditions exert little or no effect on voting patterns is consistent with evidence from other advanced industrial democracies. See, for example, Michael Lewis-Beck, "Comparative Economic Voting: Britain, France, Germany and Italy," *American Journal of Political Science* 30 (1986): 315–46.

13. Detailed data are available from the authors on request.

14. Gregory Markus, "The Impact of Personal and National Economic Conditions on the Presidential Vote: A Pooled Cross-Sectional Analysis," *American Journal of Political Science* 32 (1988): 137–54.

15. Monroe and Erickson, "The Economy and Political Support," 622–23.

16. Data are not presented in tabular form.

17. Keith Archer, "A Simultaneous Equation Model of Canadian Voting Behaviour," *CJPS* 20 (1987): 553–72.

18. Lawrence LeDuc, Harold Clarke, Jane Jenson and Jon Pammett, "Partisan Instability in Canada: Evidence from a New Panel Study," *American Political Science Review* 78 (1984): 470–84.

19. Clarke et al., *Political Choice*, 352–55.

20. Gregory Markus and Philip Converse, "A Dynamic Simultaneous Equation Model of Electoral Choice," *American Political Science Review* 73 (1979): 1059.

21. Lacking panel data, this approach introduces some measurement error through recall data. For an estimate of the error introduced see Robert MacDermid, "The Recall of Past Party Identification: Feeble Memories or Faulty Concepts?" (Paper presented at the annual meeting of the Canadian Political Science Association, McMaster University, Hamilton, 1987).

22. See, for example, Angus Campbell, Philip Converse, Warren Miller and Donald Stokes, *The American Voter* (New York: Wiley, 1960) and also Clarke et al., *Political Choice in Canada*, chap. 5.

23. See Clarke et al., "Voting Behaviour and the Outcome of the 1979 Election."

24. We recognise, of course, that one could apply a much less stringent operational definition, the effect of which would be to increase the measured effect of leadership and to reduce further the observed effect of economic performance. However, as we shall argue, even using the stricter definition, the importance of inflation has deteriorated markedly.

25. See, for example, Clarke et al., *Political Choice in Canada*, 243–72.

26. Note that the discriminating criterion in panel 5-B is whether the respondent always felt close to the party voted for in 1984. The 1984 National Election Study does not contain a question asking whether the respondent always voted for that party, as does the 1979 study. The question selected was closest available approximation.

section

5

RECENT FEDERAL ELECTIONS

---

o

VOTING BEHAVIOUR AND THE OUTCOME OF THE 1979 FEDERAL ELECTION: THE IMPACT OF LEADERS AND ISSUES[◇]

HAROLD D. CLARKE
JANE JENSON
LAWRENCE LeDUC
JON PAMMETT

Given the Liberal party's dominant position in Canadian federal politics, it has been extremely difficult for the Progressive Conservatives to effect an electoral breakthrough and win enough parliamentary seats to form a government. In this century, the Conservatives have been in power for only 22 years. The last time the party formed a majority government was in the spectacular Diefenbaker victory of 1958 which gave the Conservatives 208 of 265 seats. After the demise of the Diefenbaker government in 1963, the Conservatives languished in opposition until 1979 when they won a plurality of seats and Joe Clark formed his short-lived government. It is the election of 1979 which provides the focus of analysis in this article, and especially the success of the Conservatives in supplanting the Liberals, although not with a majority government.

The article uses data from the 1979 Canadian national election and panel study[1] to investigate the impact of issue perceptions and party leader images on voting behaviour and the outcome of that election. Using the conceptual framework and methods of analysis developed in our previous work on Canadian elections,[2] it will be argued that issues played a particularly important role in producing a Conservative victory in 1979. The limited nature of that victory, however, reflected not only a complex mix of issue effects on voter choice, but also the manner in which various segments of the electorate reacted to the party leaders. By considering issue and party leader effects in the 1979 election, the article illustrates and amplifies previous arguments regarding the sensitivity of substantial

◇ *Canadian Journal of Political Science* 15, 3 (September 1982): 517–52.

numbers of Canadian voters to short-term forces in the electoral arena. In the conclusion, it will be argued that this sensitivity rendered the Conservatives extremely vulnerable in the subsequent 1980 election.

THE CANADIAN ELECTORATE

Given the change in government that resulted from the 1979 election one might be tempted to infer that fluctuations in *individual* voting behaviour were atypically large. In this regard, earlier research has documented that considerable individual level instability has accompanied Liberal electoral victories as well.[3] In 1979, although the official election returns show the Liberals lost only three percentage points and the Conservatives picked up only one point compared to their 1974 standings, survey evidence indicates that individual changes in vote and party identification were several times greater than the aggregate results would suggest. Of those participating in both the 1974 and 1979 elections, 27 per cent report switching their vote, and 15 per cent of all those with partisan attachments in 1979 recall changing their party identifications since 1974.[4] For the 1972–1974 election pair, comparable figures were 22 per cent and 18 per cent, respectively. Thus, the extent of individual-level change in party identification and vote between 1974 and 1979 appears substantial, but not atypical, of those elections when there has been no change of government.

Such changes in party identification and voting preference are intimately related to the "flexible" nature of partisanship for many Canadians. In *Political Choice in Canada*, we classified as *flexible* partisans those respondents who deviated in any one of three ways from strong, stable, and consistent party identifications. All three of these conditions were found to be related to the volatility of past voting behaviour, as well as to a number of attitudinal variables.[5] Individuals with strong, stable and consistent party identifications were designated as *durable* partisans. Previous research indicates that much of the vote switching which takes place between any two elections is concentrated among flexible partisans, a group which constitutes a majority of the electorate in federal elections.[6] Also, levels of political interest condition the sensitivity of flexible partisans to particular short-term forces. In 1974, the flexible-low interest group was more sensitive to the effect of leaders, while flexible-high interest partisans responded more strongly to the influence of issues.[7] In contrast, long-term forces explained all but a very small proportion of the variance in voting behaviour for durable partisans.

Also vital for understanding electoral results is a consideration of the composition of the electorate, which can be conceptualized as consisting of three distinct components—the permanent electorate, transient voters, and new voters. In any election, the size of these components and the direction of their choice will be critical. The permanent electorate can be defined as eligible voters who report that they "always" or "usually" vote in federal elections.[8] The net impact of the second component considered here—the transient voters—will be determined by patterns of voter turnout in any given election. Transients are not consistent nonparticipants in the electoral process but rather persons who vote sometimes, but not always. A given pair of elections will show some previous nonvoters moving back into the active electorate and a number of previous voters not exercising their franchise.[9] In the present context, the increase in turnout from the relatively low 71 per cent recorded in the 1974 federal election to the slightly above average 76 per cent of 1979[10] suggests that, in an analysis of the outcome of the latter contest, the behaviour of transient voters entering or re-entering the electorate should be carefully examined because of their numbers. Finally, any given election will see the infusion of a number of new voters into the electorate, the total impact of which will be determined by patterns of population growth and by the length of the interval between elections. In 1979, the potential impact of this group was significant because of the unusually long span of nearly five years between the 1974 and 1979 elections. Approximately 2.3 million new voters (comprising 15 per cent of the total eligible electorate of 15.1 million in 1979[11]) came of age between these two contests. Overall, 11.5 million Canadians cast ballots in 1979—an increase of 19 per cent over the 9.7 million voting in 1974.[12] Of these additional 1.8 million votes, approximately one-third are accounted for by the higher turnout while the remainder were new voters who became eligible after 1974 and went to the polls in 1979.[13]

The distribution of respondents in the 1979 national election study in terms of patterns of voting participation, partisanship and political interest is displayed in table 1. The large percentages of transient and new voters (17.9 per cent and 16.8 per cent respectively of those classified in table 1) indicate the potential importance of these groups for understanding the 1979 election outcome. Also significant is the fact that substantial majorities of all three participation categories (that is, permanent, transient and new voters) are flexible partisans. The large number of such partisans in these groups suggests the possible importance of short-term forces associated with issue perceptions and party leader images for comprehending both the nature of voting choice in 1979 and the outcome of this contest. The potential sensitivity of flexible partisans to such forces is further indicated in that sizable numbers of these voters have moderate or high levels of political interest. In sum, 42.9 per cent of those surveyed in 1979 combined partisan flexibility with moderate or high levels of political interest. A further indicator of the electoral significance of this group is the fact that nearly three-fifths of them were members of the permanent electorate. As noted, previous analyses of the 1974 election survey data indicate that flexible partisans respond strongly to short-term forces associated with party leader images and/or issue perceptions, and their behaviour is most significant for comprehending processes of political stability and change. As will be demonstrated below, this also is the case in 1979. First, however, we will consider how these and other voters perceived party leaders and important issues in this election.

PARTY LEADER IMAGES

It is ironic that as media attention to party leaders increases, and popular explanations of election results focus ever more sharply on comparative evaluations of the leaders, there is little evidence that they are becoming any more popular with the electorate. Indeed, much evidence points the other way.[14] In table 2, "feeling

TABLE 1 *A TYPOLOGY OF THE 1979 CANADIAN ELECTORATE, BASED ON PARTISANSHIP, POLITICAL INTEREST, AND VOTE HISTORY* (Percentages)*

		The Permanent Electorate** Partisanship		The Transient Electorate* Partisanship		The New Voters** Partisanship	
		Durable	Flexible	Durable	Flexible	Durable	Flexible
Political Interest	*High*	9.7	16.4	1.0	2.6	1.2	1.6
	Moderate	6.8	11.9	1.8	2.9	1.2	2.5
	Low	7.8	12.6	2.8	6.8	4.1	6.2
		24.3	40.9	5.6	12.3	6.5	10.3

* Total N (weighted) for all types = 2595.
** Persons who "always" or "usually" vote in federal elections and who voted in both 1974 and 1979.
* Persons who "seldom" vote in federal elections, but who did vote in one of the 1974 and 1979 elections.
** Persons first eligible to vote in 1979.

TABLE 2 MEAN PARTY LEADER THERMOMETER SCORES, BY PROVINCE, 1968, 1974 AND 1979

	Trudeau			Stanfield/Clark			Douglas/Lewis/Broadbent		
	1968	1974	1979	1968	1974	1979	1968	1974	1979
Newfoundland	67	66	57	70	48	50	54	51	41
Prince Edward Island	58	66	60	71	59	54	66	52	51
Nova Scotia	61	56	54	71	62	56	56	52	58
New Brunswick	61	65	54	71	57	51	54	48	43
Quebec	72	69	60	52	40	41	42	44	38
Ontario	69	62	54	56	48	47	58	51	53
Manitoba	72	50	45	53	49	48	62	45	56
Saskatchewan	56	55	47	58	43	55	61	52	58
Alberta	61	54	41	58	45	61	53	42	48
British Columbia	68	57	49	53	48	51	57	46	50
Total	68	62	56	56	46	48	54	47	49

thermometer" scores[15] for the leaders of the three main parties are arrayed for the elections of 1968, 1974 and 1979. These data show that nationally the mean scores for the three leaders in 1979 did not stray very far from the neutral mark (50). Pierre Trudeau continued to be the highest rated of the party leaders, but his 1979 mean score of 56 was 6 points lower than his score in 1974, and 12 points lower than 1968. Joe Clark and Ed Broadbent, both new leaders at the time of the 1979 election, achieved marginally higher overall scores than their predecessors had in 1974. Even so, neither topped the neutral mark nor equalled the popularity levels registered by Robert Stanfield and Tommy Douglas in 1968, a year in which the public's view of all the leaders seems, in retrospect, to have been quite benevolent.

In attempting to determine the potential magnitude of "leader effects" on voting, it is instructive to subtract the leader thermometer scores from thermometer scores for the parties as a whole. Such scores show whether a leader runs ahead or behind his party in popularity, and thus give a preliminary indication of how much impact a leader might have.[16] Empirically, the leader-minus-party scores show that in most provinces thermometer ratings of Trudeau and the Liberal party are very similar (data not shown in tabular form). Patterns for the other two leaders are quite different, however, with Broadbent scoring consistently higher than the NDP, and Clark generally running behind the Conservative party. Clark trails his party in several provinces such as Ontario and British Columbia where the Conservatives made major electoral gains, and thus it would seem that his potential for attracting votes on the basis of his own appeal was rather low. Broadbent, on the other hand, runs far ahead of his party in most places. It should be noted, however, that his predecessors also did this, and that this is partially due to the relatively low ratings given in many provinces to the NDP.

When considering possible party leader effects it is also noteworthy, if not unexpected, that thermometer scores for leaders are highly correlated with voters' partisan attachments. For example, Trudeau is given a mean score of 77 by Liberal identifiers, but only 34 by Conservatives and 46 by New Democrats. Conservative identifiers place Clark at the 70 degree mark, but Liberals and New Democrats only grade him 39. Broadbent is given a score of 77 by New Democrats, and 47 by identifiers with the other two parties. Yet, Clark scores somewhat lower in these instances than the other two leaders, and this is reinforced when the subtraction of leader minus party scores is arrayed by party identification (data not shown in tabular form). Here, Clark runs behind the Conservative party for all groups, but particularly among Conservative identifiers. Broadbent, on the other hand, runs virtually even with his party among NDP identifiers, but 12 degrees ahead of the party among Conservatives and 8 ahead among Liberals.

As another indication of the possible impact of party leader images in 1979, one may examine levels of affect for the leaders among the extraordinarily large group of newly eligible voters. While Trudeau and Broadbent received *higher* ratings from this new voter group than from the rest of the electorate (mean thermometer scores of 58 and 51 respectively), Clark received a *lower* score (45). Similarly, when the leader-minus-party thermometer scores are computed, Clark ran further behind the Conservative party in popularity among new voters than among other electors. For new voters in the pivotal province of Ontario, Clark's mean score on the thermometer was only 44, compared to 57 for Broadbent and 56 for Trudeau. The possibility that Clark's unpopularity among these voters may have cost the Conservatives dearly in their quest for a majority government is a subject that will be considered in subsequent analyses.

ISSUE PERCEPTIONS

Elections are frequently identified in the public mind with the main issues discussed or the campaign strategies attempted by the parties. For example, the 1974 federal election was generally perceived to be about inflation, since that issue was dominant in the campaign and prominent in party strategy. Our previous analysis of the 1974 election has shown, however, that such a label is in many ways misleading, since neither inflation nor any other single issue was responsible for producing the result. Instead, the Liberals succeeded in attracting enough of the permanent, transient and newly eligible components of the electorate through a series of small effects to make victory possible. Some of these effects were issue-related and some were not, but their cumulative effect was a Liberal success.[17]

The 1974 situation would not appear atypical. For a large majority of federal elections it can be hypothesised that the impact of issues on the result will be made through such a series of relatively minor effects of several issues, rather than by a dramatic single issue which sweeps most of the voting public into one party's camp. The basic reason for this lies in the nature of the three conditions which must be met if an issue is to have an electoral impact. An issue must be salient for the public; it must be a valence issue, that is, skewed in its distribution such that the bulk of public opinion favours one side of it; and it must be an issue which is positively or negatively associated by the public (or at least, the public to whom it is salient) with at least one political party.[18] In 1974 none of the issues decisively met all of these conditions.[19] However, to the extent that some issues partially met the conditions (for example, inflation was salient for many voters and characterised by a skewed distribution of opinion; leadership had a skewed opinion distribution; majority government was strongly linked to one party), they had small effects on the overall election outcome.

When designing their campaign strategies, parties may be quite sensitive to the ways in which issues can affect election results. Thus they may, at times, deliberately follow a strategy of aggregating several "issue publics" rather than trying to rely on the overall impact of one or two dramatic issues. In order to implement such a strategy, a party must choose either to create or emphasise issues which are salient, not necessarily to the electorate as a whole, but to selected groups whose support will make a meaningful net addition to party strength. Second, the issues must have skewed opinion distributions so that opposing parties cannot nullify their effects by adopting the "other side." Third, the party must succeed in connecting the issues to itself, claiming them as its own. In the 1979 election, we find several issues which the Conservatives attempted to emphasise in such a way as to maximize these three conditions. The Liberals, in contrast, concentrated on the issue of national unity and thereby attempted to increase the salience of an issue on which opinion was heavily skewed in their favour.

Beginning with the salience condition, table 3 displays the issues cited by respondents as most important in the 1979 election.[20] The contrast with 1974, when one-third of all respondents mentioned inflation,[21] is immediately apparent. In 1979, no *single* issue was cited by even 10 per cent of respondents as most important, and only references to the Quebec situation reach 20 per cent when both issue mentions are aggregated. In more general terms, however, both economic and Confederation issues, stressed during the campaign, were mentioned by substantial groups of people as most important. Leaders and leadership also captured considerable attention, as did the general feeling that it was "time for a change." A number of other issues were salient for small segments of the electorate. That not everyone had issue concerns is suggested by the fact that slightly over a quarter of the sample could think of no issue which was important. The question of whether the distributions of opinion on various issues are skewed or not is more difficult to determine.

This condition for an issue to be important in affecting an election result is relevant, it will be recalled, because parties risk having their opponents take opposite positions on issues on which opinion is divided so as to obviate any appreciable gain that might be realised. The ideal issue for a party is one where the population takes one side. For example, in 1974 and 1979, overwhelming proportions of those mentioning inflation as an issue were opposed to it. Indeed, in Canada and elsewhere, inflation may be *the* classic contemporary example of a valence issue.[22] Of the issues which appear in table 3, several are "naturally" of the valence type for the population as a whole, and others may well have been valence issues for those concerned with them as election issues. The general economic issues—inflation, the state of the economy—did not have divided opinion distributions because an overwhelming proportion of the references to them were complaints about current conditions. Confederation issues, at least in their "national unity" manifestation, were similarly "one-sided," since most of the people who raised them were concerned with the possible collapse of the Canadian political system, and were in favour of national unity. Finally, "time for a change" is by definition a valence issue prejudiced against incumbents.

Other issues in the 1979 campaign met the valence condition in varying ways. Mortgage deductibility, for instance, is not naturally a valence issue, since there is an argument that allowing the deduction of mortgage interest payments from income tax is not good economic policy and is unfair to low income persons who cannot afford to purchase a home. These were in fact the arguments advanced by the Liberals in their critique of the Conservative policy. However, it appears from poll data gathered prior to the campaign that mortgage deductibility was in fact a valence issue, with a large majority of the population in favour of it.[23] The "issue" of leaders and leadership is something of a different story. Such issues were promoted by the NDP and the Conservatives on the assumption that there was a ground-swell of public opposition to the prime minister. Although there was a good deal of dissatisfaction with Trudeau, it is doubtful if the whole "leaders and leadership" issue was characterised by a highly skewed opinion distribution in 1979. As we have seen in the preceding section, Trudeau was still more popular overall than the other leaders.[24] Additionally, although the "important issues" question

TABLE 3   *IMPORTANT ISSUES IN THE 1979 ELECTION (Percentages)*

Issue	First Mention	All Mentions+
Economic Issues		
Inflation	8.3	18.1
Economy generally	7.5	14.6
Unemployment	5.6	14.6
Specific economic issues	3.5	9.3
Mortgage deductability	4.3	8.4
Social services	1.7	4.7
Energy		
Energy generally	2.4	6.6
Petro-Canada	2.3	6.1
Confederation		
National unity	5.3	13.2
Bilingualism	1.6	4.4
Quebec	9.1	20.1
Leaders		
Trudeau	7.2	12.1
Clark	.9	2.0
Leadership	2.1	4.1
Time for a change	5.4	10.5
Other Issues		
Foreign policy	.6	5.3
Other specific issues	2.6	8.1
Other	1.2	2.3
None	28.4	
N =	2669	1910

+ Multiple mentions, excluding missing data.

reveals some people who thought Trudeau was the issue and who took a position against him, it also reveals a group that designated "leadership" as the issue and thought the Liberals were the party that could provide it.

The third condition which an issue has to satisfy if a party is going to be able to use it to mobilize support is that the party's position must be linked to the issue, and its position must be preferred. Table 4 shows which parties the electorate saw as closest to them on what they perceived as the most important election issue. Several issues favoured one party. Confederation and social services issues favoured the Liberals, with the former being considerably more salient to the public than the latter (table 3). In the case of economic issues the Liberals did less well. The Conservatives were closest to the preferred position of more of the respondents who made general references to the state of the economy, or who referred to a specific economic issue, like the dollar, the deficit, taxes or interest rates. The NDP was closer for more of the people who were concerned about unemployment. These economic issues, however, were not strongly linked to one party. While pluralities favoured the Conservatives' positions on them overall, substantial minorities

TABLE 4   PARTY CLOSEST ON MOST IMPORTANT ISSUES
(Row Percentages)

Issue	Liberal	PC	NDP	None	N+
General economic	25.1	35.1	23.1	15.8	374
Unemployment	25.9	25.3	33.5	11.6	124
Specific economic	32.5	44.5	11.6	10.1	77
Mortgage deductibility	10.8	71.9	15.5	1.8	106
Social Services	39.6	23.1	25.7	5.5	51
Energy	38.6	33.9	18.6	7.8	115
Confederation	64.0	18.6	6.0	9.4	378
Leaders	30.5	54.0	6.4	8.3	253
Time for a change	12.7	62.5	10.0	11.6	126
Other	36.8	37.8	16.6	7.0	101

+ May not add to 100 per cent because other parties (not shown) are included in the percentages.

preferred the Liberals' or NDP's. Moreover, a sizable number of respondents perceived no party as closest to them on economic issues, perhaps reflecting a feeling that the economic situation was beyond the capabilities of any of the parties to alleviate. It seems unlikely, then, that issues of this type could have been used to mobilize large numbers of supporters behind a single party, even though the issues were both reasonably salient and opinion about them was substantially undivided.

Table 4 reveals that majorities of those persons concerned with three issues—mortgage deductibility, "time for a change," and leaders—saw the Conservatives as closest to their position. As argued above, however, within the entire electorate the "leaders and leadership" issue did not have a strongly skewed opinion distribution because while many people did not like Trudeau, others did and felt that only the Liberals could provide the leadership required by the country. The other two, mortgage deductibility and "time for a change," however, did have skewed opinion distributions, and would seem therefore to have held greater potential for mobilizing support for the Conservatives.

LEADERS, ISSUES AND ELECTORAL CHOICE

Overall, when expressing their "reasons for voting" in 1979, respondents indicated that they were motivated by a multiplicity of considerations. Many voters made explicit reference to specific issue concerns, whereas others spoke in more global terms about parties, leaders or local candidates without elaborating their reasoning in any detail. In some cases such general references to parties or political figures likely reflect simple but powerful affective feelings rooted in traditional party loyalties or perceptions of the personality and stylistic characteristics of leaders or candidates. For a sizable proportion of voters, however, electoral judgements about party, leaders and candidates may be influenced by issue considerations. Illustrating the potential importance of issue concerns in 1979 are responses to a series of questions where respondents were requested to indicate the relative importance of party leaders, local candidates and parties as a whole as factors in their voting choices, and to specify if issue positions formed the basis for their judgement. Those

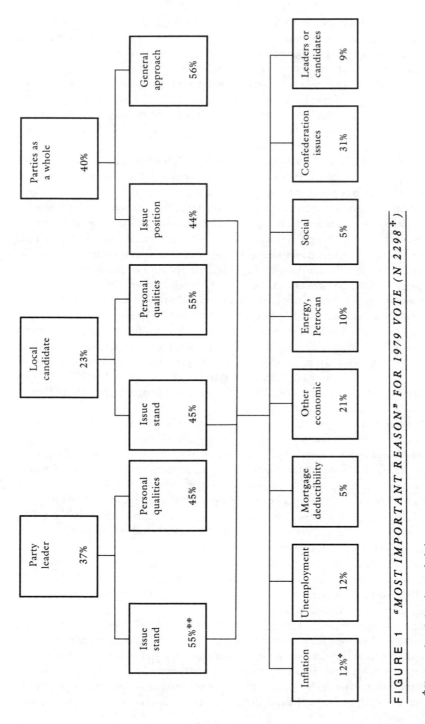

FIGURE 1 *"MOST IMPORTANT REASON" FOR 1979 VOTE (N 2298⁺)*

⁺ Voters only, missing data excluded.
⁺⁺ Percentages based on subset immediately above.
✦ Combined "issue streams," selected issues only, multiple response.

indicating the importance of issues were requested to designate the issues they had in mind.[25]

Regardless of whether leaders, candidates or parties as a whole were ranked most important, many respondents stated that there was an issue basis underlying their choice. Altogether, 48 per cent placed themselves in an "issue stream," with 52 per cent referring to the "personal qualities" of leaders or candidates or a party's "general approach" (figure 1).[26] Those placing themselves in an "issue stream" cited a broad range of specific issues as their principal concerns. The eight most frequently referenced issue categories are displayed in the bottom row of figure 1. Several economic issues plus the Confederation issues were cited most often, with the latter forming the largest single category.

The potential of issues, the personal qualities of leaders and candidates, and the "general approaches" of the parties to influence voting behaviour and the overall election result can be investigated by examining the direction of the vote for various leader, local candidate and party streams. Generally, the Liberals did best among persons citing party leader as the principal factor in their voting choice, the Conservatives were strongest among those mentioning local candidate or party, while the NDP accumulated its strongest support among respondents citing the party factor. Specifically, the Liberals captured 50 per cent of the votes of persons citing party leaders, 36 per cent of those mentioning local candidates, and 31 per cent of respondents referring to parties as a whole. Comparable percentages for the Conservatives are 28, 43 and 47 per cent, and for the NDP are 12, 14 and 21 per cent. A more detailed analysis of these data shows that the Liberals did particularly well among those voters citing the personal qualities of leaders (64 per cent), while the Conservatives were strongest among voters referring to the general approach of the party (50 per cent) as well as its issue stands (42 per cent). The NDP had its best showing among voters concerned with issues, particularly with the issue positions of the parties (26 per cent).

Two points are noteworthy about these data. First, respondents in the combined issues streams were not overwhelmingly anti-Liberal in their voting behaviour. Although the Liberals trail the Conservatives by 11 per cent (33 per cent to 44 per cent) and 13 per cent (29 per cent to 42 per cent) in the two issue streams for local candidate and parties respectively, this margin is substantially offset by their large lead of 24 per cent (54 per cent to 30 per cent) in the leader-issue category. Thus, although the issue concerns of many voters likely hurt the Liberals in 1979, issue impacts, nonetheless, were far from unidirectional. Indeed, the ability of the Liberals to gain (or retain) the votes of a sizable proportion of those voters motivated by issues was a significant factor in explaining both the relatively small overall erosion in the party's popular vote percentage between 1974 and 1979 (from 43 per cent to 40 per cent), and by extension, the failure of the Conservatives to secure a majority government.

Second, voters' reports of their "reasons for voting" are imperfect guides to the actual weight of various factors on electoral choice. For example, votes cast on the basis of reactions to perceptions of the personalities or styles of party leaders or local candidates may be rationalized post hoc in issue terms. Again, some voters may project their own issue preferences and concerns onto parties or politicians already approved (or disapproved of) on other grounds.[27] That such rationalization and projection effects were likely at work for at least some segments of the electorate in 1979 is suggested by the observation that large numbers of *all* categories of partisans placed themselves in one of the issue streams in the party-leader-candidate question sequence. Among flexible partisans (persons with weak, unstable or inconsistent party identifications), no less than 49 per cent are in the issue streams. For durable partisans (those with strong, stable and consistent partisan ties), the comparable percentage is 46 per cent. Durable partisans are, however, voters for whom the independent effects of issues on voting choice are most doubtful, for they constitute that element in the electorate most prone to view the political world through the distorting lens of partisanship. The possibility that many voters, particularly durable partisans, are subject to rationalization and projection effects, indicates the need for considerable caution when making inferences about the strength of various possible determinants of electoral choice.

Regarding the relative strength of different variables on voting decisions, we have argued elsewhere that it is useful to analyse voting behaviour in Canada *within* categories of partisanship and political interest.[28] The fact that many electors are flexible partisans lacking strong, stable and consistent ties with parties is of primary importance. Previous research has shown that issue and party leader effects are stronger for these voters than for those with durable partisan attachments. This research also has demonstrated the effects of political interest as a variable differentiating responsiveness to party leader and issue effects. In 1974, voters with higher levels of political interest, particularly flexible partisans, were especially sensitive to issues, whereas those with lower interest levels responded more strongly to the styles and personalities of party leaders.[29]

Finally, the nature of partisanship in Canada makes it difficult to separate long-term and short-term effects on voting behaviour. When assessing party leader or issue effects in the context of a particular election, one cannot simply control for the direction of party identification. For at least some flexible partisans, current partisan ties may reflect rather than affect perceptions of party leaders and issues. To circumvent, if not resolve, this problem, voting behaviour in a previous federal election can be used as a surrogate measure of long-term forces on electoral choice. For some voters, the 1974 vote, for example, will reflect the operation of genuine long-term forces, whereas for others, it will represent the impact of short-term forces working at an earlier point in time. In any case, the 1974 vote has the advantage of encapsulating the impact of variables operating prior to the 1979 election campaign.

For each of the partisan-political interest categories in the permanent electorate, multiple regression analyses of Liberal, Conservative and NDP voting were performed using 1974 vote, party leader and local candidate thermometers, perceptions of party closest on most important issue, and party thermometers as predictors. In each case, 1974 vote was entered into the analysis first to provide a statistical control for possible long-term effects. To measure the unique effects of issues and leaders, these variables were entered next. The regressions were performed twice with the order of entry of these variables being reversed to assess unique and joint issue and leader effects. Local candidate and party thermometers were then entered. Local candidate thermometers were entered after the issue and party leader variables on the assumption that long-term forces and feelings about issues and party leaders

TABLE 5   MULTIPLE REGRESSION ANALYSES OF 1979
           VOTE BY PARTISAN-POLITICAL INTEREST
           TYPES

| | | Proportion of variance explained for | | | | |
| | Durable- | | | Flexible- | | |
	Low	Moderate	High	Low	Moderate	High
Panel A: Dependent variable—Liberal vote						
Long-term forces						
1974 vote (Liberal—other)	.72	.78	.71	.16	.16	.19
Short-term forces						
Leaders (unique)	.00	.00	.00	.05	.04	.05
Issues (unique)	.01	.00	.04	.10	.18	.18
Leaders and issues (joint)	.01	.00	.00	.04	.04	.04
Local candidates (unique)	.01	.00	.01	.01	.02	.01
Campaign (unique)	.00	.01	.01	.01	.02	.00
Candidates and campaign (joint)	.00	.01	.00	.00	.00	.01
Total	.75	.80	.77	.37	.46	.48
Panel B: Dependent variable—Conservative vote						
Long-term forces						
1974 vote (PC—other)	.66	.91	.78	.21	.13	.26
Short-term forces						
Leaders (unique)	.00	.00	.00	.01	.04	.03
Issues (unique)	.02	.00	.03	.12	.19	.19
Leaders and Issues (joint)	.00	.00	.01	.02	.03	.05
Local candidate (unique)	.01	.00	.00	.01	.01	.00
Campaign (unique)	.00	.00	.00	.02	.01	.01
Candidates and campaign (joint)	.00	.00	.00	.00	.00	.00
Total	.69	.91	.82	.39	.41	.54
Panel C: Dependent variable—New Democratic party vote						
Long-term forces						
1974 vote (NDP)—other	.51	.95	.60	.22	.15	.13
Short-term forces						
Leaders (unique)	.00	.00	.00	.02	.02	.02
Issues (unique)	.00	.00	.01	.06	.10	.17
Leaders and issues (joint)	.01	.00	.01	.01	.00	.01
Local candidate (unique)	.00	.00	.00	.01	.01	.01
Campaign (unique)	.00	.00	.00	.00	.00	.00
Candidates and campaign (joint)	.00	.00	.00	.01	.01	.01
Total	.52	.95	.62	.33	.29	.35

may influence perceptions of local candidates, but that the latter seldom influence how voters react to the former. Again, the order of entry of the local candidate and party thermometer variables was reversed in two regressions to measure the unique and joint effects of local candidates and residual campaign effects not captured by other variables.[30]

The results of this procedure (table 5) indicate that the effects of party leader images and issue perceptions are quite different for durable and flexible partisans. Among the durables, the mean percentage of variance explained by all predictor variables is 76 per cent. Long-term forces (as summarised by the 1974 vote) account for virtually all of this explained variance (97 per cent on average). In contrast, for flexible partisans, the total explained variance has a mean value of 40 per cent, with long-term forces accounting for an average of 45 per cent. Party leader and issue effects are strongest among flexible partisans. Consonant with previous analyses of factors affecting voting in the 1974 federal election, the pattern of issue effects differs markedly according to political interest levels. Specifically, the unique effects of issue perceptions are greatest among flexible-moderate and flexible-high interest partisans. Unlike 1974, however, issue effects in 1979 are greater than those for party leaders among all political interest categories of flexible partisans, and one cannot detect a tendency for leader effects to be concentrated among flexible-low interest partisans.[31] Rather, the 1979 analyses show relatively small unique leader effects of approximately equal strength for all types of flexible partisans.[32] Finally, similar to 1974, for all analyses of the durable partisans, issue and leader effects are either miniscule or nonexistent.

In terms of understanding voting behaviour in the 1979 election and the outcome of that contest, the size of issue and leader effects, and the ratio of the former to the latter among all categories of flexible partisans deserves additional comment. Perhaps particularly noteworthy is the fact that these rations are largest in the Conservative and New Democratic party analyses. For the Conservatives, the weakness of leader effects may have proved especially important in terms of preventing them from attracting the additional votes required to win the seats needed to form a majority government. In this regard, the relative strength of issue versus leader appeals as forces prompting a Conservative vote in 1979 is, of course, consistent with data presented previously concerning low levels of affect for Clark and the tendency for feelings about the Conservative leader to be more negative than those for his party in every region of the country including Ontario and the West—areas where Conservatives fared extremely well. It also will be recalled that the Conservatives ran relatively poorly among voters citing party leaders as "most important" in their vote decisions. Indeed, if the latter data were examined in terms of the composition of the group voting for each party, only 28 per cent of Conservative voters, as compared to 52 per cent of the Liberals, cited party leaders as "most important." Thus, the findings of the regression and other analyses presented above all suggest that the low levels of affect generated by Clark may have cost the Conservatives dearly in 1979. This topic will be considered below as part of a more general investigation of how leader images and issue perceptions influenced the 1979 election outcome.

CONVERSION AND REPLACEMENT IN THE 1979 ELECTION

As noted earlier, for purposes of understanding the outcome of the 1979 election, the electorate may be usefully divided into three major groups—the permanent

TABLE 6   COMPARISONS OF TOTAL CONTRIBUTION TO
ELECTORAL CHANGE IN 1974 AND 1979
(Column Percentages)

		As Per Cent of Total Electorate		As Per Cent of Voters in Two Elections Only	
		1974	1979	1974	1979
Permanent electorate	Voting for the same party in both elections (1972–74 or 1974–79)	60	55	78	73
	Voting for different parties (1972–74 or 1974–79)	17	20	22	27
Transient voters	Previous nonvoters re-entering electorate	5	7		
	Previous voters leaving electorate	13	6		
New voters	entering electorate	5	12		
	N =	2060	2276	1586	1691

electorate, comprising those voters who normally participate in federal elections and who voted in both 1974 and 1979; the transient voters, including those re-entering the electorate in 1979 and previous voters who failed to vote in this election; and the new voters, entering the electorate for the first time. The effects on the election caused by new voters and by transient voters entering or leaving the electorate, as well as the effects of attrition, are generally referred to as *replacement*, thus identifying any change that takes place as a result of turnover of voters rather than of votes. In contrast, *conversion* refers to a change in behaviour by members of the permanent electorate, whether brought about by long-term or short-term forces. Analyses of the 1974 election showed that conversion and replacement worked in different directions in producing their net effects, and replacement was, in total, a more important factor in explaining the result of that particular election.[33] In 1979, the potential for changes of both types was relatively large. As discussed above, there was a broad distribution of salient issues in 1979, three of the four parties fought the election under new leaders, and issue, and to a lesser extent, leader effects on individual voting behaviour were discernible among a broad segment of the electorate. Thus, the possibility of short-term conversion effects would seem high. The increased turnout and large infusion of new voters in 1979 also indicate replacement effects may have been substantially greater in 1979 than in 1974.

Our analysis of conversion and replacement effects in 1979 begins with the data presented in table 6. This table shows that slightly more than half of the electorate is comprised of persons supporting the same party in 1979 as in 1974. This

TABLE 7   1979 VOTE BY BEHAVIOUR IN THE 1974
ELECTION+ (Diagonal Percentages)

		1974 Behaviour				
		Liberal	PC	NDP	Social Credit	Not Voting	Not Eligible
	Liberal	30.2	1.6	1.2	0.4	2.6	5.9
1979	Conservative	9.2	19.7	1.7	0.4	3.0	4.0
Vote	NDP	3.5	1.5	6.5	0.1	1.5	2.5
	Social Credit	0.4	0.1	0.2	1.2	0.4	0.7

+ As measured by 1974–1979 panel and 1979 cross-section sample. Voters in the 1979 election only. N = 2135. Votes for other parties included in percentages but not shown in table.

represents a drop of 5 per cent from the comparable proportion of the 1974 electorate, brought about both because of a modest increase in the incidence of switching, and because the larger infusion of new voters and transient voters increases the base on which the percentage is computed. As noted above, among participants in both elections only, the incidence of switching is found to be 27 per cent in 1979 compared to 22 per cent in 1974.

Unlike 1974, when the net contribution of conversion to the election outcome was small, patterns of switching in 1979 heavily favoured the Conservatives. As seen in table 7, fully 9.2 per cent of those voting in the 1979 election had voted Liberal in 1974 and opted for the Conservatives in 1979. In exchanges with all other parties, Conservative gains totalled 11.3 per cent of the 1979 electorate, while losses amounted to only 3.2 per cent, a net advantage of 8.1 per cent. The Liberals, however, suffered a net loss of 9.9 per cent of the total vote, gaining only 3.2 per cent from past supporters of the other three parties while losing 13.1 per cent of the electorate that had supported the Liberals in 1974. Gains and losses for the other parties were somewhat more balanced, although the NDP's net gain of 2.0 per cent among 1974 voters in the 1979 electorate (5.1 per cent–3.1 per cent) came mainly from 1974 Liberals. Those abandoning the NDP in 1979 tended slightly more often to opt for the Conservatives than the Liberals.

The contribution of replacement to the 1979 result also may be assessed by examining the net impact of the transient and new voters as proportions of the total electorate. Liberal losses among the permanent electorate were partially offset by the nearly 3 to 2 advantage that the party enjoyed over the Conservatives among new voters. The Conservatives, on the other hand, did marginally better than the Liberals among transient voters. The NDP realised a portion of its net gain from each of these groups, but did somewhat better among the new voters. A slightly different way of looking at the behaviour of various groups in the 1979 electorate is provided by table 8. The Conservatives were considerably more successful than the other parties (and more successful than any of the parties in the 1974 election) in retaining their past supporters. The NDP did slightly better than in 1974 by holding more than 60 per cent of its past voters, while the Liberals did somewhat worse (they retained 70 per cent of their 1972 voters in 1974). A substantial proportion of the NDP's total vote in 1979, however, came from former Liberals

TABLE 8 WHERE THE 1974 VOTE WENT IN 1979
(Column Percentages)

		1974 Behaviour					
		Liberal	PC	NDP	Social Credit	Not Voting	Not Eligible
	Liberal	64	7	11	19	26	36
	Conservative	20	80	16	16	30	24
1979	NDP	7	6	61	6	15	15
Vote	Social Credit	1	1	2	51	4	4
	Did not vote	8	7	8	8	25	19
	N* =	1013	528	229	51	214	348

* Twenty-four respondents voting for other parties in 1979 are included in percentages but not shown in the table. The analysis shown in the table is based on all respondents in the 1979 sample, with missing data removed.

and new voters. In both elections, Social Credit displayed greater volatility than any of the other parties, retaining only about half of its previous support while picking up new support from other sources. As in 1974, the Liberals did well among new voters (36 per cent of whom voted Liberal), although their margin in 1979 within this group was not as great as in the previous election (45 per cent of the new voters in 1974 supported the Liberal party). Among transient voters, the Conservatives enjoyed a narrow plurality in 1979, while this group favoured the Liberals by a margin of more than 2 to 1 in 1974. Three-quarters of those who reported not voting in the 1974 election entered or re-entered the electorate in 1979. Among 1974 voters leaving the electorate, there is no discernible pattern in terms of past voting behaviour—each party appears to have lost approximately the same percentage of its past supporters (7 per cent of the Conservatives and 8 per cent in the case of each of the other parties) to nonvoting.

Of those in the partisan/voter groups who switched parties in 1979, by far the largest share consisted of flexible partisans. These patterns of movement heavily favoured the Conservatives (table 9), with the Conservative advantage being greatest among switching flexible-high interest partisans. This was the case both in terms of the total share of the electorate accounted for by this group (6.1 per cent) and in terms of the size of the net Conservative advantage. It is noteworthy also that the NDP did significantly better than the Liberals among all three groups of flexible partisans. The pattern of switching displayed by the three flexible partisan groups and by the small number of durable partisans who switched indicates the significance in terms of aggregate electoral change of the short-term forces acting on individual behaviour examined earlier. In an election in which these forces are highly favourable to the opposition parties, the aggregate effects are potentially large. It is not surprising, therefore, that in 1979 the group accounting for the most net change and the greatest differential impact is the flexible-high interest partisans, a group shown earlier to be relatively sensitive to issue effects. In contrast to the 1974 election, in which a substantial amount of switching by flexible partisans produced only modest aggregate effects on the election outcome, the 1979 election

TABLE 9 CONTRIBUTION TO AGGREGATE ELECTORAL CHANGE OF ALL PARTISAN/VOTER GROUPS IN 1979 (*As Per Cent of Active 1979 Electorate**)

	Percentage switching to					Percentage remaining				
	Liberal	PC	NDP	SC	Total**	Liberal	PC	NDP	SC	Total
Partisan types										
Durable-high interest	0.4	0.9	0.2	—	1.6	5.7	3.7	0.7	0.1	10.2
Durable-moderate interest	0.1	0.1	0.2	♦♦	0.5	3.8	2.0	1.1	—	6.9
Durable-low interest	0.5	0.6	0.3	♦♦	1.6	5.8	2.4	1.0	♦♦	9.3
Flexible-high interest	0.8	3.8	1.4	0.1	6.1	5.1	5.4	1.3	0.2	12.0
Flexible-moderate interest	0.7	2.6	1.1	0.2	4.6	3.4	2.1	0.9	0.3	6.8
Flexible-low interest	0.7	2.6	1.4	0.4	5.1	4.9	2.8	1.3	0.5	9.5
	3.2	10.6	4.6	0.8	19.5	28.7	18.4	6.3	1.2	54.7
Transient voters										
Re-entering 1979 electorate	2.5	2.8	1.4	0.3	7.1					
Leaving electorate♦ in 1979	3.4	1.7	0.8	0.2	6.2					
New voters										
Voting in 1979	5.4	3.7	2.3	0.6	12.1					

* Excluding nonvoters in *both* 1974 and 1979 elections and new voters not voting in 1979. N = 2244.
** Votes cast for other parties are included in totals but not shown in table.
♦ Indicates vote in previous (1974) election.
♦♦ Less than 0.1 per cent

was one in which the impact of short-term forces on both individual behaviour and the election outcome was substantial.

The pattern of voting by the groups of voters who switched parties in 1979 contrasts sharply with that shown by those who did not switch (table 9). Among all groups of nonswitching durable partisans, the Liberals maintained a substantial advantage over their opposition, and the net effect of this advantage was sufficient to offset much of the gain by the Conservatives among switchers. Among flexible partisans the pattern is also quite different for those remaining with their 1974 party than for the same groups who switched in 1979. Only among flexible-high interest partisans did the Conservatives enjoy a net advantage, and even in this group the advantage was very small. Hence, although flexible-high interest partisans remaining with their 1974 parties account for a total of 12 per cent of the active 1979 electorate, their net effect on the election outcome was almost nil. Among the moderate- and low-interest groups of flexible partisans, however, the Liberal advantage was slightly greater and acted to offset some of the net advantage gained by the Conservatives among switchers.

The net effect of the various groups of flexible and durable partisans who constitute the permanent electorate should of course be considered in the context of the replacement effects which formed an important part of the pattern of aggregate electoral change in 1979. As noted, the number of new voters entering the electorate was much larger than normal, due both to patterns of population growth and the long interval between the 1974 and 1979 elections. Even allowing for the fact that turnout among new voters is normally lower than for other groups, the Liberal advantage among new voters in 1979 was large enough to offset some of the losses sustained among switchers. This is particularly true when the net change is considered as a proportion of the total electorate (table 9).

Among transient voters participating in the 1979 election, the net effect on the election outcome was, by contrast, very small since this group divided nearly equally between Liberals and Conservatives with New Democrats running a modest third. Some potential effect on the outcome is seen, however, among transient voters who failed to vote in 1979. This group was heavily Liberal in 1974. While it is, of course, far from certain that these transient voters would have supported the Liberals in the same proportion had they voted in 1979, this element of the electorate nevertheless appears to constitute a group of "stay at home Liberals" who, in total, exerted at least a potential if not an actual effect on the outcome. However, this observation must be balanced against the fact that the transient voters as a group were quite favourable to the Liberals in 1974,[34] and the increased turnout in 1979 brought into the electorate transient voters who might not have been expected to vote in lower turnout elections. Since there is some evidence that this group tends to behave in a manner similar to the flexible partisans in the permanent electorate, it might be expected that they would have been more favourable to the Conservatives in 1979 than in the previous election given the thrust of the short-term forces working against the Liberals in 1979.

In general, it is clear that while the Conservatives owed their 1979 victory to the willingness of 1974 Liberals to switch parties (particularly in Ontario and the West), their failure to improve their appeal substantially among the large number of new voters in 1979 had a significant moderating effect on the result. In part at least, the failure of the Conservatives to gain a majority in the 1979 election may have been due to this weakness among new voters. While the analysis of a national sample does not permit discussion of the result in terms of parliamentary seats, it is clear that a better showing among new voters and transients would have helped the Conservative cause significantly.

There is reason to believe that the Conservative party's weakness among new voters is not something peculiar to the circumstances of the 1979 election. Analyses of age-related differences in party identification using the 1974 and 1979 national surveys show that the Conservatives have failed to maintain their position in the two youngest cohorts in the sample—those coming of voting age in the Diefenbaker/Pearson era and those entering the electorate during the Trudeau years.[35] Given that more than 40 per cent of the entire electorate has come of voting age *since* Trudeau became prime minister in 1968, it is evident that the Conservatives' continuing inability to replenish their electoral strength among the younger age cohorts may have long-range consequences for the party system. While an analysis of the decline of the party's fortunes in the 1980 election is beyond the scope of this article, one might argue that had the Conservatives been stronger among younger voters, their victory in 1979 might have been sustained in the 1980 sequel. In addition, had they won a majority in 1979, it is possible that they might have been able to strengthen their appeal to younger persons over a four- or five-year period. However that might be, the point remains that Conservative weakness among younger voters in 1979 meant that the party's victory depended primarily on the conversion of voters already in the electorate. This new-found support was not solid. As noted, many of those converted to the Conservative cause in 1979 were flexible partisans whose vote reflected the operation of short-term forces associated with issue perceptions and party leader images. How these forces contributed to the 1979 election outcome can be explored in greater detail.

ISSUES, LEADERS AND THE 1979 ELECTION

We have already discussed attitudes toward party leaders in 1979 as well as the distribution of salient election issues. With respect to issues, we have argued that certain conditions must be met in order for an issue to affect the outcome of an election, namely salience, skewness, and a link to a party. With minor modifications, these conditions might also be applied to understanding how party leaders influence election outcomes.

There is little *prima facie* evidence that leadership or attitudes toward the individual party leaders were more important in explaining the outcome of the 1979 election than was the case in 1974. The proportion of the sample naming "leader" as the most important reason for their voting choice increased only slightly in 1979 over the comparable figure in 1974, (37 per cent compared to 33 per cent) and the proportion within that group defining this to mean personality rather than issue positions likewise increased only slightly (45 per cent compared to 42 per cent). Also, the percentage mentioning "leadership" in response to the open-ended issues questions (table 3) was low (2.1 per cent) although an additional 7.2 per cent of the 1979 sample mentioned Prime Minister Trudeau as the most important "issue."

TABLE 10   SUMMARY OF POSSIBLE ELECTORAL EFFECTS
OF PARTY LEADERS IN THE 1979 ELECTION
(Percentage of Total Electorate*)

Respondents mentioning leader/ personality as "most important factor" in vote and...	Liberal	PC	NDP	Social Credit
Switching to	1.1	1.2	0.5	0.1
Remaining	7.7	2.3	0.4	0.1
New voters/transients	1.5	0.5	0.4	—
	10.3	4.0	1.3	0.2

+ Voters in the 1979 election only. N = 2135. Votes for other parties included in percentages but not shown in table.

One method of assessing the total impact of leaders or of specific issues on the election outcome is to inspect the behaviour of specific groups within the sample who, by reason of their responses, indicate that attitudes toward the leaders or feelings about a particular issue played a greater role for them than for the sample as a whole. If the behaviour of such groups is examined in the context of the total electorate a measure of both the direction and magnitude of possible electoral effects may be obtained. Table 10 indicates the pattern of movement of those who defined leaders as most important for their vote and who chose the personality rather than the issues branch of the party-leader-candidate question (see figure 1). The data suggest that leadership did not motivate a pattern of switching in 1979 favourable to any one party—the number of voters within the group switching to the Liberals being almost exactly equal to the number moving to the Conservatives. However, a sizable advantage to the Liberals did occur among those *remaining* with that party in 1979, indicating that the leadership question may have had a reinforcing effect on past Liberal voters, and thereby inhibited some voters in that group from switching to another party. The Liberals also enjoyed an advantage on the leadership question among new voters and transients, although the total proportion of the electorate accounted for by these subgroups was not as large.

The overall pattern of behaviour of this leadership-oriented group of voters is very similar to that shown by the 1974 data with the single exception that the total performance of the Conservatives within this group in 1979 was significantly better, and the net Liberal advantage on the leadership question was therefore less.[36] Since the examination of the thermometer scores presented above indicates that Clark was only slightly more popular than his predecessor, Stanfield, the most likely explanation of this pattern is the decline of Trudeau's popularity and the animosity that he provoked among at least some voters. Although this contrast is important, it does not modify the conclusion that leadership was basically a Liberal issue in 1979, and that its main effects were to keep at least some voters in the Liberal fold who might otherwise have been motivated to switch, as well as to enhance the Liberals' attractiveness to new voters and transients.

TABLE 11 *SUMMARY OF POSSIBLE ELECTORAL EFFECTS OF SELECTED ISSUES IN THE 1979 ELECTION (Percentage of Total Electorate)*

Respondents mentioning _____ as most important issue and . . .	Liberal	PC	NDP	Social Credit
(a) *Economic issues* (general)				
Switching to	0.2	1.9	1.3	1.3
Remaining	4.4	3.3	1.8	*
New voters/transients	1.1	1.1	0.9	0.1
	5.7	6.3	4.0	0.4
(b) *Unemployment*				
Switching to	0.1	0.7	0.4	—
Remaining	1.5	1.0	0.7	0.1
New voters/transients	0.3	0.4	0.4	0.1
	1.9	2.1	1.5	0.2
(c) *Mortgage deductibility*				
Switching to	0.2	0.7	0.2	0.1
Remaining	0.9	0.8	0.5	—
New voters/transients	0.4	0.4	0.5	—
	1.5	1.9	1.2	0.1
(d) *Energy* (including Petro-Canada)				
Switching to	0.3	0.8	0.2	—
Remaining	1.4	0.8	0.6	—
New voters/transients	0.4	0.4	0.2	0.1
	2.1	2.0	1.0	0.1
(e) *Confederation issues*				
Switching to	0.8	1.3	1.0	0.2
Remaining	6.9	2.3	0.5	0.3
New voters/transients	2.0	1.1	0.3	0.1
	9.7	4.7	1.8	0.6

* Less than 0.1 per cent

A similar analysis may be applied to a subset of issues which, on the basis of the frequency of their mention in response to the open-ended issues questions, might be hypothesised to have influenced the 1979 election result. The salience of these issues may be assumed, either in the aggregate sense if they were mentioned by large numbers of voters, or in the sense that a particular group of individuals, even if small, defined them as "most important." Voting then is indicative of both the link to party and skewness of opinion acting together. In other words, an issue may have affected the fortunes of a particular party if it was identified with that party in the public mind *and* characterised by a sufficiently skewed opinion distribution so as to move voters in one direction. In the absence of either of these conditions, we should expect to find approximately equal proportions of voters moving simultaneously in opposite directions. Table 11 applies this test to selected issues of the 1979 election campaign—economic issues, unemployment, mortgage deductibility, energy (including Petrocan), and Confederation issues.

Voters switching parties in 1979 and mentioning any of several general economic issues ("inflation," "the economy," and so forth) were substantially more likely to choose the Conservatives or the New Democratic party than the Liberals (table 11). However, the net effect of this shift was partially offset by the tendency of those who did not switch to be slightly more favourable to the Liberals. The new voters and transients mentioning economic issues split almost evenly among the three parties. Thus, while the net contribution of economic issues to electoral change in 1979 favoured the Conservatives, the effect could hardly be said to have been decisive. While few voters switched to the Liberals because of the economy, a significant number were willing to remain with the party for this reason, and the Liberals succeeded in gaining at least an even split of new voters and transients expressing concern about general economic issues. Thus, as in 1974, issues that might seem on the surface to be heavily biased against the government did not consistently have this effect. On balance, however, the Conservatives fared better on economic issues, particularly among switchers.

The same type of pattern is shown by voters mentioning unemployment as the most important issue in 1979 (table 11), although the total percentage of the electorate accounted for by these respondents is much lower. Voters mentioning unemployment and switching parties were significantly more likely to choose the Conservatives, while those maintaining the same vote as in 1974 were slightly more favourable to the Liberals. New voters and transients split evenly among the three parties. The net effect of the three groups acting together was that no party had a clear advantage on this issue. While one might expect that an issue such as "unemployment" virtually by definition would have an anti-government effect, this was not true for all groups of voters in 1979.

Two other issues which also might be seen to have motivated small groups of voters in 1979 were the mortgage deductibility and energy issues. Mortgage deductibility, a prominent plank in the Conservatives' platform, was clearly associated with that party, while energy policy was associated with the Conservatives only to the extent that it involved their commitment to "privatize" Petro-Canada (about half of the mentions in the energy group). As with the other economic issues, those switching parties and mentioning mortgage deductibility were more likely to move to the Conservatives, although the actual number of voters following this pattern was small (table 11). New voters and transients, as well as voters not switching parties, display no clear pattern, thus moderating any advantage that the Conservatives may have gained among switchers on this issue. The fact that mentions of mortgage deductibility were concentrated more heavily in Ontario is potentially of some importance, however, as it was the high turnover of seats in this province that contributed heavily to the Conservative victory. The energy issue, like mortgage deductibility, displays a mixed pattern of small effects but is less favourable in total to the Conservatives (table 11).

In some respects the most interesting and potentially the most important group of issues in the 1979 election campaign are those in the "Confederation" category. These issues include references to national unity, constitutional reform, specific constitutional issues, bilingualism, Quebec, separatism, and the referendum. The possible significance of these issues derives from the fact that the number of respondents identifying them as most important in the 1979 campaign was relatively large, and although Quebec residents were more than twice as likely as those in other provinces to identify such issues as most important, the percentages of respondents in other regions of the country mentioning them was sufficiently great to suggest a potentially widespread impact on the election result.[37] As with other issues, there is a difference with respect to the behaviour of the three electoral groups identifying Confederation issues as most important. As may be seen in table 11, the pattern of switching benefited the Conservatives slightly (although less so when only specific references to Quebec are included). However, this advantage was more than offset by those not switching parties in 1979 and by the new voters and transients. When the three groups are totalled, the net effect of Confederation issues was highly favourable to the Liberals, both in direction and in the number of voters involved.[38]

The pattern of voting displayed by respondents mentioning the five sets of issues considered above reflects, in many ways, the nature of the treatment of issues in the 1979 campaign. The Conservatives sought to fight the campaign on economic issues and to develop in the voters' minds an association between these issues and the record of the government, thereby creating the link to party which is a necessary condition of issue voting. Although the total effect of these issues was only slightly favourable to the Conservatives, their partial success with this strategy is indicated by the fact that many of those who reported switching and who identified economic issues as "most important" opted for them. The Liberals, on the other hand, sought to seize one of the most important of the Confederation issues already known to be favourable to them—national unity—and make it more salient to the electorate as a whole. That they were at least partially successful is indicated by the number of respondents mentioning national unity as the most important issue of the campaign and by the proportion of the electorate remaining Liberal and mentioning a Confederation issue. This pattern is particularly noticeable in Quebec, but it can be detected in other parts of the country as well.

CONCLUSION: A LIMITED CONSERVATIVE VICTORY

Although the Conservatives won the 1979 election, the 136 seats they captured were only sufficient to form a minority government. It will be useful to consider in conclusion how the various issue, leader, conversion and replacement forces combined to make the 1979 election an exercise in the politics of limited change. Although we cannot pinpoint the particular constituencies which the Conservatives might have won and hence secured a parliamentary majority, we can indicate the degrees of weakness shown by the party in each of the areas mentioned above. The party's shortfall from majority government status was so small (6 seats) that a stronger showing in any of the areas cited above would likely have made the difference.

Regarding leader effects, in the period prior to the election, Clark, a compromise choice for the leadership of his party, performed well in the House of

Commons, improved the party organisation, and managed to overcome at least temporarily many of the factional disputes that have plagued the Conservatives in recent years.[39] The fact that a majority of the electorate are flexible partisans sensitive to short-term forces associated with issues and party leader images provided the new leader with the opportunity to play an important role in moving voters into his party's camp. The significance of this opportunity is underscored by data showing that the popularity of the Liberal leader, Trudeau, had slipped to (for him) record lows in every region of the country. However, although Clark appears not to have inhibited a Conservative vote among those positively disposed to the party on other grounds, it does seem that he provided little positive help to his party. Clark's image was unfavourable in relative terms, being overshadowed by those of the Liberal or NDP leaders in every province but Alberta and British Columbia. Perhaps especially significant was the low level of affect for Clark among the large cohort of new voters, particularly those in Ontario. On balance, party leader images and leadership as an issue remained factors which favoured the Liberals.

The Conservative strategy of attempting to aggregate a number of moderate and small issue effects did work to their advantage to some extent. They avoided their 1974 mistake of putting extensive campaign resources into an issue such as wage and price controls over which the electorate was deeply divided. The analysis of conversion effects at work in 1979 shows that a number of issues were positively related to voters' propensity to switch to the Conservatives—these ranged from general economic issues to specific concerns with the dollar, taxes and government spending, mortgage deductibility, energy, as well as the general feeling that it was "time for a change." However, if one considers voters remaining with their party, the impact of issues for the Conservatives was in many cases either blunted (in the case of economic issues) or reversed (in the case of national unity). Overall, they were not able to loosen the electorate's party-issue ties sufficiently to persuade more voters to abandon the Liberals, and the number of voters switching to the Conservatives fell short of that needed to produce a majority.

The final area of Conservative weakness concerns replacement effects, and it is one that was particularly important in the 1979 election. The party's inability to appeal to new voters cost it dearly in this election since such voters made up over 15 per cent of the electorate. As a result, their cohort of voters in 1979 contained a large number of persons in the permanent electorate who had switched from the Liberals and New Democrats. These people were very important to the Conservatives because of the party's limited appeal among the large new voter group. More success with the forces of replacement in 1979 would have lessened the extent to which the Conservative voting coalition was a product of the difficult and often fickle processes of electoral conversion. Reliance on such processes left them especially vulnerable to a sharp reversal of their fortunes with the desertion of many of their 1979 converts. The potential for such desertions was strong, given that most of the voters switching to the Conservatives in 1979 were flexible partisans, many of whom lacked strong attachments to the party. And the opportunity for such desertions was to come sooner than anyone foresaw.

NOTES

1. In this study a national probability sample (N = 2744) of the 1979 electorate was interviewed immediately after the election. Included in the survey were 1295 respondents originally interviewed as part of the 1974 national election study. The 1974 survey design is described in Harold D. Clarke, Jane Jenson, Lawrence LeDuc and Jon Pammett, *Political Choice in Canada* (Toronto: McGraw-Hill Ryerson, 1979), Appendix A, 397–400. Details regarding the 1979 survey design are available from the authors upon request. These studies were supported by the Social Science and Humanities Research Council of Canada. All analyses and interpretations are the responsibility of the authors.

2. Clarke et al., *Political Choice in Canada*, passim.

3. Ibid., 148.

4. These figures are based on respondents' recalled voting behaviour and party identification. Analyses of the 1974–1979 panel data also suggest considerable instability in both party identification and voting. For example, if one analyses panel members voting in at least one of the 1974 and 1979 elections, 65 per cent have the same identifications in 1974 and 1979, 18 per cent have different identifications, 14 per cent have moved to or from the status of nonidentifier , and 3 per cent are nonidentifiers in both years. Sixty per cent report voting for the same party in 1974 and 1979, 22 per cent report switching their vote, and 18 per cent voted in only one of the two elections. Altogether, 48 per cent report stable party identifications *and* stable voting behaviour.

5. Clarke et al., *Political Choice in Canada*, 309–16.

6. Ibid., 315.

7. Ibid., 343–48.

8. Conceptually, this treatment differs from a truly "permanent" pool of eligible voters to the extent that attrition due to death, disability or emigration must be taken into account in analyses extending over a substantial period of time. Between a pair of elections, however, such effects will be relatively small and can reasonably be disregarded in an examination of electoral turnover. Such effects should not be overlooked in analyses of long-term electoral trends. Butler and Stokes, for example, have demonstrated the importance of demographic variables in accounting for the decline of the Liberal party in Britain in the early part of this century and the concomitant rise of the class alignment in modern British politics. See David Butler and Donald Stokes, *Political Change in Britain* 2d ed. (New York: St. Martin's, 1976), chaps. 7, 8 and 9.

9. Because the treatment here is confined to the 1974–1979 pair of elections, transient voters not voting in both of these elections are excluded from the analysis. For a general analysis of the attitudes and behaviour of transient voters see Clarke et al., *Political Choice in Canada*, 309–16.

10. Chief Electoral Officer, *Report, 1979* (Hull: Ministry of Supply and Services Canada, 1980), x.

11. The number of new voters is calculated from the *Census of Canada 1976*, v. 8, bulletin 8SD.1, catalogue 92-832, 1–3.

12. Chief Electoral Officer, *Report, 1979*, xi.

13. An increased turnout of 5 per cent among surviving 1974 voters would have brought an additional 646 000 of these voters to the polls in 1979, or 34 per cent of the 1.9 million increase in the total vote. Estimated from *Census of Canada 1976*, ibid., and Chief Electoral Officer, *Report, 1974*, ix.

14. See, for example, Allan Kornberg, Harold D. Clarke and Arthur Goddard,

"Parliament and the Representational Process in Contemporary Canada," and Allan Kornberg and Judith D. Wolfe, "Parliament, the Media and the Polls," in *Parliament, Policy and Representations,* ed. Harold D. Clarke, C. Campbell, F. Quo and A. Goddard (Toronto: Metheun, 1980), chaps. 1 and 3.

15. The feeling thermometer scales range from 0–100, with 50 explicitly designated as the neutral point. See Clarke et al., *Political Choice in Canada,* 406–7.

16. We must treat these results with some caution, however, for two reasons. First, for many respondents the score on one variable may be affected by the other; for example, if someone likes Trudeau that person might give the Liberal party a high score as well for that reason, thus causing Trudeau to appear similar to the party on the thermometer ratings. Second, a high score for a leader may not necessarily translate into votes for his party if the party itself is particularly disliked, or if the voter is making the decision without reference to leader images.

17. Clarke et al., *Political Choice in Canada,* chap. 12.

18. Ibid., 243–44; Butler and Stokes, *Political Change in Britain,* chap. 13. The distinction between "position" and "valence" issues first appeared in Donald E. Stokes, "Spatial Models of Party Competition," in *Elections and the Political Order,* ed. Angus Campbell et al. (New York: Wiley, 1966), 170–71.

19. Clarke et al., *Political Choice in Canada,* chap. 8.

20. Respondents were asked: "Now I would like to ask you some more specific questions about the recent [1979] *federal* election. What, in your opinion, was the most important issue in that election?" Respondents who cited an issue then were asked three follow-up questions: (a) "How do you feel about the issue?" (b) "Which party is closest to you on this issue?" and (c) "How important was that issue to you in deciding how to vote in the election?" These respondents then were questioned about whether or not another election issue was important to

them and the remainder of the sequence [(a)-(c)] was repeated for those citing such an issue.

21. Ibid., 246.

22. This assumes voters consider inflation and other issues in isolation from one another. However, if voters perceive inflation as being tied to other issues (for example, levels of unemployment), then depending upon how these issues are presented to the electorate in the context of a specific election campaign, inflation may take on positional qualities. On this point see James E. Alt, *The Politics of Economic Decline: Economic Management and Political Behaviour in Britain Since 1964* (New York: Cambridge University Press, 1979), 8–12.

23. A Gallup survey on the mortgage deductibility question found 74 per cent in favour, 15 per cent against, and 11 per cent with no opinion. Canadian Institute of Public Opinion, *The Gallup Report* (27 December 1978).

24. Additional evidence in support of this conclusion is provided by individual-level comparisons of leader popularity. Pairwise comparisons of voters' thermometer ratings of Trudeau and Clark show that 53 per cent preferred the former, 38 per cent the latter, and 9 per cent rated them equally. For Trudeau and Broadbent, comparable percentages are 48 per cent, 38 per cent, and 13 per cent respectively. Indicative of Clark's relative unpopularity is the finding that when compared to Broadbent, 48 per cent of the electorate gave higher thermometer scores to the NDP leader, whereas Clark was favoured by 38 per cent (15 per cent rated them equally).

25. The question asked was "In deciding how you would vote in the recent 1979 *federal* election, which was the *most* important to you: the *party leaders,* the *candidates* here in this constituency, or the *parties* taken as a whole?" For those citing party leaders or local candidates the follow-up question was: "When you say that _____ was the *most* important to you, are you thinking of this person's personal qualities or this person's stand on certain issues?" For persons mentioning party the follow-up question

was: "When you say that party was the *most* important to you, are you thinking of the party's general approach to government or its position on certain issues?" Those in either question sequence who cited "issues" were asked: "Which issues are you thinking of specifically?"

26. These percentages are very similar to those obtained in the 1974 survey. In 1974, 49 per cent (58 per cent of the "party leader," 48 per cent of the "local candidate" and 43 per cent of the "parties as a whole" streams) of the respondents cited an issue basis for their answers regarding the "most important factor" in their voting choices, and 51 per cent selected the "personal qualities" or "general approach" options.

27. A useful discussion of the problems such effects pose for analysing voting behaviour is Richard A. Brody and Benjamin I. Page, "The Assessment of Policy Voting," *American Political Science Review* 66 (1972): 450–58.

28. Clarke et al., *Political Choice in Canada*, chaps. 10 and 11.

29. Ibid., 343–48.

30. This method of multiple regression is known as the analysis of commonalities. For a brief nontechnical discussion of this technique see N. Nie, S. Verba and J. Petrocik, *The Changing American Voter* (Cambridge: Harvard University Press, 1976), 303, note 8.

31. In 1974, issue effects were greater than those of party leaders among flexible-high interest partisans in the analyses of voting for all three parties. Leader effects were greater than issue effects among flexible-low interest partisans in every case (Clarke et al., *Political Choice in Canada*, 346). In this respect, the 1979 results appear to be a mirror image of those for 1968. In that election, leader effects consistently exceeded those for issues among all categories of flexible partisans (ibid., 354–55).

32. Multivariate stepwise logit analyses yield results very similar to those produced by the regression analyses. The logit procedure shows that the impact of short-term leader and issue forces was almost wholly confined to flexible partisans; that issue effects were invariably greater than those for leader images among all political interest categories of flexible partisans; and that leader effects were, relatively speaking, greater in analyses where Liberal rather than Conservative or NDP voting was the dependent variable. For a description of the logit procedure used see the *SAS Supplemental Library User's Guide, 1980 edition* (Cary, NC: SAS Institute, 1980), 83–102.

33. Clarke et al., *Political Choice in Canada*, 373–80.

34. Ibid., 367.

35. For data on the partisanship of various age cohorts see Lawrence LeDuc, "Sources of Long-Term and Short-Term Electoral Change in Canada" (Paper presented at the Conference on Critical Electoral Forces: Changing Mass Politics in Advanced Industrial Societies, Florida State University, Tallahassee, Florida, 23–24 May 1980), 11–15.

36. Clarke et al., *Political Choice in Canada*, 374–75.

37. By region, the percentage of respondents mentioning one of these issues as most important was: Atlantic (13), Quebec (25), Ontario (12), Prairies (15), BC (12).

38. Of course, the pattern is partly accounted for by the combination of the greater salience of this issue in Quebec and the strong tendency of Quebec voters to support the Liberal party. However, more detailed analyses show that the Confederation issues were basically favourable to the Liberals in all parts of the country.

39. George Perlin, *The Tory Syndrome: Leadership Politics in the Progressive Conservative Party* (Montreal: McGill-Queen's University Press, 1980).

GREAT DEBATES: THE TELEVISED
LEADERSHIP DEBATES OF 1979◊

LAWRENCE LₑDUC
RICHARD PRICE

᳁

The 1979 federal election campaign was only the second occasion in our political history when the nation's three federal party leaders participated in a televised debate. That event, entitled Encounter '79, thus represented a significant departure from conventional campaign strategies, and one that did not recur in the 1980 campaign. The first televised debate between Canadian federal party leaders took place in 1968. A joint CBC–CTV proposal for a 1974 debate was rejected by the parties. That Encounter '79 took place at all undoubtedly derived from electoral considerations and strategies, as did the 1984 debates. In the Gallup poll prior to the 1979 debate, the two major parties held a near tie in popular vote—Liberals 39 per cent, Progressive Conservatives 38 per cent, and New Democratic party 16 per cent. In such a tight contest, and with the knowledge that short-term factors might tip the election to either party, all actors perceived the event in terms of potential political advantage.

Debates rarely take place under any other circumstances. Incumbents almost never agree to debate unless they find their party in danger of losing an election. Similarly, a party enjoying a wide lead in the polls (such as the Liberals in 1980) can generally find a reason to avoid the risk of a debate. The presidential debates in the United States between Ford and Carter in 1976 provide a similar example of a closely fought contest and a vulnerable incumbent, although the two Reagan–Mondale debates in 1984 would appear to be a contrary case. Generally, political leaders view televised campaign debates as a means of shoring up a campaign and reinforcing traditional allegiances or alliances.

◊ *Canadian Journal of Political Science* 18, 1 (March 1985): 135–53.

LEADERSHIP DEBATES: SOME GENERAL CONSIDERATIONS

While there has been little study of televised debates in Canada, there are well developed examples available in the literature of other countries, notably the United States and Germany. In the 1960 US presidential debate, about 55 pert cent of the adult population listened to or watched each debate, while about 80 per cent were exposed to at least one of the series. At the same time, audience size varied appreciably over the series, with some estimates placing the audience for the first 1960 debate at 60 to 65 per cent of the total adult population, declining over the remainder of the series. This same pattern was again evidenced in the 1976 US debates, with about 75 per cent of all adults watching the first Ford–Carter debate, and 67 per cent and 56 per cent respectively viewing the second and third.[1] Baker and Norpoth[2] suggest that the audience for the 1972 West German debates was equally large, with about eight out of ten respondents in a national survey reporting having viewed at least one of a series of three scheduled debates.

The question of who watches such debates involves two basic considerations: audience size and audience composition. Literature on television and politics relevant to mass audience events such as debates would suggest few sociodemographic differences at the level of the individual viewer. However, potential regional variations obtaining from geographic or linguistic factors might be expected.[3] Also, "debate watching" should properly be considered in a broader context of political participation. Given the relatively modest commitment involved in watching a debate on television, we might expect debate watchers to be "participants" at the lowest level of a standard political participation scale, but nevertheless sufficiently participant so as to be likely voters. The nature of the mass audience for the debates, and its "participant–spectator" role in the 1979 election campaign is one theme that we explore here.

Observers of leadership debates in other countries have attempted to assess the electoral effects of such events, both at the individual and aggregate levels.[4] Leadership debates are, however, idiosyncratic events, which are only one part of a much larger political campaign. The televising of such events is, from the point of view of the participants, explicitly partisan. By publicizing the skills, talents, philosophies, and personal leadership qualities of the party leaders, such events may tend to accentuate the centrality of leadership in the calculus of individual voter decision making. Because much of the literature on debates is American, the analysis of this topic naturally focusses on individual candidates for the presidency. Whether debates affect voting behaviour in a system in which leaders are only one element in the matrix of voting choice is more problematic, and will be an important concern of this analysis. In the American case, evidence suggests that debates have generally tended to reinforce pre-existing candidate and party preferences.[5] There is some reason to believe that such may also be the case in Canada, given the existence of pre-debate party and leader images, and the more limited coverage of the debates.

Encounter '79 was a single two-hour media event, unlike the more extended series of debates in the US in 1960 and 1976, or the German debates of 1972. Further, all participants in the Canadian debates were experienced parliamentarians, who received a considerable amount of media coverage between elections by reason of their party positions and parliamentary roles.[6] This single event, then, must be considered in a context somewhat wider than that of the election campaign alone. Based exclusively on post-election survey data, however, this analysis will be unable to separate easily different campaign effects from those of the debates specifically, or to measure changes in attitudes which may have occurred between the day of the debates (13 May) and election day (22 May). Within these limitations, however, we will be concerned with the extent to which the debates may or may not have affected individual voting behaviour and, if they did, whether they may also have had an impact on the outcome of the 1979 federal election.

ENCOUNTER '79 STRUCTURE AND SUBSTANCE

The actual structure of the leadership debates of 1979 was both similar to and different from the American experiences of 1960, 1976, and 1980. Like American presidential debates before and after 1979, Canadian leaders were called upon to respond to questions posed to them by representatives of the media: David Halton, Peter Desbarats, and Bruce Phillips. Exchanges between the leaders were controlled by the moderator, David Johnson, dean of law of the University of Western Ontario. Unlike the three presidential debates in the United States, however, Encounter '79 represented a structural compromise between the American tradition of "joint appearances"[7] and the tradition of adversarial politics more akin to question period in the House of Commons. Thus, while the panelists asked questions of the leaders, the leaders were able to ask questions of each other as well. Not surprisingly, the number of exchanges between leaders ranged from two to ten for a single topic, and the number of different issues debated in each round varied from three to seven—three in Round 3 and seven in Round 1.

The format of the 1979 debates was surprisingly simple. Each party leader was allowed three minutes for an opening statement, Joe Clark, Conservative leader, first, Prime Minister Pierre Trudeau, Liberal leader, second, and Ed Broadbent, New Democratic party leader, third. The main component of the debates consisted of three rounds, each of which lasted thirty minutes. Round 1 involved Clark and Broadbent, Round 2 Trudeau and Broadbent, and Round 3 pitted Trudeau against Clark. Finally, each participant was allowed four minutes for closing remarks. The order of the closing remarks was the reverse of that followed for the opening statements: Broadbent, Trudeau and Clark. Following are brief synopses of the three rounds of the debates.

Round 1: Clark and Broadbent debated seven different topics in the opening round of the debates. These included, in order 1. the practicality of a stimulative deficit and a balanced budget; 2. the future of Petro-Canada; 3. the conditions, if any, under which a cabinet minister could violate the law; 4. whether or not the government should impose a temporary moratorium on construction of nuclear power plants; 5. the possibility of the New Democratic party supporting a Progressive Conservative minority government; 7. the appropriate role of a prime minister in the event that voters of Quebec supported a separatist option in a referendum; and 7. whether a vote for the NDP was really a vote for the Liberals. Both Clark and Broadbent exchanged opinions 33 times; that is, Clark stated his or his party's position 16 times and Broadbent spoke 17 times.

Round 2: Trudeau and Broadbent debated four issues in Round 2. These included: 1. each party's conception of nationalism, national unity, and national identity in French and English Canada; 2. unemployment and job creation, given 900 000 unemployed Canadians; 3. the erosion of accessibility to medicare; and 4. the failure of Parliament to deal with the decriminalization of marijuana. Broadbent and Trudeau exchanged opinions 20 times, Trudeau speaking 11 times and Broadbent 9 times.

Round 3: Trudeau and Clark were questioned by panelists on only three issues in the third round, although they also discussed related subjects. Trudeau and Clark were asked: 1. to comment on the fact that the Canadian public has reservations about both of them. This opening question prompted disagreements about Loto Canada, the consequences of moving the Canadian embassy in Israel, the reform of Parliament, committee review of estimates, and political accountability. In response to a question on 2. controls on government spending, the participants exchanged views on the Lambert Commission, the Glassco Commission, the Office of the Auditor General, the position of comptroller general, zero based budgeting, sunset laws, and freedom of information. Finally, Trudeau and Clark debated 3. patriation of the constitution, and the question of federal–provincial relations, particularly with respect to the office of prime minister. In sum, the panelists asked only these three questions, and the two leaders for their part spoke 13 times: Trudeau 7, and Clark 6.

Viewers of the debates were confronted with an obvious problem of comparability, in that all three party leaders did not have to debate the same issues. Further, the substance of each round of the debates varied substantially. The informational potential of televised debates is partly a function of the extent to which the agenda of voters, politicians, and media overlap.[8] The content of the 1979 debates does suggest some congruence, given information also available on voters' perceptions of issues in 1979.[9] However, it is likely that the debates would have tended to frustrate strict issue-by-issue comparisons of parties and leaders.

WHO WATCHED THE DEBATES?

The debates attracted a large audience, and evidence from network sources suggests that a large proportion of those watching were tuned for the entire two hours. The total audience has been estimated at 7.5 million viewers which, allowing for the fact that this excludes much of the French-speaking population, is a substantial majority of the potential audience.[10] Even without taking into account the linguistic selectivity of the debates, the official estimates would indicate that about one-half of the 15 million Canadians eligible to vote in the 1979 election watched the program.

The 1979 National Election Study confirms these estimates. Fifty-one per cent of a national half-sample of the electorate taken immediately after the 1979 election reported having watched the debates:[11] among those whose primary language is English, 61 per cent reported; among those whose primary language was French, 26 per cent. Respondents in Ontario and the Atlantic provinces watched the debates

TABLE 1   WATCHING THE DEBATES COMPARED WITH
OTHER ACTS OF POLITICAL PARTICIPATION
(Percentage of a National Sample)+

Voting	89
Read about politics in newspaper	70
Discuss politics with others	64
Watched televised leader debates	51 (61)++
Convince friends how to vote	20
Attend a political meeting	17
Contact a public official	17
Work in a political campaign	11
Contribute money to a party or candidate	9
	(N = 1311)

+ Percentage of respondents who report performing act "often" or "sometimes" in federal politics—1979 half-sample.
++ Percentage for anglophone respondents only.

in slightly greater numbers than did those in the West (66 per cent, 64 per cent, and 53 per cent, respectively), while those in Quebec (29 per cent) were less likely to watch because of the unilingual format.[12] Women and men watched in approximately equal numbers according to the sample, as did those in large cities, suburbs, smaller towns and rural areas.

The act of watching the debates, as well as any possible effects on the outcome of the 1979 election, must be examined in the context of the full range of political activities in which respondents were engaged, both at the time of the debates and afterwards. Not surprisingly, watching the debates was most highly correlated with other types of passive political activities, such as reading about the campaign in the newspapers or discussing it with family and friends. In table 1, we fit the act of watching the debates to a set of different political activities which are commonly included in standard political participation scales.[13] The percentage of the national sample who reported that they watched the debate is only slightly lower than the percentage who read about politics in newspapers (70 per cent) or discuss politics with others (64 per cent); but the percentage is considerably higher than the proportion who engage in acts involving a higher level of commitment, such as attempting to persuade others how to vote (20 per cent), attending political meetings (17 per cent), or contacting public officials (17 per cent).

Although the act of watching the debates correlates more strongly with passive political activities than with other political acts, such relationships are not overwhelmingly strong.[14] This suggests that, while watching the debates overlapped other passive political activities for some people, there are many others for whom the act of turning on the television set on 13 May 1979, bore little relationship to any established pattern of political activity. Watching the debate, therefore, bears some characteristics of both an established pattern of political activity and of a "chance" occurrence for the sample as a whole. The absence of alternative programming in many parts of the country might well have contributed to the latter tendency, just as in the US when presidential addresses are carried on virtually all channels.

The activity that watching the debates *does* relate to most strongly is exposure to other aspects of the 1979 election campaign through the medium of television.

TABLE 2   RELATIONSHIP BETWEEN WATCHING THE
           DEBATES AND FREQUENCY OF EXPOSURE TO
           OTHER POLITICAL TELEVISION PROGRAMS
           DURING THE 1979 ELECTION CAMPAIGN*

Saw other programs during campaign...	Watched debates	Did not watch
Quite a few (row percentages)	70.1 (78.6)	29.9 (21.4)
(column percentages)	59.3 (59.7)	26.4 (24.5)
(diagonal percentages)	30.3 (35.9)	12.9 (9.8)
Some	43.4 (53.4)	56.6 (46.6)
	30.2 (29.7)	41.1 (39.0)
	15.4 (17.8)	20.1 (15.6)
Almost none	25.3 (30.5)	74.7 (69.5)
	10.6 (10.6)	32.5 (36.4)
	5.4 (6.4)	15.9 (14.6)

N = 1293 (868)
Chi sq. sig. at .001
Gamma = .56 (.59)

+ Percentages for anglophone respondents only shown in parentheses.

Respondents in the 1979 study were also asked whether they watched "quite a few," "some," or "almost no" television programs dealing with the 1979 federal election campaign.[15] Of those who reported watching the debates, 59 per cent (30 per cent of the total sample) indicated that they watched "quite a few" other programs dealing with the campaign (see table 2). Only 11 per cent of the debate-watchers responded that they watched almost no other political television during the course of the 1979 campaign. The overall correlation (gamma) between the two activities is +.56 for the sample as a whole and +.59 for anglophone respondents only. Not only does this indicate the nature of exposure to the debate as a political activity, it also suggests that any possible influence that the debates may have had on individual voting behaviour must be placed in the context of general campaign influences. For only a small fraction of the electorate is exposure to the debates divorced both from other political involvement and other campaign influences, particularly those involving the medium of television.

Given that the act of watching the debates correlates with other passive political activities and campaign exposure, it is not surprising to discover that it is correlated modestly with various sociodemographic attitudes in much the same way as are other passive political activities. Persons in upper socio-economic status groups, those with higher education, and those in the older age brackets were all somewhat more likely to have watched the debates than were their opposites.[16] These relationships are very modest, however, and it is perhaps more accurate to say that the debates were viewed by a broad cross-section of the Canadian public. As with political participation measures, only a small proportion of variance is explained by sociodemographic variables alone.

There is no relationship between direction of party identification and watching/not watching the debates, except that those respondents without any identification

TABLE 3   RESPONDENTS' GENERAL IMPRESSIONS OF DEBATES+

Question (if watched debates): "What were your impressions of the debates, in general?"

General positive:	Good debates, enjoyed them, interesting, informative, all good speakers, all did well, came out even, said the same things, didn't influence me	49%
General negative:	Disappointing, poor debates, waste of time, proved nothing, silly, too much fighting, evasive, showy	41
Broadbent positive:	Broadbent won, was very good, spoke well, strong showing, spoke to issues, made sense	20
Trudeau positive:	Trudeau won, was good, very smooth, intelligent, speaks well, experienced, confident	17
Clark negative:	Clark was disappointing, not impressive, lost the debate, was weak, nervous, poor image, poor speaker	17
Clark positive:	Clark did well, more honest, stood up to questions, had more to say, won the debate	10
Trudeau negative:	Trudeau was arrogant, tricky, did poorly, too aggressive, lost the debate	9
Broadbent negative:	Broadbent didn't speak well, unsure of himself, sided with Trudeau, didn't care for him	2
Neutral reference to specific debate or leader		2
Don't know, none		5
	(N = 660)	

+ Multiple response question. Illustrative responses are listed in order of frequency of mention

with a party (about 10 per cent of the sample) were less likely to have watched (40 per cent) than were those holding an identification with a party (54 per cent)— Liberal, Conservative, and NDP identifiers were almost equally likely to have watched (52 per cent, 57 per cent, and 56 per cent, respectively). There is, however, a weak positive relationship (gamma = .13) between intensity of party identification and watching the debates. Strong identifiers (56 per cent) were somewhat more likely to have watched than were those with weak party identification (48 per cent). It should not be assumed that party identification is necessarily causally prior to the act of watching the debates, or indeed of voting. There is considerable evidence that, for a significant portion of the Canadian electorate, party identification displays a tendency to travel with vote and to be responsive to a variety of short-term forces.[17] Nevertheless, it is fair to say that, if party identification is treated in the traditional manner, those whose partisan attitudes were such as to make them more resistant to change[18] were more likely to be found among those watching the debate on 13 May. We shall return to this point in our subsequent discussion of the potential impact of the debates on individual voting behaviour and on the outcome of the 1979 federal election.

IMAGES OF THE DEBATES: WINNERS AND LOSERS

In the 1979 post-election survey, the attitudes of those respondents who had watched the debates were probed by means of a broad open-ended question. Attitudes toward the performance of specific party leaders were not probed directly, nor were specific questions directed at the content of the debates.

Most respondents gave a general evaluation of the debates as a whole in at least one of their answers. Many, however, commented spontaneously on the performance of one or more specific party leaders. Although not asked specifically to do so, most respondents phrased answers in evaluative terms. Table 3 summarises responses to the "impressions" question, with answers coded along a positive–negative dimension. It may be seen that the sample is about evenly divided between positive and negative impressions with respect to the debates in general. Of those who watched the debates, 49 per cent reported a favourable impression, while 41 per cent gave a negative one. Only 5 per cent of those who reported watching the debates were unable or unwilling to give any impression of them. Issues were not specifically probed in the wording of the question and there was little issue content in these responses. Better than one-half of those sampled did volunteer an impression of at least one specific party leader in response to this question. While this does not provide a measure of leaders' performance in the debates for all respondents or leaders, the frequency and direction of these responses, taken together, do indicate the nature of the impressions of specific leaders which were formed by the mass public via the debates.

The favourable comments received by Ed Broadbent in the press regarding his performance in the debates are evident, too, in these responses. Far more respondents reported a positive impression of Broadbent's performance (20 per cent) than reported a negative one (2 per cent). Broadbent and Trudeau were both frequently mentioned as "winners" of the debate by respondents, and indeed Broadbent's total number of positive responses is slightly higher than Trudeau's. Trudeau also had a proportion of negative responses (9 per cent), although few of our respondents identified the prime minister as the "loser" of the debates.

Perceptions of Joe Clark's performance in the debates are more difficult to evaluate. In the negotiations that took place regarding the scheduling and format of the program, it was evident that Conservative strategists would have preferred to avoid the debates, but there was also a sense that scuttling the debates might exact even greater political costs.[19] Thus the hesitation with which the Conservatives approached the debates left Clark open to the charge that he was "afraid to debate" with Trudeau and Broadbent, a perception that may itself have shaped expectations of Clark's performance. The same number of respondents commented on Clark's performance as on Trudeau's, but the direction of these comments was much more negative. Many noted Clark's apparent nervousness, or said that he projected a "weak" image. There were positive perceptions as well, but few went so far as to say that Clark had "won" the debate. Among the 10 per cent of the sample who made positive comments on Clark's performance are found comments that he was "more honest" or that he "stood up well" to attacks by his opponents. Nevertheless, it is

TABLE 4   *PARTY LEADER, PARTY, AND LOCAL CANDIDATE THERMOMETER SCORES FOR WATCHERS AND NONWATCHERS OF THE DEBATES (Mean Scores)* *

	Liberal		Conservative		New Democrat	
Leaders						
Watched debates	58.0	(55.1)	50.9	(52.8)	60.0	(61.3)
Did not watch	57.4	(48.1)++	49.8	(53.3)	50.2++	(53.1)++
Parties						
Watched Debates	57.0	(51.2)	56.7	(58.6)	49.1	(49.3)
Did not watch	58.3	(54.8)	54.6	(58.8)	44.6++	(45.2)
Local Candidates						
Watched Debates	54.1	(52.6)	56.3	(58.0)	46.9	(48.3)
Did not watch	56.6	(49.9)	54.5	(59.6)	43.5	(46.3)

+ Thermometer scores for anglophone respondents only shown in parentheses.
++ Difference between watchers and nonwatchers significant at .01.

evident that in comparison with Trudeau and Broadbent, perceptions of Clark's performance in the debates were decidedly negative, even if not entirely so. In spite of this, the general tenor of the open-ended responses suggests that the common argument that Clark had only to "get through" the debates without serious political damage may have been correct. He did not have to "win" the debates in the conventional sense, but rather needed only to avoid the major political blunder that the Conservatives feared might cost them an election that they otherwise expected to win.

There are other indicators which suggest that the debates did not inflict any lasting damage on the Conservative leader, in spite of his comparatively weak performance. The 1979 national survey contains thermometer measures of affect for all three party leaders which can provide some clues to any impact that the debates or other short-term factors may have had on the general feelings of the public about each of the three party leaders.[20] Such indicators cannot measure the effects of the debates specifically, however, as to do so would require a sampling immediately before *and* immediately after the event. Neither can the debates be effectively separated from other possible short-term effects emanating from the campaign. Within these limitations the thermometer scales do provide a general indication of the image which the public held of each of the party leaders.

Table 4 displays the mean thermometer scores for each of the three party leaders calculated for both watchers and nonwatchers of the debates, together with a standard test for significance of the difference between watchers' and nonwatchers' scores. Also included, in order to provide an interpretative base line, are the thermometer scores for local candidates and the parties in general. Although the latter of these could also be subject to effects from the debates, the local candidate scores might be presumed to be relatively free of such contamination.

For the sample as a whole, there is no statistically significant difference between watchers and nonwatchers of the debates in the degree of affect that respondents felt for Trudeau and Clark, or for their respective parties (see table 4). Given this pattern, it would not seem plausible to single out the debates as the source of Clark's relatively low overall rating. Similarly, while Clark is rated lower than his party, he is placed lower by watchers and nonwatchers alike. Again, it would not seem plausible to attribute the fact that Clark runs behind his party to anything specifically associated with his performance in the televised debates.[21] Although Clark fares slightly better among anglophones, the similarity of the pattern for watchers and nonwatchers persists. Trudeau, on the other hand, does better among anglophone watchers of the debates than among nonwatchers. While his score in this group is a modest 55.1, there is, unlike the case of Joe Clark, at least the possibility that anglophone respondents' opinions of Trudeau could have been influenced by the debates.

The NDP leader, Ed Broadbent, presents a more compelling pattern. Here, the difference between watchers and nonwatchers of the debates is statistically significant, both for anglophones and for the sample as a whole. The spread between watchers and nonwatchers is a full 10 points on the thermometer scale for Broadbent, and about eight points for anglophone respondents only. One must be cautious in attributing this to the debates alone. Unlike Trudeau and Clark, Broadbent in 1979 ran consistently ahead of his party among virtually all groups, including nonwatchers of the debates.[22] But the fact that the spread is significantly greater among those who watched the debates, coupled with the much lower ratings accorded the NDP and local NDP candidates, is highly suggestive of a "debates effect" favourable to Broadbent. Given the magnitude of the positive comments on Broadbent's performance found in the "impressions" question (table 3), it is not surprising to find additional evidence of a positive debates effect on the image of the NDP leader.

VOTING BEHAVIOUR: DID IT MAKE A DIFFERENCE?

The most difficult research question to pose regarding the debates is "Did they make a difference?" either with respect to individual voting behaviour or to the actual outcome of the 1979 election. Could Broadbent's strong performance have accounted for the NDP's above-average showing (18 per cent of the total vote and 26 seats), or is this better explained by issues, other short-term forces, and demographic factors?[23] Might the more negative perception of Clark's performance have damaged the Conservatives, and perhaps in the process accounted for their failure to win a parliamentary majority—a failure that was to prove so disastrous to the party a mere nine months later? These are complex questions that are not easily answered by survey data alone. Nevertheless, the survey data provide perhaps the only real opportunity to address such questions in an empirically reliable manner.

Our task is complicated by the fact that the debates are not easily divorced from the myriad of other short-term factors that operate in elections. We know that short-term forces are potentially quite powerful determinants of voting behaviour in Canadian elections generally.[24] We are not dealing with an electorate which, in the aggregate, will tend to be highly resistant to influence by short-term variables, or for whom campaign effects might be expected to be only reinforcing.

TABLE 5 VOTING BEHAVIOUR IN THE 1979 FEDERAL
ELECTION FOR WATCHERS AND NON-
WATCHERS OF THE DEBATES*

Voted...	Watched		Did Not Watch	
Liberal (column percentages)	37.6	(32.1)	47.8	(31.0)
(diagonal percentages)	20.7	(20.7)	21.4	(11.0)
Conservative	44.2	(50.0)	31.1	(46.3)
	24.4	(32.3)	13.9	(16.4)
New Democrat	16.1	(17.6)	13.7	(21.2)
	8.9	(11.4)	6.1	(7.5)
Social Credit	1.3		5.2	
	0.7		2.3	
Other	0.9	(0.3)	2.3	(1.5)
	0.5	(0.2)	1.0	(0.6)

N = 1059 (722)
Chi Square sig. at .001 (N.S.)
Cramer's V = .18 (.09)

* Percentages for anglophone respondents only shown in parentheses.

   While a large proportion of voters are in theory "switchable" from previous partisan attachments, many of these will already have decided how they will vote at some earlier stage of the campaign. Given that the debates took place only a week before the election, the hypothesis that they could or did influence actual voting decisions depends in part on the supposition that voters remain uncommitted until the final week of the campaign. In 1979, 21 per cent of the national sample report that they made up their minds how they would vote in the final week or on election day itself. The remainder had, according to their own reports, already decided how they would vote at the time that the debates took place.[25]

   The fact that as much as 20 per cent of the electorate *might* have been influenced by the debates does not, of course, mean that they *were* so influenced. While it is difficult to isolate pure debate effects, we can establish the types of patterns that ought to be found in the data if the debates were truly responsible for switching any appreciable number of votes. First, we would expect to find differences in behaviour between watchers and nonwatchers of the debates. If identical patterns exist among those who watched the debates and those who did not, the hypothesis that the debates may have affected the election outcome appears less persuasive. Second, we would expect to find some commonality between patterns of voting and the perceived outcome of the debates themselves. If those who watched the debates prove to be *more* likely to have voted Conservative, for example, even though the perceptions of Clark's performance in the debates were clearly on the negative side, we might also be inclined to reject the argument that the debates were influential in voting decisions on any large scale.

Table 5 provides an initial test of these arguments. It may be seen that there is a statistically significant difference between watchers and nonwatchers of the debates in 1979 voting behaviour, but also that the direction of this difference is not entirely consistent with the perceptions of the debates reported earlier. Those who watched the debates were more likely to vote Conservative than those who did not watch (44 per cent and 31 per cent), and those who did not watch the program were more likely to be Liberal voters. Among anglophone respondents only (parentheses, table 5) the Conservatives continued to do better among watchers of the debates. That the overall pattern, however, is *not* statistically significant for this group, suggests that the debates may have influenced voting behaviour, if at all, only within the context of more traditional forces in Canadian elections.

It is obvious that some of these patterns are counter-intuitive, at least in so far as possible effects of the debates themselves on individual voting behaviour are concerned. It does not seem reasonable to conclude that Clark's performance would have caused his party to do better among those who watched the debates, given what we know about the impressions given by the sample regarding Clark's performance. One possibility is that the effects of the debates, if any, are primarily reinforcing. If so, then the patterns observed may be correct but the direction of causality is reversed. Watchers of the debates were not more likely to have voted Conservative, but Conservatives were more likely to have watched the debates.

The panel component of the 1979 study is useful in testing such an explanation, because past voting behaviour (in this case 1974) is causally prior to anything which might be connected with the debates, or even with the present Conservative and NDP leaders. In this sense, it is analytically superior to party identification, which is less easily disentangled from voting behaviour for those who switch over time on both variables.[26] The panel is also useful for determining whether the debates may have had any effects on vote switching, regardless of the possible direction of the switch.

An analysis of the 1974–1979 panel component of the study discloses that watchers of the debates were only slightly more likely to have switched between the two elections (27 per cent) than were nonwatchers (24 per cent), and the difference between the two groups is not statistically significant on this variable, either for anglophone respondents only or for the sample as a whole. It would seem then that the argument that the directional effects are primarily reinforcing is the more compatible with the panel data.[27]

While watchers of the debates were no more likely to have switched their votes overall than were nonwatchers, some interesting patterns were observed in the panel among those groups who *did* switch between 1974 and 1979 (data not shown). Liberal or NDP voters of 1974 who watched the debates and who switched were much more likely to go to the Conservatives than were nonwatchers, and the NDP does slightly better among defecting nonwatchers than among those who watched the debates. Both of these patterns are again counter-intuitive, given what is known about the potential advantage of the debates to any of the parties.

There is, however, an apparent effect on voting participation. Nonvoters of 1974 who watched the debates were likely to have voted in the 1979 election, while those who did not watch were somewhat less likely to have done so, and the difference between the groups is statistically significant at the .01 level. However, the problem of direction of causality must again be raised. While it is possible that past nonvoters may have been spurred to vote by the debates, it is more probable that those with a strong intention to vote were also more likely to have watched the program. Such an explanation is not only more plausible intuitively, but is also consistent with the patterns of correlation between watching/not watching the debates and other indicators of political participation discussed earlier.

This explanation of the patterns of correlation between watching/not watching the debates and voting behaviour in the 1979 election can be tested further by introducing controls for the key variables that are known to have influenced watching the debates in the first instance. As noted earlier, the fact that the debates were conducted entirely in English is a factor that must be considered, because the bulk of the French-speaking population is found in the province which also voted most heavily Liberal in 1979. Similarly, it is known that socio-economic factors are related to watching the debates, and that these same factors are also related to voting choice, even though the latter predictors are weaker in Canada than in many other Western democracies.[28]

As is seen in table 6, the introduction of controls for language and socio-economic status all but fully accounts for the relationships observed between direction of vote in 1979 and watching/not watching the debates. None of the relationships, not even that with the NDP vote, is statistically significant after these controls are introduced. The relationship between watching the debates and voting/nonvoting, however, remains significant. It must then be concluded that the effects of the debates on behaviour, if any, are on participation rather than on direction of vote.

CONCLUSION

The analysis suggests that watching the debates in itself had little effect on individual voting behaviour in 1979, or on the outcome of the 1979 election. While it appears initially that watchers of the debates were somewhat more likely to have voted Conservative or NDP and less likely to have voted Liberal, these patterns are fully accounted for by sociodemographic variables related to exposure to the debates rather than to their content. The effects on behaviour, if any, must be described at most as reinforcing. This interpretation appears reasonable when it is considered that a high proportion of debate watchers had already decided on their vote at the time of the debates.

There is an apparent relationship between watching the debates and voting participation in the 1979 election beyond that which can be explained by socio-demographic variables alone. However, it is unlikely that the debates themselves actually stimulated greater voting participation. Rather, it is more plausible that persons already intending to vote were more likely to have watched the debates, a pattern which might also be interpreted as reinforcing. On the basis of the evidence examined here, it seems unlikely that the election was won or lost in the television studio on 13 May 1979.

TABLE 6 ZERO ORDER AND PARTIAL CORRELATION COEFFICIENTS BETWEEN WATCHING–NOT WATCHING THE DEBATES AND VOTING BEHAVIOUR IN THE 1979 FEDERAL ELECTION

Correlation between Watching the Debates and Voting...	Liberal	Conservative	New Democratic Party	Not Voting	Switching*
Zero order	-.10**	.13**	.03	.14**	.03
First-order partials					
controlling for SES	-.10**	.13**	.03	.12**	.01
controlling for language	-.01	.04	-.02	.13**	.03
Second-order partials					
controlling for language and SES	-.01	.04	-.02	.11**	.01

* Panel respondents only
** Significant at .01

NOTES

1. Steven Chaffee and Jack Dennis, "Presidential Debates: An Empirical Assessment," in *The Past and Future of Presidential Debates* ed. Austin Ranney (Washington: American Enterprise Institute, 1980), 75–101.

2. Kendall Baker and Helmut Norpoth, "Candidates on Television: The 1972 Electoral Debates in West Germany," *Public Opinion Quarterly* 45 (1981): 329–45.

3. See Russell Middleton, "National TV Debates and Presidential Voting Decisions," *Public Opinion Quarterly* 26 (1962): 426–28; Arthur Miller and Michael MacKuen, "Learning About the Candidates: The 1976 Presidential Debates," *Public Opinion Quarterly* 43 (1979): 326–46; Richard Hofstetter and Terry Buss, "Politics and Last Minute Television," *Western Political Quarterly* 33 (1969): 24–37; and Thomas A. Kazee, "Television Exposure and Attitude Change: The Impact of Political Interest," *Public Opinion Quarterly* 45 (1981): 507–18.

4. Sidney Kraus, ed., *The Great Debates* (Bloomington: University of Indiana Press, 1962), and *The Great Debates: Carter vs. Ford 1976* (Bloomington: University of Indiana Press, 1979). See also, George Bishop, Robert Meadow, and Marilyn Jackson-Beeck, eds., *The Presidential Debates: Media, Electoral, and Policy Perspectives* (New York: Praeger, 1978), and Ranney, ed., *The Past and Future of Presidential Debates.*

5. Kurt Lang and Gladys Engel Lang, "Immediate and Delayed Responses to a Carter–Ford Debate: Assessing Public Opinion," *Public Opinion Quarterly* 42 (1978): 322–41; Miller and MacKuen, "Learning About the Candidates"; Douglas Rose, "Citizen Users of the Ford–Carter Debates," *Journal of Politics* 41 (1980): 214–21; Lee Becker, Idowu Sobowale, Robin Cobbey, and Chaim Eyal, "Debates' Effects on Voters' Understanding of Candidates and Issues"; and Paul Hagner and Leroy Rieselbach, "The Impact of the 1976 Presidential Debates: Conversion or Reinforcement?" in *The Presidential Debates* ed. Bishop, et al., 129–39 and 157–78; and Steven Chafee and Sun Yuel Coe, "Time of Decision and Media Use During the Ford–Carter Campaign," *Public Opinion Quarterly* 44 (1980): 53–69.

6. See Allan Kornberg and Judith Wolfe, "Parliament, the Media, and the Polls," and Richard Price and Harold Clarke, "Television and the House of Commons," in *Parliament, Policy, and Representation* ed. Harold Clarke, Colin Campbell, F. Q. Quo, and Arthur Goddard (Toronto: Methuen, 1980), 35–58 and 58–84.

7. Evron Kirkpatrick, "Presidential Candidate Debates: What Can We Learn from 1960?" in *The Past and Future of Presidential Debates*, 1–50.

8. Robert Meadow and Marilyn Jackson-Beeck, "Issue Evolution: A New Perspective on Presidential Debates," *Journal of Communication* 27 (1979): 84–92.

9. Jon Pammett, Harold Clarke, Jane Jenson, and Lawrence LeDuc, "The Politics of Limited Change: The 1979 Federal Election," Carleton University, Occasional Papers Series, no. 8. See also Harold Clarke, Jane Jenson, Lawrence LeDuc, and Jon Pammett, *Absent Mandate: The Politics of Discontent in Canada* (Toronto: Gage, 1984).

10. Frederick J. Fletcher, "Playing the Game: The Mass Media and the 1979 Campaign," in *Canada at the Polls 1979 and 1980* ed. Howard Penniman (Washington: American Enterprise Institute, 1981), 280–321.

11. The 1979 National Election Study was directed by Harold Clarke, Jane Jenson, Lawrence LeDuc and Jon Pammett, and was funded by the Social Sciences and Humanities Research Council. Field work was conducted by Canadian Facts, Ltd. The study consisted of extensive personal interviews with a national sample of 2743 eligible Canadian

voters immediately following the 1979 federal election. Included in this sample was a panel of 1338 respondents who were first interviewed in 1974, and a supplementary sample of 149 new voters between the ages of 18 and 23 who were eligible to vote for the first time in 1979. Two questions regarding the debates were asked of a random half-sample of the electorate in this study. The first of these was asked as part of a sequence of campaign activity items: "Did you see the debates between the party leaders on television on Sunday, May 13?" The second, asked only of those who responded affirmatively to the foregoing question, was: "What were your impressions of the debates, in general?" Responses to the second question were recorded literally, and up to three answers were coded for each respondent.

12. Because language is such an important correlate of exposure to the debates, all subsequent analyses will be conducted for a subset of anglophone respondents only, as well as for the complete half-sample.

13. See William Mishler, *Political Participation in Canada* (Toronto: Macmillan, 1979), and Mike Burke, Harold Clarke, and Lawrence LeDuc, "Federal and Provincial Political Participation in Canada: Some Methodological and Substantive Considerations," *Canadian Review of Sociology and Anthropology* 15 (1979): 61–75.

14. The Pearson correlations between watching/not watching the debates and the set of activities shown in table 1 range from a high of .22 for "discuss politics with others" to a low of .10 for "contact a public official." There is also a modest relationship between watching/not watching the debates and such variables as political interest and political efficacy. The Pearson correlations were respectively .29 and .16 against standard scales of political interest and political efficacy.

15. This question was asked of the same random half-sample of the 1979 electorate in the sequence dealing with exposure to the campaign. The exact

wording was: "How about television? During the election campaign, did you watch programs or advertisements about the parties or candidates or other aspects of the campaign? Would you say that you saw quite a few, some, or almost none?"

16. The Blishen scale was employed here as a summary measure of socio-economic status, and the correlation (Pearson r) between watching the debates and this scale was .14. When the Blishen scale was recorded into four categories (HI, MED-HI, MED-LO, and LO), 64 per cent of those in the highest category were found to have watched the debates, compared with 42 per cent in the lowest SES category. Education produces a similar pattern. Among those with post-secondary education, 60 per cent watched the debates while only 44 per cent did so in the lowest education group. The correlation (Pearson r) between education and watching the debates is .10. Age produces a weak pattern (Pearson r = .09). Sixty per cent of those over age 45 watched the debates, and there is no significant difference in this respect among various age groupings over 40. However, only 47 per cent of those under age 30 watched the debates. All of these patterns are similar in both strength and direction to relationships between sociodemographic variables and other passive political activity measures.

17. See Jane Jenson, "Party Loyalty in Canada: The Question of Party Identification," *Canadian Journal of Political Science (CJPS)* 8 (1975): 543–53; and Lawrence LeDuc, Harold Clarke, Jane Jenson, and Jon Pammett, "Partisan Instability in Canada: Evidence from a New Panel Study," *American Political Science Review* 78 (1984): 470–84.

18. Philip Converse, "Of Time and Partisan Stability," *Comparative Political Studies* 2 (1969): 139–71.

19. Fletcher, "Playing the Game," 286.

20. Respondents were presented with a card depicting a "thermometer," and were

asked to indicate their feelings toward each of the parties, leaders, and local candidates on a 100-point scale. The 50° mark is given as the neutral point on the scale. This measure is explained in some detail in Clarke et al., *Political Choice in Canada*, 406–7.

21. Clark ran behind his party among virtually all groups and in all parts of the country, but not so far behind as did his predecessor, Robert Stanfield, in the 1974 election. See Pammett, et al., "The Politics of Limited Change," 11–19.

22. A more detailed analysis of the thermometer scores for Broadbent in comparison to those for the NDP generally may be found in Pammett, et al., "The Politics of Limited Change," 11–19.

23. Harold Clarke, Jane Jenson, Lawrence LeDuc, and Jon Pammett, "Voting Behaviour and the Outcome of the 1979 Federal Election: The Impact of the Leaders and Issues," *Canadian Journal of Political Science* 15 (1982): 517–52. See also Clarke et al., *Absent Mandate*.

24. Clarke, et al., *Absent Mandate*.

25. In 1974, 19 per cent of a national sample reported deciding how to vote as late as the last week of the campaign. See the more detailed discussion of "time of vote decision" in Clarke, et al. *Political Choice in Canada*, 275–78.

26. Ibid., 343–50.

27. Hagner and Rieselbach, "The Impact of the 1976 Presidential Debates."

28. Clarke et al., *Political Choice in Canada*. See also Lawrence LeDuc, "Canada: The Politics of Stable Dealignment," in *Electoral Change in Industrial Democracies* ed. Russell Dalton, Scott Flanagan, and Paul Allen Beck (Princeton: Princeton University Press, 1985), 402–23.

THE CHARACTER OF ELECTORAL CHANGE: A PRELIMINARY REPORT FROM THE 1984 NATIONAL ELECTION STUDY[◊]

BARRY J. KAY
STEVEN D. BROWN
JAMES E. CURTIS
RONALD D. LAMBERT
JOHN M. WILSON

Our understanding of federal Canadian voting has been enriched through the detailed study of successive elections over the past two or three decades. Importantly, the widening time band for which we have individual-level data has enhanced our appreciation of the complexity of the subject matter. Each new research encounter with the Canadian voter has necessitated some manner of re-assessment of our assumptions concerning such basic matters as the roles of candidates, leaders and issues in the voter's calculus, the nature and strength of sociodemographic cleavages in the vote, the nature of party identification in Canada, and the stability of the electorate.[1]

The survey of the Canadian electorate following the General Election of 4 September 1984 continues in this tradition. This election and the year which preceded it had several unique, and even remarkable, features that should prompt a refinement of our thinking about Canadian elections. Remarkable first and foremost was the net effect of strong short-term partisan forces in favour of the Progressive Conservatives. A number of scholars have noted that the Canadian electorate is comparatively stable in its voting across elections in terms of net *aggregate-level* patterns, but that this masks relatively high levels of vote switching at the *individual-level*.[2] In 1984, individual vote switching remained high—indeed, at 31 per cent, it surpassed the levels for any of the elections previously studied—but

[◊] Paper prepared for the 1985 Annual Meeting of the Canadian Political Science Association, University of Montreal, Montreal, Quebec, 31 May–2 June 1985.

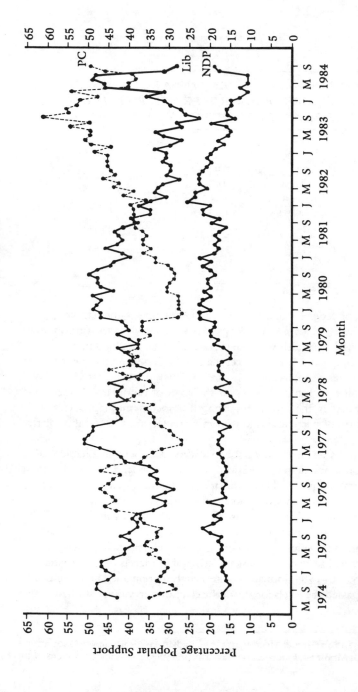

FIGURE 1   *TRENDS IN SUPPORT FOR FEDERAL POLITICAL PARTIES JULY 1974–SEPT. 1984*

Note: Responses to question: "If a federal election were held today, which party's candidate do you think you would favour?"

Source: Gallup Poll, monthly surveys.

the mask was removed. At the aggregate-level, the Liberals lost 16 percentage points compared with their 1980 performance, while the Tories had a 17 point gain. At the constituency level, 42 per cent of the districts—118 federal constituencies in all—changed their partisan representation in the 1984 election. Not since 1935 had an election produced a turnover rate of this magnitude.

Also noteworthy was the manifest instability of electoral preferences over a very few number of months. Researchers in the past have commented on the frequency of shifting party loyalties in Canadian politics.[3] However, probably few, if any, were prepared for the extreme volatility that characterised public attitudes in the twelve months preceding this election. As figure 1 shows, over the period from September 1983 to September 1984 support for the Liberal Party rose from over 23 per cent of "decided voters" to a high of 49 per cent in June 1984, before plummeting again to 28 per cent just prior to election day.

The wide fluctuations in intended vote during the election campaign were also extraordinary for Canadian politics. In the 13 previous election campaigns for which pre-election polls were conducted, no party had ever gained or lost more than eight per cent during the campaign. In 1984, however, the Liberal Party lost 20 percentage points between the first week of July and the first week of September.

A full explanation for these dramatic changes in the electorate is some time off, if attainable at all. Nevertheless, the survey data collected as part of the National Election Study have just now come to hand. Some of the results, coupled with secondary analyses of previous election survey data, will provide a basis for some tentative answers. The purpose of the present paper is to begin the task of these analyses. The strategy followed here, given the very recent arrival of the survey data, is to limit attention to tests of a number of conventional wisdoms concerning the making of the 1984 election results. Analyses bearing on four key topics are presented: (a) the comparative magnitude of individual-level vote switching in the election, the directions of switching for the various categories of the electorate, and the net consequences of the switching for regional and other sociodemographic correlates of voting; (b) the timing of Canadians' voting decisions and the influence of campaign events and other events upon those decisions; (c) the effects of perceptions of the candidates, parties and issues upon the vote; and (d) the apparent implications of the election for the underlying partisan distribution of the electorate. Many of the analyses remain at the zero-order level for the time being. Multivariate analyses will follow in due course.

DATA SOURCES

The 1984 data reported in this paper were collected as part of a single-wave post-election survey of 3377 respondents from across Canada. The field work, by Canadian Facts, Ltd., was conducted over a period of five months beginning in early October 1984. Personal interviews lasting between one and two hours covered a range of topics pertaining to the respondents' recollections of the federal election just past, and to their more general political perceptions and orientations.

The sample design for the study was a multi-stage, stratified cluster sample of the Canadian electorate, with systematic oversampling of the smaller provinces. The raw sample of 3377 respondents has been reweighted for these analyses to reflect the relative population size of each province and the proportionate age, gender and urban-rural composition within each province. More details concerning the sampling procedures, and the weighted and unweighted Ns by province, are presented in Appendix A.

The previous national election studies for 1974, 1979 and 1980, which are drawn upon in secondary analyses here, employed substantially the same procedures as the 1984 study and permit some accurate temporal comparisons.[4]

THE NATURE OF VOTER CHANGE

What constitutes a significant level of change in voting behaviour is as much a relative as an absolute judgement. An unusually high level for Canada may be the norm elsewhere, and what is a comparatively high level for Canada will still involve stability for the vast majority of voters. There is, though, the common supposition that the 1984 election had a high proportion of individual-level vote switching compared with other elections, and that this switching was overwhelmingly in the direction of the Tories. The basis for these expectations is the magnitude of the Tory landslide coupled with the healthy Liberal victory in the previous election.

The aggregate 1984 election results provide a case-in-point for the realisation of the "potential" for great electoral change implied in LeDuc's "stable dealignment" image of Canadian politics.[5] According to LeDuc, the appearance of stability in overall levels of party support in Canada tells us little about the behaviour of individuals. Beneath this surface, he emphasises, there has been a great deal of individual-level switching in recent elections; the parties are dealigned in this sense. The individual-level switching has not been apparent, though, because of the absence of large-scale upsets. He suggests that this situation "is due primarily to the difficulty any party finds in harnessing the many regional and subnational trends operating in Canadian politics."[6]

The data analyses will address the question of whether such a harnessing took place in 1984. They will show whether voter switching was relatively similar in magnitude for supporters of Liberals or the NDP in 1980 and for other categories of voters. The analyses will also yield an assessment of whether the various sub-groups of the country were, by virtue of a common direction in their vote switching, made more similar in their pattern of voting than in previous elections. It is known from the election results by province that this took place for the variable of region. But what of social sub-groups defined by social class, by religion, by age, and so on? Was there a "homogenizing" trend, compared with previous elections, for these groups as well? And, which groups showed the least effects of homogenizing? Were they the categories (other than Quebec residents who swung heavily to the Tories) that have provided the strongest support for the Liberals over the years? Or, did the homogenization extend strongly to all social sub-groups? Our data will allow us to speak to these questions.

TABLE 1 STABILITY OR CHANGE OF VOTING
BEHAVIOUR COMPARED TO PREVIOUS
ELECTION 1974–1984

	1974	1979	1980	1984
Voted for same party	60%	58%	68%	52%
Switched parties	17	20	17	24
Previous non-voters re-entering electorate	6	3	6	9
Previous voters not participating	13	6	9	7
New voters	5	13	*	9
(N=)	(2080)	(2228)	(1561)	(2684)

Percentages are rounded.
Voter behaviour for elections previous to 1974, 1979 and 1984 is based upon respondent records, but for 1980 it is taken from the respondents' previous behaviour recorded in the past.
* No new respondents were added to the sample in 1980.

To provide a context in which to assess voters' changes in 1984, comparisons can be made with recent elections for the proportions who (a) remained with their previous party vote, (b) switched parties, and (c) moved in and out of the active electorate. Table 1 provides comparisons across data from the 1984 election survey and from three previous election surveys conducted by the Windsor–Carleton team.

The results indicate that the proportion of defectors relative to those who remained loyal to their previous party certainly increased in 1984, but the level of individual change is not at all as great as that suggested by the very large net aggregate shift in party support. The 31 per cent level of individual change registered between 1980 and 1984—the highest found in any of the national election studies—exceeds the changes registered between 1974 and 1979 by six percentage points.[7] It can be seen, then, that this election was not unique for the amount of individual switching, but remarkable for the aggregate-level pattern and the magnitude of its landslide victory for the winning Conservatives.

Table 2 gives additional information on voting changes over two points in time for the past four elections. Comparisons are made for each party's bloc of supporters defined by their previous vote, for those not participating in the previous election, and for newly eligible voters. Particularly noteworthy is the 1984 performance of the 1980 Liberals who abandoned that party for the PCs in a proportion almost double that in 1979 (39 per cent versus 20 per cent). This was the previous high for desertion of a major party by its former supporters. In 1984, the Conservative Party also benefited by unprecedented infusions from every category of previous nonsupporters, although the Liberal migrants constitute by far the largest group of defectors.[8] It is from this group, because of their numerical superiority, that the PC landslide was fashioned. For this reason, the analyses below will focus on selected sources of Liberal defection.

TABLE 2   ELECTORAL BEHAVIOUR BY PREVIOUS VOTE
1974-1984

Previous Vote	Subsequent Vote (%)					
	Liberal	PC	NDP	Other	No Vote	N =
Liberal						
1972 → 74	70	11	3	1	14	(1012)
1974 → 79	64	20	7	2	7	(1093)
1979 → 80	83	7	4	0	7	(597)
1980 → 84	43	39	6	1	10	(1027)
PC						
1972 → 74	15	69	3	0	13	(516)
1974 → 79	4	83	5	1	7	(500)
1979 → 80	11	69	9	1	11	(577)
1980 → 84	4	86	6	2	6	(822)
NDP						
1972 → 74	17	12	55	6	16	(248)
1974 → 79	7	14	70	3	7	(233)
1979 → 80	14	10	66	1	10	(239)
1980 → 84	3	17	67	1	11	(343)
Other						
1972 → 74	14	9	7	49	22	(81)
1974 → 79	11	21	7	53	9	(59)
1979 → 80	24	11	13	36	17	(60)
1980 → 84	4	49	6	37	4	(29)
No Vote						
1972 → 74	42	20	10	3	26	(140)
1974 → 79	21	24	13	7	35	(107)
1979 → 80	25	21	8	3	42	(153)
1980 → 84	15	34	8	3	40	(388)
Ineligible						
1972 → 74	55	21	13	7	4	(107)
1974 → 79	36	25	15	6	19	(351)
1979 → 80	–	–	–	–	–	(–)*
1980 → 84	24	34	1	1	32	(340)

Percentages are rounded.
Voter behaviour for elections previous to 1974, 1979, and 1984 is based upon respondent records, but for 1980 it is taken from the respondents' previous behaviour recorded in the past.
*No new respondents were added to the sample in 1980.

Table 2 also shows that, compared to the changes for the Liberal voters, there is surprising consistency in the defection rates from the other two major parties. As far as the other classifications of voters are concerned, previous voters re-entering the electorate appeared to vote, in each year, in proportions approximating the voting patterns of the overall population; on the other hand, newly eligible voters have tended in the past to be more Liberal than the population as a whole and they continued this pattern in 1984.

TABLE 3   WHERE THE 1980 LIBERAL VOTE WENT IN 1984
            BY SOCIO-DEMOGRAPHIC GROUPS

	Lib → Lib	Lib → PC	Lib → NDP	Lib → Other	(N=)
Canada	48%	43	7	2	(917)
Region					
Atlantic	61%	31	8	0	(60)
Quebec	40%	55	4	1	(370)
Ontario	56%	33	8	3	(353)
Prairies	51%	44	4	1	(75)
B.C.	40%	41	19	1	(58)
Community Size					
500 000+	44%	47	7	2	(448)
30–500 000	52%	39	9	1	(154)
1–30 000	53%	39	8	0	(142)
Rural	52%	41	5	2	(172)
Sex					
Men	48%	44	7	1	(427)
Women	48%	42	7	2	(491)
Education					
Post Secondary	40%	48	9	3	(354)
Secondary	50%	43	6	1	(424)
Primary	64%	32	4	0	(138)
Income					
High	45%	45	6	4	(278)
Medium	48%	43	9	1	(310)
Low	56%	38	5	1	(183)
Subjective Class					
Upper Middle	41%	49	11	0	(90)
Middle	48%	46	4	3	(518)
Working	49%	39	12	0	(273)
Religion					
Catholic	48%	46	5	2	(593)
Protestant	51%	38	11	0	(242)
Other	37%	48	4	11	(27)
None	43%	37	16	2	(49)
Language Spoken					
English	49%	39	9	2	(479)
French	44%	50	5	1	(372)
Other	60%	31	6	3	(67)
Age					
18–24	45%	43	13	0	(47)
25–34	40%	44	12	3	(208)
35–44	44%	47	8	1	(185)
45–54	48%	47	4	2	(172)
55–64	53%	43	2	2	(164)
65+	65%	29	6	0	(126)

Percentages are rounded.

TABLE 4   PER CENT DEVIATION FROM NATIONAL PARTY VOTE BY REGION FOR FEDERAL ELECTIONS 1968–1984

	Liberal						PC						NDP					
	1968	1972	1974	1979	1980	1984	1968	1972	1974	1979	1980	1984	1968	1972	1974	1979	1980	1984
Popular Vote (%)	(45)	(38)	(43)	(40)	(44)	(28)	(31)	(35)	(35)	(36)	(33)	(50)	(17)	(18)	(15)	(18)	(20)	(19)
Region																		
Atlantic	−4	+1	+1	0	+1	+8	+22	+15	+7	+5	+4	+2	−11	−10	−5	+1	−2	−7
Quebec	+9	+11	+11	+22	+26	+7	−11	−18	−14	−23	−20	0	−9	−11	−8	−13	−11	−10
Ontario	+2	0	+2	−3	−2	+2	+1	+4	0	+6	+3	−3	+4	+4	+4	+3	+2	+2
Prairies	−10	−11	−16	−18	−20	−11	+10	+12	+16	+17	+17	+6	+5	+5	+4	+5	+4	+4
B.C.	−3	−9	−10	−17	−22	−12	−12	−2	+7	+9	+9	−3	+16	+17	+8	+14	+15	+16
Mean Deviation	5.6	6.4	8.0	12.0	14.2	8.0	11.2	10.2	8.8	14.0	10.6	2.8	9.0	9.4	5.8	7.2	6.8	7.8

Percentages are rounded.
Based upon official election figures presented in Hugh Thorburn, *Party Politics in Canada* (Scarborough, ON: Prentice-Hall, 1985).

Table 3 focusses upon the 1980 Liberal voters who acted so distinctively in 1984. In order to simplify the table, those not voting in 1984 have been eliminated (the recalculated distribution of the 1980 Liberal vote is presented in the top row of the table). Even after the nonvoters have been omitted, the Liberals were able to hold less than one-half of their 1980 supporters. A more detailed analysis of these Liberal defectors indicates that the trend to the Conservatives was most pronounced among Quebeckers (55 per cent) and the largely overlapping category of Francophones (50 per cent). Of course, Quebeckers and Francophones traditionally have been among the most staunchly Liberal of all regional and language groups. Thus, their disproportionate conversion to the Tories highlights the fact that the Conservative victory was truly a national one, manifested in every area of the country.

Other sociodemographic characteristics strongly associated with Liberal movement toward the PCs in 1984 included having a post-secondary education, a higher income, and a residence in the larger urban centres. These defections brought the Conservative support levels in these sub-groups more closely into line with the support levels for the remainder of the Canadian electorate. An examination of the defection rates from the major parties in the earlier elections (data not presented) indicated that, while the levels of change were much lower, region had tended to be the variable associated with the greatest degree of turnover. In addition, a relatively modest degree of shifting with some consistency over the past decade is associated with the post-secondary education category, a sub-group which other studies have shown to be highly volatile in its voting.[9] This has been attributed to the fact that better educated voters are less dependent upon party allegiances as voting cues because they are better positioned to follow election events. The voters who most resisted the trend away from the Liberal Party in 1984 tended to be the elderly (65 per cent stayed Liberal), the less well-educated (64 per cent remained), those lower in income, non-English and non-French speakers, and residents of the Atlantic provinces. From this list of social correlates of vote switching, one might be tempted to conclude that the lack of political interest or political awareness is associated with remaining Liberal. However, further analyses have yielded little support for this hypothesis.

A more detailed examination of the electorate is provided in tables 4 and 5 which depict the performances of the three major parties across the most prominent sociodemographic divisions for the 1984 election and recent elections. The figures in these tables represent percentage deviations from the national party vote for each sub-group in each election.

Table 4 documents the substantial decline of regional distinctiveness as a basis for describing the support bases of the Liberal and Conservative parties. In addition to the record number of seats won by the PCs, there was a clearly evident pattern of uniformity in results across Canada. Never before, not even in John Diefenbaker's massive 1958 victory, have the Conservatives won parliamentary majorities in every province of the country. The PC victory even extended into such provincial sub-regions as northern Ontario, Acadian New Brunswick, and Montreal's west end where the party has not been victorious for many years. The election was a marked departure from the pattern of increasing regional polarization that developed during the Trudeau years. Table 4 depicts the remarkable consistency

TABLE 5   PER CENT DEVIATION FROM PARTY VOTE BY SOCIO-DEMOGRAPHIC GROUP FOR FEDERAL ELECTIONS 1974-1984

	Liberal				PC				NDP			
	1974	1979	1980	1984	1974	1979	1980	1984	1974	1979	1980	1984
Community Size												
500 000+	+5	+4	+1	+1	-4	-8	-6	-2	+4	+2	+4	0
30–500 000	+4	-2	0	+1	-4	0	0	-2	+1	+2	0	+3
1–30 000	-8	-5	-6	+1	+9	+2	+9	+2	-2	-6	-3	-1
Rural	-7	-3	+1	-4	+9	+7	+4	+5	-3	-4	-4	-1
Sex												
Men	-3	-3	-4	-2	+1	+2	+4	+2	+2	0	0	0
Women	+3	+3	+4	+2	-1	-2	-4	-2	-2	0	0	0
Education												
Post Secondary	+1	-2	-4	-2	0	-2	+1	0	+2	+1	+1	+1
Secondary	-3	-2	-1	0	+2	+3	+2	+1	+1	+1	+1	0
Primary	+4	+8	+9	+8	-2	-5	-6	-5	-5	-3	-2	-1
Income												
High	+1	0	+5	0	0	-1	-4	+2	-3	0	-2	-2
Medium	-3	+1	+1	+1	-1	-2	-2	-2	+3	+2	+2	+2
Low	+1	-2	-5	-1	+2	+3	+5	+1	-2	-1	0	-1
Subjective Class												
Upper Middle	+11	-2	-3	-3	-1	+6	+7	+5	-8	-4	-4	-2
Middle	0	+1	-1	+3	+1	0	+2	+1	0	-1	-2	-4
Working	-2	0	+2	-4	-1	-4	-7	-2	+3	+4	+5	+7
Religion												
Catholic	+15	+16	+19	+8	-16	-18	-19	-5	-3	-2	-3	-4
Protestant	-12	-15	-17	-7	+15	+19	+17	+7	+1	0	+2	0
Other	-10	+16	+14	+1	-13	-15	-8	-3	+5	+1	-6	+1
None	-9	-16	-12	-12	0	-4	+1	-4	+12	+21	+10	+16

TABLE 5 CONTINUED

	Liberal				PC				NDP			
	1974	1979	1980	1984	1974	1979	1980	1984	1974	1979	1980	1984
Language Spoken												
English	-7	-10	-11	-5	+8	+10	+10	+2	+2	+3	+4	+3
French	+16	+23	+25	+8	-19	-24	-24	-2	-6	-9	-7	-7
Other	+13	+8	+6	+18	-7	-8	-5	-18	-3	+5	+1	0
Age												
18–24	0	0	+4	+6	-7	-9	-9	-4	+2	+6	+3	-1
25–34	-3	-3	0	-6	-4	-5	-6	-2	+6	+4	+3	+5
35–44	+1	+1	-5	-4	0	+1	+4	+3	0	0	+2	0
45–54	+3	+4	+3	0	+3	+2	0	+4	-5	-3	-2	-4
55–64	-2	-1	-4	+3	+3	+4	+6	0	0	-2	-2	-2
65+	0	-1	-1	+6	+6	+9	+7	-2	-4	-6	-5	-2

Percentages are rounded.
Deviation scores are based on estimates taken from the respective National Election Studies. The data for other parties have been omitted due to space limitations.

in Conservative support across Canada in 1984, as evidenced by mean deviations in regional support. These deviations are one-quarter those of the average over the five previous elections. The Liberal vote can also be seen to register less regional variation in 1984; however, that party's previous pattern was one of a steady increase in regional polarization over the Trudeau years.[10] For the NDP vote, regional consensus is much less evident.

In table 5, this trend away from factional cleavage toward more consensual voting patterns is also apparent for most of the sub-groups defined by community size, religion and language. These are the sub-groups where some of the greatest deviations have been found for previous elections. The most notable exceptions to this consensual trend are found among the sub-groups which were shown above to have remained most loyal to the Liberal Party. These included the elderly, the less well-educated, non-English and non-French speakers, and residents of Atlantic Canada. There are also some other interesting observations to be discerned from table 5. The youngest age cohort, many of whose members were voting for the first time, maintained its disproportionate support for the Liberals even more so than in the past. Also, the NDP's sources of support in the various sociodemographic categories remained remarkably similar in 1984, compared with previous elections, despite the unprecedented level of volatility displayed by the populace in general during the last election. Finally, the socio-economic categories of education, income and subjective class appeared to register less change than the regional, ethnic and religious sub-groups.

Deviation scores are based on estimates taken from the respective National Election Studies. The data for other parties have been omitted due to space limitations.

THE TIMING OF THE VOTE

The circumstances of the 1984 election raise a number of interesting questions regarding the timing of voters' decisions. As has already been mentioned, the twelve month period preceding the 1984 election was characterised by extreme volatility in public support for each of the national parties. This fluctuation in the mood of opinion was witnessed both prior to and during the election campaign, and it is likely that it was influenced by a number of significant political events that occurred during the year. Pierre Trudeau's retirement from politics provides a good example. The announcement on February 29th, 1984 preceded by about four weeks the greatest one-month change in party support recorded by the Gallup organisation in its 40 years of polling—a 14 per cent swing to the Liberal Party.[11] The subsequent party convention and the selection of John Turner as Liberal leader and Prime Minister only seemed to enhance the party's standing in the opinion polls, which in turn encouraged the party to go immediately to the electorate for a new mandate. The Gallup data shown in figure 1 suggest that parties holding leadership conventions typically experience an increase in their level of public support leading up to and immediately following these gatherings. This is suggested by the increases in the levels of acceptance of the PCs following their leadership conclaves in 1976 and 1983, as well as by the Liberals' increase in popularity, if only short-lived, in

1984. The extent to which these events have a lasting impact upon public opinion is but one aspect of the subject of the timing of the vote.

Among the conventional wisdoms that are heard about the timing of the final decision on how to vote in 1984 is that, compared to previous elections, it must have come late (near the election) for a high proportion of voters.[12] This hypothesis follows from the evidence of considerable change of opinion during the election campaign, indicating the continued drop in the stock of Turner and the Liberals, and the concomitant rise in the fortunes of Mulroney and the Tories. There is also the issue of the influence of campaign/media events upon the electorate. The conventional wisdom, in the main, seems to be that campaigns very seldom have much impact in altering party support levels—that, largely, they just function to firm up leaning supporters.[13] This extends to the impact of televised debates in Canada, and in the USA.[14] Yet, given the apparently marked changes in the fortunes of the Liberals and Conservatives during the campaign, it seems that this election may have been different in its explanatory dynamics, and that events such as the debates may have been uncommonly important. The data presented below bear on this working hypothesis.

With regard to the timing of the vote decision, the survey showed that almost one-half of all Canadians made their choice during the campaign period. This represented an increase from 5 to 10 per cent compared to the three previous elections. Interestingly, most of this difference is attributed to later decision making in the province of Quebec.[15] Voters who decided after the election was called were also distinguished in their partisan composition. They included only 32 per cent of 1980 Conservatives among them, but 54 per cent of the 1980 Liberals. This suggests that more 1980 Liberals entered the campaign feeling ambivalent toward their party, or else they were led to reassess their attitude by events during the campaign. This observation is consistent with the fact that only 40 per cent of 1980 Liberals who decided after the election was called remained with that party, while 56 per cent of 1980 Liberals deciding before the campaign stayed Liberal. An additional characteristic of those deciding during the campaign is that they were more likely to cite leadership as the primary factor in determining their vote, while early deciders were more likely to emphasise the importance of the party in their decision.

Table 6 turns to the matter of various influential events, and looks at the political preferences of those attributing their votes to these events. Not surprisingly, the vast majority of those influenced by the PC leadership convention supported that party, but the Tories also did quite well among those influenced by the Liberal convention. Particularly noteworthy is the fact that those voters citing Trudeau's departure as a political stimulus were also seen to vote Conservative by a decisive margin. When the same relationships are considered for the 1980 Liberals only, it can be seen, curiously, that citing almost any event in this context rendered the voter more likely to defect from the Liberals than was the case with 1980 Liberals as a whole. Presumably, those remaining loyal to the party are less apt to recall the events which confirmed their loyalty than those who were led to defect. Indeed, 78 per cent of the defectors recalled a seminal event of this kind, whereas only 40 per cent of the loyalists could do so.

TABLE 6   DIRECTION OF 1984 VOTE FOR THOSE
           INFLUENCED BY SPECIFIC EVENTS

	All Voters				
	PC Convention	Trudeau Retirement	Liberal Convention	July Debates	Women's Debate
Liberal	10%	18%	41%	21%	18%
PC	85	70	51	62	46
NDP	2	11	8	14	34
Other	3	1	0	3	3
(N=)	(263)	(320)	(168)	(206)	(150)

	1980 Liberals				
	PC Convention	Trudeau Retirement	Liberal Convention	July Debates	Women's Debate
Liberal	23%	27%	49%	35%	35%
PC	76	64	49	58	38
NDP	0	7	1	4	25
Other	3	1	0	3	3
(N=)	(79)	(137)	(87)	(83)	(55)

Percentages are rounded.

At first glance, these results—particularly those pertaining to Trudeau's retirement—seem to be inconsistent with the earlier Gallup results. However, a possible interpretation would be that most Liberals who returned to the fold at the time of Trudeau's resignation departed again after Turner became leader. The presence of so many Quebeckers among those Liberals adversely affected by Trudeau's departure suggests that this event was very much a mixed blessing for the party, since a number of Quebeckers were alienated by it and many others that might have been attracted in the short-term eventually defected again.

During the campaign, the events probably receiving the greatest popular attention were the leadership debates. Two-thirds of Canadians watched at least one of the debates, but the distribution of their party preferences was little different from the distribution for those not watching, after taking into account the latter group's tendency to vote less. Table 6 shows that among those whose voting decisions were determined by the debates, the July encounters overwhelmingly favoured the Conservatives, and the women's debate in August provided disproportionate support for the NDP.

Other data reinforce this point. Of those who watched any of the debates, 78 per cent thought that Mulroney outperformed Turner. Among this latter group, the PCs were supported by 64 per cent compared to 19 per cent for the Liberals. Those who believed that Mulroney did not outperform Turner supported the Liberals (44 per cent) more than the Conservatives (35 per cent).[16] In addition, other data not presented here indicate that 1980 Liberals who saw the debates were somewhat more likely to switch to the Tories in 1984 (46 per cent) than their counterparts who did not see the debates (36 per cent).

Having cited this evidence concerning the impact of the debates, it should be added that for a sample interviewed some two to six months after the events, there may be difficulties in their recalling the events and separating their evaluations of them from their general impressions of the campaign and from their votes. It is also probably the case that the above data provide an underestimate of the importance of the debates in the sense that nonwatchers are not considered. Many of this latter group are likely to have been instructed on who won the debates by a very active media, with consequences for some of their votes.

SOURCES OF THE VOTER CHANGE

In the months since the September election, there have arisen a number of plausible interpretations of different sources of the 1984 vote and voter shifts that go beyond the effects of the specific events discussed above. Each of the following interpretations, for example, have had some currency.

First, some have argued that the 1984 election was largely won on differences in the leaders' "images," or perceptions of the leaders' "personalities." The argument is that, in 1984, Mulroney ended up with a considerably more positive evaluation than Turner on such dimensions as "competence," "sureness," "warmth," and "responsiveness." Turner is thought also to have been hurt at the polls by the perception among voters who wanted new policy initiatives that he was not "a candidate of change," that he was a prisoner of policies initiated by his predecessor. In short, for many, Turner may not have been seen to offer significant policy alternatives compared to Mulroney and the PCs.

Second, it has been said that an important factor in the election results was differential perceptions of the capacities of the parties to govern well. The reasoning here is that the Liberals, given their years of limited success with the issues confronting the nation, were viewed by many as a "tired" government, one not as competent as it should be, or probably not as competent as the PCs would be.

Third, issues, too, are said to have been important in voters' decisions at the 1984 polls. For example, the problems of the deficit and unemployment, along with competent government, received heavy play during the campaign by the parties and by the media. Among voters for whom such issues were important, a high proportion may have concluded that the winning Conservatives were best able to address them properly.

Finally, the view has been advanced that the 1984 election involved a change of "mood" in the country. There are at least two variants of this view. Some say that the essence of the mood was simply that it was "time for a change," a time to try other hands at the helm of government. Others have suggested that there was an ideological direction to the mood change. The question here is whether the electorate had made something of a swing in a "conservative" direction so that, for example, government interventions to redress social inequality and to manipulate economic affairs had come to have less support than they once had. There may have been, as well, parallel changes in attitudes on moral issues, with shifts to less liberal views on abortion, capital punishment, gay rights, and so on. Assuming that the PCs were perceived to be more "conservative," such attitude changes could have helped to account for the Conservatives' support on election day.

TABLE 7   RESPONDENTS' REPORTS ABOUT THE MOST
IMPORTANT FACTOR AFFECTING THEIR
VOTING DECISION 1974-1984

Factors	1974	1979	1980	1984
Party leaders	30	35	34	28
Candidates	24	21	19	20
Parties	38	38	42	45
(N=)	(2261)	(2502)	(1677)	(3145)

Percentages are rounded.

All of these interpretations, or some subset of them, may be involved in a full explanation of the election results. Fortunately, the 1984 survey data allow us to gain some purchase on tests of various working hypotheses implied by these interpretations. For the present, because of time constraints, attention is focussed upon hypotheses concerning comparisons of Liberal voters in 1980 who remained Liberal in 1984 with those who switched from the Liberals to the Conservatives.[17] That is, an assessment is done of the comparative perceptions of the set of voters who were most responsible for the Conservative victory. Among the questions to be addressed are whether Liberal defectors versus Liberal loyalists were (a) more positive in evaluating Mulroney (versus Turner) as competent, representative of change, and so on; (b) more likely to see the PC Party as high on competence at government; (c) more likely to see the PCs as best suited to address important issues; and (d) higher in subscription to conservative economic and social attitudes. Set aside for now is the task of multivariate analyses to test for the relative effects of leaders' evaluations, party images, issue perceptions, and political attitudes upon vote switching. The zero-order analyses will suggest, however, whether each in this set of four factors may be involved in an explanation of the election results and should be pursued in further analyses.

A useful preliminary is to look at what voters themselves believed to be the principal determinants of how they voted or would have voted. They were asked which factor—party leaders, candidates or parties—contributed most to their voting decisions. Table 7 displays the relevant findings for 1984, along with results produced by the same question used in the 1974, 1979, and 1980 election surveys. In 1984, about 28 per cent of the respondents keyed on the party leaders, compared to 45 per cent who cited the parties. These figures were the lowest and the highest, respectively, in the series of four surveys. Candidates, apart from leaders, were consistently less important in people's thinking about why they voted as they did; these were generally in the range of 20 per cent.

A somewhat different picture of the relative importance of leadership is suggested by data from those who switched from Liberal votes in 1980 to Conservative votes in 1984, compared with Liberals who remained loyal in 1984. Nearly one-half of the defectors claimed that the party leaders had the greatest impact on their voting decisions. This compares with slightly less than a fifth of the loyalists who credited leaders with this much influence. In contrast, nearly one-half of the Liberal loyalists explained their voting decision in terms of parties. These

TABLE 8 THERMOMETER RATINGS (*Mean Scores*) FOR
PARTY LEADERS GIVEN BY LOSING PARTY
LOYALISTS AND DEFECTORS TO THE WINNING
PARTY 1974–1984

Year	1974	1979	1980	1984
Winning party	Liberal	PC	Liberal	PC
Winning leader	Trudeau	Clark	Trudeau	Mulroney
Loyalists	PC, 40	Lib, 39	PC, 29	Lib, 52
Defectors to	Lib, 58	PC, 61	Lib, 63	PC, 76
Losing leader	Stanfield	Trudeau	Clark	Turner
Loyalists	PC, 65	Lib, 81	PC, 65	Lib, 66
Defectors to	Lib, 57	PC, 47	Lib, 38	PC, 47

striking differences are confirmed by the pattern of results produced by the question asking about "the least important component" affecting the vote. In response to this question, about one-third of the loyalists and one-tenth of the defectors offered a leadership explanation.

The 1984 survey also asked respondents what it was about the party leaders that they had in mind when they claimed that the leaders had contributed the most to their votes. They were asked whether they were thinking about the leaders' stands on issues or about their personal qualities. There were no differences of note in the findings. All categories of voters—loyalists, defectors, Liberals in general, and Tories in general—split approximately in half between stands on issues and personal qualities.

The relative importance of leadership was gauged by comparing the results for 1984 with the components mentioned by defectors from the Liberal or the Conservative party to the winning side in each of the three previous election surveys. Less than 20 per cent of those who voted Conservative in 1972 and who switched to the winning Liberals in 1974 offered leadership as an explanation. Approximately 31 per cent of respondents who voted Liberal in 1974 and who moved to the winning Conservatives in 1979 offered this explanation. In 1980, however, 44 per cent of those who voted Tory in the preceding year and who switched to the winning Liberal side explained their move in terms of leadership. In a comparative sense, then, it is clear that leadership was a central consideration overall in 1984, at least among those Liberals who provided the Conservatives with their landslide majority.

Further evidence on the role of leadership in voters' calculations is provided by the "feeling thermometer" used to measure how much the party leaders were liked or disliked. Respondents who switched from the Liberals to the PC party in 1984 gave Mulroney a mean rating of 76 compared to a much lower rating of 47 for Turner. People who continued to support the Liberal party in 1984 assigned its new leader a score of 66—a higher rating than the defectors gave him—but still less than they awarded Mulroney. The comparable figures were also computed from the 1974, 1979, and 1980 surveys and then two kinds of difference scores were calculated on the basis of these figures. The relevant findings are presented in table 8. First,

TABLE 9   PERCEPTIONS OF MULRONEY AND TURNER BY
           LIBERAL LOYALISTS AND DEFECTORS TO THE
           PC PARTY 1984

Traits	Loyalists		Defectors		Tau-C[a]
Arrogant	M	21[b]	T	33	−.27♦
Competent	T	15	M	70	.44♦
Ruthless	M	20	T	2	−.13*
Commands respect	T	13	M	47	.34♦
Nervous	T	51	T	66	−.08*
Decent	T	27	M	25	.32♦
Slick	M	48	M	44	−.03
Sincere	T	50	M	33	.45♦
Shallow	M	36	T	28	−.35♦
Sure of himself	M	28	M	71	.23♦
Dull	T	7	T	42	−.20♦
Warm	T	9	M	64	.39♦
Represents change	M	36	M	86	.27♦
Listens to the views of people in my province	T	0	M	63	.36♦

a Positive correlation means that defection to the PC party is associated with the judgement that
   Mulroney possesses more of a trait than Turner.
b T or M means that Turner or Mulroney possesses more of a trait than the other leader; figures are
   percentage gaps between the two leaders.

Percentages are rounded

Significance levels: * < .05
                      ** < .01
                       ♦ < .001

the mean rating given to winning leaders by defectors minus the mean rating given
to the losing leaders by the same people yielded scores of 1, 14, 25, and 29 for 1974,
1979, 1980 and 1984, respectively. This means that voters in 1980 and 1984 were
much more likely to favour the leader to whom they moved than they were the
leader whom they abandoned. This finding is consistent with the greater weight
placed by respondents on the leadership component in 1980 and 1984, compared
to 1974 and 1979, as noted above. Second, the mean rating given winning leaders
by defectors minus the mean rating for the losing leaders given by loyalists produced
differences of −7, −20, −2 and 10 in 1974, 1979, 1980 and 1984, respectively. Thus,
the 1984 data, in contrast to the data from the earlier elections, seem to suggest a
relative lack of enthusiasm for the losing leader, even among people who remained
loyal to his cause.

Given the central importance of leadership to people who switched from the
Liberals in 1980 to the Conservatives in 1984, the defectors and loyalists who cited
leadership as the most important component in their votes were compared further.
Analyses were done for their evaluations of the party leaders on 14 leadership traits.
Selection of these traits was based largely on descriptions of the leaders current in
the mass media during the campaign, plus some supplementary ideas obtained in
our pretest interviews. The characteristics of leaders, as perceived by Liberal loyalists
and defectors, are displayed in table 9.

TABLE 10 *MOST IMPORTANT ISSUES, 1974–1984*[+]

	1974	1979	1980	1984
Economic Issues				
State of economy	5%	11%	9%	20%
Inflation	38	13	14	2
Wage and price controls	8	1	—	—
Taxes	3	8	3	3
Government spending, hiring	1	2	—	3
Budgets, the currency	2	2	17	11
Unemployment, jobs	3	10	4	43
Other economic issues	3	1	1	4
Confederation Issues				
National unity	2	8	4	1
Intergovernmental relations	—	2	3	2
Bilingualism	3	3	—	1
Quebec, separatism, referendum	1	15	6	3
Resource Issues				
Natural resources	—	5	1	2
Energy, oil development	2	4	18	1
Energy pricing	—	—	13	1
Social Issues				
Housing, health, pensions, women's issues, etc.	12	5	2	13
Other Issues				
Foreign relations, defence	2	2	3	3
Leadership	6	14	15	9
Electoral change, parties	1	8	8	15
The election itself, majority government	7	1	4	1
Other	3	2	2	5
None	30	28	22	12
(N=)	(2445)	(2668)	(1786)	(2858)

Percentages are rounded.
Columns run to more than 100% because of multiple responses.
+ 1974, 1979 and 1980 figures are taken from H. Clarke, J. Jenson, L. LeDuc, and J. Pammett, *Absent Mandate*, p. 81.

The strongest relationships are for "sincerity" and "competence." In the case of "sincerity," for example, loyalists saw Turner as much more sincere than Mulroney (the gap between them was 50 per cent) and defectors saw Mulroney as more sincere than Turner (the gap was 33 per cent). Although the relationship was pronounced for "competence," this was largely attributable to defectors who saw the Tory leader as much more competent (a gap of 70 per cent), compared to the loyalists for whom the differential in Turner's favour was only 15 per cent.

It is also striking that respondents did not simply attribute positive traits to their preferred leader and denigrate the other leader. This can be seen in the clear

TABLE 11   *1984 VOTE OF 1980 LIBERALS BY SINGLE MOST IMPORTANT ISSUE*

	All 1980 Liberals	Unemployment	State of Economy	Electoral Change	Social Issues
Liberal	48%	51%	39%	37%	38%
PC	43	38	51	57	45
NDP	7	10	9	3	11
Other	2	1	1	3	6
(N=)	(917)	(266)	(132)	(92)	(54)

Percentages are rounded.

tendency for both categories of voters to perceive Turner as more "nervous" and "dull" than Mulroney, while Mulroney was perceived as more "sure of himself," "representative of change" and "slick" than Turner. Since the picture of Turner that emerges here is not especially flattering, even among respondents who continued to vote Liberal in 1984, it is not surprising that loyalists tended disproportionately to emphasise the parties as the centrepiece in their voting decisions.

On the perceptions of which leader represented change, over 80 per cent of the total sample thought that Mulroney represented change, while about one-third felt similarly about Turner. These perceptions held even among 1980 Liberals, and, of course, for 1980 Conservatives. Those 1980 Liberal voters who saw Turner as representing change stayed with the party by a proportion of 66 per cent as compared to 27 per cent who moved to the Conservatives. However, if they did not think Turner represented change, only 32 per cent stayed Liberal and 59 per cent switched to the PCs. Perceptions of Mulroney as the candidate of change or not produced parallel levels of Liberal switching (52 per cent versus 41 per cent). The small number of 1980 Liberals who did not think that Mulroney represented change stayed Liberal in an overwhelming proportion (73 per cent).

Before looking at how respondents used issues to evaluate parties we should consider, first, what they thought the issues in the campaign were. The issues cited by the sample as being most important in the 1984 election are presented in table 10 in categories comparable to those employed by the Windsor–Carleton team in their studies of the three previous elections. The overwhelming issue in frequency of mention in 1984 was unemployment, cited by over one-third of the sample as the most important issue, and by 43 per cent as one of the two most important issues. This proportion was greater than that for any other issue during the past four elections. Other issues receiving substantially greater mention than in the past included the state of the economy, social issues (including women's concerns), and the "electoral change" category, the vast majority of whose mentions had to do with "time for a change." Those issues that dropped most compared to past elections were inflation, concern with Confederation, and concern with resources. It might also be added that the proportion not mentioning any issue fell precipitately.

The relationship of issues to the 1984 voting preference of 1980 Liberals is depicted in table 11. This table is limited to the single most important issue

TABLE 12   FIRST AND SECOND MOST IMPORTANT
CRITERIA CITED BY RESPONDENTS IN
EVALUATING THE LIBERAL AND PC PARTIES

Criteria	Most Important	Second Most Important
Controlling inflation	25	19
Dealing with the provincial governments	3	5
Dealing with the US	2	2
Handling relations with Quebec	2	3
Running the government competently	21	10
Dealing with unemployment	27	22
Providing social welfare measures	2	4
Protecting the environment	1	3
Limiting the size of government	1	3
Dealing with women's issues	1	2
Working for world peace	7	11
Handling the deficit	9	15
(N=)	(3222)	(3209)

Percentages are rounded.

reference of previous Liberal voters, together with their 1984 voting behaviour. One observation to be drawn is that the widely cited unemployment issue is less related to switching from the Liberal Party than the average, but those who mentioned "time for a change," the state of the economy, or social issues as being most important were more likely to abandon the Liberals.

Turning now to perceptions of the parties, the 1984 respondents were also asked to "forget for a moment the likelihood of each party getting elected to government" and to judge which parties would do the best and the worst jobs in dealing with each of a series of 12 tasks were they to form the government. Having done this, respondents were then requested to specify which two tasks were most important in their assessments of the parties.

Table 12 summarises the frequencies with which each task was named as "most important" and "second most important" by the entire sample. It is interesting to note that, when given this list of issues, unemployment, inflation, and running the government competently were chosen as most important in evaluating the parties. Dealing with unemployment was listed by 27 per cent of the sample as most important and by an additional 22 per cent as second most important. Virtually half of the sample mentioned the challenge of unemployment either first or second out of 12, making this, by this measurement procedure too, the overriding consideration for judging the parties. The further economic matter of controlling inflation was cited first by 25 per cent and second by another 19 per cent of the sample. In third place was running the government competently, which may also have been perceived as an economic matter by many; this was mentioned first by 21 per cent and second by 10 per cent of the sample.

Next, the relationships between loyalists versus defectors and their evaluations of the Liberal and Conservative parties were examined. This was done, first, for

TABLE 13   *EVALUATIONS OF WHICH PARTY (Liberal or PC) WOULD BETTER HANDLE A TASK AMONG RESPONDENTS WHO SAID PARTIES WERE THE MOST IMPORTANT FACTOR IN THEIR VOTING DECISIONS*

Criteria	Loyalists	Defectors	Tau-C[a]
Controlling inflation	L 26[b]	PC 72	−.58✦
Dealing with the provincial governments	L 8	PC 74	.44✦
Dealing with the US	L 33	PC 54	.45✦
Handling relations with Quebec	L 31	PC 44	.39✦
Running the government competently	L 57	PC 84	.77✦
Dealing with unemployment	L 41	PC 66	.60✦
Providing social welfare measures	L 69	PC 0	.34✦
Protecting the environment	L 47	PC 25	.44✦
Limiting the size of government	PC 6	PC 63	.31✦
Dealing with women's issues	L 42	PC 46	.48✦
Working for world peace	L 84	L 50	.19✦
Handling the deficit	L 1	PC 89	.53✦

Percentages are rounded.

[a] Positive correlation means that defection to the PC party is associated with the judgement that the PC party will perform a task better than the Liberal will.

[b] L or PC means that the Liberal or PC party is judged superior than the other party in performing a task; figures are percentage gaps between the two parties.

Significance levels: ✶ < .05
            ✶✶ < .01
            ✦ < .001

respondents who cited parties as the most important component in their votes and, second, for respondents who judged a given task as an important factor in their voting evaluations of the parties.

Table 13 summarises the results for respondents who judged that parties were more important than leaders and candidates in shaping their votes. Running the government competently was most strongly associated with defections to the Tories. Among defectors, the gap between the Liberals and the Conservatives was 84 per cent in favour of the Tories. People who voted Liberal produced a gap of approximately 57 per cent in the direction of their preferred party. This kind of polarization occurred also for unemployment. Both Liberal and Conservative voters thought that their party could best deal with this problem (a gap of 41 per cent for Liberals in favour of the Liberals, and a gap of 67 per cent for Conservatives). There were only two exceptions to this tendency to flatter one's own party. Both categories of voters believed that the Tories would do a better job of limiting the size of government and that the Liberals would do a better job of working for peace.

The relationship between loyalists versus defectors and evaluations of parties' probable performances was specified also by whether a task was selected as an important consideration in judging the parties. Looking at evaluations without regard to the importance of the criteria leaves respondents open to a "halo effect"—that is, describing the party they like in a generally favourable manner and doing the opposite for disliked parties. Controlling for the importance of the criteria used, however, should more clearly reveal the fundamental assessment that may lie lack of any halo effect. The findings for this analysis are presented in table 14. There was less of a tendency for respondents to flatter their preferred parties overall,

TABLE 14 JUDGMENTS OF WHICH PARTY (Liberal or
PC) WOULD BETTER PERFORM A TASK
AMONG RESPONDENTS WHO SAID A GIVEN
TASK WAS MOST OR SECOND MOST
IMPORTANT AS A CRITERION

Criteria	Loyalists	Defectors	Tau-C
Controlling inflation	L 28	PC 65	.54♦
Dealing with the provincial governments	PC 34	PC 82	.28♦♦
Dealing with the US	L 29	PC 72	.53♦♦
Handling relations with Quebec	PC 21	PC 95	.43♦
Running the government competently	L 61	PC 71	.78♦
Dealing with unemployment	L 34	PC 79	.69♦
Providing social welfare measures	L 81	PC 0	.50♦♦
Protecting the environment	PC 4	PC 10	.03
Limiting the size of government	L 9	PC 88	.55
Dealing with women's issues	L 15	PC 56	.38*
Working for world peace	L 87	L 26	.36♦
Handling the deficit	PC 17	PC 90	.42♦

Percentages are rounded.
Significance levels: * < .05
♦♦ < .01
♦ < .001

presumably on the grounds that it is the issue in question that matters to respondents rather than the party as such. In five comparisons, both loyalists and defectors tended to agree that one of the parties was superior to the other party in handling a task. The Tories were seen as superior to the Liberals by both categories of voters in dealing with the provinces, Quebec, the environment, and the deficit. Both groups were in agreement that the Liberals would do a better job working for peace. In all of these comparisons, however, it should still be noted that the gaps in favour of voters' preferred parties continued to exceed the gaps for voters' non-preferred parties. Where there was polarization in respondents' perceptions, the strongest relations appeared for the issues of running the government competently and dealing with unemployment.

The question of whether defectors from the Liberals to the Tories differed in political attitudes compared with Liberal loyalists can best be addressed using responses to a battery of 15 questions on economic and social issues from the survey, each of which called for opinions on the propriety of governmental actions, either to address social inequalities, to maintain social control, or to strengthen military defences.[18] Table 15 reports on the covariation between these attitudes and staying with, versus switching from, the Liberals. Eight of 15 relationships were statistically significant, but the magnitude of each was small (taus of .10 in two cases and less than that for the others). If there was a pattern in the stated attitudes of the two groups of voters, it was that those who abandoned Turner and the Liberal Party for the Conservatives were more "libertarian" in their outlook than were the loyal Liberals. Defectors to the Tory camp were more likely to favour a "pro-choice" position on abortion, the position that homosexuals should be able to teach in schools, and superiority in nuclear weapons; they were more likely to oppose

TABLE 15   *CORRELATIONS BETWEEN LIBERAL
LOYALISTS VS. DEFECTORS AND ATTITUDES*

Attitude Statement	Endorsed by	Tau-C
Government guarantee adequate housing	—	-.02
No medical extra billing	Loyalists	.06*
Rich/poor gap too great	—	.05
No right to strike for civil servants	Defectors	-.06*
No hire scabs	—	-.04
Government not responsible for jobs for the unemployed	—	-.02
Increase NATO contributions		.04
Higher taxes for high incomes	Loyalists	.08*
Government ensure money for the elderly	—	.02
US nuclear superiority	Defectors	-.10**
Government increase women's job opportunities	Defectors	-.08*
Favour capital punishment	—	.02
Favour censorship	Loyalists	.07*
Favour freedom of abortion	Defectors	-.10**
Permit gay teachers	Defectors	-.07*

Significance levels: * < .05
                      ** < .01
                      ♦ < .001

banning of extra-billing by doctors and hospitals, increased taxation for high income people, strikes in the public sector, and censorship of pornography; the defectors were also more likely to favour government efforts to increase the occupational opportunities available to women. This last finding provides the only exception to a "libertarian" pattern in attitude differences (see table 15).

CHANGES IN PARTISAN COMPOSITION?

It is clear that the 1984 election was one characterised by a set of strong short-term forces combining to create a net partisan advantage for the Progressive Conservative Party some 16 percentage points above their typical vote.[19] Not clear are the longer term implications of this election for the nature of the Canadian party system. That is, to what extent was the underlying partisan distribution of the electorate altered by this election? Did Liberal defectors regard their behaviour as a response to short-term and remediable conditions such that their defections might well be temporary, or did their switch to the Tories reflect a more basic reassessment of partisan interests?

Speculation on such matters at this point is fraught with difficulties. The most impenetrable of these is the possibility that the voting change has initiated a process of realignment, the fruits of which are not yet discernible. A second problem is the possibility that partisan interests are defined primarily in terms of immediate short-term conditions, such that current partisanship has only weak implications for the longer term. Along this line, a number of scholars have suggested that partisanship in Canada tends to be less firmly rooted in the social fabric of the

TABLE 16   DISTRIBUTION OF FEDERAL PARTY
IDENTIFICATION+ 1974-1984

	1974	1979	1980	1984
Liberal	49%	43%	44%	34%
PC	23	28	27	41
NDP	10	13	15	14
Other	3	4	2	1
No identification	15	12	12	9
(N=)	(2445)	(2435)	(1692)	(2965)

Percentages are rounded.
+ Distributions are based on responses only to the initial question in the standard party
identification battery. Thus, nonidentifiers who expressed a leaning in subsequent probes
are still treated as nonidentifiers in this table.

community than in some other countries; as a consequence, party identification is freer to travel with the vote when short-term forces produce a shift in behaviour.[20]

This is clearly the case with some voters, as LeDuc and his colleagues have demonstrated. For other voters, however—those labelled "durable partisans" by the Windsor–Carleton researchers—partisanship does seem to function as a more enduring orientation with significance for future behaviour.[21] Given this finding, and in the absence of an alternative, the 1984 distribution of partisanship is examined against the backdrop of earlier distributions.

Table 16 displays the distribution of party identification in Canada as reported in each of the four post-election surveys over the past decade.[22] On the surface, at least, these data suggest that the 1984 election produced significant changes in the partisan alignment of the electorate. While the proportions aligning themselves with the NDP and those professing no identification are almost identical to those found in the immediately previous period, the Liberal proportion has dropped 10 percentage points, and the Progressive Conservative proportion has increased a total of 14 percentage points. These shifts are sufficient to reverse the rank of the two major parties in Canada, and to make the Conservatives the "plurality" party for the first time since surveys of this kind were initiated 20 years ago.

As indicated above, however, these data may not provide a reliable basis for generating longer term voting expectations. At least some of those who have left the Liberal fold, or who are now calling themselves Conservatives, are simply expressing their current evaluation of the alternatives—an evaluation that could easily change with conditions. A partial solution to this problem may be to strengthen the criteria by which partisans are identified. That is, by eliminating from the analysis those who are least likely to hold the traditional "reference group" conception of partisanship, we may gain a better appreciation of how much the changes in 1984 have altered the support bases of the parties.

Table 17 attempts to do this. Respondents represented in this table are limited to those who jointly satisfied the following conditions: (a) they freely identified themselves with one party or another; (b) they indicated that they identified "very" or "fairly strongly" with the party in question; and (c) they indicated that they had never felt closer to any other federal party. Thus the table includes only respondents

TABLE 17   DISTRIBUTION OF FEDERAL PARTY
            IDENTIFICATION FOR "HARD-CORE"
            PARTISANS ONLY 1974–1984

	1974	1979	1980	1984
Liberal	61%	56%	58%	40%
PC	25	29	28	45
NDP	11	12	13	14
Other	4	3	2	2
(N=)	(1132)	(1183)	(807)	(1311)
"Hard-core" partisans as % of total electorate	(46%)	(49%)	(48%)	(44%)

Percentages are rounded.

TABLE 18   DISTRIBUTION OF FEDERAL PARTY
            IDENTIFICATION FOR "HARD-CORE"
            PARTISANS ONLY, BY REGION, 1974–1984

	1974	1979	1980	1984
Atlantic Region				
Liberal	69%	58%	58%	42%
PC	28	35	36	54
NDP	3	7	7	4
Other	—	—	1	—
(N=)	(109)	(127)	(76)	(114)
Quebec				
Liberal	78%	84%	86%	61%
PC	9	7	5	29
NDP	4	4	6	7
Other	9	6	3	4
(N=)	(338)	(356)	(265)	(347)
Ontario				
Liberal	53%	52%	49%	43%
PC	33	32	26	42
NDP	14	16	16	15
Other	—	1	—	—
(N=)	(371)	(431)	(277)	(485)
Prairies				
Liberal	40%	24%	33%	12%
PC	42	57	49	70
NDP	15	15	17	16
Other	4	5	2	2
(N=)	(144)	(189)	(126)	(259)
British Columbia				
Liberal	51%	35%	30%	24%
PC	22	30	38	41
NDP	25	30	29	35
Other	4	5	3	1
(N=)	(93)	(100)	(69)	(138)

Percentages are rounded.
Ns for each region subsample are the region's weighted N for the national cross-section.

who approximate a conception of "durable" or "hard-core" partisans.[23] The percentages in parentheses at the bottom of the table indicate the proportion of the entire electorate which passed this tougher test of partisanship. It can be seen from these figures that so-called "hard-core" partisans constitute a large, albeit a minority, proportion of the electorate. If we assume that these respondents are the most resistant to a change in identification, and are the least likely to defect temporarily to support another party, they might be regarded as the parties' underlying bases of support in "normal" times.

Within the table itself, comparisons over the four election periods reinforce the view that 1984 produced a major shift in the partisan composition of the electorate. From a solid majority position in the previous three election periods, the Liberal Party has sustained a net loss of 18 percentage points—a loss of almost a third of its 1980 core of supporters—and has fallen behind the Conservative Party which gained 16 percentage points over the same four year period. Again, the size of the NDP support base is altered little in 1984, and has been quite stable over the ten year period.

To explore the nature of this shift further, table 18 replicates table 17 for each of the five regions in Canada. The data in this table suggest that the realignment, if such it was, is dramatic in three of the five regions of the country. Only in the regions of Ontario and British Columbia were the changes in partisan distribution modest, and in neither case was the ranking of the parties altered. Although the Liberals managed to retain majority status in Quebec, their drop of 25 percentage points together with a similar Tory gain will surely have implications for the character of competitive party politics in that province.

Clearly, the methodological characteristics of this tougher measure of partisanship must be examined in greater detail, and its relationships to other criteria explored, before we use it further as a speculative tool. Suffice it to say at this point that the voting shifts in 1984 were accompanied by rather dramatic shifts in voters' partisan self-descriptions.

DISCUSSION AND CONCLUSIONS

An election as decisive as the one discussed here might normally be expected to provide a clearer portrait of Canada's polity than appears to be the case. As has been pointed out, the placement of the findings described above within the context of previous Canadian voting research is not a straightforward matter. The massive electoral change registered at the aggregate level was not reflected by a corresponding rate of change at the individual level. The extent of individual-level switching exceeded that seen in any of the other national post-election studies, but not to a substantial degree.

Change in 1984 differed from past elections in that it was mostly in one direction. The bulk of those changing their vote consisted of former Liberals moving to the Conservative Party, by a proportion almost twice that of any previous movement between major political parties. A sociodemographic analysis of the election indicated that the Conservatives won a national mandate by gaining disproportionately among groups previously disaffected from the party such as Quebeckers and Francophones. The Liberals lost voters to the Tories among all social sub-groups, but this effect was less evident among the elderly, the less well-educated, residents of the Atlantic provinces, and the non-English and non-French speakers. The election was characterised by much less cleavage between regional or other sociodemographic divisions than was the case during the Trudeau era.

The 1984 election differed from past votes in the extreme volatility of the public displayed both prior to and during the campaign. More Canadians made their voting decision during the campaign than in recent elections, and this group was composed disproportionately of Quebeckers and of people influenced by leadership. Among other political events, the leadership debates contributed substantially to Brian Mulroney's enhanced image by comparison with John Turner.

An examination of the sources of the voters' change revealed that leadership was a particularly important factor among former Liberals switching to the Conservative Party. Mulroney's image was seen as more positive than Turner's on a variety of traits including such evaluative characteristics as competence, warmth, responsiveness, and representing change. On representing change, though, it was not clear if Mulroney's favourable image was a cause or an effect of partisan preferences.

The most widely mentioned election issue was unemployment, but reference to it was not associated with leaving the Liberal Party. Issues that were associated with vote switching included "time for a change," the state of the economy, and social concerns. The evaluation of party performance in a series of closed-ended, issue-related tasks showed that respondents again rated unemployment as their most important concern, and this concern was strongly associated with the distinctive behaviour of Liberal loyalists and defectors as was the issue of competence. Because of the closed-ended format, there were differences in the frequency of some of the other issues mentioned by comparison to the open-ended question.

An attempt to discern the attitudinal orientation of Liberal switchers showed that, although such relationships were not strong, there was a somewhat greater libertarian aspect to their views.

The discussion of partisanship moves into the potentially more speculative area of future implications from the election. Without intending to suggest very much in that direction, it is of interest to note that the Conservative Party emerged from the election with a much greater proportion of "hard-core" partisans than had previously been the case.

Some may be tempted to overstate the future implications of such a dramatic election outcome, but this should probably be resisted. What the Conservative Party has gained is an opportunity to try to re-establish a sustaining national base that it has lacked since the First World War. The advantage that party now has is that it can determine its own political fate, rather than having to depend upon the Liberals to make mistakes. To those who feel there is an inevitability to electoral realignment, it should be remembered that despite John Diefenbaker's landslide of comparable proportions in 1958, the Conservatives were out of power within five years.

APPENDIX A: SAMPLE DESIGN

The sample design for the study was a multi-stage stratified cluster sample of the Canadian electorate, with systematic oversampling of the smaller provinces. Sampling proceeded through four stages. First, the localities within each province were stratified by urban–rural composition, and a random selection of localities from each of the five urban–rural strata was made. Localities were selected proportional to size. In this way, a total of 245 localities from across the country were selected into the sample. For reasons of cost, the localities found in the Northwest and Yukon Territories, those found in Labrador, and those located in the extreme northern portions of Quebec, Ontario, and the western provinces were systematically excluded from the sample. It is estimated that these exclusions account for no more than 3 per cent of the Canadian population.

The second stage of the sampling procedure involved randomly selecting Census Enumeration Areas (EAs) from within localities. The 483 Enumeration Areas selected at this stage constitute the primary sampling units for the study. Within each of these EAs, a block was selected at random. On the block, interviewers were given a random start at a specific address, and were instructed to seek an interview from fifteen households selected at a fixed interval around the block. Finally, within selected households, a version of the Troldahl-Carter-Bryant sampling technique was used to select the respondent from among the eligible voters in the household.[24] Up to four call-backs were permitted to complete an interview.

The raw sample of 3377 respondents has been reweighted for these analyses to reflect the relative population size of each province and the proportionate age, gender, and urban–rural composition within each province. The weighted N is 3380 respondents. Both unweighted and weighted Ns by province are presented in table A1.

TABLE A1   *UNWEIGHTED AND WEIGHTED PROVINCIAL SAMPLE NUMBERS IN THE 1984 NATIONAL ELECTION STUDY*

	Unweighted Sample Sizes	Weighted Sample Sizes
Newfoundland	134	70
PEI	112	16
Nova Scotia	132	116
New Brunswick	136	93
Quebec	779	906
Ontario	967	1213
Manitoba	251	142
Saskatchewan	252	130
Alberta	263	304
British Columbia	351	390
Total	3377	3380

NOTES

1. The series of National Election Studies has spawned a plethora of published research works. Some of the most significant of these are John Meisel, *Working Papers on Canadian Politics* (Toronto: McGill-Queen's Press, 1972); Harold Clarke, Jane Jenson, Lawrence LeDuc and Jon Pammett, *Political Change in Canada* (Toronto: McGraw-Hill Ryerson); and Harold Clarke, Jane Jenson, Lawrence LeDuc and Jon Pammett, *Absent Mandate: The Politics of Discontent* (Toronto: Gage Publishing Co., 1984).

2. See, for example, Lawrence LeDuc, "Canada: The Politics of Stable Dealignment," in *Electoral Change in Advanced Industrial Democracies: Realignment or Dealignment?* ed. Russell J. Dalton et al. (Princeton, N.J.: Princeton University Press, 1984), 402–24. See also Harold Clarke et al., *Absent Mandate*, 55–76.

3. See William P. Irvine, "The Canadian Voter," in *Canada at the Polls, 1979 and 1980* ed. Howard R. Penniman (Washington, D.C.: American Enterprise Institute, 1981), 55–85; Lawrence LeDuc, "The Dynamic Properties of Party Identification: A Four Nation Comparison," in *Controversies in Voting Behavior* ed. Richard G. Niemi and Herbert F. Weisberg (Washington, D.C.: Congressional Quarterly, 1984), 424–36.

4. For a description of the 1974 survey design, see Lawrence LeDuc et al., "A National Sample Design," *Canadian Journal of Political Science* (*CJPS*) 7 (1974): 701–708. The 1979 and 1980 designs are described in Harold Clarke et al., *Absent Mandate*, 1–5.

5. Lawrence LeDuc, "The Politics of Stable Dealignment."

6. Ibid., 423.

7. These figures are based upon recall of previous votes by respondents, a comparable question in both election studies. The 1979 figure varies slightly in magnitude from the figure for degree of change that is recorded in the panel.

8. If the 1980 Liberal voters had defected in 1984 in the same proportion as their average over the previous three elections, and if other patterns were as they were, the Liberal Party would have had a slight edge in popular vote over the Conservatives.

9. Jerome Black, Michael Coveyou and Jane Jenson "Federal Provincial Voting Behaviour: An Examination of Electoral Migration." (Paper presented at the 1972 annual meeting of the Canadian Political Science Association, Montreal, Quebec). Gerald Pomper, *Voter's Choice* (New York: Dodd, Mead and Co., 1975), 31 refers to the greater independence in party identification of the better educated in the USA.

10. Public evaluations of the three party leaders in 1984 based upon "feeling thermometers" revealed ranges for each leader of approximately 5 per cent over Canada's different regions. By contrast, in the previous elections featuring Trudeau and Clark, the differences across regions in leader evaluations exceeded 15 per cent. These data suggest that the declining regional polarization in patterns of party support coincided with a declining regional polarization in perceptions of party leadership.

11. At the time, many observers questioned the accuracy of this poll, but the next poll yielded virtually the same results.

12. The party leading in pre-campaign Gallup polls had had its popular support change by an average of only 3 per cent in the five elections from 1968 to 1980, and 4.5 per cent in the 13 elections from 1945 to 1980. See Val Sears, *Toronto Star*, 1 September 1984.

13. See, for example, Harold Clarke et al., *Political Choice in Canada*, 275–99; and Bernard Berelson, Paul Lazarsfeld, and William McPhee, *Voting* (Chicago: University of Chicago Press, 1954).

14. See Lawrence LeDuc and Richard Price, "Great Debates: The Televised Leadership Debates of 1979," *CJPS* 18 (1985): 135–53. For a recent U.S.A. example, see Kathleen Frankovic, "The 1984 Election: The Irrelevance of the Campaign," *PS* 18 (1985): 39–47.

15. Among Quebeckers, over 58 per cent decided during the campaign, while the corresponding figure for non-Quebeckers was 47 per cent. In previous elections, the proportion deciding after the election was called was in the range of 45 per cent or lower.

16. Mulroney clearly defeated Turner in the debates with an average rating of 6.8 to 4.2 on a ten-point scale. Broadbent had a score of 6.4, but voters impressed with his performance were not as likely, as in Mulroney's case, to translate that into support for his party.

17. We know that voters tend to see the Liberal and Progressive Conservative parties as quite similar in ideological terms, while both of them are seen as quite distinct from the New Democratic Party. See, for example, R. D. Lambert, "Questionnaire design, response set and the measurement of left/right thinking in survey research," *CJPS* 16 (1983): 135–44. We mention this because focussing on the two ideologically similar parties may have the effect of altering the relative importance of leadership and party in voters' calculations. We have focussed on these two parties for two reasons. First, there is much less traffic between the NDP and each of the other parties, making estimates based on these few cases questionable. Second, the heavy traffic between voting Liberal in 1980 and voting Conservative in 1984 seems to account for the Tory landslide.

18. The attitude statements employed in the 1984 survey can be roughly classified under five rubrics. The statements appear verbatim as follows: (1) *Duties of government*: (i) The government should see that everyone has adequate housing; (ii) It is not the responsibility of government to assure jobs for unemployed Canadians; (iii) The government should see to it that older and retired people have enough money to live on; (iv) The government should increase the employment opportunities available to women; (v) Doctors and hospitals should not be allowed to extra bill or charge patients more than the government health plans pay them. (2) *Wealth*: (i) The difference between the rich and the poor is too great in Canada; (ii) People with high incomes should pay a greater share of the taxes than they do now. (3) *Rights of Labour*: (i) Government employees should not have the right to strike; (ii) During a strike, management should not be allowed to hire workers to take the place of strikers. (4) *The military*: (i) Canada should increase its military contributions to NATO; (ii) The US and its allies should aim for superiority in nuclear weapons. (5) *Morality*: (i) There should be capital punishment for anyone convicted of murder; (ii) Pornographic magazines and movies should be censored; (iii) The decision to have an abortion should be the responsibility of the pregnant woman; (iv) People who are homosexuals should be permitted to teach school.

19. This estimate of a typical support level for the Progressive Conservatives is based on their average support over the previous five elections from 1968 through 1980.

20. See, for example, William Irvine, "The Canadian Voter"; and Lawrence LeDuc, "The Politics of Stable Dealignment."

21. The notion of "durable" partisanship is developed most fully in Harold Clarke et al., *Voting Choice in Canada*, chaps. 5 and 10.

22. The measure of party identification employed here is respondents' initial answers to the question, "Do you usually think of yourself as a Liberal, Progressive Conservative, NDP, or what?" Any nonidentifiers who admitted a leaning in subsequent probes are still treated as nonidentifiers for the purpose of this analysis.

23. This stricter measure of partisanship differs from that defining "durable" partisanship for the Windsor–Carleton researchers in that we have not incorporated in our construction a criterion demanding consistency of identification across both the federal and provincial levels. To signal this difference, we use the term "hard-core" rather than "durable" in the current analysis.

24. For a description of this selection technique, and a comparison of its performance with alternative techniques, see Ronald Czaja, Johnny Blair, and Jutta P. Sebestik, "Respondent Selection in a Telephone Survey: A Comparison of Three Techniques," *Journal of Marketing Research* 19 (1982): 381–85.

FREE TRADE AND THE DYNAMICS OF THE 1988 CANADIAN ELECTION◇

RICHARD JOHNSTON
ANDRÉ BLAIS
HENRY E. BRADY
JEAN CRÊTE

On 1 October 1988, Conservatives could reasonably assume that they would be returned to government with a comfortable majority. This was so in spite of the fact that Parliament was dissolved over an issue, Free Trade with the USA, which had brought down one government in 1911 and which none since had dared touch. One month later, the Conservatives stared into the abyss of defeat; 1911 seemed about to repeat itself. By election day, the Conservatives had recovered most of their original advantage. How did they dissipate their early lead? How did they restore it?

The 1988 Canadian National Election Study was designed to address such questions. Its pre-election component was a "rolling cross section," in which interviews were distributed roughly evenly over the campaign. The campaign wave was administered by a form of computer assisted telephone interviewing (CATI) which, among other things, accommodated experiments to mimic the rhetoric of the campaign.

This paper reports an early pass through these data. They suggest that the Conservative collapse at mid-campaign was indeed a recapitulation—of sorts—of 1911. The collapse revealed the Conservatives' chief strategic weakness. Their recovery bore witness to the fact that the election was not just a referendum on Canadian–American relations. It was also, as elections are, a choice of government. Putting the choice in these terms played to the Conservatives' chief strength. And the choice also reflected strategic and dynamic factors. Most notably the campaign saw a bandwagon to the Liberal party. But the bandwagon stalled.

◇ Paper prepared for the American Political Science Association Annual Meeting, The Atlanta Hilton, Atlanta, Georgia, 31 August–3 September 1989. Copyright by the American Political Science Association.

The authors acknowledge the generosity of the Social Sciences and Humanities Research Council of Canada, under grant 411-88-0030, and of the computing centres at the University of British Columbia and l'Université de Montréal. Fieldwork for the 1988 Canadian National Election Study was carried out by the Institute for Social Research, York University. Critical to the whole enterprise were David Northrup, John Tibert, and David Bates. None of the foregoing individuals or institutions are responsible for any errors of analysis or interpretation.

THE COURSE OF PARTY SUPPORT

Over the campaign we completed roughly 77 interviews per day from 4 October to 20 November inclusive. The day on which a respondent happened to be interviewed was, to all intents and purposes, a random event.[1] With daily tracking, the sample can be partitioned pretty much at will. The partition adopted here splits the sample at the day following the leaders' debates and isolates the last two weeks.

The path of vote intentions over the campaign appears in table 1. Our data reflect the pattern familiar to attentive observers of polls published over the campaign: before the debates, a strong Conservative lead with the other two parties virtually level pegging; in the weeks immediately after the debates, a Tory crash and a Liberal surge[2] such that these two parties were tied, with the NDP consigned to its accustomed, distant third; no more than modest shifts into the penultimate week; and a Conservative surge at the last.[3]

The debates, obviously, must have been critical to Conservative reverses. At the same time, the debates gave a decisive advantage to the Liberals over the NDP. But what was it that made the debates critical? The Tory recovery in late campaign appears to coincide with an advertising blitz by Conservatives and their allies. If that advertising did indeed hold the key to Tory recovery, what themes in it resonated in the public?

THE FALL AND RISE OF FREE TRADE

THE PATH OF SUPPORT

The obvious place to begin is with what seemed to be the overriding issue: Free Trade. According to table 2, opinion on the Free Trade Agreement (FTA) ebbed and flowed much as did Tory support.[4] The debates marked a critical transition in support for the Agreement. Support was sliding before the debates, a slide hinted at by the difference of proportions between the first two periods. The days immediately after the debate produced an immediate ten-point drop.[5] But the 26 October–6 November average incorporates a gradual recovery of Free Trade support, a recovery which the table records as continuing into the last two weeks of the campaign.[6]

The recovery was partial and asymmetric. Only about half the drop in the percentage supporting the FTA was made good. And virtually all of the recovery was confined to the support side of the ledger. The percentage opposed to the FTA

TABLE 1   VOTE INTENTIONS BY PERIOD

	Conservative	Liberal	NDP	Other	
4–14 October	45.6	25.0	23.7	5.7	(491)
15–25 October	47.8	26.4	21.6	4.2	(655)
26 Oct.–4 Nov.	37.2	35.6	22.3	4.9	(795)
7–13 November	38.9	36.3	21.9	2.8	(435)
14–20 November	46.6	34.5	16.0	2.9	(433)

TABLE 2 FREE TRADE AGREEMENT OPINION BY PERIOD

	Support FTA	Neither Support/Oppose	Oppose FTA	
4–14 October	43.2	22.9	34.0	(661)
15–25 October	38.8	21.2	40.0	(856)
26 Oct.–6 Nov.	32.7	20.7	46.6	(960)
7–13 November	37.9	16.4	45.7	(532)
14–20 November	38.4	16.5	45.1	(527)

did seem to slide in late campaign but only by a couple of points. This asymmetry between support and opposition will crop up again in analyses reported below.

What produced the shift against the FTA? We believe that the campaign and, in its especially focussed way, the debate tapped uncertainty about the FTA, an uncertainty that before the campaign had been only latent. Our design picks this uncertainty up in two ways, each in the form of an experiment.

UNCERTAINTY OVER THE AGENT

If the debates had a decisive moment, it arrived when Mr. Turner confronted Mr. Mulroney directly with his responsibility for the Free Trade Agreement. His words were: "I happen to think you've sold us out." These words and the rivetting exchange which followed echoed and brought to fruition weeks of preparatory rhetoric by both opposition parties and by nonparty advocates.

The rhetoric sought to take advantage of voters' natural tendency, in the face of uncertainties and complexities, to look to proxies, in this case to ask who was responsible for the negotiations. Liberal and NDP strategists believed that such a process could only work to the agreement's disadvantage: they repeatedly styled the FTA as "the Mulroney Free Trade deal." The Mulroney government had regularly been attacked by the opposition as mendacious and unreliable. Much was made of contradictions between 1984 campaign promises and post-1984 policy initiatives; retreats by the government in face of such criticism only seemed to confirm its untrustworthiness. The government was plagued by conflicts of interest and petty corruption. Harmful in themselves, these problems sat poorly with the 1984 campaign's emphasis on honesty. The Prime Minister himself is typed as in the habit of telling his immediate audience whatever it wants to hear, heedlessly contradicting promises made to other audiences. And the Prime Minister seems to have gained a reputation as someone who will do anything to close a deal, even at the expense of his own bottom line, if indeed he has one. The Free Trade Agreement thus seemed vulnerable to the reputed untrustworthiness of the agent principally responsible for it.

To assess this vulnerability, we administered (as hinted above in a footnote) not one FTA support/oppose item to our respondents but two. Assignments of respondents to one or the other version was at random. The basic item was:

As you know, [fill] has reached a Free Trade Agreement with the United States. All things considered, do you support the agreement or do you oppose it?

TABLE 3   FREE TRADE SUPPORT/OPPOSITION BY
          NEGOTIATING RESPONSIBILITY AND PERIOD

| | | Negotiator | | | |
		"the Mulroney Government"	"Canada"	Difference	2-Tail Prob*
4–14 October	Support	39.4	47.1	–7.7	0.048
	Oppose	36.5	30.4	6.1	0.097
		(368)	(298)		
15–25 October	Support	36.0	40.2	–4.2	0.200
	Oppose	40.5	37.9	2.6	0.417
		(456)	(416)		
26 Oct.–6 Nov.	Support	30.1	33.9	–3.8	0.193
	Oppose	46.0	45.4	0.6	0.855
		(480)	(499)		
7–13 November	Support	36.7	37.4	–0.7	0.871
	Oppose	43.4	45.9	–2.5	0.553
		(254)	(290)		
14–20 November	Support	39.8	33.0	6.8	0.099
	Oppose	42.8	43.8	–1.0	0.811
		(308)	(241)		

* From t-test with pooled variance estimate of standard error

The experiment lay in the fill for who precisely reached the agreement.

Half the sample was given the word, *Canada*. This places a mild burden of proof on rejecting the agreement. To the extent that it does, this version mirrors Conservative late-campaign rhetoric which asked: what would be the effect of rejecting the FTA on Canada's image abroad as a good-faith negotiator? The other half of the sample was supplied the words, *the Mulroney government*. This treatment goes straight to the Prime Minister's reputation.

The opposition rhetoric's greatest impact should have come in early campaign. Indeed much of the impact may have been absorbed by the time our fieldwork began, so intense over the summer had been the opposition's attempts to link the FTA to the Prime Minister. To the extent that opinion remained unmobilized in October, however, the "Mulroney" treatment should have had an adverse impact on support for the FTA. As the campaign wore on this impact should have weakened. A consideration which in early campaign might not be ordinarily accessible to the respondent's consciousness, and thus which if introduced into that consciousness might move survey response, may in late campaign already be factored into the latent response disposition. At this point, invoking it serves only to reinforce opinion on one side and is likely to be discounted by the other side.[7]

For the FTA in particular, this expectation is reinforced by our sense of the government's late-campaign rhetoric. In early campaign, the government adopted what might be called a third-party approach to the FTA. They appear to have been sensitive to precisely the concerns outlined in the two preceding paragraphs. Rather than emphasise their own responsibility for the Agreement, the government recited the number of endorsements that the FTA had received from independent groups. The debate nullified this approach. Forced at last to acknowledge paternity, the government proceeded to defend its progeny vigorously. Worrying aloud about the implications of tearing up an agreement reached after painful negotiations did promise to shift the burden of proof. The FTA itself started to become the status quo, departure from which required justification.

Our experiment suggests that the opposition's pre- and early-campaign strategy was well conceived. In the first fortnight, respondents given the "Mulroney" treatment were nearly eight points less likely than respondents given the "Canada" treatment to support the FTA and over six points more likely to oppose it.[8]

By mid-October, this difference was cut nearly in half and in the last week the difference was, if anything, reversed. The mid-campaign extinction of the experiment's effect derived primarily from the "Canada" group: their drop in support from early to mid-campaign was nearly twice that of the "Mulroney" group and their growth in opposition nearly half again as large. In contrast, *all* the FTA's post-debate recovery was generated by the "Mulroney" group.

The trajectory of the two treatment groups to 13 November bears testimony to the early campaign effectiveness of the opposition attack on the agreement and to the accuracy of Mr. Turner's salvoes in the debate. Respondents in the "Mulroney" treatment were receiving the essential message of the campaigns and of the English debate before respondents in the other group were. For the "Canada" group, the campaign had to be a few weeks old before it could supply respondents the consideration which we had, by lot, withheld from them. The debates, of course, reinforced this message.

UNCERTAINTY OVER THE AGREEMENT'S IMPACT

Debate over the agreement also addressed its substance. Three lines of attack seemed especially promising as the campaign began: the apparent abrogation of *sovereignty* over key elements of the economy;[9] threats to Canada's *social programs*, and fear of *job displacement*. Arguments available to supporters of the FTA seemed politically weaker. Two such arguments, nonetheless, had emerged by the eve of the campaign: a standard comparative-advantage claim in terms of *lower prices*, and an historically specific argument in terms of insurance against *American protectionism*.[10]

Each of these arguments was mirrored in a challenge contingent on initial FTA opinion. Supporters were given, at random, one of the three opposition arguments and asked if this made them less supportive. Opponents were given one or the other of the two supportive arguments and asked if this made them less opposed. Respondents were not asked if they changed their minds, just if they felt less of whatever it was they initially claimed to be.[11]

Again, we should expect the impact of challenges to follow the logic in Zaller[12] and diminish as the campaign wore on. Early in the campaign, the consideration embedded in the challenge might seem novel and thus have considerable marginal impact. Late in the campaign, the argument should be better rehearsed by respondents and more likely to be discounted into the opinion as initially revealed. That is, by late campaign the rhetoric's impact should be not so much *internal* to the

TABLE 4   IMPACT OF CHALLENGES BY PERIOD

	To Supporters: (Entry is percentage less *supportive*)			To Opponents: (Entry is percentage less *opposed*)	
	Control Key Sectors	Social Progs	Loss of Jobs	US Protection	Price of Goods
4–14 October	29.8 (98)	35.0 (74)	29.0 (99)	11.6 (109)	12.7 (107)
15–25 October	22.3 (114)	39.6 (90)	34.9 (111)	3.8 (168)	12.1 (168)
26 Oct.–6 Nov.	27.1 (98)	27.3 (104)	24.5 (105)	10.9 (203)	10.7 (222)
7–13 November	25.1 (84)	25.4 (47)	14.5 (60)	9.5 (118)	14.0 (120)
14–20 November	10.0 (67)	21.6 (55)	14.7 (75)	12.3 (122)	14.0 (99)

experiment, in the percentage saying that they feel less supportive or less opposed upon exposure to a challenge, as *external* to the experiment, in the ebb and flow of pre-challenge support respondents express for the FTA.

Table 4 suggests that opponents did indeed have the rhetorical advantage. Before 6 November, the weakest opposing argument moved nearly two times as many FTA supporters as did the strongest supporting argument move FTA opponents. In the last week of the campaign, however, the corresponding ratio was less than 1:1. If we compare strongest to strongest, probably the most relevant comparison, the early and late-campaign ratios are around 3:1 and 1.5:1. All of the decay in impact is on the opposing-argument side, however. By the last week the job-loss and sovereignty challenges were no more powerful than either challenge on the other side. The campaign had done its work, evidently, by helping FTA supporters cope with opposition arguments and by moving erstwhile supporters who were truly vulnerable to opposition considerations to the place where they belonged: in the opposition camp. Only the social programs challenge retained any appeal over and above what looks like the 10–14 point baseline right down to the end. Of all considerations bearing upon the FTA, the concern for the integrity of Canada's welfare state seems to have been the most powerful. At its early campaign peak, this consideration moved two FTA supporters in five to reconsider.[13]

The greater part of the decay in impact from our challenges occurred as respondents internalized the bigger arguments of which ours are but a shadow. One of the reasons, then, that late-campaign FTA supporters were less sensitive to a challenge may have been that there were fewer such supporters to challenge in the first place. Many respondents whose characteristics produced a weak disposition to support the FTA in early campaign may have been blown off that position by the rhetorical winds of mid-campaign and thus were not longer around to be chal-

TABLE 5 *FREE TRADE OPINION AND VOTE INTENTIONS BY PERIOD*

	Support	Neither	Oppose		Support	Neither	Oppose	
	A. 4–14 October				B. 15–25 October			
Con	67.6	52.9	11.7	45.6	72.7	48.9	18.3	47.8
Lib	13.9	23.2	40.8	25.0	14.7	25.1	40.8	26.5
NDP	13.4	17.4	41.3	23.7	9.0	20.4	36.5	21.4
Other	4.1	6.5	6.1	5.7	3.6	5.6	4.5	4.3
	45.4	20.7	33.9	(491)	44.8	16.9	38.3	(647)
	C. 26 Oct.–6 Nov.				D. 7–13 November			
Con	77.1	41.9	5.0	37.2	80.9	30.7	7.0	39.6
Lib	9.3	36.8	54.9	35.4	12.4	45.4	53.9	36.3
NDP	8.2	18.6	34.6	22.4	4.4	18.0	37.1	21.5
Other	5.3	2.7	5.6	5.0	2.3	5.9	1.9	2.7
	36.2	16.5	47.4	(785)	39.4	14.6	46.0	(428)
	E. 14–20 November							
Con	88.3	56.0	7.3	47.5				
Lib	6.4	28.1	61.0	33.8				
NDP	2.8	10.5	29.0	15.7				
Other	2.6	5.5	2.7	3.0				
	42.3	12.3	45.4	(417)				

lenged. Those remaining were quite likely already to have incorporated the consideration in the challenge by late campaign if not before.[14]

Challenges on the other side underline just how hard the pro-FTA arguments were to make. Typically, they failed to move all but one in ten of the agreement's opponents. Toward the end, they seemed to gain some bite but it is not clear what to make of this. Over the last three weeks the proportion of opponents was declining modestly from its post-debate peak (see table 2) and thus ought not to have been heavily laden with diffident new converts. Perhaps this is just sampling variation at work. In any case the overriding fact seems inescapable: in rhetoric, at least, supporters of the FTA occupied a strategically vulnerable position.

But hold the position they evidently did. Indeed, they even regained some ground. Nearly all of the gains were at the net expense of the "undecided" share; the percentage opposed to the FTA slipped by only one to two points.

MOVEMENT IN PARTY SUPPORT: THE FREE TRADE CONTRIBUTION

Our experiments avail us little in unpacking the recovery in FTA support.[15] For now, we shall just go directly to the next obvious question: how much of the

Conservative fall and subsequent recovery is attributable to the rehabilitation of Free Trade and how much came from other sources? What about the Liberals and New Democrats? Information on these questions appears in table 5.

The first thing to note is that support for the Agreement was higher through-eout the campaign among those who volunteered a party preference than in the sample as a whole. To see this, compare the column marginals by period in table 5 with the row entries in table 2. Table 5 also suggests that less pre-debate movement in pro-FTA opinion occurred among respondents with a party preference than among respondents without one.[16] But as FTA support crashed and opposition mushroomed just after 24–25 October, a net mobilization of FTA opponents into party preference also occurred.[17]

Now we turn to the shifting course of FTA opinion and vote intention, beginning with the contrast between period 2, just before the debates, and period 3, just after. To estimate the period-2-to-period-3 vote gain or loss purely attributable to gain or loss in FTA support, take the period-2 transition pattern and apply it to the period-3 FTA numbers to compute a notional period-3 Conservative share. The difference between this notional period-3 share and the actual period-2 share is the "pure" compositional shift, the shift purely attributable to movement in FTA opinion. It will also be useful to discuss the compositional shift as a percentage of the total shift, although, as we shall demonstrate later, the estimate here will overstate the compositional impact.

Had the Conservative party attracted period-3 FTA supporters at the period-2 rate, the party would have incurred a gross loss of 6.3 points.[18] But the party slightly increased its efficiency at tapping the pro-FTA group and thus contained the loss on the left side of the table to 4.7 percentage points. The party lost 1.4 points from the "neither" pool, of which 0.2 per cent was attributable purely to the shrinkage of the group. Finally, had the Conservatives continued to tap the opponent pool at the period-2 rate, the 9.1 point increase in that pool's size would have netted the Conservatives a 1.7 point gain in support on the right side of the table. But the conservative vote rate among FTA opponents dropped by more than two-thirds. The party thus lost 4.6 points here. The shift in support for the FTA accounted directly for just under half the total Conservative period-2-to-period-3 drop: –6.3 –0.2 + 1.7= –4.8 points, as compared with a total Conservative drop of –10.6 points. The rest came from the party's declining ability to recruit in the neutral and opposed categories.[19]

To account for the Conservative recovery, compare period 3, the party's nadir, with period 5. Imagine now that the Conservatives maintained their period-3 recruitment pattern into period 5. What would the shifts in FTA support and opposition do to their share? FTA support grew by 6.1 points over the interval and at a 77.1 per cent recruitment rate, this growth would have given the Conservatives 4.7 more percentage points of the vote. The neutral category shrank by 4.2 points; at a 41.9 per cent recruitment rate, this would have cost the Conservatives 1.8 points of the total vote. FTA opposition dropped by 2.0 points; at the period-3 recruitment rate of 5.0 per cent, this drop in the anti-FTA share would have cost the Conservatives 0.1 per cent of the vote. Shifts in the FTA margin alone, then, would have accounted for only 2.8 (+ 4.7 –1.8 –0.1) points of the total period-3-to-period-5 gain of 10.3 points.

The other 7.4 points came from dramatic increases in the party's ability to squeeze support from each FTA category. From FTA opponents, the party was able to attract 7.6 per cent, in contrast with a period-3 rate of only 4.8 per cent. The increase in this recruitment rate was only slightly offset by shrinkage of the corresponding base and thus by this particular route the Conservatives pulled to themselves 1.2 per cent more of the total body of committed respondents. In the neutral category, instead of a 1.8-point loss from the category's shrinkage, growth in Conservative recruitment produced a null shift.

The biggest Conservative gains came within the party's natural base, supporters of the FTA. Over the first four periods, the Conservatives were markedly less efficient than the combined efforts of Liberals and New Democrats at tapping into their core. The Combined Liberal–NDP recruitment rate hovered around 80 per cent before the debate, shot up close to 90 per cent in period 3 and stayed there right to the end. The Conservatives, in contrast, started off by pulling in only two-thirds of FTA supporters. The percentage crawled up period by period but in period 3 was still lower than the combined Liberal–NDP rate had been two periods before. By period 5, however, the Conservative rate was virtually equal to the Liberal–NDP one. At the end, pro-FTA Conservatives constituted 37.4 per cent of committed respondents where they had been only 27.9 per cent of the total in period 3. Thus 9.5 points of the total Conservative gain came from a combination of growth in the pro-FTA base and increased efficiency in tapping that base. Of this 9.5 per cent total, 4.7 points came from pro-FTA share growth (see the calculations in the previous paragraph) and 4.8 points, from the efficiency gain.[20]

Now turn to the Liberals and New Democrats. From period 2 to period 3, both the anti-FTA share and the joint Liberal–NDP efficiency in tapping that share went up. Had the transition rates not shifted, the two parties together would have gained 6.9 points from the surge in the anti-FTA share, lost 0.2 points from the shrinkage (such as it was) in the neutral share, and most 2.0 points from the shrinkage of the pro-FTA share, for a net gain of 4.7 points. Instead, of course, the two parties became rather more efficient at tapping the anti-FTA and neutral pools and only slightly less efficient on the pro-FTA side. The total gain over the period thus was 9.9. Of this, the real beneficiary was the Liberal party. The NDP roughly held its own from period 2 to period 3. The Liberals, however, increased their catch dramatically among both opponents and neutrals.

From period 3 to period 5, the Liberals roughly held their own, while NDP support wasted. By itself, the small drop in the percentage opposed to the FTA robbed the combined Liberal–NDP camp of 1.8 points. Thanks to a small increase in recruitment, the two parties actually contained the loss to 1.6 points. The depletion of the neutral share would have robbed the Liberals and NDP of a further 2.3 points had they continued to tap this pool at the period-3 rate. But as the neutral share dropped, so did Liberal and NDP recruitment in the neutral group also drop. The combination of these factors took 4.4 points off the Liberal–NDP total share. Had the two parties continued to recruit pro-FTA voters at the period-3 rate, the growth in the pro-FTA share would actually have netted them 1.2 per cent more of the total vote. But their joint recruitment in this group was cut in half and so 2.4 more points were shaved from the Liberal–NDP total. Of the total ground lost by Liberals and New Democrats from period 3 to period 5, less than one-half, 3.0 of a total 8.3 points, was attributable to simple shifts in the FTA margin. Most critical was the parties' diminished ability to tap the neutral and the pro-FTA groups.

Virtually all of this loss was incurred by the NDP. A 1.6:1 edge for the Liberals among opponents of the FTA grew to 2.1:1. The corresponding edge among neutrals grew from about 2:1 to 2.7:1. Among supporters of the FTA, the figures were 1.1:1 and 2.3:1. The Liberal party's shares among FTA supporters and neutrals shrank in absolute terms but this shrinkage was partly offset by a consolidation of FTA opponents in the Liberal camp.

Clearly, shifts in support for the FTA do not afford a full accounting for the dynamics of the campaign. This is especially so for the Conservative recovery. If pro-free trade sentiment had grown from period 3 to period 5 but nothing else had happened, the Conservatives would have made a modest recovery. By our reckoning, their share of total party commitments would have been just over 40 per cent, not quite enough for a parliamentary majority.[21] And by failing to control factors related to FTA opinion we have almost certainly exaggerated its significance in the overall scheme of things. Most of the Conservative recovery came from factors separate from (even if related to) the FTA. What were these factors?

TOWARD A FULL ACCOUNT

The campaign of 1988 was not a referendum, after all, but an election. Its most immediate entailment, at least should a one-party majority emerge, would be the identity of the government. As the end of the campaign approached, Conservative rhetoric increasingly seemed to emphasise this fact. *Leadership*, in the sense of fitness to lead a government, thus is a fruitful theme to examine.

The 1988 election saw the publication of a record number of polls.[22] As the number of published polls grew, so did concern over the possibility of an electoral *bandwagon*. Aside from hand-wringing about the general susceptibility of Canadians to the contentless appeal of frontrunners, there was a specific interest in Quebec. One piece of Canadian political folklore has it that Quebec always goes with the winner.[23] This time the winner's identity may have shifted and then shifted back.

Finally, opponents of the FTA faced a *strategic* dilemma: which of the two parties in opposition provided the locally most effective instrument for blocking the agreement? Was the psychological cost of second-choice voting worth paying?

In the rest of this section, we review each of these arguments a little further, discuss measures appropriate to each, and conclude with our general estimation strategy. In the next section will appear the actual estimations.

LEADERSHIP

Canadian elections have commonly been typed as referenda on leadership. Such an emphasis fits the domination of parliament by the executive, a domination which predates the party system[24] and which, indeed, the party system evolved to accommodate. As Siegfried put it in 1906:

... it is of the first importance to the success of a party that it should by someone who inspires confidence, and whose name is a programme in itself. ... in accordance with the Anglo-Saxon [*sic*] habit, the Canadians attach themselves rather to the concrete reality than to the abstract principle. They vote as much for the man who symbolizes the policy as for the policy itself.[25]

The emphasis continues into recent analyses. Electability is clearly important to delegates at Liberal and Conservative leadership conventions.[26] Voters themselves evidently validate the delegates' criterion.[27] Of course, our own analyses, above, of the impact of Mr. Mulroney's name on FTA support are consistent with this emphasis. The wording experiment embodied the belief—in keeping with Siegfried—that it matters how the FTA is presented: as an abstract principle or as symbolized by Mr. Mulroney.

In the campaign itself, much of the rhetoric turned on facets of party leaders. This may have been especially true of Liberal and Conservative leaders, but even the NDP encouraged citizens to vote not so much for the party as for Ed Broadbent. What was important about leaders?

Leadership as such seemed to be one critical factor. Here the leader with the biggest problem was obviously John Turner. Voters were encouraged to ask themselves if someone who could not run his own party should be entrusted with the running of the government. More to the immediate point, questions could be raised about Mr. Turner's ability to lead an anti-Free Trade coalition. Mr. Turner's *ability* to lead the anti-FTA fight also carried implications for his *motives* in the fight: could he be *trusted* to carry it on? Could he even be trusted as an interpreter of the agreement? Were his negative judgements on the content of the agreement the sincere product of a careful, balanced reading, or were they just a tactically motivated gambit to stake out a clear location for the Liberal party, a gambit which would, not incidentally, reinforce his own shaky position within the party? The Conservatives' late-campaign "streeter"[28] question captured both the leadership and the trust facets of Mr. Turner's problem brilliantly: "He's out to save *his* job, not mine."

But trust was dangerous ground for the Conservatives. If Mr. Turner's credibility as an interpreter of the Agreement was suspect, so was Mr. Mulroney's credibility as a negotiator, at least in early campaign, as our experiment suggested. Conservatives were well advised not just to attack Mr. Turner's trustworthiness but to shore up that of Mr. Mulroney as well.

Table 6 summarises the course of leader evaluations over the campaign. Entries are mean feeling thermometer ratings.[29] The table suggests what many observers believed: that a big problem for the Liberal party was its leader. Before the debates, Mr. Turner trailed Mr. Mulroney by 6 to 10 "degrees." He was even further behind Mr. Broadbent. The campaign affected Mulroney and Broadbent ratings hardly at all. There is a hint of mid-campaign decay and late campaign recovery for Mr. Mulroney. The mid-campaign rating hardly differs from that in early October, however, and is less than two standard errors below the grand mean.

TABLE 6   *PERIOD VARIATION IN THERMOMETER RATINGS*

	4–14 October	15–25 October	26 Oct.– 6 Nov.	7–13 November	14–20 November
Mulroney	50.0 (494)	53.4 (665)	49.9 (771)	51.8 (407)	53.3 (441)
Turner	44.0 (494)	44.4 (665)	51.0 (769)	50.1 (408)	48.5 (443)
Broadbent	53.1 (494)	54.2 (665)	53.2 (771)	51.4 (409)	52.7 (442)

Entries are Period Mean Ratings.

The pattern for Mr. Turner, in contrast, is very clear. He gained no ground over October.[30] After the debate he moved up into the same range as his competitors. Indeed, he may even have outrated Mr. Mulroney. He then proceeded to dissipate something like one-third of his gains. By campaign's end, he was clearly back in third place among leaders, although not as distant a third as before.[31]

THE POSSIBILITY OF A BANDWAGON

We framed items on parties' perceived national chances. These expectations items were adapted from recent American National Election Studies.[32] The national items were worded:

> Now let's talk about how the election is going for each party. We will be using a scale which runs from 0 to 100, where 0 represents *no* chance for the party, 50 represents *an even chance*, and 100 represents *certain victory*.
>
> (Using the 0 to 100 scale), what do you think the [party name] party's chances are of winning the election *in the whole country?*[33]

Respondents' probability ratings were rescaled to total 100 for the three parties. Many respondents took us at our word and rated two or more parties at 50. The mean total of raw ratings thus exceeded one hundred. The modal three-party totals were 100 and 150. Response was dominated by two groups: those who anchored their response by the 50 rating and those who imposed a 100-point constraint on themselves. Under the circumstances, it seemed unwise not to rescale.[34]

We argue that expectations measured in this way should mediate, among other things, the impact of published polls. One simple way of representing this mediation is as follows:

$$E_{it} = \alpha + \delta_1 P_t + \delta_2 P_{t-1} + \sum \beta_i X_{ijt} + \in_{it}$$

Where

E_{it} is the i-th respondent's expectation for a given party at t;

P_t is the party's share of committed respondents in the most recently published poll;

P_{t-1} is the party's share of committed respondents in the second most recently published poll;

X_{ijt} is any variable which might affect party expectations; and

$\in_{it}$ is the disturbance term, which subsumes all unmeasured variation.

Putting two poll readings in gives the system some memory. Putting more than two in, with twenty-four distinct poll readings, would leave us prey to outliers. Note that t does not measure time linearly as in days, but refers to the period beginning with the day after the most recently published poll and ending with the day of publication of the next poll. Many of the other variables, X, will not vary over time, but opinions on the Free Trade Agreement and leader ratings did, as we have just seen, vary with time and were likely to affect expectations; hence the subscripting of X-variables by time as well as by respondent. The details of the various X_{ijt} are a matter for discussion later.

Consider what the expectations setup implies. The continued dependence of E_{it} on the earlier poll smooths its movements. Response to the latest poll is damped by the continued relevance of its immediate predecessor. And even if the t + 1-th poll brings no further perturbation in the party's share, the expectation will adjust further as the t-th-period datum becomes the lag observation for t + 1. The smoothing spans only two periods as the setup is not lagged in E_i and thus an observation at t does not continue to have an impact at t + k akin to some δ^k. It would have been ideal to let a lagged E value represent respondents' memories, but measures were not, of course, repeated for individuals within the campaign. On the other hand, to the extent that expectations shift votes, the first-round dynamic impact of polls at t and t–1 should be reflected in polls at t + 1. Thus the expectations logic should ultimately spin out to an asymptote larger in absolute value than the first-round displacement.

Ideally, we would enter expectations directly into vote equations and enter the poll readings only in equations with expectations on the left-hand side. Unfortunately, the expectations terms are likely to be contaminated with variance from elsewhere in the system, from unmeasured aspects of leadership, for example. Prudence dictates, for now at least, entering the poll terms directly into vote equations. Even if we do not look at how expectations affect votes we can still estimate the impact of polls on expectations, with the setup above, as error in the expectations variable is not a particularly compelling consideration when the latter is on the left-hand side.

FREE TRADE IN A STRATEGIC CONTEXT

Supporters of the FTA did not face a strategic dilemma. Deviations from the simple imperative to support the Conservatives may have occurred but not in response to local strategic considerations.[35] For Conservative preference, then, all FTA effects are main effects.

Liberals and New Democrats, in contrast, were competing for the same turf. Vote expectations for FTA opponents should be conditioned on some representation of local likelihoods of Liberal and NDP success.[36] To this end, our expectations battery included items about parties' local chances:

> (Using the 0 to 100 scale), what do you think the [party's name] party's chances are of winning *in your riding?*

The local ratings were rescaled according to the same logic as for national ratings. The rescaled items were then multiplied by a dummy variable indicating opposition to the FTA. Support for the FTA was also dummied out; on the support side, of course, no interaction was called for. Direct representation of the two sides seems indicated by the repeated evidence of asymmetry between FTA support and opposition.

In accounting for strategic effects, each anti-FTA party's local expectations should appear in each party's estimation. This is indicated by the rather complicated geography of Canadian party competition. Each of the pairwise possibilities— Liberal v. Conservative, Liberal v. NDP, and Conservative v. NDP—has its set of constituencies, as has the full three-cornered competition. Direct representation of the local ratings seems unavoidable; unlike the case with expectations and un- published polls, we lack external strategic information which is unequivocally predetermined relative to the vote.

ESTIMATION STRATEGY

Although leader ratings and FTA opinion moved through the campaign in ways that we can make sense of, assessing their impact on party choice requires that we control factors which confound individual-level estimations.

Leader ratings, for example, are powerfully affected by party identification. Omission of the latter would lead us to overestimate the independent effect of leader ratings and thus to overplay the electoral implications of the variation in table 6. Estimation of effects from FTA opinion also calls for controls. Left to themselves, the anti-FTA interaction terms which involve local Liberal and NDP expectations would overestimate strategic effects. Places of Liberal strength have dispropor- tionate numbers of Liberal identifiers. The same is true, *mutatis mutandis,* for NDP strongholds.[37] Even on the pro-FTA side, controls make sense. Table 5 indicates a profound issue polarization in the electorate, to be sure. But some of this issue division may have been a consequence as much as a cause of party division. We might even worry about the coefficients on the poll terms.

Accordingly, the coefficients which appear in tables 7 and 8 are extracted from an elaborate estimation in which virtually every plausible geographic, demographic, occupational, and ethnoreligious factor in the data set appears.[38] Identification with each of the three parties was also controlled.[39] The simultaneous estimation of effects of central interest—leader ratings, bandwagon, and FTA support and opposition—also provides mutually necessary controls. The core items all covary longitudinally or cross-sectionally. The omission of any one could lead to the overestimation of impact from the others.

The disadvantage of this setup is that coefficients are constrained not to vary over the campaign. We have already from table 5 a *prima facie* indication that FTA effects widen over the campaign. The same—or the opposite, for that matter— could well be true for leader effects.[40] Nor can we exclude the possibility that impact

TABLE 7 *IMPACT OF FTA OPINION, LEADER RATINGS, AND EXPECTATIONS ON VOTE INTENTIONS, FROM SATURATED LONGITUDINAL ESTIMATION*

	Conservative	Liberal	NDP
Pro-FTA	0.147♦ (0.018)	−0.099♦ (0.019)	−0.047++ (0.017)
Anti-FTA	−0.193♦ (0.018)	0.123++ (0.033)	0.082++ (0.030)
Anti-FTA x Lib Loc Rating	—	0.211♦ (0.054)	−0.220♦ (0.049)
Anti-FTA x NDP Loc Rating	—	−0.353♦ (0.056)	0.315♦ (0.051)
Mulroney Thermometer	0.0036♦ (0.0003)	−0.0018♦ (0.0004)	−0.0018♦ (0.0003)
Turner Thermometer	−0.0024♦ (0.0004)	0.0050♦ (0.0004)	−0.0027♦ (0.0003)
Broadbent Thermometer	−0.0012++ (0.0004)	−0.0026♦ (0.0004)	−0.0039♦ (0.0004)
Poll(t)	0.0014 (0.0016)	0.0022 (0.0015)	0.0015 (0.0021)
Poll (t−1)	0.0001 (0.0018)	0.0024 (0.0015)	0.0038+ (0.0020)
Intercept	0.379♦ (0.084)	0.185♦ (0.055)	0.093 (0.061)
R^2-adj. df	0.625	0.540	0.514

Entries in parentheses are standard errors; (N = 2673).
$^+ p < 0.05$
$^{++} p < 0.01$
$^♦ p < 0.001$ (one-tailed test)

from polls also shifts over the campaign. They may increase in importance as the stakes rise. Or they may become less important as voters acquire more substantive information on which to base their choice.[41] A setup adequate to the full complexity of campaign dynamics must await further research.

FREE TRADE

Here we have drained the blood from the subtleties of the issue. We have forced the issue to have the same effect over the whole campaign, rather as we did above in estimating pure "compositional" shifts from table 5. The coefficients in table 7 represent, in effect, the average FTA-induced cleavage for the campaign as a whole.

TABLE 8   *THE IMPACT OF PUBLISHED POLLS*
ON EXPECTATIONS, FROM SATURATED
LONGITUDINAL ESTIMATION

	Conservative Expectation	Liberal Expectation	NDP Expectation
Poll(t)	0.0029♦ (0.0008)	0.0055♦ (0.0006)	0.0044♦ (0.0009)
Poll(t–1)	0.0037♦ (0.0009)	0.0046♦ (0.0006)	0.0015+ (0.0009)
Intercept	0.236♦ (0.041)	0.007 (0.022)	0.023 (0.027)
R^2-adj. df	0.209	0.268	0.173

Entries in parentheses are standard errors; (N = 2572).
+ $p < 0.05$
++ $p < 0.01$
♦ $p < 0.001$ (one-tailed test)

Moreover, they represent an approximation to the "pure" FTA effect.[42] Factors related to opinion on the FTA are now allowed to have a direct effect on party choice. Some of these factors—region and party identification most notably— are natural complements to FTA opinion. Conflict over the agreement was another phase in the continuing and intensifying argument between the Conservatives, on one hand, and the Liberals and NDP, on the other, over social and economic policy. Thus, to control for such factors is not to suggest that their covariance with FTA opinion indicates that the cleavage in table 5 was somehow fake. It is to suggest, however, that the conflict was not entirely novel. To the extent that our controls siphon off direct impact from FTA opinion they leave as a residue an estimate of just how much the cleavage over the agreement represented a shift in Canadian electoral choice.

For FTA effects, the easiest comparisons involve the Conservative party. Both the pro- and anti-FTA coefficients in the Conservative equation give the difference between the indicated category on the FTA and the neutral category. Where the table 5 differences between the neutral and pro-FTA camps in the percentage Tory vary from 15 to 50 points and average around 30 points, the coefficient from table 7 on the pro-FTA dummy variable indicates a *ceteris paribus* impact of just under 15 points. The anti-FTA/neutral difference, from table 5, in Conservative vote share fluctuated from 30 to 49 points. The average difference was something over 35 points. In table 7, the difference is, once again, cut by half.

Accounting for shifts on the Liberal and NDP side is more complex. For dynamic estimates, we shall look only at the pro-FTA side. Table 5 suggests that the anti-FTA/neutral cleavage in Liberal choice varied from 9 to 33 points and averaged around 20 points. Again, table 7 suggests that this estimate should be cut in half. The same thing happens to the NDP difference. In table 5 this fluctuates from 4 to 14 points and averages about 9.5 points. The table 7 estimate is under 5 points.

By this accounting, the impact of FTA opinion movement on party shares as calculated from the bivariate arrays of table 5 was overestimated, on average, by a factor of about two. For instance, if we apply the coefficients from table 7 to the FTA marginals in table 5, we estimate that shifts in the latter accounted for 3.0 points of the Conservative party's period 2-period 3 drop and 1.3 points of the period 3-period 5 recovery. This only confirms the point which we extracted from that table, however: movement in FTA opinion was only one factor—and a far from determinative one at that—in the flow of the vote.

The other story about FTA opinion is the conditionality of party choice among FTA opponents. Averaged over the campaign the likelihood of supporting each anti-FTA party was affected by both parties' perceived local chances. The impact of local expectations for the NDP was especially great. Having established a strategic effect, how much should we make of it? The strategic choices here largely replicated the historic pattern of Liberal and NDP support: Liberal shares increased as one moved eastward and NDP shares increased as one moved to the west, roughly speaking (although the coefficients are orthogonal to province of residence, given the controls). The historic pattern itself may be the product of strategic choices. But whether the 1988 polarization increased the strategic component in election returns is a question for further analysis.[43]

LEADERS

Ratings of each leader played a significant role in choice of each party. Not surprisingly, for any given party's estimation, the party's own leader played the biggest role. But Mr. Turner played the biggest role overall. This was true in two ways. His average coefficient was larger than for either of the other leaders. Thus, quite apart from dynamics over the campaign, Mr. Turner was the most important independent, personal factor in party choice. On balance, this was unfortunate for his party. But we also recall from table 6 that Mr. Turner was the only leader whose standing was affected discernibly by the campaign. Translating from table 6, the 5.6 degree rise in Mr. Turner's personal standing from period 2 to period 3 accounted for 2.8 points of the total 8.9-point Liberal gain. By the same reasoning, the decline in Mr. Turner's rating accounted for 1.25 points of the party's 1.6 point slippage from period 3 to period 5.

BANDWAGON

Estimations for the direct impact of polls on preference are shaky but suggestive. The easiest conclusion to reach is for the Conservatives: we have no reason to believe that at any point their share was affected by prior published polls.

At the other end are the NDP. Their share did indeed respond to a poll, the second most recent one. Table 7 suggests that a one point jump in the NDP standing in a published poll will, after another poll has intervened, induce almost four-tenths of a point gain in the NDP share of the electorate at large. Of course, this logic also works on the down side. Arguably, some of the NDP's slide in late campaign was dynamically induced. Alternatively, the NDP's strength in early campaign may have reflected not so much the party's intrinsic appeal as its apparently favourable strategic position.

The Liberals present a more difficult case. Neither poll coefficient is significantly different from zero, although the effect of the latest poll just fails to clear the threshold. Collinearity could be part of the reason for this weakness, as of all poll pairings the Liberal one is the most highly correlated.[44] If one looks at the impact of poll readings one at a time, each Liberal reading has a significant impact: for each the β is 0.0038 with a standard error of 0.0011.[45] However we get to it, the conclusion does seem to be that the Liberals, like the NDP, were susceptible to dynamic effects from polls. As with the NDP, a unit shift in Liberal standing in published polls seems to be worth about four-tenths of a point shift in the subsequent Liberal share.[46]

Published polls are not just a passive record of the event. But did they produce a bandwagon? The answer seems to be yes, but it stalled. Before the debates, Liberal poll readings fluctuated in the upper 20s, sometimes just ahead of the NDP, sometimes just behind. On the morrow of the debates, the last poll reading gave the Liberals 28 per cent of committed response. The second-to-last poll gave them 25 per cent. The first reading after the debate had the Liberals at 37 points. If we take our two-poll estimation at face value, this shift ought to have netted the Liberals a further 2.7 percentage points.[47] Subsequent poll readings fluctuated considerably. Although the cumulative impact would have been to the considerable benefit of the Liberals, the marginal effect of published polls seemed to have been exhausted by 6 November.

Then came the Gallup poll of 7 November. This poll gave the Liberals 43 per cent of committed respondents, 6 points more than the immediately preceding poll. The second-most recent poll was, in turn, 3 points below its immediate predecessor. By our two-poll reckoning, the perceptual shifts of 7 November ought to have been worth a further 0.6 points, as the positive impact of the 7 November poll was offset by the negative impact of the one before. Within days, however, new readings came in. These placed the Liberals back in the high 30s, roughly level pegging with the Conservatives. Most of the impact from the 7 November poll ought to have been erased within a week.[48]

In the end, countless dynamics could take the Liberals only so far. Even though Liberal poll standings rose through early November and held until the last week, the forces which initiated their surge were playing out. Support for the FTA was going up and Mr. Turner's rehabilitation had stalled and then reversed.

FURTHER OBSERVATIONS ON EXPECTATIONS

Do the published polls drive expectations? The answer, from table 8, seems to be yes. Current expectations for each party are fed by standing from at least the two most recent polls. For Liberal and Conservative expectations, the power of the second most recent poll is very impressive.

A percentage point gain in the Liberal party's published poll standing translates into the equivalent of a 0.55 point gain in expectations. The impact from the second most recent poll is almost as large.[49] The cumulative impact for the other parties is not as large as for the Liberals, but the effect is still impressive.[50]

TABLE 9   *PERIOD VARIATION IN EXPECTATIONS*

	4–14 October	15–25 October	26 Oct.– 6 Nov.	7–13 November	14–20 November
Cons	0.468 (494)	0.509 (665)	0.453 (770)	0.417 (408)	0.431 (437)
Liberal	0.295 (493)	0.265 (665)	0.355 (770)	0.406 (407)	0.389 (437)
NDP	0.225 (494)	0.217 (665)	0.182 (770)	0.163 (408)	0.156 (437)

Entries are Period Mean National Probability Ratings.

To get a sense of how ratings moved consult table 9. Ratings move with events, but, reassuringly, with a discernible lag. The Conservatives, for instance, began with a big margin over both other parties. The Liberals' opening margin over the NDP was less than half as large as the Conservatives' margin over the Liberals. The Conservative lead widened in period 2, sensibly so in light of the unanimity of early poll evidence. The perceptual ground began to shift in period 3. Expectations for both the Conservatives and the NDP slipped. Liberal gains at the expense of both other parties put the Liberals much closer to the Tories than before and much closer to the Tories than to the NDP. Period 4 brought a reinforcement of the immediate post-debate shifts. Expectations for the Liberals were almost as high as for the Conservatives at this point. The last week saw some regression to earlier patterns. The final shift was modest but did put the Conservatives clearly in front.

To get a sense of the lag in respondents' expectations, compare movement in expectations with movement in vote intentions, from table 1. The Liberal peak and Conservative trough in expectations arrived *after* the corresponding points in vote intentions. Voters evidently needed time to digest the dynamically relevant information. It should also be noted that the Liberal peak and Conservative trough came in the week which began with the Gallup poll which showed the biggest Liberal lead of the campaign.[51]

The modest reversal of direction in the last week was consistent with the small widening of the Conservative lead that our data record for the preceding week and with the chorus of published polls contradicting the Gallup result. The modesty of the expectations reversal was *not* in accord with the final week's underlying reality, the Conservative surge.

CONCLUSIONS

The campaign moved opinion on the core issue, the Free Trade Agreement, in dramatic ways. The early campaign unleashed latent fears, most pointedly, our experiments suggest, about the negotiator and about the integrity of Canada's social programs. The recovery in FTA support was more modest than the fall which preceded it. The basis of the recovery remains elusive, but our first cut at the evidence points to a possible rehabilitation of the Prime Minister.

In any case, the recovery in FTA support explained only a fraction of the total Conservative recovery. More important was the Conservatives' sharply increased ability to squeeze support out of all camps, but especially to rally their natural base, FTA supporters. Only in the last week did the party finally recruit votes from that base at a rate comparable to Liberal and NDP recruitment from their own base. The Conservatives' biggest barrier in mid-to-late campaign may have been psychological: for a brief span they came close to losing the expectations game and in doing so may have fallen victim to a Liberal bandwagon. If there was such a bandwagon, however, it stalled.

Part of the Liberal failure reflected a leadership gap which they could not, in the end, close. Mr. Turner closed the gap after the debates but fell back even as Mr. Mulroney recovered. Why specifically Mr. Turner fell back we cannot yet say.

Indeed, we have hardly begun to unpack the campaign. For most purposes, we have confined ourselves to a crude periodization of events. And among factors external to our survey we have examined only polls. The volume and content of advertising and media coverage remain to be explored as does the individual-level flow of pre-election vote intentions to election-day behaviour.

NOTES

1. A fresh sample was released each day. The release was large enough to yield about 80 ultimate completions. The bulk of the completions were recorded within three days of release but numbers were kept open for two weeks and for as many as 15 callbacks (a few completions took even more callbacks than this). The first few fieldwork days saw fewer than 80 completions, as the system warmed up. By about day 4 (7 October) the daily pattern was set: 40–50 completions from that day's release, 10–20 from the previous day's sample, 5–10 from two days before, and scattered completions from a range of earlier releases. As the end of campaign approached, the clearance period for new daily samples shortened and thus the response rate tailed off. The impact of this was small until the last two days, however.

2. The suddenness of the shift is not just an artifact of the way in which our data are partitioned. The daily record indicates a shift clearly visible within 48–72 hours of the English debate.

3. Although the Conservatives do better than the NDP, worse in our tracking and the late surge to the Conservatives is more dramatic than in published polls, the path of preferences in the data as we report them corresponds roughly to that in published polls. But the path of party shares over the campaign can be made to look quite different.

Our reading of vote intention combines response to two items, an initial query about vote intention and a probe for leaners. Something like this seems to be the norm in commercial polls. If leaners are excluded, the Conservative recovery looks more rapid than table 1 suggests. On a daily tracking, the Conservatives appear to have made all their postdebate gain by about 11 November. No last minute surge appears. How the time path of Conservative recovery is characterised will be critical to more sophisticated analyses in later papers. It will be especially critical to analyses of strategic voting and of bandwagons. To the analyses here, the choice of measurement does not seem so critical.

4. Table 2 combines response to two versions of the FTA support/opposition item. Respondents were assigned at random to one or the other version of the item, on which see table 3 and the accompanying discussion.

5. This drop is calculated from a daily tracking and thus is not represented in table 2 directly.

6. The daily tracking brings this out more clearly than does table 2, which indicates a statistically insignificant difference between the last two weeks.

7. Howard Schuman and Stanley Presser, *Questions and Answers in Attitude Surveys: Experiments in Question Form, Wording and Content* (New York: Academic Press, 1981) and John Zaller "Toward a Theory of the Survey Response" (Paper presented to the American Political Science Association 1984 Annual Meeting, Washington, DC). As Zaller puts it: "question wording changes which introduce new ideas, stimulate memory, or otherwise alter the context in which an issue is viewed often influence survey responses. Question wording changes which cannot plausibly be argued to have done any of these things less often affect survey responses" (p. 23).

8. As table 3 indicates, however, only the support-side difference was significant.

9. Sovereignty was also raised in relation to Canadian culture, but the cultural sovereignty argument did not strike us as having as much mass-public bite as did arguments about economic or social policy.

10. Later in the campaign, a theme emerged which we had not anticipated correctly: a concern over access to a large market. The usual form of the argument went: but for the FTA, Canada would be the only industrialized country without guaranteed access to a market of 100 million or more. In its substance, this argument overlaps the "American protectionism" challenge which we did pose. But the emphasis in the large-market argument seems structural, on an abiding characteristic of the market for Canadian products. Rhetorical emphasis on the American protectionism seemed more in terms of active harassment, under countervail proceedings, which could go on irrespective of the tariff level. Recall that the FTA both lowered US tariff levels and set in place a dispute resolution system. In our post-election survey, we have framed an item in terms of market size.

11. The challenges to supporters were:
    i) Some people say that under this agreement Canada will lose its ability to control key sectors of the economy, such as energy.

    ii) Some people say that this agreement will make it very hard for us to maintain our social programs, such as medicare.

    iii) Some people say that under this agreement many Canadians will lose their jobs, in industries such as textiles, automobiles, and services.

    The challenges to opponents were:

    i) Some people say that this agreement will defend us against *American* protectionism, such as happened in the softwood lumber dispute.

    ii) Some people say that this agreement will lower the cost of many of the goods that Canadian families need.

    After the challenge the respondent was asked:

    Does this make you *less supportive* of (*opposed* to) the agreement, or does it make *no difference* to how you feel?

12. Zaller, "Toward a Theory of the Survey Response."

13. Reassuringly, respondents who claimed that the challenge's consideration might make them reconsider were more likely to report a pre-post election change than were respondents who said that the challenge would make no difference.

14. This interpretation still requires substantiation. It sits rather awkwardly with the exact time path decay in challenges' effectiveness: anti-FTA challenges declined in impact only after the debates even though the slide in FTA support began before the debates.

15. One hint comes out of preliminary work with the post-election wave, however. We recast the challenges as agree–disagree items about the FTA and asked all

respondents about them. After the campaign, the social programs item evoked the *lowest* level of agreement. The item which evoked the highest level of agreement was the one, mentioned above, which referred to the size of the North American market.

16. The arithmetic of this sentence and the one before are similar. In periods 1 and 2, FTA opponents were 2 to 3 times more likely than supporters not to express a party preference. From period 1 to period 2 the ratio of FTA opponents to supporters among uncommitted voters rose from just under 2:1 to just under 3:1. The ratios in this and the next footnote are calculated from data not reported in a table.

17. In periods 3, 4, and 5, FTA opponents were only slightly more likely than supporters to avoid party commitment: opponent:supporter ratios among nonpartisans hovered around 6:5.

18. That is:
72.7% × 36.2 − 72.7% × 44.8 = −6.3.

19. Of course, the total drop of 10.6 points is smaller than it would otherwise have been because of the party's increased efficiency in tapping the pro-FTA pool.

20. By efficiency we mean nothing more than the size of a transition rate in the table. We do not mean to suggest that the Conservative campaign, as an organisation or strategic phenomenon, was less efficient than the other party's campaigns. No doubt, one reason the combined Liberal–NDP rate was higher than the Conservative rate was the simple fact that the number of parties in question was two, not one. If an FTA opponent could not stomach one party, he or she could support the other. That the Conservatives finally were able to tap their base nearly as fully as Liberals and New Democrats did theirs is testimony to the power of the Conservative campaign. Nothing has been said yet about the strategic wastage of Liberal and NDP votes in competition with each other.

21. Not enough, that is, according to seat–vote relationships estimated from official returns from 1935 to 1984 inclusive. Moreover, the 40 per cent

level is probably an overestimate, given our general propensity to overstate the Conservative share.

22. Alan Frizzell, "The Perils of Polling," in *The Canadian General Election of 1988* ed. Alan Frizzell, Jon H. Pammett, and Anthony Westell (Ottawa: Carleton University Press, 1989), 95, reports 24 published polls, twice as many as in the 1984 campaign.

23. Another bit of folklore always has Quebec voting for one of its own. These rival claims can be squared with each other, but the issue is quite complex.

24. Gordon T. Stewart, *The Origins of Canadian Politics: A Comparative Approach* (Vancouver: University of British Columbia Press, 1986).

25. André Siegfried, *The Race Question in Canada* (Toronto: McClelland and Stewart, 1966; Carleton Library Edition).

26. See, for example, Patrick Martin, Allan Gregg, and George Perlin, *Contenders: The Tory Quest for Power* (Scarborough, Ont: Prentice-Hall, 1983) and George Perlin, ed., *Party Democracy in Canada: The Politics of National Party Conventions* (Scarborough, Ont: Prentice-Hall, 1988).

27. On which see Harold Clarke, Jane Jenson, Lawrence LeDuc, and Jon Pammett, *Political Choice in Canada* (Toronto: McGraw Hill-Ryerson, 1979) and *Absent Mandate: The Politics of Discontent in Canada* (Toronto: Gage, 1984).

28. Strictly speaking it would be more correct to refer to the advertisement in question as an "alleged streeter." See Hugh Winsor, "Last ad blitz costing PCs $2 million," *Globe and Mail* (16 November 1988), A1.

29. The preamble for the thermometer items was:

Now let's talk about your feelings towards the political parties, their leaders and their candidates. I'll read a name and ask you to rate a person or a party on a thermometer that runs from 0 to 100 degrees. Ratings between 50 and 100 degrees mean that you feel favourable toward that person. Ratings between 0 and 50 degrees mean that you feel unfavourable toward that person. You may use any number from 0 to 100 to tell me how you feel.

The order in which thermometers were presented was randomized. Those unable to rate leaders were placed at 50.

30. The late-October reading spans the period of the—real or imagined—aborted coup by his own advisors. For one account of the event, see Gerald Caplan, Michael Kirby, and Hugh Segal, *Election: The Issues, the Strategy, the Aftermath* (Scarborough: Prentice-Hall, 1988), chap. 9.

31. A similar story emerges from a battery of leader traits which we adapted from recent American National Election Studies. For an example of the dynamics of traits in primary elections, see Henry E. Brady and Richard Johnston "What's the Primary Message: Horse Race or Issue Journalism?" in *Media and Momentum: The New Hampshire Primary and Nomination Politics* ed. Gary R. Orren and Nelson W. Polsby (Chatham, NJ: Chatham House, 1987). For their original rationale, see Donald R. Kinder, *Presidential Traits* (Ann Arbor, Mich.: Pilot Study for the 1984 NES Planning Committee and the NES Board of Overseers, 1983). The battery had to be adapted to Canadian conditions, specifically to the need for French–English parallels.

Trait ratings for Messrs. Mulroney and Broadbent were relatively insensitive to the course of the campaign. Mr. Mulroney's ratings as "trustworthy" troughed right after the debates, however. And Mr. Broadbent's ratings for providing leadership and as a "man of vision" decayed after the debates. For neither man did the slippage amount to much, however. Mr. Turner's ratings on every trait peaked in the period right after the debate. We had hoped to see a focussed peaking on his leadership traits, but such was not the case. Although respondents are perfectly capable of providing ratings differentiated by trait, the dynamics of trait

ratings, at least for Mr. Turner, were quite undifferentiated. For this reason, we have decided simply to employ the summary thermometer evaluation.

32. For analyses with the American items see Larry M. Bartels, *Presidential Primaries and the Dynamics of Public Choice* (Princeton, NJ: Princeton University Press, 1988) and Brady and Johnston, "What's the Primary Message."

33. The battery also includes local-expectations items. Within the battery, item locations were varied randomly with respect to both local/national orientation and party.

34. A case could be made to anchor the scales directly at 0.33, rather than at 0.50, by dividing raw response (in integers) by 100 and taking the quotient to the appropriate power. Response could then be further rescaled to bring the totals to unity. This was the strategy in Bartels, *Presidential Primaries*, and may yet become ours. Our simpler rescaling has much the same effect and will suffice for now. Respondents unable to assign a probability were given a value of 0.33.

35. At least not to strategic considerations that we could measure. Our focus in designing the survey was on the three-party battle. The Conservatives were vulnerable, it seems, to third-party competition, from the Reform Party in the West and the Christian Heritage Party in a number of regions. Anecdotal evidence suggests that a strategic logic governed some of the third-party response, especially by potential supporters of the Reform party. The latter were susceptible, it is claimed, to arguments that even in Alberta the Conservatives needed Reformers' votes to save the FTA. Interestingly, once the Conservative majority had been secured, voters in Beaver River, a northeastern Alberta riding, felt licenced to return a Reformer in an early by-election.

36. On the general logic of which see Jerome H. Black, "The Multicandidate Calculus of Voting: Application to Canadian Elections," *Canadian Journal of Political Science* 22 (1978): 609–38.

37. As a reflection of this local variation, party identifier groups differed even more over local expectations than over national ones.

38. For a preliminary discussion of the variables, see Richard Johnston, André Blais, Henry Brady, and Jean Crête, "Free Trade in the 1988 Canadian General Election" (Paper prepared for delivery at the PIPES seminar, University of Chicago, 12 April 1989).

39. The need to control party identification demands comment. The 1988 Canadian survey uses a subtly different item from earlier ones. The new item is conceptually closer to the American original than the old one was. On the logic of the change see Richard Johnston, "The Equivalence of Party Identification Measures: A National Survey Experiment" (Paper prepared for delivery at the American Political Science Association 1988 Annual Meeting, Washington, DC).

Over the campaign the distribution of party identifications shifted not at all. This was so even though vote intentions moved around dramatically. Outside Quebec, Conservative identifiers outnumbered Liberal identifiers about 6 to 5. In Quebec Liberals outnumbered Conservatives 3 to 2. Identifiers, as indicated by response to the first identification item (that is, not including leaners), were about 65 per cent of the non-Quebec sample (about the same percentage as in the USA) and just over 50 per cent of the Quebec sample.

40. Indeed, in estimations not reported here we found effects from ratings of Mr. Broadbent to diminish in impact as his party fell out of contention.

41. The latter relationship dominates choice in primary elections, according to Bartels, *Presidential Primaries*, and Brady and Johnston, "What's the Primary Message." Canadian general elections are more intense from the beginning than are primaries, and the leading players tend to be better known.

42. On the logic of this approximation see Carol A. Cassel and Robert C. Luskin, "Simple Explanations of Turnout Decline," *American Political Science Review* 82 (1988): 1321–30.

43. The parties themselves breathed not a word about strategic accommodation. Neither party saw strategic voting as consistent with its long-term party-building interests.

44. The correlation for Liberal poll readings is 0.654, not in itself all that high, while for the NDP the correlation is 0.521. The correlation for the Conservative readings is only 0.375.

45. Separate estimation for the NDP also yields significant coefficients in each case. For the most recent poll reading β is 0.0036 with a standard error of 0.0018. For the second most recent poll reading, β is 0.0045 with a standard error of 0.0017.

46. If nothing else changes and thus the initial impetus behind that unit change is sustained, the single-period lag coefficient of 0.38 would generate a cumulative impact of 0.61 ($\delta/1- \delta$) points as later polls register and retransmit the first-round impact.

47. The increment in Liberal share at the most recent poll was 9 points (37 v. 28). The increment in the second most recent poll was 3 points (28 v. 25). The calculations thus are: $(9)(0.22) + (3)(0.23) = 2.7$. The impact from the one-poll estimation mentioned in the body of the text would have been larger: 3.4 points.

48. Impact from the single-poll estimation would have been much larger, 2.3 points, but would have been erased the moment the next poll was published.

49. We did estimate a coefficient for the impact of expectations on the vote, notwithstanding our methodological ruminations in the text. The coefficient in the Liberal equation was 0.37. Combining this coefficient with those in table 8 suggests that a unit shift in poll standing is worth a 0.2 unit shift in subsequent party share. Now if that unit shift stands up in the next poll but no further shift occurs, another 0.17 points (0.46)(0.370) will be added to the Liberal share. The cumulative impact of that unit increment in poll share would thus be 0.37 points, far from trivial. This is uncannily close to the estimate from table 7.

50. If we repeat the exercise in the previous footnote for the NDP and Conservatives, the results are less satisfying. The directly estimated impact of polls from table 7 is rather larger than that coming out of an equation with expectations on the right-hand side in the case of the NDP. The reverse is true for the Conservatives: no impact from table 7 and an impact from the two-stage estimation almost as large as that for the Liberals.

51. See the discussion above. This poll gave the Liberals, as we have noted, 43 per cent of committed respondents and the Conservatives only 31 per cent. Gallup projected a Liberal majority at this point. By all accounts, the immediate impact on Tory campaign workers, particularly in Quebec was devastating (in contrast with the apparent lack of effect on their own share in the electorate at large, at least from our estimation in table 7). Conservative strategists seriously contemplated publishing their own polls, but decided to await events. See Caplan et al., *Election*, 187ff.

section 6

VOTING AND GENDER

---

o

DOES GENDER MAKE A DIFFERENCE
IN VOTING BEHAVIOUR?

PETER WEARING
JOSEPH WEARING

ɔ

It is difficult to know why this question has received so little attention in Canadian voting studies, which have preferred to till the unfertile fields of class cleavage or to explicate the religious cleavages that are relics of a bygone era. Differences between men and women are both obvious and eternal. Moreover, issues of particular interest to women—such as abortion, equal pay for work of equal value, and daycare—are now important items on the political agenda. Recently there has been a good deal of popular speculation about whether the parties and their leaders have had differing degrees of success in appealing to female voters. Is there a "gender gap" between men's and women's support for the major parties? Do women assess politics differently from men? Are women's positions on issues different from men's? Can women harness their political power in order to extract concessions from government as other interest groups do? If the answers to these questions are "yes," then their political pressure could be very formidable indeed. But if, on the other hand, women are not yet a voting bloc, can they be organised as one?[1] If such a feminist strategy were successful, would it risk producing a counteraction from politically aware men? We cannot hope to answer all these questions within this short article, but we hope at least to provide an initial investigation of the territory.

Historically, women in western democracies—after being enfranchised earlier in this century—voted for conservative parties in larger proportions than men. The difference was not large and was probably related to other factors such as age and religion. Older people and regular church-goers also tend to be more conservative. Since women live longer than men and attend church more frequently, their conservatism may have been related as much to these other social factors as to gender. A particularly striking example is the Italian Christian Democratic party, whose electorate was 60 per cent female, while the other major Italian parties were

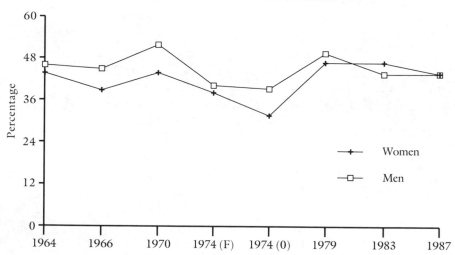

Conservative Vote in British Elections

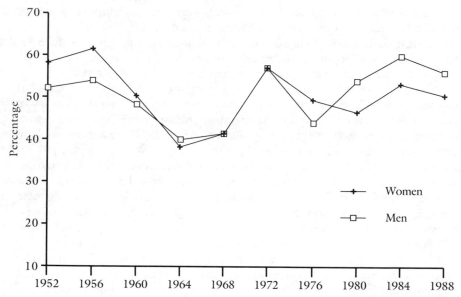

Republican Vote in Presidential Elections

FIGURE 1 *"CONSERVATIVE" VOTE BY SEX, USA AND BRITAIN*

Source: Adapted from Pippa Norris, "The Gender Gap in Britain and America," *Parliamentary Affairs* 38 (1985): 192–201.

TABLE 1   *MEN'S AND WOMEN'S*
          PARTY VOTES, 1974-88

	Male	Female
1974		
Liberal	48.0	56.8
PC	33.2	28.3
NDP	13.4	9.6
1979		
Liberal	38.2	46.0
PC	43.9	34.6
NDP	14.3	14.0
1980		
Liberal	43.0	52.1
PC	40.6	28.8
NDP	15.4	17.0
1984		
Liberal	23.3	26.7
PC	58.9	55.8
NDP	15.3	15.3
1988		
Liberal	22.4	29.0
PC	46.2	38.6
NDP	16.7	17.7

Source: National Election Studies, 1974–79–80, 1984, 1988.
Columns do not total 100 due to exclusion of other parties,
refused, and don't knows.

TABLE 2   *PARTY VOTE BY RELIGION AND BY SEX*

	Protestant		Catholic		Other		None	
	Male	Female	Male	Female	Male	Female	Male	Female
1984	(534)	(572)	(582)	(624)	(53)	(27)	(151)	(93)
Liberal	17.2	19.0	31.8	34.8	25.5	34.9	11.3	17.0
PC	66.2	63.4	53.6	50.8	50.7	35.9	55.9	49.0
NDP	14.1	16.2	11.5	11.9	21.6	23.8	32.1	30.1
1988	(448)	(491)	(572)	(526)	(91)	(55)	(149)	(102)
Liberal	21.6	22.9	25.0	36.0	27.5	29.1	12.2	25.3
PC	43.8	46.0	49.4	34.3	35.2	32.7	49.7	27.2
NDP	17.6	17.6	13.2	14.5	19.8	18.2	26.1	31.9

Source: National Eledction Studies, 1984, 1988.
Columns do not total 100 due to exclusion of other parties, refused, and don't knows.

quite predominantly male. Studies done in the 1970s, however, found that "the most important reason for this high level of female support for the DC was the greater degree of church attendance among women." When church attendance was held constant, the difference between men and women's voting became much smaller.[2] A similar situation existed with respect to German women, who were also more "statist"—they supported whatever party formed the government.[3]

In the last decade or so, however, women in most western democracies have become less inclined to support conservative parties. As shown in figure 1, US women are now less likely to vote Republican than men, and British women have abandoned their age-old allegiance to the Conservative party—ironically when it was headed by a woman.

In Canada, women have supported the Liberal party more enthusiastically than men in all five elections from 1974 to 1988, although the difference was small in 1984 (see table 1). There also seems to be some growing female support for the NDP. It used to do better among the male electorate than among the female,[4] but the party now gets more or less the same support from male and female voters. The NDP, like parties of the left elsewhere, is no longer at a disadvantage in appealing to women voters.

Various avenues can be explored in order to explain the differing responses given by women to the three parties. Is the phenomenon related to another socio-demographic factor, as it was in some European countries? Or do Canadian women have different policy concerns from men? Have activist women begun to mobilize their fellow female voters in accordance with a feminist agenda? We argue that the gender gap is real and cannot be explained away with other socio-demographic factors. While men and women do share many policy concerns, they diverge on several key concerns of present-day politics. It appears, however, that the policy preferences of men—and especially of men with higher education—are the ones making a distinctive contribution to the current political agenda.

Historically, the social characteristic that was most closely linked with party preference was religion. One might have expected that, as in the European examples referred to earlier, religious affiliation might be a surrogate for the gender gap. But table 2 shows that the age-old link between religion and voting is finally beginning to dissipate. Moreover, *within* religious groups, differences between men and women are not great, especially in the two large Protestant and Catholic groups in 1984. In 1988, Protestant men and women divided among the three parties in more or less equal proportion, although Catholic women were more Liberal and Catholic men were more Conservative.

Another possible area of explanation lies in marital status. A study of US women voters found that single women and working women were more Democratic than married women and women not in the work force. In other words, the latter group was not only more conservative, but also more closely aligned with men, who were strongly Republican.[5] Something similar happens in Canada. As table 3 shows, men and women who are or who have been married are much more similar in their voting behaviour than those who have never married. It is never-married females who diverge most sharply from the rest of the population.

In some instances, education is a social factor that can explain a variation in vote among females. Some writers have suggested that, as women gain more access to higher education, their "life experience" will come to resemble men's and so their political views will converge.[6] Data from the 1984 and 1988 elections on voting by level of education and by sex indeed show that men and women with only elementary education diverged greatly: women were more Liberal than men; men

TABLE 3   *PARTY VOTE BY MARITAL STATUS AND SEX*

| | Never Married | | Ever Married | |
	Male	Female	Male	Female
1984	(276)	(219)	(1043)	(1097)
Liberal	30.0	36.5	21.5	24.7
PC	52.3	47.9	60.6	57.4
NDP	14.7	13.5	15.5	15.7
1988	(267)	(222)	(1008)	(996)
Liberal	20.8	42.4	22.9	26.0
PC	46.3	29.1	46.1	40.7
NDP	17.9	21.1	16.4	16.9

Source: see table 2.

were more inclined than women to vote NDP (table 4). The gap narrowed for those with high school education and virtually disappeared for those who had been to a community college. At university level, however, the gap widens—women are more likely to vote Liberal or NDP than men, while men are more Conservative. The most striking differences occurred in 1988. The margin within this group of men over women voting PC was 16 per cent. Women preferred the Liberal party by 11 per cent. The sexes split in an even more startling way when the university-educated are broken down by region. In western Canada, men and women hardly diverged. In Ontario and Quebec, they split sharply with Quebec men more than women favouring the PCs by a 2:1 ratio. In Ontario, the sexes divided into opposing camps: the Liberals received the most votes from women, and the PCs the most from men.

Various explanations can be advanced to account for this unexpected gender gap separating the most highly educated men and women of central Canada.

TABLE 4   *PARTY VOTE BY LEVEL OF EDUCATION AND SEX*

| | Elementary | | High School | | College | | University | |
	Male	Female	Male	Female	Male	Female	Male	Female
1984	(187)	(139)	(531)	(656)	(244)	(246)	(357)	(273)
Liberal	30.5	36.9	22.7	26.3	22.0	23.1	21.3	25.6
PC	52.1	51.6	60.6	56.9	61.7	61.9	57.9	49.9
NDP	16.8	11.2	15.0	14.9	13.0	13.5	16.7	20.2
1988	(99)	(77)	(586)	(563)	(217)	(245)	(367)	(293)
Liberal	20.3	34.7	24.2	25.4	21.5	30.5	20.8	33.5
PC	50.3	42.3	40.9	37.7	43.6	39.9	55.3	38.5
NDP	11.2	7.8	20.8	19.1	16.8	17.2	11.7	17.6

Source: see table 2.

TABLE 5   *REPLIES OF UNIVERSITY-EDUCATED MEN AND WOMEN ON ISSUES RELEVANT TO THE 1988 ELECTION*

Statement	Percentage Agreeing with Statement		
	Males	Females	Net Difference Males/Females
Free Market/Competition:	(327)	(246)	
i General principle	77.9	66.0	+11.9
ii Market set energy price	52.6	31.5	+21.1
iii Let poor farmers go into another line of work	39.9	22.4	+17.5
Ways to Reduce Deficit:			
iv Family allowance to needy	73.6	62.1	+11.5
v Restrict unemployment insurance	70.8	62.0	+8.8
vi Reduce welfare payments	36.9	30.9	+6.0
vii Sell PetroCanada	61.2	52.9	+8.3
viii Sell CNR	58.6	46.6	+12.0
ix Reduce defence budget	59.9	58.1	+1.8
Workers and Management:			
x Important decisions made by management	45.2	29.3	+15.9
xi Wages for unskilled about right for skill required	59.1	42.3	+16.8
xii Working people earn what they deserve	57.2	26.2	+31.0
Civil Liberties/Morality:			
xiii Catholic hospital not required to perform abortions	35.9	30.4	+5.5
xiv Encourage immigration from countries like us	47.5	24.0	+23.5
xv Capital punishment never justified	35.5	36.9	–1.4
xvi Not prevent adults from buying pornography	58.4	32.4	+26.0

Source: National Election Study, 1988.

Perhaps it is because these women come face-to-face with the harsh realities of discrimination as they attempt to establish careers in the male-dominated upper echelons of the business world. As such, they may consciously distinguish themselves from their male counterparts and become, in a sense, "feminized" voters with different attitudes, policy agenda, and voting patterns.

The National Election Studies pose questions about policy and the proper role of government, where women's views can be compared with men's. Studies in other countries show that, while men and women do agree on a wide range of issues, they differ significantly in a number of areas. In the US, women tend to be more "dovish" on foreign policy issues and men more "hawkish"; women support gun control and oppose capital punishment.[7] In Britain, women are more concerned about protecting the environment and getting rid of nuclear weapons.[8]

TABLE 6   *FIRST AND SECOND MOST IMPORTANT*
TASKS OF GOVERNMENT: PERCENTAGE
MENTIONING...

Tasks	All		University Educated	
	Men	Women	Men	Women
	(1653)	(1725)	(410)	(327)
Controlling inflation	39.5	43.2	32.2	36.9
Dealing with provincial governments	8.3	7.0	8.1	9.4
Dealing with the US	4.8	2.6	4.3	2.2
Handling relations with Quebec	4.5	3.3	3.6	2.6
Running the government competently	30.0	28.1	34.8	38.4
Dealing with unemployment	47.0	47.0	44.2	43.4
Providing social welfare measures	6.1	6.0	7.6	7.1
Protecting the environment	4.5	4.1	5.9	4.4
Limiting the size of government	3.9	3.0	5.7	2.8
Dealing with women's issues	1.3	4.8	1.5	4.8
Working for world peace	13.6	21.4	13.2	25.8
Handling the deficit	28.0	18.6	34.9	22.0

(N = 3380)

Source: National Election Study, 1984.

As in the US and Britain, Canadian men and women hardly differ in their degree of support or opposition that they show for many issues. On abortion, for example, where given the nature of the issues, the sexes might be expected to divide, the percentages in favour and in opposition are quite similar. Nor do gender differences appear on other issues, such as whether government should be responsible for ensuring adequate housing or for providing sufficient income for older people. Women, however, are particularly more inclined to support censorship of pornographic magazines and movies, while men are more apt to favour increased contributions to NATO.[9]

In particular, we want to address the policy priorities of university-educated men and women in order to explain their divergence in voting as outlined above. An analysis of these data, however, lend little support to the hypothesis that the split among the well educated is a female-driven gender gap—rather, it would appear to be male initiated. Specifically, university-educated male voters appear to have a relatively cohesive and fairly conservative policy agenda which they, in the last two federal elections, have been able to harness consistently and to translate into voting power, whereas university-educated women would appear to have been less successful in establishing political policy priorities and in transferring these priorities to the ballot box.

The 1988 National Election Study raised a host of issues and table 5 sets out a number of these where university-educated men and women mostly differed.[10] Men, much more than women, inclined towards giving free reign to market forces and competition. They were prepared to cut back on social programs as a means of reducing the deficit and they took a hard-nosed approach to those at the bottom of the economic system.

How do these differing opinions on issues manifest themselves in opinions of government in general? In 1984, respondents in the National Election Study were asked to state the most important tasks of government.[11] Those tasks mentioned as the first- and second-most important by all men and women and by university-educated men and women are set out in table 6. Only five of these tasks reached double digit figures. Most frequently mentioned was the task of dealing with unemployment, and on this men and women differed not at all. On the next most frequently mentioned items, women rated more highly the task of controlling inflation, while men were slightly more concerned that government be run competently. The biggest gap between the sexes occurred on the fourth and fifth most frequently mentioned tasks of government. By a substantial margin (7.8 per cent) women gave high priority to working for world peace, while men by a margin of 9.4 per cent gave paramount importance to handling the deficit. Among the university educated the split was even wider on these two issues: 12.6 and 12.9 per cent respectively.

Respondents were also asked to state which party was the best for each specific task. We tried to assess the consistency of voters by establishing which individuals voted for the party they identified as being "best" on their highest priority task. Thus a "consistent" voter would be someone who, for example, identified unemployment as the most important task of government, considered the NDP as the most appropriate party to address this and then voted NDP. Of course, when examining National Election Study data we cannot be certain that attitudes precede behaviour in this way. However for comparative purposes we make this assumption.

To a certain extent, these expectations of attitudinal differences were borne out. Men appear to have been much more successful than women in harnessing voting power behind their issues. Of those university-educated males who believed that handling the deficit was the most important task of government, two thirds actually voted for the party best able, in their opinion, to do it. On the other hand, only one third of university-educated women with world peace as their paramount issue atually voted for the party cited as doing the best job on that. On the issue that set them apart from female voters, this group of men more often voted according to what they said was important to them.

CONCLUSION

Differences in political behaviour between males and females, while not overly pronounced, consistently surface in national election studies. On most major questions of policy and government priority, women and men in aggregate tend to concur with each other. The areas in which there tends to be disharmony are usually less relevant to the electorate as a whole. One area of striking divergence occurs between highly educated men and women, although education level appears to have a greater impact on men's political attitudes and behaviour on women's. In 1988, university-educated men tended to have a somewhat different political agenda than either their less well-educated counterparts or women. This group's agenda tends to be more free-market oriented and perhaps, due to a greater cohesiveness of attitudes, they have been more successful in establishing their agenda as the government's agenda.

This is not to say that the agenda of university-educated men will always be more prominent; rather in the past they seem to have been more successful in identifying issues of importance to them and harnessing their voting power in a more united fashion. In the future, however, as we enter an era when government will have to make decisions on disarmament and the environment, women (the larger portion of the electorate) could have significant influence on government policy because these are the very issues of particular concern to them.

NOTES

1. Two thoughtful discussions of these and related questions are Thelma McCormack, "Examining the Election Entrails: Whatever Happened to the Gender Gap?" *This Magazine* (March-April 1989), 31–35; Naomi Black, "Where Does the Gender Gap? or: The Future Influence of Women in Politics," *Canadian Woman Studies* 6 (Spring 1985): 33–35.

2. Douglas A. Wertman, "The Christian Democrats: Masters of Survival" in *Italy at the Polls, 1979: A Study of the Parliamentary Elections*, ed. Howard R. Penniman (Washington: American Enterprise Institute for Public Policy Research, 1981), 74–76.

3. David P. Conradt, *The German Polity*, 2d ed. (New York: Longman, 1982), 131–32.

4. Harold D. Clarke, Jane Jenson, Lawrence LeDuc and Jon H. Pammett, *Political Choice in Canada*, abridged ed. (Toronto: McGraw-Hill Ryerson, 1980), 88. The National Election Studies used in this analysis were made available by the Inter-University Consortium for Political and Social Research. Neither the original investigation nor the Consortium bear any responsibility for the analysis or interpretation presented here.

5. N.W. Polsby and A. Wildavsky, *Presidential Elections: Contempory Strategies of American Electoral Politics*, 7th ed. (New York: Free Press, 1988), 171–72.

6. Marian Sawer and Marian Simms, *A Women's Place: Women and Politics in Australia* (North Sydney: Allen & Unwin, 1984), 161–62; McCormack, "Examining the Election Entrails," 33.

7. Polsby and Wildavsky, *Presidential Elections*, 171.

8. Pippa Norris, "The Gender Gap in Britain and America," *Parliamentary Affairs* 38 (1985): 192–201.

9. National Election Study, 1984.

10. For items ii, iii, xiii, and xvi, respondents were given two alternative policy positions and they could also indicate "Neither" or "Undecided." For items iv–ix, we combined those strongly approving with those approving. The policy statements referred to in the table were as follows:

    i. Competition, whether in school, work, or business leads to better performance and a desire for excellence.

    ii. The price Canadians pay for energy should be left to the market.

    iii. Farmers or fishermen who cannot make a living should shift into another line of work just like any other small business has to do.

    iv–ix. Below are listed some ways in which government could cut their deficits. Please indicate if you strongly approve, approve, disapprove, or strongly disapprove of each way by writing the number that best represents how you feel in the space provided to the right of each statement.

       iv. Make Family Allowance payments only to low-income families.

vi. Reduce welfare payments.

vii. Sell Petro-Canada to private investors.

viii. Sell Canadian National Railways to private investors.

xi. Reduce the defence budget.

x. When it comes to making decisions in industry, the important decisions should be left to management.

xi. Unskilled workers (such as janitors, dishwashers, and so on) usually receive wages that are about right, considering the amount of skill required.

xii. Working people in this country usually earn what they deserve.

xiii. If the only hospital in a region is run by Roman Catholics it should be required to provide abortion services, because it would be unjust to deny women in this region the same rights that women enjoy elsewhere.

xiv. Canada should try harder to encourage immigration from countries most like us, such as those in Europe.

xv. Capital punishment is never justified, no matter what the crime.

xvi. Adults should not be prevented from buying pornographic books and movies, because it is impossible to define what is pornographic.

11. The question was worded as follows: Which of these tasks is the most important in how you personally judge the parties?

FURTHER READING

o

CJPS *Canadian Journal of Political Science*

CRSA *Canadian Review of Sociology and Anthropology*

1. Two books that first broke the ground in studying Canadian electoral behaviour are by John Meisel, *Working Papers on Canadian Politics*, 2d ed. (Montreal: McGill-Queens University Press, 1975); and by Peter Regenstreif, *The Diefenbaker Interlude: Parties and Voting in Canada* (Toronto: Longman, 1965). Two of the most important recent books are jointly authored by Harold D. Clarke, Jane Jenson, Lawrence LeDuc, and Jon Pammett. They are *Political Choice in Canada*, abridged ed. (Toronto: McGraw-Hill Ryerson, 1980) and *Absent Mandate: The Politics of Discontent in Canada* (Toronto: Gage, 1984).

2. John Courtney's edited collection of articles, *Voting in Canada* (Toronto: Prentice-Hall, 1967), provides a good overview of research up to that date and it has been followed by Sylvia Bashevkin's recent compilation: *Canadian Political Behaviour: Introductory Readings* (Toronto: Methuen, 1985).

3. The pioneering study on voting behaviour in a Canadian federal election is John Meisel, ed., *Papers on the 1962 Election* (Toronto: University of Toronto Press, 1964). An important series, entitled *At the Polls*, began in the 1970s to examine individual elections in the world's leading democracies. The Canadian studies, edited by Howard R. Penniman, are *Canada at the Polls: The General Election of 1974* (Washington: American Enterprise Institute, 1975); *Canada at the Polls, 1979 and 1980* (Washington: American Enterprise Institute, 1981); *Canada at the Polls, 1984* (Durham, N.C.: Duke University Press, 1988). A group at Carleton University, Alan Frizzell, Jon H. Pammett and Anthony Westell, have produced *The Canadian General Election of 1988* (Ottawa: Carleton University Press, 1989). Articles on specific elections include G. R. Winham and R. B. Cunningham, "Party Leader Images in the 1968 Federal Election," *CJPS* 3 (1970): 37–55; Jon H. Pammett, Lawrence LeDuc, J. Jenson, and H. D. Clarke, "The Perception and Impact of Issues in the 1974 Federal Election," *CJPS* 10 (1977): 93–126; Steven D. Brown, Ronald D. Lambert, Barry J. Kay, and James E. Curtis, "The 1984 Election: Explaining the Vote" (Paper presented to the Canadian Political Science Association annual meeting, 1986); R. H. Wagenberg, W. C. Soderlund, W. I. Romanow, and E. D. Briggs, "Campaigns, Images and Polls: Mass Media Coverage of the 1984 Canadian Election," *CJPS* 21 (1988): 117–29.

4. Out of the multitude of books that provide a comparative survey of voting studies, two of the most useful are: Richard G. Niemi and Herbert F. Weisberg, eds., *Controversies in Voting Behavior*, 2d ed. (Washington: CQ Press, 1984) and Martin Harrop and William L. Miller, *Elections and Voters: A Comparative Introduction* (London: Macmillan, 1987). Within this comparative, international framework,

Canadian voting behaviour may appear less idiosyncratic than is often supposed. H. D. Clarke, Kai Hildebrandt, L. LeDuc, and J. Pammett, "Issue Volatility and Partisan Linkage in Canada, Great Britain, the United States and West Germany," *European Journal of Political Research* 13 (1985): 237–63. Lawrence LeDuc, "Partisan Change and Dealignment in Canada, Great Britain, and the United States," *Comparative Politics* 17 (1985): 379–98. Arend Lijphart, "Religious vs. Linguistic vs. Class Voting: The 'Crucial Experiment' of Comparing Belgium, Canada, South Africa and Switzerland," *American Political Science Review* 73 (1979): 442–58. J. Myles, "Differences in the Canadian and American Class Vote," *American Journal of Sociology* 84 (1979): 1232–37.

5. Party identification is discussed in a number of articles. Donald E. Blake, "The Consistency of Inconsistency: Party Identification in Federal and Provincial Politics," *CJPS* 15 (1982): 691–710. David J. Elkins, "Party Identification: A Conceptual Analysis" *CJPS* 11 (1978): 419–35. Two articles by Jane Jenson: "Party Loyalty in Canada: The Question of Party Identification," *CJPS* 8 (1975): 27–48 and "Party Strategy and Party Identification: Some Patterns of Partisan Allegiance," *CJPS* 9 (1976): 27–48. Two articles by Lawrence LeDuc: "Canada: The Politics of Stable Dealignment," in *Electoral Change in Advanced Industrial Democracies* ed. Russell J. Dalton, Scott C. Flanagan, and Paul Allen Beck (Princeton: Princeton University Press, 1984), 402–24, and his article on partisan change referred to in paragraph 4. Ronald D. Lambert, James E. Curtis, Steven D. Brown, and Barry J. Kay, "Effects of Identification with Governing Parties on Feelings of Political Efficacy and Trust," *CJPS* 19 (1986): 705–28. Vincent Lemieux, "La composition des préférences partisanes," *CJPS* 2 (1969): 397–418; Paul M. Sniderman, H. D. Forbes, and Ian Meltzer, "Party Loyalty and Electoral Volatility: A Study of the Canadian Party System," *CJPS* 7 (1974): 268–88.

6. One of the conundrums of Canadian voting behaviour that has received a good deal of attention by political scientists is the effect of class on voting. Why does it apparently have so little impact? Or, alternatively, might careful analysis unearth a link that has hitherto gone unnoticed? Janine Brodie and Jane Jenson, *Crisis, Challenge and Change: Party and Class in Canada Revisited* (Ottawa: Carleton University Press, 1988). Linda M. Gerber, "The Federal Election of 1968: Social Class Composition and Party Support in the Electoral Districts of Ontario," *CRSA* 23 (1986): 118–35. Elisabeth Gidengil, "Class and Region in Canadian Voting: A Dependency Interpretation," *CJPS* 22 (1989): 563–87. Barry J. Kay, "An Examination of Class and Left–Right Party Images in Canadian Voting," *CJPS* 10 (1977): 127–43. V. Keddies, "Class Identification and Party Preference among Manual Workers," *CRSA* 17 (1980): 24–36. Ronald D. Lambert and A. A. Hunter, "Social Stratification, Voting Behaviour, and the Images of Canadian Federal Political Parties," *CRSA* 16 (1979): 287–304. Ronald D. Lambert, James E. Curtis, Steven D. Brown, and Barry J. Kay, "Canadians' Beliefs about Differences between Social Classes," *Canadian Journal of Sociology* 11 (1986): 379–99. Lynn McDonald, "Social Class and Voting: A Study of the 1968 Canadian Federal Election in Ontario," *British Journal of Sociology* 22 (1971): 410–22. Rick Ogmundson, "Party Class Images and the Class Vote in Canada," *American Sociological Review* 40 (1975): 506–12 (and a related article in *CRSA* 12 (1975): 565–76). Michael D. Ornstein, H. M. Stevenson, and A. P. Williams, "Region, Class and Political Culture in Canada," *CJPS* 13 (1980): 227–71. E. M. Schreiber, "Class Awareness and Class Voting in Canada," *CRSA* 17 (1980):

37–44. K. W. Taylor and N. Wiseman, "Class and Ethnic Voting in Winnipeg: The Case of 1941," *CRSA* 14 (1977): 174–87 (and two related studies by the same authors in *CJPS* 7 [1974]: 314–28 and in *CRSA* 16 [1979]: 60–76). John Wilson, "Politics and Social Class in Canada: The Case of Waterloo South," *CJPS* 1 (1968): 288–309.

7. Related to the class perceptions of the electorate are its ideological perceptions. David J. Elkins, "The Perceived Structure of the Canadian Party Systems," *CJPS* 7 (1974): 502–24. Ronald D. Lambert, James E. Curtis, Steven D. Brown, and Barry J. Kay, "In Search of Left/Right Beliefs in the Canadian Electorate," *CJPS* 19 (1986): 541–64. Neil Nevitte, Herman Bakvis, and Roger Gibbins, "The Ideological Contours of 'New Politics' in Canada: Policy, Mobilization and Partisan Support," *CJPS* 22 (1989): 475–550. J. A. Laponce, *Left and Right: The Topography of Political Perceptions* (Toronto: University of Toronto Press, 1981). John F. Zipp, "Left–Right Dimensions of Canadian Federal Party Identification: A Discriminant Analysis," *CJPS* 11 (1978): 251–77.

8. Several articles examine the various socialization factors that influence voting behaviour, including religion, political knowledge, and parental influence. Religion is discussed by Lijphart in his article referred to in paragraph 4 and by Donald Forbes and Paul Sniderman in "Religion and Partisanship in Canada, 1965 to 1984" (Paper presented to the Canadian Political Science Association annual meeting, 1988). Ronald D. Lambert, James E. Curtis, Steven D. Brown, and Barry J. Kay, "The Social Sources of Political Knowledge," *CJPS* 21 (1988): 359–74. Michael D. Martinez, "Intergenerational Transfer of Canadian Partisanships," *CJPS* 17 (1984): 133–43.

9. Although over half the electorate is female, the impact of women on voting has so far received lamentably little attention. Two articles that deal with this in different ways are by André Blais et Jean Crête, "Les ménages et le vote [au Québec]," *Recherches sociographiques* 28 (1987): 393–405; and by Alfred A. Hunter and Margaret A. Denton, "Do Female Candidates 'Lose Votes'?: The Experience of Female Candidates in the 1979 and 1980 Canadian General Elections," *CRSA* 21 (1984): 395–406.

10. The electorate's perceptions of various issues, including the economy, majority government, and leadership are discussed in several articles. Lawrence LeDuc, "Political Behaviour and the Issue of Majority Government in Two Federal Elections," *CJPS* 10 (1977): 311–39. Keith Archer and A. Kornberg, "Issue Perceptions and Electoral Behaviour in an Age of Restraint, 1974–1980," *American Review of Canadian Studies* 15 (1985): 68–89. J. R. Happy, "Economic Performance and Retrospective Voting in Canadian Federal Elections," *CJPS* 22 (1989): 377–87. Steven D. Brown, Ronald D. Lambert, Barry J. Kay, and James E. Curtis, "In the Eye of the Beholder: Leader Images in Canada," *CJPS* 21 (1988): 729–55.

11. Regionalism, language and residence are dealt with in previously mentioned articles by Ornstein et al., (paragraph 6) and by Elkins (paragraph 7). Two other relevant articles are J. A. Laponce, "Assessing the Neighbour Effect on the Vote of Francophone Minorities in Canada," *Political Geography Quarterly* 6 (1987): 77–87; and André Blais, "Politique agricole et résultats électoraux en milieu agricole au Québec," *CJPS* 11 (1978): 333–81.

12. Voting behaviour at the provincial level is the subject of two books by Donald E. Blake: *Two Political Worlds: Parties and Voting in British Columbia* (Vancouver: University of British Columbia Press, 1985); and *Small Worlds: Parties and Provinces in Canadian Political Life*, which he wrote with Richard Simeon, published in Toronto by Methuen, 1980. Richard Hamilton and Maurice Pinard have written three important articles on Quebec elections in the 1970s: "The Basis of Parti Québécois Support in Recent Quebec Elections," *CJPS* 9 (1976): 3–26; "The Independence Issue and the Polarization of the Electorate: The 1973 Québec Election," *CJPS* 10 (1977): 215–59; "The Parti Québécois Comes to Power: An Analysis of the 1976 Quebec Election," *CJPS* 11 (1978): 739–75. Peter McCormick, "Voting Behaviour in Alberta: The Quasi-Party System Revisited," *Journal of Canadian Studies* 15, 3 (1980): 85–97. Two articles by John Wilson, "The Decline of the Liberal Party in Manitoba Politics," *Journal of Canadian Studies* 10 (1975): 24–41; and with the collaboration of David Hoffman, "The Liberal Party in Contemporary Ontario Politics," *CJPS* 3 (1970): 177–204.

13. The role of the party system is the subject of Janine Brodie and Jane Jenson, *Crisis, Challenge and Change: Party and Class in Canada Revisited* (Ottawa: Carleton University Press, 1988); Joseph Wearing, *Strained Relations: Canadian Parties and Voters* (Toronto: McClelland and Stewart, 1988); and John Wilson, "The Canadian Political Cultures: Towards a Redefinition of the Nature of the Canadian Political System," *CJPS* 7 (1974): 438–83. The impact of party organisation on voting—more specifically the extent to which door-to-door canvassing affects the vote—is dealt with by Robert Cunningham in "The Impact of the Local Candidate in Canadian Federal Elections," *CJPS* 4 (1971): 287–90 and by Jerome Black in "Revisiting the Effects of Canvassing on Voting Behaviour," *CJPS* 17 (1984): 351–74. A related question is "Does the Candidate Make a Difference? The Macro-Politics and Micro-Politics of Getting Elected," which is examined by William Irvine in an article from the *CJPS* 15 (1982): 755–82. The effect of incumbency is the subject of two articles by M. Krashinksy and W. J. Milne: "Some Evidence on the Effect of Incumbency in Ontario Provincial Elections," *CJPS* 16 (1983): 489–500 and "Additional Evidence on the Effect of Incumbency in Canadian Elections," *CJPS* 18 (1985): 155–65.

14. Within Canadian writing on voting behaviour, a unique attempt to combine both the long- and the short-term components of the electoral decision appears in an article by Keith Archer, "A Simultaneous Equation Model of Canadian Voting Behaviour," *CJPS* 20 (1987): 553–72.

15. Colourful portraits of two leading Canadian pollsters appear in Robert Fulford, "This Brain for Hire," *Saturday Night* 100 (December 1985): 29–37; and Jeffrey Simpson, "The Most Influential Private Citizen in Canada," *Saturday Night* 99 (July 1984): 11–18.

16. Finally, how reliable are voting studies? Opposing points of view are taken by Nelson Wiseman, "The Use, Misuse, and Abuse of the National Election Studies," *Journal of Canadian Studies* 21, 1 (1986): 21–37 and by Lawrence LeDuc, "On Abusing the National Election Studies" (Unpublished manuscript, n. d.).

294

An honest attempt has been made to secure permission for all material used, and if there are errors or omissions, these are wholly unintentional and the publisher will be grateful to learn of them.

Lawrence LeDuc, Harold D. Clarke, Jane Jenson and Jon H. Pammett, *"Partisan Instability in Canada: Evidence from a New Panel Study,"* American Political Science Review 78 (1984): 470–84. Reprinted with permission of the American Political Science Association.

Harold D. Clarke and Marianne C. Stewart, *"Short-term Forces and Partisan Change in Canada: 1974–80,"* Electoral Studies 4 (1985): 15–35. Reprinted with permission of Butterworths, London.

H. Michael Stevenson, *"Ideology and Unstable Party Identification in Canada: Limited Rationality in a Brokerage Party System,"* Canadian Journal of Political Science (CJPS) 18 (1985): 813–50. William P. Irvine, *"Explaining the Religious Basis of the Canadian Partisan Identity: Success on the Third Try,"* CJPS 7 (1974): 560–63. Richard Johnston, *"The Reproduction of the Religious Cleavage in Canadian Elections,"* CJPS 18 (1985): 99–114. William P. Irvine, *"Comment on 'The Reproduction of the Religious Cleavage in Canadian Elections,'"* CJPS 18 (1985): 115–18. Keith Archer, *"The Failure of the New Democratic Party: Unions, Unionists, and Politics in Canada,"* CJPS 18 (1985): 353–66. Keith Archer and Marquis Johnson, *"Inflation, Unemployment and Canadian Federal Voting Behaviour,"* CJPS 21 (1988): 569–84. Harold D. Clarke, Jane Jenson, Lawrence LeDuc and Jon Pammett, *"Voting Behaviour and the Outcome of the 1979 Federal Election: The Impact of Leaders and Issues ,"* CJPS 15 (1982): 517–52. Lawrence LeDuc and Richard Price, *"Great Debates: The Televised Leadership Debates of 1979,"* CJPS 18 (1985): 135–54. Reprinted with the permission of the Canadian Political Science Association.

Richard Johnston, *"The Geography of Class and Religion in Canadian Elections,"* Paper reprinted with permission of the author. Represented to the Canadian Political Science Annual Meeting, 1987.

Jon H. Pammett, *"Class Voting and Class Consciousness in Canada,"* The Canadian Review of Sociology and Anthropology 24, 2 (1987): 269–90. Ronald D. Lambert, James E. Curtis, Steven D. Brown and Barry J. Kay, *"Social Class, Left/Right Political Orientations, and Subjective Class Voting in Provincial and Federal Elections,"* The Canadian Review of Sociology and Anthropology 29,4 (1987): 526–49. Reprinted with permission of the journal.

Kristen Monroe and Lynda Erikson, *"The Economy and Political Support: The Canadian Case,"* The Journal of Politics 48, 3 (1986): 616–47. Reprinted with permission of the University of Texas Press.

Barry J. Kay, Steven D. Brown, James E. Curtis, Ronald D. Lambert and John M. Wilson, *"The Character of Electoral Change: A Preliminary Report from the 1984 National Election Study,"* Paper presented to the Canadian Political Science Annual Meeting, 1985. Reprinted with permission of Barry J. Kay, Wilfred Laurier University.

Richard Johnston, André Blais, Henry E. Brady and Jean Crête, *"Free Trade and the Dynamics of the 1988 Canadian Election,"* Paper prepared for the American Political Science Association Annual Meeting, 1989. Reprinted with the permission of The American Political Science Association.

843042